the **politics** companion

robert leach

your course ... one source

palgrave
macmillan

First published 2008 by
PALGRAVE MACMILLAN
Houndmills, Basingstoke, Hampshire RG21 6XS and
175 Fifth Avenue, New York, N.Y. 10010
Companies and representatives throughout the world

PALGRAVE MACMILLAN is the global academic imprint of the Palgrave
Macmillan division of St. Martin's Press, LLC and of Palgrave Macmillan Ltd.
Macmillan® is a registered trademark in the United States, United Kingdom
and other countries. Palgrave is a registered trademark in the European
Union and other countries.

ISBN-13: 9780230517905 paperback
ISBN-10: 0230517900   paperback

This book is printed on paper suitable for recycling and made from fully
managed and sustained forest sources. Logging, pulping and manufacturing
processes are expected to conform to the environmental regulations of the
country of origin.

A catalogue record for this book is available from the British Library.
A catalog record for this book is available from the Library of Congress.

10 9 8 7 6 5 4 3 2 1
17 16 15 14 13 12 11 10 09 08

Printed and bound in China

the **politics** companion

Palgrave Student Companions are a one-stop reference resource that provide essential information for students about the subject — and the course — they've chosen to study.

Friendly and authoritative, **Palgrave Student Companions** support the student throughout their degree. They encourage the reader to think about study skills alongside the subject matter of their course, offer guidance on module and career choices, and act as an invaluable source book and reference that they can return to time and again.

Palgrave Student Companions — your course ... one source

Published
The MBA Companion
The Politics Companion
The Social Work Companion

Forthcoming
The Cultural Studies Companion
The English Language and Linguistics Companion
The Health Studies Companion
The Literary Studies Companion
The Media Studies Companion
The Nursing Companion
The Psychology Companion
The Theatre, Drama and Performance Companion

Further titles are planned

www.palgravestudentcompanions.com

Brief contents

Contents

Part VI   What Next?   265

Part VII   Resources for Studying Politics   275

Boxes

Preface

This book was conceived as a one-stop guide for all undergraduates studying politics. I cannot claim that it will answer all the questions a politics student might ask. In truth, no single book could do that. Yet I do hope that students will find it of real use to them in negotiating the fascinating but increasingly complex subject of politics. Much of the study of politics has become highly specialized. Scholars in particular fields employ their own specialist vocabulary and methodologies, and often only engage with each other. It has become difficult for those embarking on a politics degree course to see the discipline as a coherent whole. If this book helps students to understand how the study of politics developed, where it is now, and how the elements of their course fit together, it will have done something. I trust also that politics undergraduates will find the advice and guidance on a wide range of topics of practical benefit, and that it will assist them in both enjoying, and succeeding in, their studies.

I did not find it an easy book to write, because it is so wide-ranging, too much so perhaps for any single author to cover the whole field of studying politics successfully. Parts of this book have involved a fascinating voyage of discovery into areas of the discipline in which my own background has been limited. I think I have a learned a great deal I did not fully appreciate before about my own subject. I hope the inevitable gaps in my own knowledge are not too glaring. At times I thought a group of academics might have tackled the project more successfully, although I know from personal experience that books written by committees carry their own problems. As a single author I have been able to conceive the book as a whole, and this may help readers also to see the wood for the trees.

I owe many debts. Some of these will be obvious, such as the considerable debt to so many authors, ancient and modern. I am, however, particularly grateful to all those who have given me practical help on the project. These include several anonymous reviewers who gave invaluable constructive, and often very detailed, advice on early drafts. Some of the advice I have gratefully taken, and some I considered extremely carefully before deciding to continue in my obstinate way, but all of it was very useful. I also have to acknowledge a debt to Steven Kennedy and Suzannah Burywood at my publishers, Palgrave Macmillan, who commissioned the book, even if there were times when I wished they had not. They have been supportive and encouraging throughout, while Stephen Wenham has been a model of patience and tact, especially in the latter stages. Susan Curran (of Curran Publishing) has been her usual extremely efficient self in translating my manuscript into page proofs. However, my biggest debt I owe to my loyal and supportive wife, Judith, whose habitual tolerance and forbearance have been strained rather more than usual on this particular endeavour.

Robert Leach

Introduction

This book is designed to provide politics students with a one-stop guide to the subject and its study. The aim is to combine, in a single volume, first, an exploration of the discipline of politics, its nature, development and key elements; second, practical advice on choosing courses and special options, developing skills, and career prospects; and third, a useful reference source on key political terms and political thinkers.

Why do students need a *Politics Companion?*

There are some useful books available on each of these topics. Thus there are some good politics dictionaries that contain a wide range of entries on political terms and political thinkers, and some rather more specialist books exploring in rather greater depth key concepts or major political thinkers. There are some handy guides available on choosing politics courses, on study skills and on careers advice. There are also some stimulating books on the nature of politics, and an invaluable broad introduction to political ideas, institutions and processes (Heywood, 2007). In addition there are books that examine aspects of the development of the discipline of politics, and the changes in emphasis in its study over time, although these are far from easy for the beginner. There are some good introductions to more specialist fields, such as international relations, comparative politics, political philosophy or research methodology (for further details, see Resources for Studying Politics on page 276).

All these are issues, topics or areas that anyone studying politics at university level is likely to encounter at some stage, and often on a regular basis. Yet until now students would have had to buy a small library of books to cover them. This *Politics Companion* is intended to provide students with a broad resource base throughout their degree. It provides extensive information and advice on many of the issues that will arise over the course of a university politics programme. Inevitably the breadth of coverage involves some sacrifice of depth. No single book can supply all you need to know to succeed on a politics course. Often, you will have to refer to other more specialist sources to develop and extend your knowledge and understanding of particular issues and topics. Reading widely is essential to success on a politics course. Yet this book should provide you with your first port of call on many of the issues and problems that you will encounter, and also with clear guidance on a range of topics, with detailed advice on further reading and references.

The book also provides an overview of the whole discipline of politics. The study of the subject has grown so extensive, and so compartmentalized, with so many specialist fields and sub-disciplines, that it is sometimes difficult for undergraduates to see the wood for the trees. Degree programmes often involve a formidable range of core politics subjects, ancillary studies and highly specialized options, and it is not easy to appreciate how all these parts fit together and interrelate. While virtually all universities offering degree courses in politics will cover much the same broad elements, particular institutions inevitably have their own distinctive slant to the study of the subject, reflecting the specialist research interests of staff, and sometimes a particular approach or methodology. Students may not always appreciate what is general and what is distinctive in their politics degree course, nor what some more specialist elements actually involve.

Moreover, politics is often studied alongside other allied disciplines in a broad social science or humanities programme, and it may not invariably be clear why these disciplines are combined and what are the implications of such combined studies for the study of politics in particular. This book should provide students with a 'map' of politics, its core elements and specialist areas, and adjoining disciplines that will enable them to make sense of their particular course and the distinctive routes and specialist options it offers, in relation to the study of politics more generally.

The plan of the book

Although the book can be read from the beginning through to the end, it is not anticipated that this is how it will normally be used. Rather, the expectation is that students will dip into particular sections as and when they need to, and follow up the extensive cross-referencing as required. It is useful for readers to learn to find their way around the book, but the order of the material in some respects is less important.

Yet the organization of the material in the book is not arbitrary. The focus is on the needs of students as they go through a politics course. Thus Part I, divided into three sections, deals with issues and questions that confront a new politics student from the outset. Anyone studying politics has to consider the question, 'What is politics really about?' because the nature and definition of politics is highly contested and influences the content and analysis of the subject. It is not an issue that can be ducked. The second section, 'What to expect from your politics course' is also addressed primarily to students beginning a course. It outlines the key elements of a typical politics degree course. It includes some advice on choosing a university that may appear redundant for those who have already made their choice and begun their course, although it may help them to understand the similarities and distinctive features of their own course. However, this section also deals with key choices you will have to make in the process of studying for your degree, over subsidiary subjects, specialized options and sometimes different pathways through a politics programme, perhaps involving distinctive degree titles, which may open up opportunities for further study or interesting careers. Specific examples are included from courses and universities around the world. Finally, a longer third section explores the skills you will need to develop to succeed, both on your politics course, and subsequently after graduating. Detailed practical advice is offered on how to tackle various forms of assessment, which in some institutions may include individual or group oral presentations, group projects and dissertations, as well as the more familiar essays, papers and unseen examinations.

The second part of the book deals with theories and approaches to the study of politics, some of which may be loosely linked with the conflicting views of the nature of the subject (outlined briefly earlier in Part I, Section 1). This section could usefully be read as a concise overview before starting your course or when deciding whether to study politics at all. But it should also be helpful to return to – and probably read in more detail – when you start confronting the theories and approaches in your studies. It is important to appreciate that politics has been studied for many centuries, and the works of great political philosophers from the ancient Greeks onwards still figure on many modern politics degree courses. Moreover, while it is universally acknowledged that the study of politics must be comparative, this has a time dimension as well as a spatial dimension. History provides a storehouse of examples of political institutions and processes that still appear relevant to the analysis of politics today.

Thus the first section of Part II provides a brief overview of the evolution of the theory and practice of politics, up to around the middle of the twentieth century. At this time the 'behavioural revolution' in the study of the social sciences in general and politics in particular led to a dramatic expansion in the scope of the subject and the numbers of those engaged in studying and researching political science across the western world. The development of the discipline over the last half century or so is described in Part II, Section 2, 'Theories and approaches to the study of politics'. The key point here is that although new theories and approaches have been hugely influential, they have not displaced older approaches, some of which have enjoyed a significant revival.

Part III defines and discusses the significance of a range of key political terms and concepts, many of which you will almost certainly encounter fairly early in your course. While some terms are relatively straightforward, others are 'essentially contested concepts' on which there are strong differences of opinion, and these are treated more fully. Part IV similarly has entries of varying length on key thinkers, some of whose names you may encounter with increasing frequency as your course progresses. These two parts together should comprise an invaluable reference guide throughout your studies.

Part V addresses 'Key research and debates' in modern political science. The scope of the study of politics has grown enormously over the last half century, and particular areas of the discipline have become increasingly specialized. Thus no single scholar (and certainly not this author) could hope to provide a comprehensive survey of cutting-edge research across the whole discipline. Yet this would not be appropriate even it was feasible. This book, after all, is designed for undergraduates. So the coverage of this part is illustrative rather than comprehensive, indicating some of the contemporary issues and debates in the discipline that may whet the appetite for specialized final year options, or perhaps postgraduate study.

Part VI, 'What next?', looks beyond graduation to prospects for careers and further study. It is argued that although it is not narrowly vocational, the content and skills involved in a politics degree can equip students for a wide variety of careers. Indeed many of the skills necessary for success on a politics degree are life skills, transferable to other contexts. However, it is also urged that the sooner students begin thinking about life beyond graduation the better, as some choices made earlier may narrow the options available, while others can lead on to satisfying and interesting careers in specific fields. Work placements or more specialized political internships may give you valuable experience, while a period of study abroad may widen your horizons. Some further study, particularly to acquire professional qualifications in such fields as law, accounting or journalism, may enhance your employability and prospects. Higher degrees may provide a satisfying educational experience without always necessarily improving your career options, unless you have the ability and interest for an academic career.

Finally, Part VII, 'Resources for studying politics', involves suggestions for further reading and other learning resources, including useful websites, and other important information for a politics student, including national and international organizations involved in the academic study of politics. A full bibliography follows.

referencing

Extensive cross-referencing is provided throughout the book. Key concepts that are defined in Part III are highlighted in **bold black type** and key thinkers discussed in Part IV are highlighted in **bold brown type**, normally when they are mentioned for the first time within a passage or section, as the frequent highlighting of common concepts and important thinkers would be repetitious and distracting. There are also cross-references to other parts of the book (in brackets, with relevant page numbers) where particular theories or the ideas of key thinkers are discussed further.

References to other books and articles use the Harvard system, with brief reference to the author, date of publication and page provided in the text, and full details in the bibliography (for an explanation of referencing systems see pages 40–2). I have sometimes slightly varied from the usual formula by proving the date of original publication in square brackets before the date of the edition used (and citing just this in the text where the date is significant). This is particularly important for older texts. For example, a reference only to the date of a modern translation of Rousseau or Tocqueville is unhelpful to students, who should be told when these works were actually written. Some less famous long-dead writers may even be mistaken by the unwary for modern authors.

introduction to part I:
studying politics

This part of book deals with some of the issues and problems that confront a new politics student from the outset. The first section on the nature and definition of politics may appear abstract and theoretical rather than practical. Yet it is an issue that needs to be confronted from the first, because different views of politics not only reflect different underlying theoretical assumptions, they involve implications for content and methods, for what sort of politics is studied and how it is studied. It is a question to which you will return throughout your course.

The second section explains what you can expect from your politics degree course. Politics degrees can differ considerably in content and style between countries and institutions, although most universities in the western world offer a broadly comparable core of politics studies, with numerous distinctive specialist options. This section begins with an account of the main elements of a politics degree course, and some explanation of what each of these elements involves. It goes on to offer practical advice on choosing a course and on the many other decisions you will have to take in the course of your studies, for example on the choice of subsidiary subjects, specialist options and sometimes different pathways through a broad politics programme. These can involve distinctive degree titles (such as, for example, international relations or public policy and administration) and may open up prospects for careers or further study.

The third section focuses on the skills you need on a politics degree course, and how to improve them. Most skills required for success in studying politics are generic rather than specific – they are similar to those needed for many subjects, particularly in other social sciences and the humanities. Yet some skills, such as coping with controversy and bias, are particularly important in studying politics. Once it was commonly assumed that students already had the skills they needed to succeed on a degree course or that they would acquire them, over time, through practice. Today, the importance of developing skills for success not only at university, but also for life and work after graduation, is generally appreciated. This section provides detailed practical advice on a wide range of skills, and clear guidance on tackling assignments and examinations.

Section 1: What is politics really about?

Most books described as introductions to politics begin by seeking to define politics. This seems sensible. After all, if anyone is going to spend part of their life in studying a subject, they need to know what it is they are studying. Yet these introductory first chapters exploring the nature of the subject are often the most difficult (and one suspects, the least read). Defining politics turns out to be far from straightforward. There are brief, snappy one-liners that are eminently quotable but often raise more questions than they answer (see Box 1.1), and longer more complex definitions using abstract terminology that are as clear as mud to the average beginner.

> *Defining politics turns out to be far from straightforward.*

BOX 1.1 views on politics

'The science and art of government' (*Shorter Oxford English Dictionary*)
'Who gets what, when, how' (Harold Lasswell, American political scientist)
'The authoritative allocation of value' (David Easton, American political scientist)
The art of the possible (R. A. Butler, British Conservative politician)
The personal is political (feminist slogan)

Students commonly want to get to grips immediately with key political issues, ideas and processes that interest and concern them rather than abstruse debates over the nature of politics. In some respects the question, 'What is politics?' might be more easily answered at the end of a book or course, than at the beginning. Certainly it is a question to come back to and reconsider, again and again, in the light of further study. Yet it is not a question that can or should be ducked at the outset.

> *There are fundamentally conflicting views of what politics is really about among some of the greatest thinkers who have analysed the subject.*

None of us comes to the study of politics with a blank sheet. We all have preconceptions, notions of what politics is about, sometimes unconscious assumptions that we have not really explored. Each of us needs to confront these preconceptions, because they will shape how we approach the subject. We also need to question the assumptions of others about politics, including the most celebrated authorities. What are their underlying assumptions about the nature of politics? Because, as you will discover, there are fundamentally conflicting views of what politics is really about among some of the greatest thinkers who have analysed the subject. It is important to know where they are coming from, and what assumptions have influenced their conclusions. Different views on the nature of the subject inevitably influence what sort of politics is studied and how it is studied. So this section addresses some different possible answers to the question 'What is politics about?'

Politics is about government?

One view is that politics is about **government**. It is a standard dictionary definition (see Box 1.1). Most people associate politics with government, to the extent that the two words are sometimes used almost interchangeably (for example, in the titles of books, courses and university departments). Certainly the institutions and personnel of government feature strongly in the treatment of politics in the media, as well as in virtually all politics textbooks.

Yet what is government? In the media and in common speech 'the government' is generally identified with those national leaders who appear to be currently in supreme charge of a country's domestic and foreign policy, such as the US President, the German Chancellor, the UK Prime Minister, aided by other ministers, advisers and officials. This 'government of the day', as it is sometimes described, is transient, and only part of the whole system of government. This includes not only the governing or '**executive**' role, but also law making (or legislating) and adjudicating on the law, the function of the **judiciary**. Additionally, those who are formally responsible for government are aided by an army of officials, who advise on and subsequently implement (or sometimes fail to implement) government policy.

Even so only relatively few people have been directly involved in government throughout recorded history. This remains true even in modern **representative democracies**. Abraham Lincoln's celebrated definition of democracy as 'government of the people, by the people, for the people' is misleading. The most that may be claimed is that the people have influence over government, but they are not, in any realistic sense, part of government. Thus if politics is identified purely and simply with government it effectively excludes the vast majority of ordinary people. If politics is for the many as well as the few, it must involve the governed as well as the governors. Government is part of politics, not the whole of it.

> *If politics is identified purely and simply with government it effectively excludes the vast majority of ordinary people.*

Politics is about governing, or governance?

> The ultimate and defining purpose of politics is governing and making public policy.
>
> (B. Guy Peters, in Leftwich, 2004: 23)

The view that politics is about governing rather than simply government is broader and more inclusive. It shifts the focus from the institutions and personnel directly involved in government to the *process* of governing and to *public policy*. Many more people and organizations may be involved in the process of governing than the government. Political parties, a huge range of interest groups, the media, private sector firms and voluntary organizations of all kinds may influence the making and implementation of public policy.

Yet governing, like government, still implies control, doing something to someone else. The few govern, the rest are governed. The fashionable term **governance** removes or at least reduces this implication. Governance blurs the distinction between governors and governed. We are all part of the process of governance. To quote a celebrated American book, 'Governance is the process by which we collectively solve our

> *We are all part of the process of governance.*

problems and meet our society's needs. Government is the instrument we use' (Osborne and Gaebler, 1992: 24). Within this broad process of governance the role of government itself is changing. Modern government increasingly involves 'steering' rather than 'rowing', to use the terminology of Osborne and Gaebler (1992: 25–48), or 'enabling' rather than 'providing'. Government leads rather than controls, and works together with other organizations from the public, private and voluntary sectors in policy networks to achieve shared goals.

One problem with the emphasis on governance is that it makes politics sound rather too cosy and consensual. It downplays political conflict, the suggestion that different groups and organizations may have sharply opposed interests, that in the making of public policy some win and others lose. The notion of a benign government 'steering' or 'enabling' rather ignores the point that governments often have to choose between unpalatable alternatives, and take unpopular decisions. Government may also sometimes have to force its decisions on those who are strongly opposed to them.

Politics is about the state?

The notion that politics is about government, governing, or governance raises a further question: government of what? Governing can take place at a number of levels, yet in practice most of the focus of the study of politics is clearly about the state, or states. It may sometimes focus on the government and politics of a specific **state**. It may involve a more systematic comparative approach, but this in practice normally consists of comparisons between states. The study of **international relations** may imply a broader approach, but still focuses principally on the interaction of states – more specifically independent sovereign states, each using its power and resources to promote its own interests. While 'supranational' government of various kinds (for example the United Nations and the European Union) may have growing influence, many would argue that real power in international relations still rests largely with states.

Thus anyone studying politics will soon have to confront the concept of the state, which seems to involve much more than government. The state may be defined as a political and governmental unit that is **sovereign** over a particular territory. However, there is little that sounds cosy or consensual in the notion that politics is about the state. Indeed, according to some definitions, the state appears rather sinister, something to fear (see Box 1.2). It is a compulsory association. You belong to it whether you want to or not. Moreover, both Max **Weber** and Leon **Trotsky** suggest that it ultimately rests on coercion or force. This matches some of our own experience and expectations. If we ignore the power of the state, and flout its laws or refuse to pay its taxes, we can be punished by fines or imprisonment. Thus the state can deprive us of our property, our personal freedom, and even, in many countries at many times, our lives. Many today would agree that politics is inseparable from force and coercion (see for example Nicholson in Leftwich, 2004: 41–52).

BOX 1.2 the state

'The state is a human community that (successfully) claims the monopoly of the legitimate use of physical force within a given territory.' (Max Weber, German sociologist).

'Every state is founded on force' (Leon Trotsky, Russian Communist revolutionary).

Yet while an element of compulsion and coercion is inseparable from the conception of the state, it is also simply a political community to which people belong, and towards which they may feel a strong sense of allegiance and identity, particularly perhaps in the relatively modern conception of the 'nation-state'. Such a state consists of a **nation**, a people bound together by some common characteristics or shared identity. Thus, from this perspective, state and people are one. Moreover the state protects its members from external threats and internal disorder. It provides law and security to enable people to go about their own business peacefully, and pursue their own lives. The framework of the state seems the precondition of economic growth and development, and of culture and civilization. Modern states can also provide other services that their people want and need – such as education, health and social security. The modern state can be a '**welfare state**'.

Different conceptions of the state – the coercive and potentially oppressive state, and the potentially benevolent state – underlie different views of the state and politics. Because the state has coercive power and may oppress its citizens, many have sought to limit its scope. Thus some **liberals** and **conservatives** would distinguish between the state and **civil society**, between a public sphere which is a legitimate field for state intervention and politics, and a purely private sphere of home, family and voluntary activities from which the state and politics should be firmly excluded. From some perspectives, the less the state does, the better. Economic liberals would distinguish between the state and the market, and seek to exclude the state from most economic activity. This is a perspective that has been at the heart of the recent privatization of many activities previously run by the state.

Yet many conservatives have emphasized the importance of maintaining the authority of the state, to preserve order and protect property. Some liberals (sometimes called social liberals) and even some conservatives have sought to use the power of the state to provide opportunities to help individuals to realize their potential. Many **socialists** in the past sought to give the state much more power, to establish a political system in which the state owned the means of production and effectively controlled the economy. **Fascism** was associated with a totalitarian theory of the state, according to which the state was all-embracing and excluded from no sphere of activity.

All these perspectives stress the real or potential power of the state for good or evil. Yet states may not always appear so very powerful in practice. A focus on the formal institutions and processes of the state neglects the contribution to the political process of non-state organizations and interests, such as financial institutions, major manufacturers and retailers, trade unions and other **pressure groups**. Some argue that it is such powerful outside interests that really determine key issues rather than states and their governments. Even very large and apparently powerful states may appear impotent in the grip of global economic forces they cannot control. Large transnational corporations (TNCs) may have more effective power than many states. One implication is that those who wish to study politics should focus on power rather than states or their governments.

Politics is about power?

The notion that politics is essentially about **power** implicitly or explicitly underpins many definitions of politics and the study of the subject. Moreover it addresses some of the criticisms of the identification of politics with government or the state. Those who argue politics is about power do not necessarily accept that power rests where **constitutions** or laws claim. Indeed, some argue that effective political power may rest outside government

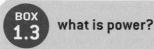

BOX 1.3   what is power?

'Political power grows out of the barrel of a gun' (Mao Zedong, Chinese Communist leader).

Power is 'the production of intended effects' (Bertrand Russell, British philosopher, 1938).

A has power over B to the extent that A can 'get B to do something that B would not otherwise do.' Robert **Dahl**, American political scientist, 1957: 201).

'A exercises power over B when A affects B in a manner contrary to B's interests' (Stephen Lukes, 1974: 27).

and the formal apparatus of the state altogether: with, for example, armed gangs, powerful economic interests, the **mass media** or religious leaders. In such circumstances government ministers and state officials may appear mere puppets of others who control the real strings of power.

However, those who argue that politics is about power often disagree over what political power is, who has it, and how far power is narrowly concentrated in the hands of the few or more widely dispersed. This is not an argument that can easily be resolved by appeal to the evidence, as the evidence is contentious, not least because there are considerable problems in defining power, and even greater difficulties in measuring it.

Some would equate power simply with physical force or coercion. This view has already been touched upon in the discussion of the state (above), and appears to match aspects of reality. There are many examples in both the recent and more distant past of military leaders using the power of the armed forces to seize control of government (Finer, [1962]). The exercise of physical force seems only too obvious an aspect of modern politics around the world today. Even so, political power can not rest for long entirely on physical force alone. Those who seize power violently commonly seek to maintain it by other means. It is noteworthy that the three most notorious twentieth-century dictators, Hitler, Mussolini and Stalin, owed neither their rise to power, nor their exercise of power, primarily on their control of the army and their readiness to use crude physical force, however ruthless they showed they could be. Instead their power rested, to a greater extent than is widely acknowledged, on the willing acquiescence of many, and perhaps most, of those over whom it was exercised.

Political power is more usually associated with other forms of influence than physical force.

Indeed, political power is more usually associated with other forms of influence than physical force. This has always been true, but is particularly apparent in the modern world, where some form of representative democracy has become the most common form of government. Democracy implies that ultimately power rests with the people or at least with the majority of the people. Indeed Alexis de **Tocqueville**, the generally sympathetic French observer of early nineteenth-century American democracy, concluded that the majority was 'all-powerful', to the extent that he was worried about the 'tyranny of the majority' (Tocqueville, [1835]: 287–322). Others since have talked (respectfully or critically) of the power of public opinion. Indeed, it is not difficult to find instances of governments altering course in response to a strong expression of public opinion. Yet others may point to the way public opinion may be influenced or manipulated, perhaps by government itself, perhaps by the media, perhaps by an influential minority. Indeed, the most subtle and sinister aspect of power, some would argue, is the power to shape how people think.

It is has been plausibly argued, particularly by **Marx** and his followers, that the ruling ideas in every age are the ideas of the ruling class. For Marx, the wealthy few, who control the 'means of production', are the real ruling class. Political power reflects economic power. Thus under **capitalism** it is the **bourgeoisie**, who own and control capital, who really control the state, whether they occupy a formal role in government or (more often) do not. It would be conceded, even by those American political scientist like **Dahl** and **Lindblom**, who argue that political power is fairly widely dispersed, that business interests nevertheless wield an influence over government disproportionate to their numbers. However, although few would deny the importance of business power in modern politics, the extent of its influence and control over government is more contestable. Ultimately, the **Marxist** hypothesis that political power ultimately reflects economic power can neither be proved nor disproved.

BOX 1.4 **who has power? various perspectives**

Bureaucracy Rule of officials

Democracy Rule of the people

Oligarchy Rule of the few

Patriarchy Rule of men (literally, rule of the father)

Plutocracy Rule of the rich

Theocracy Literally rule of God, in practice rule of priests or religious leaders

---

Others have different perspectives on who really exercises power (see Box 1.4). It has often appeared throughout history and across the world today that there is a power behind the throne. It may appear in some societies, both in the past and today, to be those who have religious authority, religious leaders who seem to have more extensive influence and real power than secular rulers, and can tell them what they can or cannot do. It may be state officials, who are in theory mere functionaries, simply implementing government policy, who really exercise power behind the scenes. It may be simply men, who, from a radical feminist perspective, exercise power over women everywhere. It may be the rich who effectively 'call the shots', buying influence without needing to exercise formal positions of power.

Besides this question of who has power, there is also the question, 'What is power for?' Is power an end in itself or a means to an end? Admittedly, power itself seems to attract some people, and it has even been claimed that power is an aphrodisiac (for how could the apparent sex appeal of some elderly and ugly politicians otherwise be explained?). Yet power is a capacity to do something, or to 'produce intended effects' in Bertrand Russell's words (Box 1.3). Holding power is not the same as exercising it. Perhaps power should be judged in

> *New rulers and new governments often discover they have less power to make real change than they expected.*

terms of outcomes. The failure to do much with power may reflect a cautious conservative political outlook, or it may reflect a failure of will. However, it may also or alternatively have something to do with the constraints on power. New rulers and new governments often discover they have less power to make real change than they expected.

Ultimately the long debate among political scientists over the nature and distribution of political power has been inconclusive. Some of the simpler definitions put forward by Dahl and others have been shown to be inadequate. However, broader and more subtle interpretations of power, including the power to set the political agenda or shape people's preferences, make it even more difficult to study its exercise. Yet ultimately, however power is defined, it is almost impossible to measure its distribution in the same way as, for example, the distribution of the population (by age, sex, occupation etc.) or the distribution of income and wealth. Thus Lincoln Allison (in McLean and McMillan, 2003: 434) pessimistically concludes, 'the concept of power has not filled the central role in the study of politics which many pioneers hoped it would'.

Politics is about conflict?

A common perspective is that politics arises out of conflict. Indeed, much of the distaste that some people feel for politics seems to be related to the conflict it involves. It is sometimes imagined that much of the conflict is unnecessary, that it is artificially stimulated by politicians and political parties, who feel bound to oppose whatever 'the other side' proposes, or who appear to love conflict for the sake of it. Indeed, politics is often identified purely and simply with party politics, and deplored for that reason. If only these partisan politicians could come together to form an all-party coalition to work for the interests of the whole country, or government could be put in the charge of some disinterested experts! Behind such hopes there is an assumption that there is often a single 'right answer' to problems, which men and women of good will, freed from partisan considerations, would discover.

> If there were universal agreements on ends and means there would be no need for politics.

Yet more commonly there is no such right answer, but irreconcilable positions reflecting conflicting interests. If there were universal agreement on ends and means there would be no need for politics. Politics arises because humans disagree over issues where collective binding decisions on the whole political community are required. We have not just different but conflicting interests.

For some, the essential conflict is between individual human beings. The English political thinker Thomas **Hobbes** (1588–1679) graphically described the natural condition of humanity as a perpetual war of every man against every man, because they want the same things that they all cannot have, because of scarcity. This view of humanity as in ceaseless competition for scarce resources is the perspective of mainstream economics, from the classical economists such as Adam Smith or David Ricardo, down to modern neoliberal economists. Most economists assume that human beings are motivated by their own rational self-interest. It is competition between countless self-interested individual consumers and producers in the market place that it is the motor of economic activity. Indeed, modern rational choice political economists (such as **Buchanan**, **Tullock**, **Olson** or **Niskanen**) are particularly scornful and dismissive of the notion that humans can behave altruistically, and prefer someone else's interest to their own. Thus they do not accept the protestations that politicians and public servants commonly make that they are serving the public or national interest. They make the (fairly common) assumption that politicians and bureaucrats are in the business of government for what they themselves can get out of it.

Yet humans appear to be naturally sociable for the most part. They belong to families, tribes, gangs and larger groups of all kinds. Thus the conflict may seem to be between not so much individuals but groups pursuing their collective interests. Much of politics seems to involve conflict between many different groups each expressing (or 'articulating') its own views and interests. The conflict can be deeply divisive, passionate and sometimes violent. There are bitter conflicts over, for example, road building, air transport, nuclear power, abortion, animal rights, civil liberties and war. Some of these reflect opposed economic interests, some conflicting values which may not easily relate to individual self-interest. Moreover, the choice, when it is made, is not one from which individuals can easily opt out. A political decision on, for example, whether or not to ban handguns, build a new airport, increase tax on alcohol, reduce speed limits on cars or declare war involves a decision that is binding on the whole community. In such conflicts, some win and others lose. Where a group feel the quality of their lives is adversely affected by a political decision, or simply that it is morally wrong, the outcome is not easily accepted.

Some would argue that such conflicts between groups mask more fundamental conflicts within humanity, such as conflict between different ethnic or religious communities, between classes or between the sexes. It appears even more obvious that politics is about conflict when we consider not just politics within states, but politics in the wider sphere. The dominant interpretation of international relations involves states using their resources to pursue vigorously their conflicting national interests in conditions of **anarchy**. Some broader perspectives have assumed rather fearsome antagonisms which threaten the future of the planet. These include the ideological 'cold war' between **communism** and capitalism (until its abrupt end around 1989), and succeeding conflicts between the west and the developing world (or between 'north' and 'south'), or between faiths, cultures or 'civilizations' (the view of Samuel **Huntington**).

Politics is about conflict and consensus?

Altogether the notion that politics is about conflict has plenty of evidence to support it. Yet if politics is only about conflict the outlook for humanity is gloomy indeed. However, some insist that politics is not just about conflict but about the reconciliation of conflict, the pursuit of compromise and **consensus** (or agreement). If politics is to succeed it has to bring people together and not just reflect their conflicting interests.

The French political scientist Maurice **Duverger** talks of the 'Janus face' of politics. Janus was a Roman god with two faces, pointing in opposite directions. Duverger argues that conflict and integration are two opposed but inseparable aspects of politics. He claims that 'politics involves a continual effort to eliminate physical violence …. Politics tends to replace fists, knives, clubs and rifles with other kinds of weapons', although, he sadly acknowledges, 'it is not always successful in doing so' (Duverger, 1972: 221). This accords with the sense in which the words 'politics' and 'political' are commonly used. When people talk of a 'political solution' to a problem (for example, Northern Ireland or Palestine) they mean a solution involving peaceful negotiation rather than violence and war. For Duverger, politics is about both conflict and the search for compromise and consensus.

This is often how politics seems to operate in **democratic** countries. Clearly individual politicians and political parties represent conflicting interests. They do not, by and large, create political conflict, but reflect real differences of interest and view in the wider community. In putting forward their own case and exposing the weaknesses of their opponents they are contributing to effective public debate, and better evidence-based public policy. This is, or should be, many would argue, what the political process is all about (Crick, 2000, and see also Crick in Leftwich, 2004).

Yet an engagement in debate almost presupposes a readiness to make concessions, to settle sometimes for half a loaf. On many issues politicians and parties must also be prepared to compromise, to accept an outcome that is, from their perspective, less than ideal, in order to secure some kind of agreement. Moreover, any political leader or party that hopes to win majority support cannot afford to articulate a single interest, but must seek to represent and 'integrate' a range of interests, which means persuading others, including their own supporters, to understand different views and interests and make concessions. So politics is not just about conflict but about resolving conflict.

> *An engagement in debate almost presupposes a readiness to make concessions, to settle sometimes for half a loaf.*

Yet while some object to the conflict involved in the political process, others criticize the search for compromise. Indeed compromise solutions are often denounced as a sell-out or betrayal, an abandonment of principle, a spineless appeasement of opponents. Thus the former British prime minister, Margaret Thatcher, boasted that she was a conviction politician who abhorred consensus. 'For me, consensus seems to be the process of abandoning all beliefs, principles, values and policies' (Thatcher, 1981, quoted in Kavanagh, 1990: 7). Even so, Mrs Thatcher was a rather more pragmatic politician than her own rhetoric suggested.

Politics is about ideas and principles?

Much of the writing on politics that has come down to us from the past has been unashamedly normative. In other words this writing is concerned with how politics should be, rather than how it is. Political philosophers for 2500 years have argued over how human beings should live together, over the best form of government, over the justification for private **property** and its distribution, over how far citizens should obey the state, and what **rights** and **freedoms** they should enjoy. Many of these questions have continued to inform political debate and influence political change down the ages and through to the present day.

Thus the US Declaration of Independence (1776) proclaimed, 'We hold these truths to be self-evident, that all men are created equal, that they are endowed by their Creator with certain inalienable rights, that among these are life, liberty and the pursuit of happiness.' The French Declaration of the Rights of Man (1789) pronounced 'Men are born free and remain equal in rights.' These were bold. ambitious claims, and it is easy to point out how far reality fell short of the rhetoric. Yet there were substantially successful campaigns to apply these rights, to abolish the slave trade and the institution of slavery, to promote freedom of speech, to end religious and racial discrimination, to emancipate women, and much else. Many of the rights and freedoms secured have been enshrined in state constitutions, the United Nations Universal Declaration of Human Rights (1948) and the European Convention on Human Rights (1951). There are also modern political creeds or ideologies commonly loosely linked with political parties, publicly committed to greater equality and social justice, or more freedom for the individual, or whatever. Ideas, values and principles seem central to much of modern political debate, yet they have been largely absent from this discussion over the nature of politics, so far at least.

There are reasons for the omission. As we have seen, at least one modern major theoretical approach to the study of politics assumes humans are motivated by rational self-interest, and that any ideals they proclaim are just a form of protective colouring, or involve simply self-delusion. Indeed there are abundant examples of political hypocrisy: politicians who extol the sanctity of marriage and family values, while conducting extra-marital affairs, or who accumulate wealth while preaching socialism, or who jet around the world to promote resource conservation.

There are also sad reminders of the way inspiring political ideals like **freedom** and **equality** can be perverted. As the French revolutionary Madame Roland mournfully observed on the way to her own appointment with the guillotine in 1793, 'O liberty! What crimes are committed in thy name' ('*que de crimes on commet en ton nom*'). One thinks of other political movements similarly inspired by high ideals that ended in tyranny, as portrayed in George Orwell's bitter satire on the 1917 Russian Revolution, *Animal Farm* (1945), in which the animals' dream of equality ends in the cynical slogan, 'All animals are equal, but some are more equal than others.' Disillusion with the fruits of communism helped influence a wider rejection of political ideologies for the politics of pragmatism ('What matters is what works').

Yet it was not just because of the betrayal of such political ideals that traditional political philosophy and political **ideologies** fell from fashion. The emergence of logical positivism in the early twentieth century revolutionized the study of philosophy, and led to the rejection of 'metaphysics', under which title was included moral and political philosophy. This was among the influences on the development of a parallel revolution in the study of social sciences, including politics, which involved the rejection of normative political theory for the positive scientific analysis of political behaviour. The behavioural revolution reached its climax in the 1950s, which saw the announcement of the death of political philosophy (Laslett, 1956) and, at the end of decade, the end of ideology (Bell, 1960). It has since become clear that the obituaries were premature. The study of political ideas is now very much alive. Even so, it remains under-emphasized in many accounts of the nature of politics, which continue to emphasize the political process over political aims and values.

BOX 1.5 normative political theory and positive political science

Normative political theory involves the prescription of norms of conduct and values, and the study of what *ought to be* rather than what *is*

Positive political science involves the 'positive' or 'objective' scientific analysis of political behaviour

Yet politics without hopes, dreams and values is ultimately a rather mean-spirited business. The growth of political apathy and alienation, particularly but not exclusively among the young, is much lamented, the reasons for it much discussed, and possible remedies put forward (Putnam, 2000; Stoker, 2006). Nevertheless, there is abundant evidence that people can still be stirred by a particular issue or cause. Much of this transcends party and parliamentary politics. There is also indeed an evident danger that where zeal for a cause becomes fanaticism it can involve a rejection of the normal democratic politics altogether and even the embrace of violence. Mainstream democratic politics faces growing apathy on

Politics without hopes, dreams and values is ultimately a rather mean-spirited business.

one side and intolerant fanaticism on the other. It has to offer some ideals, inspiration and hope which encourage people to engage with it.

We are perhaps in danger of forgetting that politics can inspire as well as disappoint. There are those who have given their lives so that others can enjoy the rights and freedoms now largely taken for granted. They include Abraham Lincoln who fought a war to abolish slavery and preserve democracy in the United States, Mahatma **Gandhi**, whose inspired non-violent campaigns of civil disobedience eventually secured the establishment of a free democratic India, and Martin Luther **King**, the black American civil rights leader who dreamed 'of a day when the sons of former slaves and of former slave owners will be able to sit down together at the table of brotherhood'. We might think also of the defiant speech of Nelson Mandela, on trial for his life in the South Africa of apartheid in 1964:

> I have cherished the ideal of a democratic and free society in which all persons live together in harmony and with equal opportunities. It is an ideal which I hope to live for and achieve. But if needs be, it is an ideal for which I am prepared to die.

He was eventually set free from his sentence of life imprisonment to become the first president of the new post-apartheid South Africa, and then modestly and freely resign the power he had never realistically anticipated. The new South Africa he did so much to establish is far from perfect, but promises a better future for the majority of its people.

There is, unhappily, abundant evidence that political ideals can be betrayed or sold short, and they can be pursued dogmatically and fanatically. Yet ideals can inspire even if they are often only imperfectly realized. Thus although proclamations of human rights may commonly be more honoured in the breach than the observance, they set a standard of conduct that has already materially influenced political behaviour for what many of us would consider the better.

So what is politics?

So what is the right answer? Some of the answers discussed (both here and elsewhere) may seem more plausible than others, but none appear totally convincing. Some are perhaps more appealing than others, but that does not necessarily make them right. There is indeed, no incontrovertibly right answer. There are many key concepts in the study of politics that are 'essentially contested', including politics itself. These essentially contested concepts reflect differing and competing interpretations of the world and human society. A politics student needs to understand these competing perspectives and different answers, and weigh them against the available evidence. But on many key issues the evidence is not conclusive. Ultimately, you will have to make up your own mind on many aspects of the subject and on the nature of politics itself. That should not be a source of anxiety. Politics is inherently controversial. To many of us it is what helps to make the subject so fascinating.

A politics student needs to understand these competing perspectives and different answers, and weigh them against the available evidence.

Section 2: What to expect from your politics course

The main elements of a politics degree course

Politics courses vary considerably, both between countries and between universities, although most offer some broadly comparable main elements. Each of these may contain several specific modules and lead on to a wide range of specialist options. These main elements are explained below. It should, however, be appreciated that they may be described under rather different titles in some institutions, and the weight attached to each element may vary considerably between institutions.

The politics and government of particular states

The politics and government of the country in which the university is situated will constitute a core element of most politics degrees around the world. For 'home' students the politics of their own country will offer a familiar introduction to the study of the subject. For foreign students such courses provide a valuable opportunity to learn more at first hand of the government and politics of the host country. Thus virtually all degrees in politics in the United States involve students in undertaking an initial course in American government and politics, commonly followed by a range of more specialized American politics modules. Most politics degrees around the world expect or require students to learn about the politics and government of their country. Thus politics students take an introductory course in Canadian politics at the University of Ottawa, in Swedish politics at the University of Stockholm, in Australian politics at Melbourne University, and in Dutch politics at Leiden University (information from university websites).

One partial exception to this near universal provision of introductory courses in the politics of the home country is the United Kingdom. Because some undergraduates have already studied British politics as part of their specialist studies at the higher (or sixth form) level of their school studies, some (but by no means all) university departments of politics prefer not to duplicate this work at the early stages of degree study. However, they invariably offer intermediate or advanced level modules on aspects of British politics in subsequent years.

> *Most politics degrees around the world expect or require students to learn about the politics and government of their country.*

Comparative politics

The in-depth analysis of a single country's government and politics can be fascinating and illuminating, but it is now universally acknowledged that the study of politics should be comparative. Thus all university politics degrees involve some comparative politics. What this involves in practice may vary considerably. It may simply involve the in-depth analysis of the politics of one or more other countries. Thus a module in British politics offered by an American university, or a module in American politics offered by a British university, might come under the heading 'comparative politics'. Such an analysis of another country's politics does involve implicit comparison, because students will inevitably compare its political institutions and behaviour with those of their own country with which they are already familiar, and similarities and differences will often be emphasized and made more explicit by tutors.

However, most specialists would argue that a truly comparative approach involves more systematic comparison across a whole range of countries on a regional or global basis. Thus legislatures or political parties, or pressure groups, or state bureaucracies may be examined across a continent or the world. The study of comparative politics can throw up considerable variations in political practice across countries. Major differences may become apparent, in, for example, levels of turnout in elections, or the finance of political parties, or checks on the power of central government, or media bias or the extent of corruption. Cross-country surveys may throw up a wide range of political attitudes, loyalties and values. Further analysis may suggest tentative hypotheses for the reasons for these variations, hypotheses that might be tested against the available evidence. Such work may help to illuminate why some peoples appear willing to engage in politics while others are more apathetic, why some political systems appear more durable than others, or why some countries have apparently managed the transition to democracy more smoothly than others (Hague and Harrop, 2007).

> The study of comparative politics can throw up considerable variations in political practice across countries.

International relations

While there is global scope for such comparison, comparative politics still focuses primarily on the government and politics of states, rather than inter-state politics, or the politics of transnational and international organizations. Yet many of the really big political issues, such as peace and war, global inequality, the conservation of the environment and the very survival of humanity, transcend state borders. They involve relations between states, and also, increasingly, international government and **non-governmental organizations** (**NGOs**) as well as powerful transnational business corporations (TNCs). The subject (or sub-discipline) of **international relations** examines the efforts of governments, organizations and peoples to tackle these vital issues of international peace and security, global inequality and the future of the planet (Brown with Ainley, 2005). These are issues that naturally interest and concern students, who rightly expect them to figure prominently in any politics degree programme. While international relations has long been treated as a core subject, the literature on **globalization** and international political economy has expanded to such an extent that they figure prominently as special fields of study in many politics degrees.

> Many of the really big political issues, such as peace and war, global inequality, the conservation of the environment and the very survival of humanity, transcend state borders.

Political theory

Political theory almost invariably figures as another core study area in a politics degree. Yet the broad label 'political theory' is somewhat problematic and can conceal considerable variations in content. It may not seem immediately obvious that political theory should be a distinctive field of study within politics. Theories are integral to the study of politics. The analysis of political behaviour inevitably involves theory. The study of comparative politics certainly includes masses of theory at every level. Radically contrasting theories underpin the study of international relations. Why should those undertaking a university degree in politics be expected to take a separate course in political theory? However, 'political theory' as a subject is commonly interpreted to mean the theories or ideas that key thinkers have had about politics over time. This time dimension can be very long – extending back to the political ideas of the ancient Greeks 2500 years ago. Thus in many universities political theory entails the study of the writings of great political philosophers of the past from Plato onwards, up to and sometimes including, the present day.

Such political theory can be fascinating but much of it is unashamedly 'normative', in other words involving how politics should be conducted, the best form of government, arguments for obeying authority, justifications for equality or inequality, rather than the more dispassionate or 'scientific' analysis of political behaviour as it is. This goes back to the distinction between normative political theory and explanatory political science discussed in Section 1 (see Box 1.5, page 16), which is a recurring theme in this book. Some of the early pioneers of the behavioural revolution in the study of politics and other social sciences rejected traditional political philosophy as unscientific. Yet the rigorous separation of 'fact' and 'value' appeared more difficult than these pioneers imagined, and much of the new political science involved implicit normative assumptions. Indeed, many of the key political issues facing the modern world clearly have an important ethical dimension (consider issues of human rights, global inequality, green politics). Moreover, political philosophy in recent decades has experienced a considerable revival and is no longer exclusively associated with the writings of 'dead white European males'.

Some political theory courses involve a thematic approach to explore issues of justice, equality, freedom, political rights and obligations, while others prefer to tackle these issues through a chronological treatment of key thinkers, such as Plato, Aristotle, Machiavelli, Hobbes, Locke, Rousseau, Kant, Mill and Marx. Others politics courses prefer to focus more narrowly on the thinkers of the last two centuries, and take in some of the pioneers of modern social science, such as Durkheim and Weber, and more recent thinkers such as Hayek, Dahl and rational choice theorists, as well as the work of modern political philosophers such as Rawls and Nozick. Other university courses distinguish between traditional political theory and the theories and methodologies of modern social and political science, and deal with these in separate introductory modules, as well as more advanced specialist options. At some stage, research methods feature in most courses, commonly involving some statistics.

Public policy and public administration

Public policy and/or public administration is a core area of study in many general politics degree courses, and is the main focus of some more explicitly vocational degree programmes, preparing students for a wide range of possible careers in public administration at various levels of government. The study of public policy and administration deals not only with political institutions and processes but with public **bureaucracies** and the outputs and outcomes of public policy. This involves examining the whole policy cycle from the identification of a problem, through the search for a solution, and the emergence of policy, and on to implementation and subsequent monitoring and review. This approach gives

> *The study of public policy and administration deals not only with political institutions and processes but with public bureaucracies and the outputs and outcomes of public policy.*

more attention to actual policies, such as transport, health or education policies, relatively neglected in some politics degree courses. Such a focus commonly reveals problems in implementing policy, and the often unintended consequences of policy decisions. It has already generated significant academic debate and an impressive and extensive body of theory (Parsons, 1995).

Choosing a university, degree course and options

Where to study?

Many readers will have already chosen a degree course and indeed may well have started it. In that case you may prefer to skip this section. However, if you have yet to make a decision, but think you would like to study politics at university, there are a bewilderingly large number of courses and institutions to choose between. It is worth considering your choice carefully. You are about to commit three or four years of your life to this course, which will cost you (and/or your family) a considerable financial sacrifice, but may have a significant effect on the opportunities open to you thereafter. It is not a decision to take lightly.

The advice here is confined to educational issues. In practice there are many factors influencing the choice of university that may have little to do with purely educational issues. Thus some students have to study near home and others want to, for personal or financial reasons, and this will considerably reduce the options available to them. Those who actively prefer to study well away from home, or even abroad, have a much wider choice. They may be more interested in what a particular city, area or country has to offer by way of amenities than the attractions of specific universities or courses. These may be important factors affecting your enjoyment of a university education but they are not issues on which advice can sensibly be offered here.

To gain initial information about politics degrees at particular universities there is no substitute for examining the detailed courses that they offer, the staff responsible for teaching them, and their research interests and publications. All this information, and much else besides, is usually available from the relevant university website. (Very useful links to the websites of university politics departments around the world are provided by the Political Studies Association (PSA) in the United Kingdom: www.psa.ac.uk)

However, to state the obvious, you cannot study anywhere you want. Choice is inevitably constrained as it is a two-way process, involving both intending students and universities. Some prestigious institutions are very selective and will only offer places to the best-qualified applicants. They may not be prepared to take you, however desperately you want to go there. Other university departments may need you more than you need them. Desperately anxious to fill courses, they will eagerly accept anyone who is minimally qualified. If they are too eager, you may reasonably wonder why, although there are some good politics departments that seem to have problems recruiting students for reasons largely outside their control.

In these circumstances you may want to attend the most prestigious institution that will offer you a place. That may make sense. Reputations matter, and a good degree from an elite university carries some weight in the jobs market. Yet if you are not accepted by your first choice institution, this may matter less than you think. A good degree from a reputable university will serve you better than a poor degree from an elite university.

BOX 1.6 — what's in a name? university schools and departments in politics

Politics courses are usually provided by academic sub-divisions of universities variously described as schools, departments, or sometimes faculties (although the term 'faculty' is more commonly reserved for groupings of schools or departments). From a student perspective these academic divisions can be confusing but are of little immediate importance. (Indeed some institutions make a habit of frequent administrative reorganization.)

Of little more significance are the names given to the relevant departments or schools. Almost everywhere in the United States and commonly in much of the English-speaking world and on the mainland of Europe, courses in politics are offered by a department (or school) of political science. However, in Britain and Ireland relatively few departments or schools employ the label 'political science' (although Birmingham, University College, London, and Trinity College, Dublin are among the exceptions). Manchester, Essex and Strathclyde have departments of government, as does the University of Cork in the Irish Republic. More common is the simple description 'department (or school) of politics' or 'politics and international relations'. The lack of reference to 'science' does not mean that the approach to the study of politics is any less scientific in these universities.

These formal titles may give some indication of the flavour and range of politics that is studied. Thus a department that specifically includes 'international relations' or 'international studies' should certainly cover these subjects more than adequately. Yet the absence of international relations from a department's title does not necessarily imply any neglect of a subject that is widely regarded as integral to the study of politics. However, some universities with a particular strength in the subject area have established separate departments of international relations (e.g. Sussex in England and St Andrews in Scotland).

A number of universities around the world have departments of public administration, public management or public policy, suggesting a particular emphasis on the institutions and processes of government and the public sector at every level.

Some elite universities, with an enviable world-wide reputation for scholarship and research, do not always attach a high priority to the education of undergraduates (although others take teaching very seriously). Some world-famous professors may not even figure on undergraduate teaching programmes, and others may not be good performers in lecture halls or seminar classes. Brilliant students may succeed anywhere, almost regardless of the quality of the teaching. However, if you are an ordinarily good, rather than a brilliant, student you may be better off in a university that does not enjoy a world-wide reputation for research and scholarly publications, but gives a high priority to good-quality teaching.

There is considerable variation in the size of university politics departments. Large departments will naturally employ more staff, with a wider range of scholarship and expertise, and may offer a greater range of courses and a far more extensive choice of specialist politics options. They will commonly be associated with much better library and other facilities, (although some popular and prestigious universities have rather over-crowded, old-fashioned and poorly-equipped lecture and seminar rooms). Smaller departments will inevitably reduce the range of choice, but there may be compensations. A more limited range of modules may fit together better in an integrated programme, and smaller institutions can be less impersonal, and enjoy better staff–student relations.

You will want to know about the university facilities, and on the academic side its learning resources, particularly its library and information technology. You should also find out what is expected of you in terms of work and attendance in lectures and seminars, and the overall pattern of assessment across the course, which can differ quite considerably between universities. What for example is the balance between unseen examinations and other forms of assessment? Does the course include a compulsory or optional dissertation or long essay? What degree classifications have recent cohorts of students obtained? What proportion of students drop out or fail? What did students do after graduating? What further courses did they undertake and what jobs did they obtain? Are there opportunities for a period of study abroad, perhaps at a partner institution, or to undertake a placement or political internship in an appropriate department or organization? (See below.)

> You should find out what is expected of you in terms of work and attendance in lectures and seminars, and the overall pattern of assessment across the course.

The answers to some of these questions may be in the university prospectus or departmental website (easily accessed, for example, via www.psa.ac.uk), although this material is of course designed to promote the institution. Other more neutral and dispassionate information on performance may be in the public domain, and is sometimes required by governments, and published in guidebooks or newspaper supplements. However, there is no substitute for sampling an institution first hand. Attend an 'open day' if you are given the chance. You will meet some of the tutors and ideally some current students, perhaps attend a sample lecture, inspect some of the teaching material, tour the library and facilities, and have the opportunity to ask questions (including some of those suggested in the previous paragraph).

Degrees of specialization

One decision that you may have to take when initially choosing your course is how much politics you want to study, and what other subjects (if any) you might want to study alongside politics. This is a decision you may not always have to take immediately, but can postpone until after you have begun your course, perhaps before you start your second level or year of studies. Commonly, university degree courses are initially broad in the first year or level, and become more specialist as well as more advanced at subsequent levels. Sometimes this will involve studying a range of disciplines or subjects at foundation level, with students only opting for specialization in a single discipline later.

In most universities you will be faced with key choices at various stages of your degree course, including whether to specialize in politics, or combine the study of politics with another discipline or disciplines, or take politics as a subsidiary subject. Thus an undergraduate in an American university may choose to 'major' in politics, or alternatively may prefer to make it a minor or subsidiary element of their degree programme, taking just a few politics modules. In Britain and some other parts of the English-speaking world there is often a choice between taking a 'single honours' (or 'pure honours') or 'joint honours'. A single honours course in politics will be devoted principally to the study of politics, although the study of some other subjects in associated disciplines, such as economics, sociology or law, may also be involved. In a joint (or combined) honours course, politics is studied in combination with one or more other discipline, commonly drawn from other social sciences or the humanities, such as politics and economics, or politics and history, or politics and law. One popular degree title, used by some leading British universities, combines three major subjects, philosophy, politics and economics (PPE). Some universities elsewhere in the English-speaking world employ the US terminology of 'majoring' in a particular subject alongside the British distinction between single and joint honours degree programmes.

A combined or joint honours degree programme course will clearly reduce the breadth and depth of the coverage of politics, although studying politics in conjunction with another allied discipline can frequently offer fresh insights into both. Partner disciplines may also significantly influence the approach to the study of politics. Thus where politics is combined with one or more other social sciences, such as sociology or economics, it is likely to be treated rather differently from politics studied alongside history or philosophy or law. The same may also be true of the disciplines with which politics is combined, particularly where they clearly overlap, as evidenced in composite subject labels, such as political economy or political sociology. Similarly, where politics is combined with a subject like law this is likely to influence the content of both, with particular emphasis on constitutions, government and the legislative process, and human rights on the politics side, and on constitutional law and administrative or public law rather than private law. (See the illustrative example of politics degrees at Essex University's Department of Government in Box 1.7).

The title of a single honours degree in politics may simply mirror the title of the department or school. However, very large departments may offer a range of specialist politics degrees, for example in public policy or international relations, as well as courses that combine the study of politics with another discipline or disciplines. (See, for example, the politics degrees provided at Essex.) These more specialist degrees may not always be quite as distinctive as their titles suggest. Thus a range of degree programmes may share some core politics modules and have access to some similar specialist politics options (as at Essex). Students who have studied many of the same modules may sometimes graduate with very different degree titles.

Decisions on more specialist politics programmes require careful consideration. You will naturally be guided by your own interests, by your performance in particular modules, and by career considerations, as well as the advice your receive.

Specialist options

Whether you take a single honours degree in politics, major in politics or take politics in combination with another subject or subjects, you will still normally have a range of politics options to choose between at some stage in your course. A large university with a big politics department will normally offer not only more choice of degree courses (both specialist single honours and various combined honours programmes), but also a far wider range of specialist options. It is only possible here to give a few examples of the politics options offered by specific universities around the English-speaking world (see Box 1.8).

The choice can seem daunting. These are some of the points you might like to consider.

What exactly does the module involve? This is not always self-evident from the title or short description. Study any relevant published material, such as module handbooks (sometimes available online), ask your personal tutor, and talk to students who have taken it.

How will it fit with the rest of your studies? You may fancy a topic that is quite outside your experience and unconnected with much of the rest of your course, and why not? It might spark off new interests. More commonly you may want to consider options that connect with previous studies, and may lead on to more advanced options (and sometimes even postgraduate courses or subsequent careers). Bear in mind that some choices may

BOX
1.7

four of the politics degrees offered by the Department of Government at Essex University (UK)

BA Politics

First year
Introduction to Politics
Two Social Sciences options
One Social Science option *or one* Humanities and Contemporary Studies option

Second year
Political Analysis
Introduction to Political Theory
Two options

Third year
Four politics options

In certain circumstances *one* politics option may be substituted by a project, a language course *or one* option in another social science department.

BA International Relations and Politics

First year
Introduction to Politics
Introduction to European Politics
Introduction to International Relations
One Social Science option *or one* Humanities and Contemporary Studies option

Second year
Political Analysis
International Relations
One Politics option from a specialist list
One Politics option

Third year
One option from Politics courses with a regional focus
One option from Politics courses with an International Relations focus
Two Politics options

BA Politics and Law

First year
Introduction to Politics
Either Introduction to European Politics *or* Introduction to International Relations
Public Law I
Criminal Law

Second year
Political Analysis
Joint seminar in Politics and Law
One Politics option
Public Law II

Third year
Legal and Political Theory
One Politics option
EC law
One Law option from:
  UK Human Rights Law
  European Human Rights Law
  Public International Law

BA Philosophy, Politics and Economics

First year
Introduction to Economics
Introduction to Politics
Introduction to Philosophy
Introduction to Quantitative Economics

Second year
Microeconomics, Macroeconomics *or* British Economic Policy
Three options from Government, Economics and Philosophy

Third year
Four options from Government, Economics and Philosophy

[Information from website www.essex.ac.uk/government/]

BOX 1.8 examples of specialist options provided in politics degrees from around the world

Princeton University (USA)
Ethics and Public Policy
Politics and Religion
Law and Society
American Constitutional Development
The Presidency and Executive Power
State, Nation and Cultural Identity
Political Systems of the Middle East
Politics in Africa
Political Islam
Human Rights
Politics After Communism
Inequalities
International Political Economy
Peacemaking
Causes of War
Research Methods in Political Science

University of Melbourne (Australia)
Australian Political Economy
American Politics and Society
West European Politics
Chinese Politics and Society
Modern Political Thought
Public Policy Making
Sexual Politics
European Integration: Politics of the EU
Europe: Identities and Citizenship
Quantitative Social Research
Political Communication
Global Environmental Politics
Terrorism: Shifting Paradigms
Democracy: Theories and Concepts
Classics of Political Thought
Contemporary Political Philosophy

University of Sheffield (UK)
The Analysis of British Politics
The Global Political Economy
Contemporary International Affairs
Contemporary Political Theory
Labour in Modern British Politics
Coercion, Consent and Ideology
Women and Politics
Equality and Justice
Contemporary Rights Theory
War and Peace
Politics and Public Policy in Germany
Elections and Voting
The Political Thought of Machiavelli
Migrants, Nations and States in Europe
The Political Economy of Africa
Nationalism and Ethnic Conflict in Asia

University of Toronto (Canada)
Politics and Government of the US
Canadian Government and Politics
Political Theory
Methods
Topics in Comparative Politics
Environmental Politics in Canada
The State, Planning and Markets
Managing International Military Conflict
Contemporary Canadian Federalism
Modern Political Thought
Comparative Foreign Politics
Ontario Politics
International Law
Politics of Global Governance
Russian Politics
Media in Politics

constrain what you can do in future. Thus some advanced options can only be taken if you have studied an earlier 'underpinning' intermediate option. Some more specialist degree titles may require that you take some relevant options.

Who is the tutor? This may be an important consideration. He or she may have a world-wide reputation in this subject, and you will have the opportunity to sit at the feet of an acknowledged expert (although he or she might not always be a brilliant and inspiring teacher!). You may have encountered the tutor previously in your course and know something of him or her. You may know nothing about him or her at all, in which case it is useful to seek information, including from students who have taken the module.

Is the option regularly available? Commonly, options only run if there is sufficient demand to make them economic. Sometimes options that feature in a university prospectus may not have been taught for years. Others may not run if the tutor is taking a period off for research (a 'sabbatical').

How is the option assessed? There is sometimes a fairly common pattern of assessment across modules, but in some universities assessment can vary quite considerably between modules. Some, for example, may be assessed entirely through an end of module unseen examination, while others might involve submitted essays, papers or projects. Oral presentations may feature as part of some module assessments. The form of assessment can be critical for some students. Yet you would be unwise to reject a module that otherwise fits in with your interests and plans solely because of the assessment. If you are worried about it, seek further advice, and find out how past students have fared.

Study abroad, placements and internships

Some universities may also offer the chance to study in another country in a partner institution for part of your course. This can be a great opportunity to broaden your horizons, although the personal, financial and academic implications will need to be weighed carefully. Inevitably, not all the modules in partner institutions will be comparable with those in your university. This can create some problems when you return to your home institution and find you have not fully covered some of the work necessary to enable you to cope easily with the next level of study. However, almost all students who undertake a period of study abroad find that the personal and academic advantages considerably outweigh any such difficulties.

Alternatively or additionally you may have the option to undertake a semester or year to gain practical experience of work in government, the public or voluntary sector as part of your degree course on a placement or 'internship'. Both the term and the practice of internships was originally applied to medical training in hospitals, particularly in the United States. It has been extended to cover practical work experience in other fields of study and in other countries, especially in the English-speaking world, although the term 'placement' is still more familiar in Britain. Such internships or placements remain less common in politics than on some other courses, such as business studies, where a 'sandwich' course involving a year placement with a business firm is regarded as key element of the degree. However, many politics courses are now offering such internships for those who wish to pursue them (see Box 1.9).

If you are not happy with your course

However much (or little) advanced thinking and planning you do, you may at some stage feel dissatisfied with your chosen course. If so, do not make any hasty decisions. You may be temporarily depressed for reasons perhaps unconnected with your course. Alternatively you may be finding problems on specific modules or pieces of work. Seek advice. Talk to your tutor, specialist advisory services, family, friends and fellow students. It is possible that this will resolve your problems or put them into perspective. You may also be able to take a year out of your studies and resume later.

If, however, you ultimately decide that the course is not for you, it is not the end of the world. You may be able to switch to another course at the same university, or to a different university. You may be better advised to drop out of university for a period, and retain the option of returning to higher education later, perhaps to study politics, perhaps something quite different. Many 'second chance' students have subsequently done very well. Make sure you get it right next time. To misquote Oscar Wilde, to screw up on one course might be regarded as a misfortune; to screw up on two looks like carelessness!

BOX
1.9
examples of political internships for students at universities in Australia, New Zealand, Canada and Scotland

The School of Political Science and International Studies at the University of Queensland, Australia 'has established internship partnerships with the Australian Federal Parliament, the Parliament of Queensland and a number of national and international, government and non-government agencies'. Its website quotes from the experiences of recent interns at the Department of Premier and Cabinet in Queensland, at the Australian Permanent Mission to the United Nations, at the International Service for Human Rights, at the United Nations in Geneva. One intern worked in the office of a shadow minister in the Australian Parliament, and also as an intern of the US Congress at Washington (www.polsis.uq.edu.au).

Victoria University of Wellington, New Zealand offers for selected students a programme of 'directed individual study' involving a parliamentary internship to learn about the parliamentary process by working at Parliament during their honours year. Assessment involves a seminar (25 per cent), a research paper (50 per cent) and a final examination (25 per cent) (www.vuw.ac.nz/pols/courses).

The Department of Political Science at McGill University, Montreal, Quebec, Canada, allows Honours, Joint Honours and Major students to arrange internships in political science with a sponsoring organization, which might include an international organization, a government agency or an NGO as part of their programme. Assessment is through 'a major research project based on the internship' (50 per cent), and a written record of the work conducted during the internship (25 per cent), both assessed by the university department, and a performance assessment (25 per cent) by a supervisor at the organization hosting the internship.(www.mcgill.ca/politicalscience/courses).

The University of Edinburgh enables up to 20 students to serve as political interns to Members of the Scottish Parliament following a short five-week academic programme at the Institute of Governance. Interns 'are required to undertake a research project and will have study space in the parliament building as well as an academic base in the Institute of Governance' (www.international.ed.ac.uk).

Section 3: Study skills

Critical thinking, objectivity and bias in the study of politics

The need for critical thinking is crucial in the study of politics. I used to advise my first-year students, 'Question everything. Take nothing on trust, least of all from me.' Some students are uncomfortable with doubt, and crave certainty. They seek right answers, and are unhappy when even their tutors do not claim to know what the right answer is, and positively invite criticism. If you feel this way, and cannot change this mindset, you would be well-advised to consider another subject!

Yet others have no difficulty in accepting that controversy is inseparable from the study of politics. Indeed, this is why many are initially attracted to the subject. They enjoy debate and argument, challenging the views and analyses of others, and advancing and defending their own ideas. Often they already have strong political convictions of their own. They may hope that studying politics will help them to further a particular cause, or promote their favoured **political party**, or even assist their own political ambitions. Indeed some of those who have studied government and politics have gone on to practise politics at the highest level (and some who have practised politics have subsequently retired to study it). It is hardly surprising that there should be such an interplay between the practice and study of politics.

> *I used to advise my first year students 'Question everything. Take nothing on trust, least of all from me'.*

Practising politics and studying politics

Yet the study of politics requires a different approach from its practice. The practising politician, like the practising lawyer, tries to make the best of his or her brief, and is sometimes skilled at 'making the worse cause appear the better'. It is not their job to present other arguments, to supply opposition to their own case. They can be as partisan and one-sided as they like. Students of politics, by contrast, are obliged to consider all sides to a question, and to seek to understand, and represent fairly, political perspectives with which they personally degree. They are not supposed to ignore or gloss over inconvenient facts that do not suit their case.

Facts and values

Indeed, as we have seen, politics today is regarded as a social science, aspiring to the same objective scientific approach as other sciences. Scientific method requires that hypotheses should be formulated in such a way that they can be tested rigorously against the available evidence. Research in politics, as in other sciences, should be capable of being replicated (or successfully repeated) by other researchers. Much scientific research is dependent on extensive quantitative analysis, and this is true of some political research, most notably on voting behaviour. With some other topics it is more difficult to test hypotheses using extensive quantitative analysis, yet a scholarly approach still requires that theories and causal explanations should be tested thoroughly against the available evidence.

Yet one of the problems with the social sciences in general and politics in particular is that we are part of what we are studying. We bring our own preconceptions, interests and preferences, sometimes unconsciously, to what we study, and scientific detachment is more difficult than with the physical sciences. Indeed, we would be (literally) inhuman if we failed to derive normative recommendations from some of our political analysis. International war, genocide, poverty, starvation and the destruction of the environment are all things that most of us would prefer to avoid. So perhaps we should also accept that the study of politics can embrace both a dispassionate analysis of political behaviour and recommendations for a better life for individuals and society (as indeed it did for Aristotle).

Yet if the discipline of politics involves both facts and values, it still demands obligations from students to examine evidence rigorously, not to ignore inconvenient facts, and to present arguments fairly. This is as true of political philosophy as it is of political science. If we study modern political philosophers such as **Rawls** or **Nozick** we may come to agree or disagree with their arguments, but we should still outline them fairly first. The same is true of the study of political **ideologies**. We may strongly oppose some ideologies, but we still need to understand what they are, and why and how they are held. That holds even for ideologies, such as **fascism** or **racism**, that most of us find abhorrent. The same is true of political behaviour. We may deplore political apathy on the one hand or **terrorism** on the other, but simply to condemn them will not enable us to explain either.

> *Always remember, when you are writing an essay, or presenting a seminar paper, that you are not making a political speech.*

A student of politics needs to adopt a sceptical, critical approach. This means you can by all means criticize particular institutions, thinkers or creeds, but do so from knowledge and not from ignorance. Always remember, when you are writing an essay, or presenting a seminar paper, that you are not making a political speech. You will often be invited to 'discuss' a particular statement. Normally this will involve exploring both sides (or all sides) of the issue, fairly and dispassionately, before finally reaching a balanced judgement. This may involve a reasoned support for a particular viewpoint. Yet how you are assessed will depend much less on the conclusion you reach than on how you arrive at that conclusion.

Media bias

Politics students are urged to keep up with current political developments. They are encouraged to make full use of the mass media, to read about politics in serious newspapers and magazines, to watch news and current affairs programmes on television, to surf the internet for a range of information and opinion. Yet they are also expected to cultivate a healthy scepticism with regard to the political news and the interpretations on offer from official sources and from the media. Indeed, an examination of government 'spin' and the sources of media bias and influence may figure strongly on their course.

Your own bias

Anyone studying politics needs to become sensitive to other forms of bias, not least their own bias. You should acknowledge that your own upbringing, education and the broader influences to which you have been exposed have inevitably shaped your political understanding and make you more predisposed to accept some political perspectives than others. Studying politics may not change your views, but should make you more aware and understanding of the often very different assumptions of others.

Tutor bias

Some students are so careful to avoid voicing their own political preferences that they go to the other extreme and suppress their own convictions, writing what they imagine will please their tutors rather than what they believe themselves. Politics students are often only too aware that their tutors and professors have their own political preferences. They may know that lecturer X is a conservative, that professor Y is a Marxist, that tutor Z is an advocate of animal rights. Often students think they will win favour (and grades!) by aping the views of those who teach them, even if it means suppressing their own.

This expectation is almost invariably wrong. Any tutor who only rewards those who agree with his or her own political views is acting unprofessionally. Almost all politics tutors would prefer a well-argued case with which they personally disagree to a badly argued essay in support of their own views. I once caught an able student (who might have been fairly described as 'New Right' or 'neoconservative') scribbling graffiti, 'Marx means marks', suggesting that Marxist views would be well rewarded (a comment that was perhaps directed more against one or two of my colleagues than at myself). After he and his fellow students had graduated I asked him whether he still thought that 'Marx meant marks' on his degree course. He grinned sheepishly and replied, 'No! Not after I've seen the results!'

> *Almost all politics tutors would prefer a well-argued case with which they personally disagree to a badly argued essay in support of their own views.*

By all means try to discern your tutors' own forms of bias – not just their party political preferences but their more subtle academic bias, including their preferences for some theories or methodologies over others. This will help you to a more detached and informed perception of their teaching. You may still appreciate them and profit from what they have to give, but learning also to criticize your tutor is part of your own education. None of us have a monopoly of wisdom.

Time management (and taking responsibility for your own learning)

It may not occur to some students that they need to think about managing their time, because in the past much of their time was organized for them. Most universities treat students as adults who should take responsibility for their own learning. They tell you the rules, provide timetables for classes and lectures, issue submission dates for assessed course work and publish the time and format for examinations. How you deal with this information is up to you. Some universities may not even check on your attendance at seminars and lectures. You are free – you may never have felt so free before in your entire life (and you may never be so free again). You are free to make what use you want of the facilities the university offers. You are also free to fail.

Many students unfortunately are ill prepared for the increased freedom they have to manage their own lives, and cannot cope with it. There are often plenty of other enticing opportunities and distractions open to you at university. There will seem to be more important things than your academic work. You may indeed learn a great deal outside your politics course, but you are sacrificing years of your life to study at university, and you (or more commonly your parents or guardians) may be making a considerable financial sacrifice for the privilege of attending university. If you perform well, you may set yourself up for life. If you do not, you may spend many years playing catch-up, and perhaps regretting lost opportunities. You do need to think about organizing your life and managing your time.

Timetabled lectures and seminars and 'free' time

On a politics course (as in most degree courses in the humanities and social sciences) the hours of class contact per week may be relatively light, with long gaps in between. There is a strong temptation to retire to the student union or coffee bar between classes, passing your time chatting, drinking or playing games. Yet the university will expect you to spend much of this 'spare time' studying – reading in the library, making notes, preparing for classes and working on essays, reports, seminar presentations and other projects. Commonly, most of the work on which your assessment and progression is based is 'end-loaded' in the form of end of semester, end of term or year examinations or course work. Even if deadlines seem pleasantly distant, you need to get started early, in plenty of time. If you do not prepare adequately for this work you are unlikely to meet the required standard. You risk failure.

You need to acquire good working habits, from the start if possible, and keep to them. Commonly you will be given course or module handbooks full of advice and instructions. Read and digest all the material you are given on what is expected of you. Make sure you know submission dates for course work, and the exam timetable. Draw up a daily schedule of work, and keep to it. You can reward yourself with planned free time, which will be enjoyed all the more if you have earned it following hours of productive study. Do not relying on 'burning the midnight oil' to complete course work or last-minute cramming before exams.

Making the most of lectures, seminars and tutorials

Unless you are studying by distance learning, you will normally be attending university or college regularly on a full-time or part-time basis. While much of the work you undertake on your course will involve private study in libraries, college rooms or at home, you will be expected (and often required) to attend a number of formal timetabled sessions for students each week. The hours of formal class contact may vary considerably between institutions, and over the period of study. (Commonly, more class contact may be expected in the first year, less in the final year.) These formal timetabled sessions may take various forms: for example, lectures, seminars and tutorials.

Lectures

A lecture normally involves one-way communication between, commonly, a single lecturer and a (sometimes very large) number of students. They are a cheap, but not necessarily very efficient form of teaching. Students have only minimal opportunities to participate beyond listening and taking notes, and research suggests they may retain very little of the material presented. Lectures are best seen as the start of the learning process. A good lecture will provide an introduction to a topic, raising issues and questions for students to explore further, individually through their own reading and course work, and collectively in seminar discussion and sometimes collaborative projects.

BOX 1.10 tips for making the most of lectures

> Adopt a questioning approach. Do not take material on trust. Sometimes lecturers seek to provide a balanced overall summary of different views, sometimes they express their own distinctive approach, sometimes they take a deliberately provocative line. What was your lecturer attempting to do? Compare the analysis of your lecturer with that in textbooks and more specialist books. Discuss lectures with fellow students formally and informally. You may find they react very differently to the same material.

> Make full use of any accompanying material supplied. Most lecturers will provide at least a list of the lecture topics, and some helpfully supply a synopsis of each lecture, either in a pre-circulated module or subject handbook, or in material distributed in each lecture, or provided online.

> Make brief notes during the lecture, concentrating on key points and important supporting evidence. If a lecture outline is provided, you may be able to make marginal notes on this. If not, most lecturers provide some hints on what is worth recording. You may want to make rough copies of any tables, charts or diagrams introduced in the course of the lecture. Do not try to record every word. If you do, you will be writing too frantically to be able to concentrate on understanding the lecturer's argument.

> Go over your notes as soon as possible after the lecture, while it is still reasonably fresh in your mind. Tidy them up, and highlight what appear to be key points. Write down any questions that occur to you or points that need clarifying in you own mind. You may have opportunities to follow these up in seminars or tutorials.

> File your notes, so that you can find them again when you might need them.

> Learn from and reflect on the style and technique of good lecturers. They may provide good role models for oral presentations (see later) that you may be required to undertake. (You might learn what to avoid from some lecturers!)

Seminars

Seminars commonly involve a seminar tutor and a small group of students, say from around a dozen to 20 or more. They may be scheduled to follow lectures, pursuing and developing material from the lecture, or they may involve a quite distinct programme of activities not closely related to the lectures. Either way, ideally seminars should involve two-way communication, with plenty of active student participation. The ideal is not always realized. Seminars may be poorly structured, so that students have no clear idea of what is expected of them. Alternatively, students may not have undertaken the preparatory work expected before the seminar, relying on others to do the work and the talking. In either case, there may not be much effective student participation and the tutor will do most of the talking, virtually delivering an impromptu mini-lecture. You may think you will learn more from simply listening to the tutor, but in politics especially you learn principally by testing your ideas and understanding in open discussion.

Seminars may be structured to achieve this by a clear specification of tasks to be undertaken both before and during the seminar. Thus the whole seminar group may address a series of questions or tasks, perhaps arising from the previous lecture or from prescribed reading. A large seminar group may be broken up into smaller groups of three or four, each given specific problems or questions to investigate, reporting back to the whole seminar. Individuals or small groups of students may be required to deliver more formally an oral presentation to begin seminar discussion. Some students regard an oral presentation as a fearful ordeal, but it is extremely useful skill that it is well worth acquiring (see below for more on oral presentations).

Active participation in seminars is valuable in itself. However, it is increasingly the case that many students take what might be described as an instrumental attitude to the work required of them. Thus they concentrate their efforts on work that is formally assessed, and will determine whether they pass or fail, and the level of their final mark, grade or class. They neglect work that is not formally assessed. This can be a bad mistake. Some seminar activities may be excellent preparation for tackling formal in-course assessments or examinations. However, on some courses extra incentives may be provided to encourage effective involvement in seminars. Thus students may be required to write up seminar logs of their activities, and these may form a (generally small) part of the assessment of the module or subject. Alternatively, or additionally, individual or group seminar presentations (see below) may be formally assessed as part of the overall assessment package. While some may deplore the need for such incentives, some formal assessment of seminar activities can significantly improve their quality.

Tutorials

Traditionally, tutorials involved meetings between a tutor and just one or two students. They are thus a very expensive form of teaching. While in some ancient universities whole courses still revolve around weekly tutorials, in most institutions they are very sparingly provided. Indeed the use of tutorials as a regular and systematic part of teaching is now commonly confined to dissertations or extended essays (if these are part of a course) often in the final year. Where such facilities are provided, use them!

In some institutions, new students may be assigned a personal tutor, who is expected not to teach them on particular topics or modules, but to take an interest in their work and progress, perhaps over the first year or over the whole course. This tutor is normally the first person you should see if you have any academic, health, family or personal problems. They will provide contact details and/or times when they may be available in their room, but most of the initiative is left to the student. Students may only be exceptionally summoned to see their tutor, usually following some reported shortcoming – poor attendance, missed work, or a more serious disciplinary problem. Relatively few students voluntarily pursue meetings with their tutors, even if they run into serious difficulty. Indeed, they may purposefully avoid any contact. This is a serious mistake. Most tutors are understanding and sympathetic. Although it is sometimes difficult to imagine, all tutors were once students, and commonly experienced similar sorts of problems themselves. If you are open with them, they can often provide constructive practical help and advice, both on issues directly concerned with your course, and on other problems affecting your work and performance. They can also put you in touch with a whole range of specialist services.

Researching topics, using books, articles, the internet and other sources

You have been set a politics assignment on a specific topic that you need to research. How do you set about it?

Commonly you will have been given a reading list. This may begin with a chapter or two from textbooks you have been advised to purchase and have to hand. Beyond that, you will almost certainly have been recommended to consult a number of more specialist books and perhaps journal articles, which can normally be consulted online. Such reading lists can vary considerably in their usefulness. Sometimes they appear mercifully brief – until you discover there are no copies of the titles recommended left in the university library, and alternatives are not suggested. You may need to search for these yourself. Sometimes the list is formidably long, so that you could not possibly be expected to consult more than a small number of sources, but there is little indication of which are the most important to look at. Rarely will you be expected to read a book from beginning to end, but specific page references are not always provided (see advice below on 'finding what you need from books and articles').

Use the library

With luck most of the books and articles you are recommended to read will be accessible in your university library, or from other libraries to which you can gain access (such as a city reference library). You should be able to access the library catalogue giving full book details, location and availability. Familiarize yourself thoroughly with the layout, facilities and regulations of your own university library and other useful libraries. You may already be aware of the Dewey cataloguing system. Most politics books will be found catalogued from 320 to 330, although you may find other useful texts under different headings (e.g. 'public administration' from 350). You will often need to look on the shelves housing subjects linked with politics, such as sociology, economics, law and history. If you cannot find the books you need in your university library, you should be able to order them on inter-library loan. Very recent books, not yet purchased or catalogued by your library, may sometimes be perused quickly in bookshops (but it is not usually easy to take notes!).

> *Familiarize yourself thoroughly with the layout, facilities and regulations of your own university library.*

Do not neglect the library reference section. The downside is that you cannot normally take reference books out, but the compensating advantage is that you are more likely to find the books you need on the shelves, or after a short wait if they are in current use. Ordinary dictionaries and even encyclopaedias may not be sufficiently specialist for your purposes, but you will find some more specific politics dictionaries, sourcebooks, yearbooks, handbooks, collections of statistics and journal abstracts. For some assignments these resources are invaluable.

You may also be expected to consult journal articles (perhaps less so initially, but more frequently as your course progresses). Current journals may be found unbound. Past journals may be found loose in cardboard files or bound in volumes by number and date. However, today many journals can be consulted more readily online. Some important developments in the discipline have sometimes first appeared in journal articles. Publication in prestigious journals is highly prized in the profession, and students who use such sources can feel they are at the frontiers of knowledge and research. Sometimes it is possible to follow the course of a major academic controversy through a series of journal articles.

Finding what you need from books and articles

Academic reading is not like reading a novel or a popular work of non-fiction. You seldom need to start at the beginning and read to the end. A book is a resource from which you take what you need. You should already have some idea of what you hope to learn from it: perhaps questions you want answered, theories or approaches for which you seek explanations or criticisms. Do not read passively, hoping to 'soak up' knowledge, but actively and thoughtfully. Some passages that are less useful for your immediate requirements may be skipped or skim-read. Other passages you may need to re-read carefully until you have fully grasped their meaning. If there are words that you do not fully understand, you will have to look them up in ordinary or more specialist dictionaries. Once you have read the relevant chapters or pages, think about them, then close the book and try to note down the key points (see section on note-making). Then go back to check that you have included all that is necessary.

BOX 1.11 parts of a book

You should also become familiar with parts of a book that you might neglect if you are reading simply for entertainment, such as publication details, tables of contents, references and the index.

> You will need full *publication details* for your own reference purposes (see the section on referencing, page 40–2).
> The *year of publication* may be particularly significant, as it tells you how up to date the book is. Not only recent political developments but important theoretical advances may be missing from older sources. This is important if your assignment requires up to date information and analysis, in which case you should also check that you have the latest edition available.
> With the classic texts of political science and political philosophy the date matters less. If they involve *translation* from another language, note that translations can vary considerably, so the name of the translator is significant. Also some editions may include useful expert *introductions*.
> An *author's preface* may give important insights into his or her intentions.
> The *table of contents* will give you a brief overview of the structure, approach and detailed coverage.
> For specific information, turn to the *index* and check the page numbers of relevant entries.
> Notice the *system of referencing* employed. You may need to follow up some of the references yourself.
> As you pursue your studies further, you may find it helpful to skim the *bibliography* to gain some idea of the source material the author has used, and perhaps underlying theoretical assumptions.

Other learning resources

Most university libraries and learning centres will contain a wide range of other resources, such as collections of video tapes, audio tapes, compact discs and DVDs, which may be particularly useful for some assignments. You will probably be able to read newspapers and watch television programmes from around the world (useful sometimes for comparative politics). The library may often record television and radio programmes for you. It will also normally contain large numbers of computer terminals, with access to expensive and sophisticated networked software not easily available on home computers.

The internet

For many students today the first port of call will be not a book or journal article, but the internet. This is admittedly a very useful resource. Indeed, you may be advised or required to use specified websites for your assignment. There are some very useful and highly respected academic websites which you can consult. Additionally, and particularly if you are studying political communication, or specific aspects of government, political parties or pressure groups, you would be well advised to consult official government department websites, political party websites, and the websites of particular interest and cause groups. Newspaper websites contain masses of information on politics around the world too recent for even the most up to date textbook. Many students will already be very familiar with searching the internet for information with Google.

Much of this can be very helpful. Some online material is not only free but excellent. Yet one problem with the internet is that there is no effective quality control. Anyone can publish material on the internet. Thus entries on Wikipedia and other similar sites are not subject to an extensive process of peer review, as journal articles are. Some material may be one-sided, or simply wrong. So do not rely on it uncritically, and check against information in published sources. Some students today are over-dependent on the internet, and do not read enough books and articles. Use the internet by all means (you would be foolish not to), but use it critically and never as a substitute for other more traditional sources of information.

Note-making

Your notes provide a potentially invaluable store of raw material for writing essays, dissertations and other assignments, preparing oral presentations, and revising for exams.

Much of the writing that students undertake on a politics degree is designed to be read, and often assessed, by someone else; but notes are generally made for our own purposes, and not scrutinized by anyone else. Indeed they are often so illegibly scribbled, with a private system of abbreviations, that anyone else might find difficulty in deciphering them.

Why do we make notes? Partly to help us concentrate and make sense of what we are hearing or reading, but largely because we feel we need a record that we can return to and use later. Lectures are fleeting and most books have to be returned. Your notes provide a potentially invaluable store of raw material for writing essays, dissertations and other assignments, preparing oral presentations, and revising for exams. Yet they will be of little use if they are not written, organized and filed so that they can easily be found and read later. Note-making is to some extent a personal thing. The style of notes that suit one student may not suit another. (See Cottrell, 2003: 126–32.) Here are some suggestions.

> **Keep notes brief.** Some students write too much, noting down every other word in a book or lecture. This is not only hard work, but counter-productive. It is impossible to understand the sense of a lecture or book chapter if you are scribbling non-stop. Also, it can lead to suspicions of plagiarism if you later expand such full notes into essay form (see 'plagiarism and how to avoid it', page 42–4).

> **Concentrate on key points.** Before reading, consider what you hope to learn from a particular book. Read with questions in mind. Then close the book and jot down the key points. Only then go back and check you have what you need. Use sensible abbreviations.

> **Clarify your notes.** Particularly after a lecture, but also after noting a book or article, you may need to spend a few minutes doing this. Number pages, and underline, circle or highlight important points. Use arrows to make connections clearer. Correct any slips. Names, dates, statistics and quotations need to be accurately recorded.

> **File your notes,** using any system that makes sense for a particular module of subject in a loose-leafed folder. You can separate topics by coloured card dividers. This makes it easier to find relevant notes later.

> **Avoid writing notes in the margins of books**, particularly library books. Librarians and tutors regard defacing library books as a serious offence. It is also distracting for later readers who may be seeking answers to different questions. (You can deface your own books as much as you like, if you really want to, unless of course you plan to sell them on later.)

Quantitative and IT skills

Quantitative skills

Quantitative skills are sometimes, rather illogically, bracketed with IT skills. Computers can certainly do some of the laborious mathematical calculations that previously had to be undertaken by students, and they can certainly present statistical information effectively and attractively in a variety of ways. To use statistical information appropriately requires some elementary understanding of statistical methods. Advanced statistical programmes (such as SPSS) facilitate the complex manipulation of data through, for example, multiple regression analysis, which was once extremely difficult and time-consuming. Yet at undergraduate level advanced mathematical skills, although potentially very useful, have not become as essential for the study of politics as they are already for the study of economics. However, they are undoubtedly important for anyone hoping eventually to undertake research on aspects of politics requiring advanced quantitative analysis, such as voting behaviour.

IT skills

Computers are now a familiar tool of education at every level, but particularly in universities. It was not always so. When computers were initially introduced, elementary courses had to be provided for the many students with no previous experience of their use. Now the vast majority of students are far more experienced and proficient in the use of computers than some more elderly academic staff. Indeed among some students who have become over-dependent on sophisticated computer software and the internet, it is more traditional skills that are more often lacking. Staff accustomed to elegantly written and beautifully presented word-processed assignments can get quite a shock when they encounter illegible and badly spelled hand-written examination scripts from the same students.

It is thus hardly necessary to emphasize the advantages of modern word-processing packages, of sophisticated programmes like Excel for manipulating and displaying quantitative data, and PowerPoint for illustrating oral presentations. In each case there are easy practical guides available, but facility grow fast with practice. It is also largely superfluous to draw attention to the extensive information available on the internet. Some politics modules and specific assignments may recommend accessing particular websites.

Writing essays and other assignments

You may be assessed in various ways on a politics degree, and other forms of assessment are discussed elsewhere. However, the traditional essay remains the principal form of assessment, both on formally assessed course work and in examinations. In some ways the essay is an extremely specialized and rather artificial form of communication. Some students may never be required to write another essay in their life after graduating, but good essay-writing technique remains of crucial importance for success on a politics degree course.

Good advice on writing essays can be obtained from general books on study skills (for example Dunleavy, 1986, ch. 5; Cottrell, 2003, chs 7 and 8). More specific books on writing include Peck and Coyle (1999), and Greetham (2001). You should also pay particular attention to any advice provided by your university, course and individual tutors. After all, they are responsible for your assessment. Beyond that, consider the following points.

> The most frequently provided advice on writing answers (and perhaps the advice that is most commonly ignored) is to *answer the specific question set*. Do not write all you know about the topic, or provide a precis of a lecture or textbook chapter.

> An essay requires not the mere regurgitation of knowledge and theory, but the *application* of that knowledge and theory to a specific question. It tests how well you can *apply* what you have learned to provide a structured argument that answers the question set.

> You should therefore *examine the question carefully*. Look for key words or phrases that tell you what you have to do, such as 'Account for', 'Compare and contrast', 'Critically evaluate', 'Discuss' and 'To what extent …?' Each 'question' requires a distinctive approach. (You may notice that only the last requires a question mark at the end of a sentence.)

> A common device is to provide a quotation with the innocent instruction, 'Discuss'. Whether the quotation is genuine (in which case the source is normally provided) or made up, you are not necessarily expected to agree with it, but to explore it, criticize it, expose any limitations and indicate alternative perspectives.

> You may need to *explain or define terms or concepts* used in the question. Make sure you know their meaning and significance.

> Plan your answer. Organize your plan around a number of key points (say five to nine) that you can support with evidence and expand into paragraphs.

> The first plan that comes into your head may not be the best. There are often different ways of tackling a question. Consider alternatives.

> Be prepared to modify your plan as you proceed. Word processing makes it easy to shift blocks of text if you conclude your initial order was wrong.

> Write your essay using your plan and other notes you have made. This will help you to use your own words. Avoid writing with books open in front of you. In this way you will avoid copying and accusations of plagiarism (see pages 42–4).

> Utilize, apply and explain any relevant theory, model or key concept.

> Support your arguments with evidence (facts, figures, quotations etc.)

> Use short quotations from reputable sources that support your own arguments. Do not use quotations as a substitute for your own analysis. (Some student essays involve little more than a series of long quotations joined with connecting sentences.)

> Use the referencing system recommended by your course or tutor, or if none is recommended, choose the system you prefer. Whichever system you adopt, you should source all quotations and research findings, as well as theories and concepts associated

with particular political scientists or thinkers (see the section on referencing, below, for detailed advice).

> Writing style is a personal matter. However, you should avoid slang, colloquialisms, and abbreviations used in everyday speech (e.g. 'didn't', 'could've'). Use other abbreviations only sparingly.

> Some advise avoiding the first person. Certainly it should only be employed sparingly, if at all, perhaps in an introductory 'signpost' paragraph. Avoid peppering your essay with 'I think' or 'I consider'. Such phrases are redundant. The whole essay should be what you think.

> Some advise writing in plain English and avoiding jargon. The advice is sound, up to a point. Do not use long rare words when short common ones will do. But all disciplines use a specialized vocabulary, and politics is no exception. Many key political concepts (see Part III) are either unfamiliar, or use familiar terms in an unfamiliar specialized sense. You do need to show you have mastered the appropriate terms.

> Write in paragraphs that each discuss and explore a single point, as part of a connected, structured argument. This should not be too difficult if you are writing to a sound plan. A series of disconnected short paragraphs or a continuous undivided text both suggest a haphazard series of disconnected points rather than a structured argument.

> Throughout, ensure that everything you write contributes to an answer to the question set. This does not necessarily mean repeating the actual words of the question at regular intervals throughout your essay (which can be tedious for writer and reader), but it is advisable to refer back explicitly to the question in your conclusion.

> Normally you will have been given a number of words for your essay (typical lengths are 1500 or 2000 words). You should be able to provide an answer to the question set within this number of words, and you may be penalized if you exceed it (check whether it is a guide to the average length expected or a limit that should not be exceeded). If your first draft is too long or much too short you may need to make appropriate changes.

> Make sure you thoroughly proofread your essay. Poor spelling and grammar and inaccurate details show a careless, unscholarly approach and will be penalized. Make sure proper names are spelled correctly, dates and other figures are accurate and quotes are exact.

> If you think you have followed all the above advice and still get a poor mark, seek a meeting with your tutor for further feedback. Try to learn from criticism.

Referencing

Scholarly academic books and articles normally provide extensive references. A reference provides the reader with the source of information that can be followed up and checked. The extent and accuracy of references is one test of scholarship. An absence of references does not mean that the information is necessarily wrong, but it does make it very difficult to check, and thus unreliable.

Increasingly many universities try to encourage good habits from the start and expect all student assignments, from first-year essays onwards, to be properly referenced. That means citing sources in the text, and providing a list of all the sources you have cited in a full bibliography at the end. Your references and bibliography provide one rough and ready initial indication of how much work you have done. A tutor marking your work will often start at the end, with your list of references or bibliography. (Of course, an impressive list of books and articles does not mean that you have actually read and understood them, but it will commonly be clear to a perceptive tutor from the evidence of the essay whether you have, so do not cheat!) The tutor will also look at your references cited in the text of your assignment, checking how they relate to the bibliography at the end. If nearly all the references cited relate to one or two sources, the tutor may, not unreasonably, conclude you have made little use of most of the other books and articles listed in your bibliography. References will be examined particularly closely if there is any suspicion of plagiarism (see the section on plagiarism, page 42–4).

There are various approved methods of scholarly referencing. One common form involves footnotes (at the bottom of the page) or endnotes (at the end of chapters, articles or books) relating to small superscript numbers in the text, thus.[1] This is a well-tried system, and has the advantage that the flow of the text is not interrupted, but it can mean much tedious repetition of details of a frequently used source in footnotes or endnotes. Such repetition can be avoided by using approved abbreviations of Latin phrases referring to earlier entries (*ibid.* to mean 'the same (as the last entry)' and '*op. cit.*' to mean 'the work already cited by this author'), but this is not easy for the reader, who has to search back for the first citation of the source. Rather more common today is the Harvard system of referencing. Here you cite just the author (or first author where there are several authors and '*et al.*' (abbreviated Latin for 'and others', to cover the others), year of publication and page number in brackets in the text: for example (Leach, 2008: 72). You then provide, at the end in 'bibliography' or 'references', a detailed reference with names and initials of all authors, full title in italics, place published and name of publisher, as follows:

Leach, R. F. (2008) *The Politics Companion*, Basingstoke and New York: Palgrave Macmillan.

With journal articles the author's name and initials and date of publication (in brackets) are provided, then the title of the article (in quotation marks, rather than italicized) followed by the journal title in italics, with volume and page references, as in the following example:

Lindblom, C. (1959) 'The science of muddling through', *Public Administration Review*, vol. 19, 79–88.

Your course may recommend a particular system of referencing, in which case you should follow this advice to the letter. Otherwise, choose the system you prefer. Modern word processing systems cope with traditional footnotes and endnotes well, automatically renumbering when you insert an extra note. Most modern books and journals, however, use the Harvard method, which is easier on the reader.

> If nearly all the references cited relate to one or two sources, the tutor may conclude you have made little use of most of the other books and articles listed in your bibliography.

studying

---

[1]   Leach, R.F. (2008) *The Politics Companion*, Basingstoke and New York: Palgrave Macmillan.

studying politics   41

What should you reference? You *must* reference any direct quotation that you provide. If you are summarizing in your own words the argument or theory of a particular writer, or comparing and contrasting the views of different writers, you should also give references. You do not have to provide a source for all the information you provide, if it is uncontroversial and reasonably well known, but if you cite data or claims from academic research you should give the source. Beyond that, you should hope to cite a range of sources in your text that will figure in the final bibliography. If you have listed a book or article in your bibliography that is not cited in the text, you may want to re-read what you have written to find a place to insert a relevant reference. If you cannot find any passage that relates to a recommended source that you have actually used, you may want to consider revising your assignment to include some relevant reference, even if – or perhaps especially if – you take a view contrary to that of the author.

What should you include or exclude? You should not dishonestly inflate your bibliography with sources you have not read or hardly used, but you should not sell yourself short by failing to list all the various sources you have consulted. It is quite legitimate to list a source you have skim-read in a library or bookshop, as long you have derived something from it. Where relevant, you may want to list websites or other relevant material, such as a newspaper article or television programme (for which you should supply relevant details and dates). Unless you have been directed specifically to such sources (for example in an assignment on political communication), you should beware of appearing over-dependent on them. A tutor will be unimpressed by a bibliography consisting largely of websites, particularly if you were recommended to consult a number of key books and/or journal articles (see under 'researching topics', page 34). You may be advised to leave out very elementary basic or pre-university sources (even if you still find it helpful to consult these sometimes). If you have been strongly recommended to use a particular source you would be well advised to list it in your references, if you can do so honestly.

It makes referencing much easier if you record the full details of sources as you use them. You can open a bibliography file for the assignment right at the beginning, adding to it as you go along. You may eventually decide that you do not want to list a particular source, as you made little or no use of it in writing your assignment, and you may then delete it. This may seem a waste of effort, yet you are likely to waste far more time looking up needed references that you no longer have to hand, if you have failed to record the details earlier. (The last point reflects bitter personal experience. I do not always follow my own advice, but I invariably regret it!)

Plagiarism (and how to avoid it)

Plagiarism is copying work from books, articles, fellow students or other people, and passing it off as your own. It is a particularly obnoxious form of cheating which is the negation of everything that education is about. It is also unfortunately a serious problem in many universities, particularly on assessed course work, long essays and dissertations. Some institutions provide their own clear guidance on plagiarism, which you should study closely. (If you still do not understand what constitutes plagiarism, see Cottrell, 2003: 133–4, which refers back to pages 46–58 and forward to page 142. It is the clearest explanation I have come across.) Universities have also developed their own checks and formal procedures for dealing with the problem. Detecting cheating has become a minor industry. Those who are caught can expect no sympathy, certainly not from university staff, and not from the vast majority of students, whose own achievements are devalued by the cheats.

I would prefer to believe that anyone reading this book is most unlikely to contemplate deliberately cheating in this way. Yet inexperienced students who have no intention of cheating can sometimes, almost unconsciously, appear to copy someone else's work, and find themselves accused of plagiarism. How could this come about, and how can it be avoided?

Inexperienced students who have no intention of cheating can sometimes, almost unconsciously, appear to copy someone else's work, and find themselves accused of plagiarism.

You should of course use your own words. There are some students, perhaps conditioned by expectations in other subjects at a lower level of education, who naïvely assume there are 'right' answers to questions they are set on politics courses (as there might be a right answer to a maths question). They further take it for granted that they will earn credit by copying out the 'right' answer, which they assume is the answer given in a lecture or textbook. Some indeed have even been taught that way. I have confronted students who have copied out whole paragraphs word for word from a book, and who protest vehemently that they have 'always written essays like that' and 'no one had ever told them it was wrong'.

There are others who understand that copying is wrong, but can be drawn into it unconsciously. It can result from writing an essay with a key book open in front of you. You may not mean to copy, but you may be drawn repeatedly into using similar phrases, because you cannot think of a better way of putting a point than as it is expressed in the book. By all means refer to books as you need them when writing an essay, but avoid writing with books continuously open in front of you. That will force you to use your own words, and help you to think about the arguments and to understand them.

Poor note-making can sometimes lead to essays that too closely resemble passages in a book or journal. A student conscientiously seeks to note a key source, perhaps a recommended textbook, and, unable to make a brief summary of the salient points, virtually copies down every other word. The essay is subsequently based on the notes, and as the latter are expanded again to make proper sentences, inevitably resembles the original text. You can avoid being accused of plagiarism in this way by improving your note-making, by not becoming too dependent on a single source or limited range of sources, and by developing your own essay-planning and writing skills (see under relevant headings elsewhere in this section).

Citing your sources with extensive accurate references (see heading on referencing) should ensure that you never face an accusation of deliberate plagiarism, although you may be urged to 'use your own words' if some of your own writing sometimes appears too close to that of a source you have cited. Those who set out to cheat commonly do not reveal the source material they have copied from, either in the text or in their bibliography. Indeed the discovery of chunks of material closely derived from an unlisted source provides fairly clear evidence of a conscious intention to plagiarize. One student who was found guilty of plagiarism at an institution with which I was connected was found to have copied almost all of his dissertation from two sources that were not listed in his bibliography, and were not even in the institution's library. Needless to say, once this was proved, he did not get a degree.

How far can you be original?

The work you produce on a politics degree course is most unlikely to be original in the sense that no one else has thought of the points you express before. Yet it should be original in the sense that you have thought for yourself about the topic, and come to your own conclusions, which you express in your own words. If you think critically right through the learning process, from an initial lecture and early reading on a topic to a final draft of an essay, you will produce work that is manifestly your own.

Sophisticated computer programs can now often trace the source of work plagiarized from published sources. Other forms of plagiarism can be more difficult to detect, but once suspicions are aroused, some tutors are remarkably persistent in pursuing the issue and bringing offenders to justice. Plagiarism cannot be tolerated because it devalues the efforts and ultimately the qualifications of honest, conscientious students. Ultimately, if it became suspected that cheating was widespread, degree certificates would become as worthless as forged banknotes. Unfortunately problems with plagiarism have already led some institutions to reduce or discard some educationally valuable forms of assessment and return to traditional unseen examinations, where cheating is much more difficult.

> *Your work should be original in the sense that you have thought for yourself about the topic, and come to your own conclusions, which you express in your own words.*

Oral presentations

Many books on study skills pay insufficient attention to formal oral presentations, and oral communication skills in general, partly perhaps because in the past these were not very important for successful performance on a degree course. The neglect of skills of oral communication has unhappily long been a feature of higher education in many countries. Formal classification has frequently depended entirely on skills of written communication in both examinations and in-course assessments. Interviews or 'vivas', where used, were often perfunctory, with significant implications only for very marginal and exceptional cases.

However, in many universities students have long been expected to give brief oral presentations in seminars. Seminars or classes, as we have seen, are supposed to require active student participation, rather than the one-way communication of more formal lectures. Yet whether because students have not completed the necessary preparatory work, or because they are nervous of criticism, it can be difficult to create a genuine dialogue and the seminar can degenerate into a mini-lecture by the tutor. One way of preventing this is to give particular students the task of introducing topics through a short presentation. That at least ensures that the designated students make a contribution to proceedings. However, as Dunleavy (1986: 171) largely accurately observed of the time he was writing:

> There are relatively few class teachers who make a concerted effort to help students give more effective oral presentations. Consequently students often approach 'giving a paper' by mumbling their way through a complete essay, or talking very loosely around a set of disorganized notes.

This situation may not have been transformed everywhere, but the major advance many of us have noticed in student skills in recent years is in the quality of oral presentations. This has been aided by a number of developments.

> **Improved guidance by institutions and tutors.** Commonly, detailed advice on general oral communication skills is provided to students in booklets or online by institutions, and this is often supplemented by more specific advice in course or module guides or handbooks. Some institutions go further and provide specialist tuition, which may involve, for example, video recordings and group analysis and discussion of student performance.

> **The formal assessment of some oral presentations as part of the overall package of student assessment.** Some tutors have been reluctant to assess presentations in this way, as they argue that marks are too arbitrary and subjective. Those with experience of such assessments argue they are no more subjective than essay marking. Normally the assessment criteria provided to students include both communication skills and content. They may feature a grid of aspects to be measured, which can also help tutors to evaluate how far the various criteria have been fulfilled. (Some tutors build in an element of peer assessment, which can work well.) The formal assessment of oral presentations has motivated students to develop their skills and has often led to a massive improvement in student performance. The skills acquired can be of immense benefit to graduates in the world of work.

> **The provision of accompanying handouts by students to support their presentation.** The circulation of material for the rest of the seminar group can provide a focus for seminar discussion. The material may take the form of notes on the presentation, a reading list, and perhaps questions for discussion. One easy way of doing this is to provide a print-out of PowerPoint slides (see below).

> **Improved technology.** Once the only equipment most students (and their tutors) used was chalk on blackboard or overhead projector transparencies. Now lecture and seminar rooms are commonly equipped with a range of sophisticated equipment enabling easy access of a wide range of audio-visual material, internet websites, and computer packages, most notably PowerPoint. The availability of such technology does not guarantee good presentations. PowerPoint presentations can look and sound impressive, but perhaps the main advantage of the package is getting students to talk to bullet points (as they could once do using cards), instead of simply reading a script. Whatever assessment criteria are used, good presentation skills should never be allowed to compensate for weak content.

> **Feedback.** Constructive feedback from tutors and fellow students can lead to steady improvement in performance in oral presentations.

> **Emulation.** A few good presentations can soon raise the general standard of what is considered acceptable.

> *Very few people find speaking in public easy. You may find some comfort in the knowledge that some outstanding political orators and effective political communicators had to overcome early failure.*

Some students fear oral presentations, and the need to perform in front of tutors and fellow students. They can be particularly difficult for students from some cultural backgrounds. These fears are worth striving to overcome, because the skills of confident oral communication are so valuable. Very few people find speaking in public easy. As a politics student you may find some comfort in the knowledge that some outstanding political orators and effective political communicators had to overcome early failure and sometimes significant speech impediments. You should pay particular heed to any advice supplied by your course and institution. However, the following guidance may be useful.

❯ Research the topic for your presentation thoroughly, until you feel *in command of your material.* The gaps in your own understanding may only become clear when you need to explain something to others (as any teacher will tell you).

❯ In your preparation, remember that an oral presentation is a very *different form of communication* from an essay, and requires different skills. You will be speaking to an audience, and you must consider their needs.

❯ Do not plan simply to read out an essay, but organize your talk around a clear framework with *headings and bullet points,* using cards, overhead projector transparencies or PowerPoint slides. The delivery may be less fluent than if you read every word from a full script, but will appear more natural, and be easier for your audience to follow, especially if the key points are on screen.

❯ Do not overload your presentation with *too much detail.* Concentrate on the main points to get across. Further supporting facts and figures may be best circulated in an accompanying handout (see page 45).

❯ Check whether you are expected to circulate copies of material to the seminar group either in advance, or on the day, and *follow any guidance that is provided.* It may form part of any assessment.

❯ Even if the circulation of such material is not required, you may still find it useful. It may help your audience to gain more from the presentation and aid subsequent discussion.

❯ You may gain credit for *effective use of technology* (e.g. PowerPoint slides, brief illustrative video or other supporting material), but try to ensure that you are not too dependent on it. Make sure any equipment you need is available and that you know how to use it. (If your seminar room lacks relevant facilities you may be able to book out relevant equipment – check well in advance.)

❯ *Rehearse* your presentation, preferably in front of a friend, and, if possible, in the room you will be using. Check *speed and timing.* You may need to make changes to keep to a recommended time. Most student presentations are too long rather than too short.

❯ When your presentation has to be delivered, *take your time.* Most nervous speakers are far too fast. Remember that you can normally count on a sympathetic audience who have either suffered a similar ordeal themselves already or have it to come.

❯ Begin by explaining what the presentation is about and how you have decided to tackle it.

❯ Throughout, hold your head up, make eye contact and *speak directly to your audience.* Try to appear confident even if you do feel it.

❯ Try to build to an effective conclusion. You may want to finish by suggesting *questions for further discussion* in the seminar. You may earn further credit if you manage to stimulate a lively debate among your fellow students, and can respond to points they make. (This may be an explicit criterion for assessment.)

Group oral presentations

Oral presentations can be made by individuals or by a group of students. Sometimes the latter is almost obligatory if seminar groups are large and the number of weeks for presentations is limited. The style of presentation for group presentations may not be very different from individual presentations, particularly if those in the group simply parcel up the topic between them, and do not meet to discuss the presentation again until the day arrives. Thus the 'group' presentation will simply involve a series of individual presentations, often involving different styles, and poor overall organization, with some overlapping material and other important aspects omitted. It may be far too long. This is not how a group presentation should ideally be organized.

Ideally, all students in the group should meet several times to prepare the presentation and exchange ideas on content and communication, culminating in a full rehearsal to check order, timing, technology and overall cohesion, allowing time for any changes that appear necessary. Admittedly, such meetings are not easy to organize, particularly for part-time students, but the advantages of full group cooperation are potentially huge. You will learn from each other, and soon appreciate the benefits of teamwork. You may each bring special skills to the group. You may divide up the work on the basis of content, with a series of individual contributions forming a coherent whole. In that case someone must provide an introduction, explaining who is responsible for what and the order of proceedings. You may have a more integrated presentation, involving an alternation of speakers, as in some television news programmes.

Depending on the assessment criteria, if the presentation is assessed, you may be able to specialize on tasks rather than content, playing to the strengths of individuals. Thus you may give the bulk of the speaking to confident oral communicators, allowing others to concentrate largely on research, devising useful accompanying material or managing the technology. You may need to explain how you divided up the work in this case, to make it clear that everyone participated.

Group projects

A group oral presentation and/or a group written report may form the culmination of a more extended group project, where a small number of students (say three to five) work on a particular topic over a period of months. This can be a extremely rewarding and enjoyable learning experience. There are many important educational and vocational advantages to be derived from such group work. In many occupations interpersonal skills and the ability to work effectively as part of a team are crucial.

However, getting everyone to participate and contribute a fair share of work can be a problem in any group project. This can be a particularly difficult if groups have been arbitrarily drawn up by tutors from lists of student names, and you have had no say in your colleagues. However, even if you are allowed some choice of your own group members, you may still find that you are let down by your best friend. Thus students may find themselves obliged to work with others who rarely attend or have low commitment. This can be a particular bone of contention when group performance is formally assessed, and all members of the group are normally given the same grade.

There is what economists call a 'free rider' problem. There is an understandable reluctance to complain to tutors about the work of fellow students (and of course there may sometimes be a serious problem inhibiting their full involvement). Yet students may feel that their marks have been unfairly dragged down by others failing to pull their weight. This is one reason that some tutors as well as students object to group assessment. It is not always fair. However, as long as it does not involve too large a share of the total marks for the module or subject, the educational benefits of group work may be considered to outweigh some of the difficulties for the fair assessment of individuals.

Dissertations and long essays

Some politics courses require or allow students to undertake, as part of their studies, a more substantial and sustained individual piece of work that might be called a long essay, or a dissertation. The difference between these terms is not just one of length (a long essay might commonly involve 5000 to 6000 words, an undergraduate dissertation around 10,000 to 12,000). A long essay is, as the name implies, a more extended, in-depth investigation of a topic than can be achieved in a standard essay of 1000 to 2000 words.

A dissertation normally involves some original research. Students select their own topic within broad parameters, conduct a literature search and choose a research question that they can proceed to test against evidence they collect and analyse. They are often provided with some instruction on research methods, and given sometimes quite detailed advice on the whole dissertation process and criteria for assessment. Commonly, students are required to submit a dissertation proposal for approval, and are then assigned a dissertation tutor, who should (but may not) have some expertise in the topic selected. From then on, they are largely on their own, apart from occasional brief meetings with their tutor.

Some students find the dissertation the most interesting and rewarding part of their whole politics course. With some it sparks an interest that determines their choice of career, or leads on to further postgraduate study. Yet for others the dissertation is a nightmare. They may not understand what is required of them, or lack the organization and self-discipline needed for the sustained commitment required. Sometimes they either do not seek, or fail to obtain, appropriate advice from the tutor assigned to them. Because it normally carries a substantial weighing in overall assessment, an excellent long essay or dissertation can raise a final degree classification, but a poor one can lead to failure. If you have a choice whether to undertake a dissertation, you need to weigh the potential costs and benefits very carefully.

> *Some students find the dissertation the most interesting and rewarding part of their whole politics course.*

Because not all undergraduate politics degrees involve a dissertation or long essay, and then not until the latter stages of the course, it seems unnecessary to provide extensive advice here. Moreover, aims and assessment criteria can vary significantly between institutions. You should therefore concentrate first on any specific advice given on your course, from dissertation handbooks and course tutors, because it is they who will be measuring your performance. There are also a number of excellent books on dissertations and social science methods (for example, Watson, 1987; Bell, 1993; Howard and Sharp, 1993; Denscombe, 1998). However, you may bear in mind the following points.

> Choose your topic with care. Choose something that interests you, as you may be involved with it for a year or more.

> You need a manageable research question, which can be tested against evidence (including both primary and secondary data) that you can collect and analyse within a clear theoretical framework.

> Do not be over-ambitious. Major national or international issues can be difficult to research. It is easy enough to obtain secondary data (information already in the public domain), but you need to think how you can provide some additional value involving primary data that you have generated yourself. You might consider a contentious local political issue. It is often easier to obtain information from local pressure groups, local politicians and local media than their national equivalents.

> For a dissertation you will commonly be required to submit a dissertation brief for approval (some of the marks may be set aside for this). This is a significant but necessary hurdle that may save you from investing time and energy in a flawed undertaking.

> Set aside time each week to work on your dissertation or long essay. Because the final submission date seems a long time ahead, there is always the temptation to neglect it while you attend to more immediate and pressing demands.

> Maintain contact with your tutor. Commonly those students who have most need of a tutor's advice make least use of it. Tutors may lack the time and energy to chase up students who fail to make or keep appointments.

> Make and file usable notes as you go. You will depend on them later.

> Start a bibliography file immediately, adding entries as you go along. This saves time and trouble later, searching for references you have failed to record. Sometimes a proportion of the final mark is given for references and bibliography. Often it is the first thing a marker looks at. Make sure your referencing meets the course requirements and looks suitably impressive. You may need to distinguish between primary and secondary sources.

> Preferably do not leave all the 'writing up' to a frenzied few weeks at the end of the process. You can compile a first draft of some of the material, perhaps the first chapter and a literature search, relatively early. You can always revise later, but it is comforting to have a few thousand words 'in the bank'.

> A dissertation normally requires some original empirical research (although some institutions allow a purely theoretical dissertation). Select your research methods with care. Commonly you will be required to explain and justify them.

> Students often choose to do a questionnaire survey, and this is certainly an option, but unless the questions are carefully selected, framed and tested, and a substantial representative sample of the target audience obtained, the results may be virtually worthless, even if they are attractively presented.

> One alternative is to conduct a small number of semi-structured interviews with, for example, local party or pressure group activists, public officials or elected councillors. Such interviews need courteous initial contacts and careful advance planning. Prepare your questions and discuss them with your tutor, but be ready to diverge from your script if the occasion demands. Note-taking can be difficult. If you can, persuade interviewees to let you tape the interviews.

> Whatever you choose to do, try to ensure that your own empirical research reflects your earlier theoretic framework, and that the whole dissertation hangs together.

> Leave plenty of time for revising, proofreading and printing. Once students had to pay to have their work professionally typed. Now word processing makes it easy to produce your own professional-looking copy, with time and care. But note that spelling, grammar, typographical and other mistakes lose marks. Persuade a friend or relation to help with the proofreading – they may spot slips that you miss.

> Acknowledge any help you have received from tutors, interviewees or other advisers. This is not just courtesy. It can draw attention to some of the work you have done for the dissertation, and may impress examiners.

> Obey all instructions on length, format, number of copies and submission arrangements to the letter.

> Make sure that at the end of the process you have a copy of the dissertation to keep. It

is not just a souvenir of your time on the course. It is an important example of the work you have undertaken, and may on occasion be useful to impress potential employers, or admission tutors for postgraduate study.

Tackling examinations

Once nearly all the assessment for a university degree consisted of unseen examinations. Among the rare exceptions were assessed dissertations, and sometimes an interview or viva. But otherwise grades and classes of degree were determined by performance in a series of examinations over a week or two at the end of the final year. This particularly rewarded students who revised effectively and were skilled at writing essays under severe time pressure, although students with other important skills who had worked assiduously throughout the course did not always secure the results they deserved.

Today there are often a variety of types of assessment that count towards the final degree. These may include traditional essays and other forms of written assignment submitted over the years, and sometimes assessed oral presentations and group projects. A dissertation or long essay still takes a key place in some degree programmes (see previous headings, above). These various types of assessment test a far wider range of skills than unseen examinations and are in general fairer to students, particularly those who have worked steadily and keenly throughout the course. Indeed, in some institutions unseen examinations have become relatively rare. However, skilfully devised examinations assess not only, or principally, knowledge, but insight and understanding. Most politics examinations still involve a choice of essays, and these test the ability to structure relevant and coherent answers to specific questions under time pressure. They also make plagiarism difficult (one reason for a return to traditional examinations in some universities).

> *Most politics examinations still involve a choice of essays, and these test the ability to structure relevant and coherent answers.*

Preparing for an examination

The prospect of examinations can provoke apprehension or terror, even among conscientious students, who fear they may not be able to do themselves justice. However, good preparation can take some of the worry out of exams. The following advice largely assumes that you are tackling the traditional unseen essay-based examinations. For other types of examinations follow the specific recommendations and advice of your tutors and look at past papers.

> ❯ Draw up a sensible revision schedule, well in advance of the exams, allowing plenty of time for sleep and recreation, and keep to it. Avoid relying on last-minute revision.
> ❯ Get hold of copies of past papers. These may be supplied on your course, or they may be available in libraries. It is important to 'know the enemy', and become familiar with the structure of the paper and type of questions.
> ❯ On many modules you will not need to revise all topics. If, for example, you are required to answer four questions from ten that roughly cover the syllabus, revising six major topics should normally be enough to ensure that you can answer four decent questions.
> ❯ Equip yourself to answer any conceivable question on your chosen topics. (You need a margin for safety in choosing topics, because sometimes a major topic may not come

up at all, or appears in a form that you had not anticipated, and cannot immediately see how to answer.)

> Be wary of question spotting, in the way gamblers pick 'winners' on past 'form'. Do not assume that a topic is bound to come up, or not to come up, on past trends. By all means take note of apparent tips by lecturers and tutors, but do not rely on them.

> Revise *actively*, not passively. Do not spend hour re-reading lecture notes and textbooks, and hoping that some of it will stick. (It usually does not!) Instead engage your mind and *practise outline answers* to past questions. When you find difficulty in answering a specific question, go back to books and notes to fill in gaps in your knowledge and understanding. The key to good exam performance is *technique*, and technique can be improved by practice in drafting answers to specific questions.

> When practising outline answers, think carefully about *what the question requires* and how it can best be tackled. Look at key words in the question. You might need to *define* terms, or make *distinctions* between different interpretations of concepts, models or relationships. There may be different legitimate approaches to answering the question. You might consider the pros and cons of each.

> Whatever approach you choose, you will need a *structured argument that answers the specific question set* (and not the question you might have preferred).

> For a short examination essay, think in terms of around five to seven paragraphs, each dealing with a specific point, with appropriate supporting evidence. This should form the basis of your essay plan. Too many short disconnected paragraphs give the impression of random thoughts rather than structured argument. The lack of any paragraphs suggests poor organization.

> Avoid 'cramming' – learning as many facts and figures as you can. Your grades and final result will depend not on how much you know, but how much knowledge and understanding you can apply in the limited time available to answer specific questions effectively.

> Even so, some limited rote learning can be useful. Learn key facts, dates, statistics, short quotations that you might be able to use to support your arguments.

> Make sure you can spell important proper names and key concepts, particularly if your spelling is weak. Misspelling key terms, such as 'bureaucracy', gives a bad impression. There is no 'spellcheck' to help you, and you will not want to waste valuable time checking dictionaries, even if they are allowed.

Coping with the examination

> Make sure you know the time and place of the exam, and allow ample time to get there. Last-minute panics and late arrivals will not help you to do your best.

> Make sure you have all you need, including spare writing implements, and any material you are allowed to bring in. If there is anything that appears unsatisfactory about the exam conditions (e.g. wobbly desk or chair, poor lighting, stuffy room, clock not visible, absence of material that should be supplied), inform the invigilator.

> Check the instructions on the exam paper (which should normally be familiar if you have studied past papers). If anything is not clear, ask.

> Where you have a choice of questions to answer, go through the paper quickly and put a cross against any question you think you cannot answer and a question mark against those you can. Then choose which of the possible questions you think you can

answer most effectively, and decide the order in which you will tackle them. You will probably want to answer the questions on which you are most confident first, but it may be sensible to choose a final answer (when you might be short of time) on a topic on which you are fairly confident you can produce an effective brief answer.

> If there are too many crosses against questions, do not panic. Go back and review them again. You may have been put off by unfamiliar wording, or a quotation you did not recognize. Think again about what specific questions might require.

> Do a brief plan – perhaps just five or six points (or even just key words) to be developed into paragraphs. If you have revised as suggested, you will have plenty of practice in planning answers. Sometimes students think there is insufficient time to plan answers in exams. It is even more important to plan in exams than in course work, when you may have time to start afresh, if you feel you are going astray. In an exam you have no time for false starts and second attempts.

> Do not waste time with 'setting the scene' or 'introductory' paragraphs. You may begin with a brief 'signpost' paragraph indicating how you are proposing to answer the question set, then get on with it.

> The key advice is to *answer the question set*, not the question you would have preferred, or one you have already answered in course work or in your revision. This is simple advice, repeatedly given, but still frequently ignored. There is no point in trying to impress an examiner with knowledge that is not asked for and is irrelevant to the question set.

> Include relevant facts, references, quotations you are sure of. Do not guess when you are not sure. A wrong date, inaccurate statistic or misquotation gives a worse impression than an absence of supporting detail.

> If, as is commonly the case, all questions carry equal marks, make sure you answer the number of questions required. The extra time given to fewer answers is most unlikely to provide marks to compensate for those you have lost by failing to answer a whole question.

> If you are desperately short of time for a final answer, resort to note form. This will almost certainly earn you more credit than an elegantly written introductory paragraph or two that fails to get to grips with the question.

> If you finish early, use the precious time left to read through your answers. Imagine your final grade is in the balance and that each mistake corrected earns you an extra mark. When you are writing fast, careless slips can change the sense completely (for example a missed negative) or give a very bad impression (such as a date a century out). More importantly you may realize you have left out a key aspect of a question. A late insertion (with clear directions as to where it should go) might make all the difference.

> When an exam is over, forget about it and concentrate on the next one. Do not waste time and peace of mind on inquests (at least, unless and until you might be required to do it again, when an honest reappraisal of your past preparation and performance may help you improve).

II theories and approaches to the study of politics

introduction to part II:
theories and approaches to the study of politics

Section 1 focuses on the evolution of the theory and practice of politics from the fifth century BC to the late twentieth century. Past political thinkers focused on the key issues and problems of their time. Thus the ancient Greeks were familiar with a wide variety of political systems and frequent regime change, so it was natural that they should speculate on the best form of government and the causes of political stability and change. Similarly, from the late Roman empire through to the end of the Middle Ages a key issue was the relationship between the temporal power of the state and the spiritual power of the church. Subsequently the religious conflicts in Europe from the sixteenth century onwards, and political revolutions from the seventeenth to the twentieth centuries, raised key concerns over the nature of political power and authority as well as the obligations and allegiance of subjects. So traditional political theory addressed big political questions that remain relevant today. Where does power lie? What is the best form of government? What are the causes of political instability and change? How should limited resources be distributed between individuals and communities? Why and how far should we obey the law? Why do states find it so difficult to live at peace with each other? How far can war ever be justified?

Yet although people have speculated on politics for 2,500 years it is only within the last century that it has become more systematically studied as a major discipline or social science in universities across the western world. Section 2 focuses on the development of modern political science and on important new theories, methods and approaches that have transformed the study of the subject, from the behavioural revolution onwards. Yet none of these theoretical revolutions have proved total or permanent. As new theories were exposed to criticism, older perspectives acquired a revived lease of life, sometimes in fresh variants. Thus all the theories and approaches discussed here remain current, and continue to shape the way politics is researched and studied today.

Section 1: The evolution of the study of politics

Some of the political analysis of writers from remote periods can seem startlingly modern, so much so that we can be in danger of forgetting the very different historical context in which they lived and worked. Today, most politics students read thinkers such as **Plato**, **Machiavelli** or **Rousseau** in modern translation. This of course makes them much easier to understand, but it can involve an element of distortion. There may be no exact modern language equivalent to the terms they use. Even apparently familiar concepts derived from ancient Greek or Latin, such as 'democracy', 'tyrant', 'republic' and 'dictator', which may bear some resemblance to the way in which they were originally employed by Greeks and Romans, also carry distinctive modern connotations.

> Some of the political analysis of writers from remote periods can seem startlingly modern.

There are similar problems even with less ancient texts written in our own language. Indeed, to an English-speaking student, seventeenth-century English texts by **Hobbes** and **Locke** can seem much more 'remote' and 'difficult' than modern English translations of Greek texts 2000 years older. These writers use some expressions that are no longer common, and employ other apparently more familiar terms, such as 'liberties' and 'rights', in distinctive ways. This is not to deny the continuing relevance of their ideas, but simply to emphasize the importance of context. Some of the great political texts of the past may appear to have a timeless quality, and indeed are often written in abstract terms without reference to contemporary political institutions and events. Yet inevitably they were strongly influenced by contemporary political practice, even where it may not be immediately apparent. We need to understand the times they lived in, the specific historic situation in which they thought and wrote.

The contribution of Greece and Rome (roughly from the fifth century BC to the fifth century AD)

Why should anyone studying politics in the early twenty-first century be expected to pay serious attention to the political practices and ideas of some ancient Greeks and Romans who lived from 2000 to 2500 years ago? One answer is that the Greeks virtually invented politics, both the term itself and its practice. Some of the key terms still employed in the study of politics today, particularly those used to describe systems of government, are derived from ancient Greek, while others are of Latin origin.

> The Greeks virtually invented politics, both the term itself and its practice.

Yet however fascinating the politics of Greece and Rome, we would know little about it but for the quality of contemporary writing that has survived. It is the historian Thucydides (460–404 BC) who brings to vivid life the political debates within and between ancient Greek states, and their very different systems of government, including the first known form of democracy, in Athens. **Plato** (427–347 BC) and **Aristotle** (384–322 BC) are widely regarded as the two of the greatest philosophers and political theorists of all time. The speeches of Demosthenes are still studied as models of political oratory. While Roman political thought was rather less original, Roman political institutions and practices have been immensely influential. The term 'Republic' is derived from the Latin *Res Publica* ('public affairs' or 'the public sphere'). The republican ideal has had a long recurring impact on subsequent political history in the west. The letters and speeches of **Cicero** (106–43 BC) illuminate the politics of the last years of the Roman Republic, and we owe our knowledge of the late Republic and early Empire to a number of outstanding Roman historians. Roman law remains today the basis of the legal systems of much of continental Europe.

Athenian democracy

Whether or not the ancient Greeks invented politics, they certainly developed its systematic study. The ancient Greek world involved a virtual laboratory of different political systems. Although the Greeks shared a substantially common language and culture, and could on occasion sink their political differences to combine against a common enemy, they lived in a large number of independent and often contending political communities, each with its own distinctive form of government. Some of these states involved government by a single ruler, a **monarchy** (rule of one) or tyranny (implying an illegitimate seizure of power). Others were ruled by a small minority, variously described as an **aristocracy** (literally, rule of the best), **oligarchy** (rule of the few) or plutocracy (rule of the rich).

Athens, followed by some other states, developed a more broad-based system of government, called **democracy**, meaning literally, the rule of the people, although this did not in practice include all adult inhabitants but only full citizens (excluding women, slaves and foreign residents). However, Athenian democracy, in marked contrast with modern representative democracy, did involve direct citizen participation in key decisions, including issues of taxation and spending, defence, trade and **international relations**.

The frequent wars between Greek states in the fifth and fourth centuries BC arose from conflicts of interest, but also from their contrasting political systems and values. Moreover, there were commonly conflicting class interests within states, some of those living under tyrannies or oligarchies casting envious eyes in the direction of Athens, while a number of rich Athenians hankered after a system of government closer to that of Sparta, the great rival of Athens. Thus the long Peloponnesian War (431–404 BC) between Athens and Sparta and their respective colonies and allies, described by the historian Thucydides, can be seen (like the recent cold war between the west and soviet communism) as an ideological struggle between rival political systems.

> *Athenian democracy, in marked contrast with modern representative democracy, involved direct citizen participation in key decisions.*

Some of the key participants were clearly conscious of this, as can been seen from the words Thucydides puts into the mouth of the Athenian leader **Pericles** (c. 495–429 BC) in a funeral oration near the beginning of the war. Although Thucydides himself was no friend of democracy, he sought to narrate the history of times he had lived through as accurately and dispassionately as possible. Whether he was recalling the words and arguments of

Pericles himself, or simply reconstructing what he might have said, hardly matters. While the historian's own political sympathies were towards oligarchy, he supplies one of the most eloquent and powerful cases for democracy ever made. The speech continues to inspire modern democrats. Even though the institutions of Athenian democracy were very different from those of modern representative democracy, the values proclaimed by Pericles still resonate.

Thus 'power is in the hands not of a minority but of the whole people' and 'everyone is equal before the law'. There is also toleration of the tastes and behaviour of others. 'We do not get into a state with our next-door neighbour if he enjoys himself in his own way, nor do we give him the kind of black looks which, though they do no harm, still do hurt people's feelings' (Thucydides, 1972: 145). Yet Pericles assumes the need for active political participation. 'We do not say that a man who takes no interest in politics is a man who minds his own business; we say that he has no business here at all.' He emphasizes the importance of rational public debate, maintaining that there is no incompatibility between words and deeds. 'The worst thing is to rush into action before the consequences have been properly debated' (Thucydides, 1972: 147).

For all its enduring eloquence, this speech of Pericles presents a rather rosy and idealistic picture of Athenian democracy which was not shared by all Athenians, or by many Greeks in other states. Athens with its strong navy was a great power in the Greek world, and often pursued its interests aggressively and ruthlessly. Thucydides was clearly very interested in inter-state politics (now explored in the semi-autonomous discipline of international relations) as well as the internal politics of particular states. One example is his account of the dialogue between the Athenians and the people of the island of Melos, in terms that anticipate the modern argument between political realists and idealists in the field of international relations (and are cited in modern works).

The Athenians wanted to persuade the Melians, who wished to remain neutral, to join their alliance in the war against Sparta. The Melians pleaded for justice and fair play. The Athenians responded that such considerations were irrelevant, for they had the power to force compliance, and the Melians should be sensible and recognize the fact and save their skins. The Athenians argued that it was 'a general and necessary law of nature to rule whatever one can …. You or anybody else with the same power as ours would be acting in precisely the same way.' A protracted resistance by the Melians was eventually overcome. Men of military age were put to death while the women and children were sold into slavery (Thucydides, 1972: 400–08). The Athenians employed the political language of self-interest and naked force (sometimes later described by the German term *Realpolitik*), repeatedly used down the centuries. While the rule of law might apply within Greek states, anarchy still prevailed in relations between states, as it has done substantially ever since.

Plato and Aristotle

Thucydides sought to provide a faithful record of the political conflicts he had lived through. He articulates a wide range of political arguments, but although he had his own political preferences, he was not essentially in the business of recommending particular institutions or ideas. Others were concerned with the ideal or best practicable form of government. Leading Greek thinkers did not divide human knowledge into discrete disciplines, but rather believed in its essential unity and inter-connection. Nor did they make the modern distinction between positive social science and normative political philosophy. They considered that the search for moral and political truths was essentially no different from the search to discover mathematical truths or knowledge of the physical universe. For both **Plato** (c. 427–347 BC) and **Aristotle** (c. 384–322 BC) moral philosophy, theorizing about the life that people should lead, was intimately connected with political theory and speculation over the best form of government.

Yet the contrasts between the two philosophers are perhaps more marked than the similarities. Plato's political philosophy was clearly influenced by his own political experience and observation, but his pungent criticism of democracy does not relate to particular institutions or events. Like his master **Socrates** (who was sentenced to death by Athenian democracy), he believed that virtue is knowledge. For Plato, democracy inevitably involved the rule of ignorance. He compares the people to a great beast. Political persuasion – oratory and other tricks of the politician's trade – has nothing to do with real moral and political wisdom that only the true philosopher possesses. This leads to his rather impractical-sounding conclusion that philosophers should be rulers. However, this is not so far away from the frequently voiced view today that government should be taken out of the hands of politicians and given to experts of one sort or another – business people, or scientists or suitably qualified bureaucrats.

Leading Greek thinkers considered that the search for moral and political truths was essentially no different from the search to discover mathematical truths or knowledge of the physical universe.

Aristotle was also a great philosopher, who took a different view from Plato on key questions. His approach to the study of politics was rather more practical or scientific. Although he, like Plato, speculated over the ideal state, he seemed more interested in actual states and the best practicable form of government, which he considered could involve a mixed system. He was less hostile to democracy than Plato, and assumed that a citizen of a free state would actively engage in public affairs, as man (but not woman!) was naturally a political animal.

Both Plato and Aristotle were, however, speculating about relatively small autonomous political communities, a form of state that was already on the way out in the face of the rise of empire, such as that of Aristotle's one-time pupil, Alexander the Great, and later that of Rome. The good life no longer self-evidently involved being a free citizen of an independent free state. There was thus some retreat from political engagement. Later Greek moral philosophy, such as the contending schools of the Stoics and Epicureans, had fewer immediate political implications. However, some Stoic thinkers such as Chrysippus developed notions of a universal natural law and universal citizenship, which almost seems to anticipate ideals of world government. Such ideas later struck a chord with some Romans, particularly when Rome's political dominion came to appear almost coterminous with the civilized world, and citizenship was extended to many whose ethnic origins were far from Roman.

The Roman Republic

Yet the subsequent growth of Rome's political empire effectively destroyed the Roman **Republic**, a development that was not only feared and lamented by those who lived through the Republic's decline, like **Cicero** (106–43 BC), but also many since who have valued the republican ideal. The Roman Republic was supposedly established after the expulsion of Rome's last king, and to some today the term 'republic' signifies simply any state that is not a monarchy. For others, the notion of a republic remains bound up with political freedom and active citizenship. For modern French and Americans, and many besides, the name 'republic' has become synonymous with democracy. Yet although the Roman Republic involved notions of public service and active citizenship, it was much less of a democracy than ancient Athens, and was really more of a mixed system of government with subordinate democratic elements. (Indeed, this limited democratic element was a positive attraction of the republican model to some, like the American 'founding father' **Madison**, who feared an unrestrained populist democracy.)

> The notion of a republic remains bound up with political freedom and active citizenship.

Recurring conflict between patricians (who normally dominated government) and plebs (the people) in the Roman Republic foreshadowed similar conflicts in some Italian, Dutch and Swiss cities from the fifteenth to the eighteenth centuries. The names of Roman institutions (e.g. Senate) and some Roman concepts have been freely adapted by later political systems, although it does not follow that these governments have necessarily much in common with that of ancient Rome. However, the more open attitude of the Romans to citizenship has been influential, while the framework of Roman law has perhaps been its greatest political legacy.

The classical legacy

Thus the political institutions and ideas of ancient Greece and Rome have had a massive impact on the political practice and theory of the western world ever since. Latin was the *lingua franca* of the educated classes in western Europe for many centuries after the destruction of the Roman empire. The ideas of the pagan philosophers **Plato** and **Aristotle** were incorporated first into medieval Christian theology (Aristotle's originally through Muslim Arabs, such as **Averroes**), before being regularly reinterpreted from the Renaissance onwards. In the eighteenth and nineteenth centuries educated Europeans commonly knew rather more about ancient Greek and Roman history, ideas and institutions than those of their contemporary neighbours (and sometimes even their own states).

Interpretations (and sometimes misinterpretations) of Greek and Roman models informed much of the political reform and revolution of more modern times (e.g. the American and French revolutions, the 1848 Roman Republic, constitutional changes over much of western Europe). In the twentieth century the words of Pericles appeared on the sides of London buses in the midst of the Great War (fought, it was claimed 'to make the world safe for democracy'). A few years later the Italian dictator Mussolini drew heavily on Roman symbols and culture in the process of establishing a fascist state and a new 'Roman' empire. Because of all this, for good or ill (and perhaps largely for good), the classical legacy can hardly be ignored today.

Church and state, the implications of religious belief for politics (from roughly the late Roman empire to the religious wars of the sixteenth and seventeenth centuries)

From the later Roman empire through to the seventeenth century some of the most potent political divisions and conflicts in the western world were linked to religious differences. Religion continued to be an important factor in politics in the eighteenth and nineteenth centuries, but appeared to be of diminishing political significance in the twentieth, at least until the irruption of conflict and terrorism around the new millennium, apparently inspired by religious convictions. A new wave of religious martyrs and calls for 'holy war' have demonstrated the survival of a mindset lately seen as obsolete in the modern world.

The rise of Christianity

The immediate cause of the increased relevance of religion for political behaviour from the late Roman empire onwards was the rise of new monotheist religious creeds that demanded full and exclusive allegiance. By and large, the polytheist religious beliefs of the ancients had not posed a significant threat to political authority. The gods were certainly worshipped, their divine aid sought, their apparent anger appeased through sacrifices. Particular states might have their own favoured divinities, their own shrines and temples dedicated to particular deities whose protection they sought. Yet this did not imply any divided loyalties. Religion was essentially an adjunct of the state. There was rarely conflict between civic and religious obligations, which were mutually reinforcing.

The new religions, of which Christianity and later Islam were to prove the most significant, were different. They had dramatic implications for personal conduct, and in some circumstances for political behaviour. Although Christians were prepared to 'render unto Caesar the things that are Caesar's', ultimately they recognized a higher authority than the state. The more devoted adherents were prepared willingly to embrace martyrdom rather than deny their faith. The power of perhaps the greatest empire that the world has seen was helpless in the face of such obstinate religious convictions.

Empire and papacy

Nor did the conversion of the emperor Constantine to Christianity solve the problem of divided loyalties, either for the Roman empire or for the successor states that arose from its destruction. This was a problem that the Christian theologian **Augustine** (354–430) wrestled with in the twilight of the empire. Emperors and kings might embrace the faith, but this did not make them the highest authority worthy of obedience for devout Christians. Medieval philosophers and political theorists like **Aquinas** (c. 1225-1274) and **Marsiglio** (c. 1275–c. 1342) were, for good reason, substantially preoccupied with the relationship between spiritual authority and temporal authority, papacy and empire, church and state. The prevailing assumption was that all power stemmed from God, and spiritual authority was higher than temporal authority. Moreover, the authority of kings and princes was limited to their own lands, while the Pope claimed authority over the whole of Christendom, which was still seen as a unity, despite its political divisions.

For a period in the Middle Ages this spiritual power was manifest rather than theoretical. Religious authority could sanction a change of ruler. Popes excommunicated and deposed emperors and kings, and authorized rebellions. They also instigated or endorsed wars, including the crusades, launched against Islam, another faith apparently requiring the total allegiance of its followers. Of course, religion often provided a cloak for other, more material interests. Princes sought the church's endorsement of their own ambitious designs. While some of the Christian crusaders were inspired by religious convictions, others were simply after loot. Later, in the early modern period of the sixteenth and seventeenth centuries, the conversion of the heathen to Christianity provided convenient cover for aggressive wars of conquest and colonization by European powers around the globe.

The impact of the Protestant Reformation

Yet if religious motives were commonly mixed with others, religious convictions still loomed large in daily life and patently influenced political behaviour. This became even more evident when the always fragile unity of western Christendom was destroyed by the Protestant Reformation, begun when Martin Luther (1483–1546) nailed his theses on the church door of Wittenberg in 1517. Rival versions of Christianity provoked religious wars in Germany, France and the Netherlands, and political upheavals in England and Scotland. Numbers of Protestant and Catholic martyrs demonstrated that some were still prepared to die for their faith, as the early Christians had done. Others were prepared to risk horrific punishments as they plotted to assassinate apostate rulers. A climate of fear and terror led to the persecution, expulsion and even sometimes extermination of religious minorities. Wars between states, particularly the Thirty Years War from 1618 to 1648, were substantially inspired by religious differences.

These religious upheavals had momentous political consequences. The old medieval debate on the relationship between the two powers was apparently ended by the subordination of spiritual to temporal authority. Conflict over religion in Germany was for a time suspended with the Peace of Augsburg (1555), under which the religious faith of the peoples of German states was to be effectively determined by their rulers. This was already the case in England, where Henry VIII declared himself the head of the church, and the religious faith of the English became subject to the changing tastes of successive rulers.

However, the challenge to the traditional authority of the church from some forms of Protestantism had potentially damaging implications for secular authority. Thus in Germany the princes had been given an early warning of the dangers posed by radical Lutheran ideas with the Peasants War (1524–5), which Luther himself disowned. In Scotland John Knox's brand of Calvinism led to the rejection of bishops and the established religious hierarchy, and ultimately the flight of the Catholic Mary, Queen of Scots. Her son, James VI of Scotland and subsequently James I of England, was to sum up the danger of extreme Protestantism to royal authority in the terse formula, 'No bishop, no king'. In the Netherlands the ultimately successful Protestant revolt against the Catholic Spanish rulers established a flourishing Dutch Republic, which provided a standing warning to kings of the potential dangers of religious freedom. In England extreme Protestants, or Puritans, formed the core of parliamentary opposition to the crown, which was to lead eventually to the English Civil War, the execution of Charles I (1649), and the temporary institution of a republic.

Early modern political theory

Despite the continued influence of religion on political behaviour, much of the political thought in the early modern period differed markedly in tone and substance from that of the Middle Ages. The moralizing of Christian theologians was replaced by the cynical political realism of the Florentine Niccolo **Machiavelli** (1459–1527), who in his best known work *The Prince* advised rulers to break promises as the occasion demanded. Flouting conventional religion and morality, he argued that it was more important for rulers to appear good than to be good, and safer to be feared than loved.

> *The scope and limits of political obligation – why and how far should we obey the state – became a dominant theme in political theory.*

Later thinkers were less concerned with the old medieval debates over the relationship between spiritual and temporal power than with the consequences of the breakdown of political authority, as witnessed in France in the late sixteenth century and in England in the mid-seventeenth century. The scope and limits of political obligation – why and how far should we obey the state – became a dominant theme in political theory. **Bodin** (1530–1596), who experienced the French religious wars, and **Hobbes** (1588–1679), who lived through the English Civil War, both argued in favour of obedience to a supreme and undivided sovereign power. In the case of Hobbes the argument was utilitarian rather than moral or religious, and grounded in a pessimistic estimate of the capacity of self-interested and acquisitive humans to live together peaceably without a common power to keep them in order. For others, such as **Locke** (1632–1704), obedience to the state was conditional rather than absolute, grounded in a contract in which both sovereign and subjects had obligations. Thus there was a limited right of rebellion if the sovereign failed to keep his side of the bargain. Locke and subsequently **Montesquieu** (1689–1755) also disagreed with Hobbes on sovereignty, championing a division of powers. This theoretical debate increasingly reflected the conflicting models of government in France under the absolute monarchy of Louis XIV (*'l'état, c'est moi'* – 'the state, that is me') and limited parliamentary monarchy in Britain.

Yet religion remained a potential and sometimes actual basis for political conflict within and between states. Religious minorities still faced persecution, partly because they seemed to offer a very real threat to political stability. Some fled to the New World. The French King Louis XIV expelled France's Protestant minority, the Huguenots, many of whom sought refuge in England. In the Netherlands and subsequently in England the case for toleration of different faiths was advanced by thinkers such as **Spinoza** (1632–1677) and **Locke**. Over time these arguments became more influential, at least for varieties of Protestantism, although anti-Catholic riots remained a feature of British politics until at least the late eighteenth century. Yet although around Europe as a whole the church remained rich and apparently powerful, by this time it no longer represented a substantial threat to the state.

The growth of secularism

With the spread of the ideas of the Enlightenment (see next section, page 63), the influence of established religion in the political sphere generally declined in the face of increased secularism. From the late eighteenth century onwards there was in some countries a deliberate severance of the state from the church. Thus the United States was established as a secular state from the beginning, the First Amendment to the Constitution proclaiming, 'Congress shall make no law respecting an establishment of religion, or prohibiting the free exercise thereof.' In France, through various regime changes following the 1789 revolution, the Catholic church was frequently in conflict with anticlerical radicals. Eventually, the

Third French Republic was established as a secular state, with a wholly secular system of state education. Nor was Islam immune from the prevailing secularism. Mustafa Kemal Ataturk's modernization of Turkey, for long the leading independent Islamic power, involved the establishment of a secular republic in 1923. The separation of the state from direct involvement with religion seemed particularly advisable for those countries with a diversity of faiths. Thus India, predominantly Hindu, but with a substantial Muslim minority as well as Christians, Sikhs and others, was established as a secular republic in 1949.

> From the late eighteenth century onwards there was in some countries a deliberate severance of the state from the church.

Not all nations have sought to separate church and state; some, like the United Kingdom retain an established religion, while others make explicit reference to religion in their constitution. However, even in these countries, the political role and influence of the church has generally significantly declined compared with previous periods. Even many believers seem to feel that politics and religion do not, and should not, mix. Religious leaders are often wary of engaging in political controversy, perhaps conscious that they might upset some of their own flock.

With the obvious exception of the Jews, who continued to suffer discrimination generally, and in some countries suffered state-sponsored persecution, culminating in the horror of the Holocaust, religious minorities have generally suffered less discrimination in most western states from the nineteenth century onwards. Specific disabilities have been removed and a right to freedom of conscience and religious observance has been recognized. Yet if the grievances of religious minorities generally declined with their increased toleration (with Northern Ireland a significant exception), religious identities commonly had continuing implications for political attitudes and behaviour in many countries, notably for party affiliation and voting. Christian Democrat parties dominated Italy and Germany for decades following the Second World War, and played a significant role in several other countries. In many states there appeared to be a significant if declining link between religious allegiance and electoral choice.

Even so, religion was not perceived to have much significance for politics in the second half of the twentieth century in the west. Few books on politics gave religion more than a cursory mention, if that. This has changed with the revival of religious fundamentalism, most obviously perhaps Islamic fundamentalism, but also Christian, Hindu and Jewish fundamentalism. Fundamentalists of all stripes are convinced that they have 'the truth', based on the literal interpretation of sacred texts, on which they are not prepared to make any concessions or compromises. This alone has implications for what many consider the whole nature and process of politics. Yet some fundamentalists go on to justify and practise political assassinations, suicide attacks, terror and war to further their objectives. This threatens stability and security within states, and peace between states. The mass murder of entire communities simply because of their religious allegiance, a lamentable feature of some earlier periods, has returned.

Enlightenment, progress and modernity (from the seventeenth and more particularly the eighteenth centuries to the late twentieth century)

The term 'Enlightenment' refers to the new climate of ideas which emerged principally in the eighteenth century, although it was substantially influenced by the scientific revolution and other new thinking in the seventeenth century (e.g. Descartes, **Hobbes**,

Newton, Pascal, **Spinoza, Locke**). While it affected Europe as a whole, and subsequently North America (Franklin, **Jefferson, Madison, Paine**) its main centre was France (e.g. **Montesquieu, Voltaire,** Diderot, **Rousseau**), but there was also a significant flowering of ideas in Scotland (**Hume, Smith**) and, subsequently, Germany (**Kant**). Moreover the impact of Enlightenment ideas continued into the nineteenth and twentieth centuries.

The Enlightenment is linked with modernity, the key assumptions, values and principles of our modern world, although in the later years of the twentieth century a movement described as **postmodernism** involved a substantial reaction against Enlightenment assumptions. The Enlightenment is associated with trust in science, reason and human progress rather than faith, tradition and authority. Some of its leading figures were, if not anti-religious, at least sceptical of established religion and critical of the power of the church. Thus the Enlightenment encouraged secularism, the separation of the state and politics generally from the church and religion (see previous section).

> *The Enlightenment is associated with trust in science, reason and human progress rather than faith, tradition and authority.*

Revolution

The wider political impact of Enlightenment ideas is rather more contentious. The Enlightenment was succeeded by a series of dramatic political **revolutions** in first North America, then Europe, and subsequently other continents. The extent and frequency of these political upheavals was relatively new. Regime change, though a marked feature of the ancient world of Greece and Rome, had become relatively rare in the Middle Ages and early modern period. **Monarchy** of one kind or another was the predominant form of government and substantially the only form in larger states. Disputed successions could lead to civil war or inter-state war, but rarely involved a fundamental transformation of the whole political system. The political upheavals in England in the seventeenth century were an exception, but they were originally inspired by religious rather than political differences, and the more radical ideas that briefly emerged were soon suppressed. In the eighteenth century Britain's constitutional monarchy remained exceptional in what is described by historians as the 'age of **absolutism**'.

The political sympathies of Enlightenment thinkers were mixed. Some favoured benevolent despotism, others a more limited or mixed system of government; few could be described as radicals or democrats. Yet questioning of authority and tradition was inherently subversive, and the debate the Enlightenment opened up gave currency to new political ideas which have helped to transform the language of politics. Key political concepts aired by the thinkers of the Enlightenment with potentially revolutionary implications included **freedom, equality, rights**, government by **consent, the separation of powers**, popular **sovereignty** and representative **democracy**. It is however contentious how far the ideas of the Enlightenment can be said to have 'caused' revolutions, which can plausibly be attributed to changes in material circumstances and in the balance of interests in society.

The American Revolution

The first great political revolution of modern times, and for many years the only one that long endured, was that of Britain's former American colonies. The 1776 American Declaration of Independence was a document that was thoroughly imbued with the ideas of

The 1776 American Declaration of Independence was a document that was thoroughly imbued with the ideas of the Enlightenment.

the Enlightenment, as were the later debates over the system of government for the new United States of America, and the constitution that emerged. The founding fathers did not necessarily wish to push the principles of liberty, equality and government by consent to their logical conclusion. Arguably they were more interested in the protection of property. Slavery was maintained, and checks and balances in the new constitution were designed to limit the influence of the people on government. Yet America did become the first modern democracy, and slavery was eventually abolished following the American Civil War (1861–5). It was on one of the battlefields of that war that Abraham Lincoln powerfully reaffirmed the values of the American Revolution.

BOX 2.1 the American Revolution: government of the people

From the American Declaration of Independence 1776

We hold these truths to be self evident, that all men are created equal, that they are endowed by their creator with certain inalienable rights, that among these are life, liberty and the pursuit of happiness. That to secure these rights, governments are instituted among men, deriving their just powers from the consent of the governed. That whenever any form of government becomes destructive to these ends, it is the right of the people to alter or abolish it, and to institute new government, laying its foundation on such principles and organizing its powers in such form, as to them shall seem most likely to effect their safety and happiness.

The preamble to the Constitution of the United States of America

We the people of the United States, in Order to form a more perfect Union, establish Justice, insure domestic Tranquillity, provide for the common defence, promote the general Welfare, and secure the Blessings of Liberty to ourselves and our Posterity, do ordain and establish this CONSTITUTION for the United States of America.

From Abraham Lincoln's Gettysburg Address 1863

Four score and seven years ago our fathers brought fourth on this continent a new nation, conceived in liberty and dedicated to the proposition that all men are created equal. Now we are engaged in a great civil war, testing whether that nation or any nation so conceived and so dedicated can long endure ...

We here highly resolve that these dead shall not have died in vain, that this nation under God shall have a new birth of freedom, and that government of the people, by the people, for the people shall not perish from the earth.

The French Revolution

Revolution proved contagious, particularly for the French monarchy, which had powerfully assisted the American rebellion, not because of any sympathy for the values of liberty, equality and government by consent, but to avenge earlier defeats by Britain in the Seven Years War. The origin and course of the French Revolution were dictated primarily by specifically French circumstances, but there was a two-way flow of ideas between America and France which helped inspire revolutionaries in both countries. Those directly involved included the American scientist and statesman, Benjamin Franklin, who became the first US ambassador to France on the eve of revolution, and the Frenchman Lafayette who fought in the American War of Independence, and was influential in the early stages of the French Revolution. The English radical thinker Tom **Paine** was actively engaged in both the American and French revolutions. Paine wrote *The Rights of Man* (1791–2) and *The Age of Reason* (1794–6), works thoroughly imbued with the spirit of the Enlightenment.

BOX 2.2 **articles from the Declaration of the Rights of Man and Citizen, 1789**

1. Men are born free and remain free and equal in rights. Social distinctions may be founded only upon the general good.
2. The aim of all political association is the preservation of the natural and imprescriptible rights of man. These rights are liberty, property, security, and resistance to oppression.
3. The principle of all sovereignty resides essentially in the nation. No body nor individual may exercise any authority which does not proceed directly from the nation.
4. Liberty consists in the freedom to do everything which injures no one else; hence the exercise of the natural rights of each man has no limits except those which assure to other members of society the enjoyment of the same rights. These rights can only be determined by law.
5. Law can only prohibit such actions as are hurtful to society. Nothing may be prevented which is not forbidden by law, and no-one may be forced to do anything not provided for by the law.
6. Law is the expression of the general will ...

Whereas the American Revolution occurred on another continent and was not initially seen as for export, the French Revolution had obvious implications for other European states. In fighting a war of survival against hostile European powers, revolutionary France sought to spread its message of **liberty**, **equality** and national **sovereignty** to countries such as Italy, Germany and Poland. The revolutionary war was, like the Peloponnesian War between the Athens and Sparta, and the cold war between the west and the Soviet Union, a war between rival political systems and values, an ideological war. Although the revolution that began in France in 1789 ultimately failed, the idea of revolution survived, particularly in France but also elsewhere in Europe, to inspire the revolutions of 1830 and 1848, the Parish Commune of 1870, and ultimately the Russian revolutions of 1917. The threat of revolution and counter-revolution has been a recurring feature of states across the globe over the last century. Regime change, rare before 1776, has become relatively common.

> *Revolutionary France sought to spread its message of liberty, equality and national sovereignty.*

The legacy of the Enlightenment

The idea of revolution inspired some but appalled others, who blamed the dangerous new thinking associated with the Enlightenment. This reaction can be seen in the **conservative** ideas of Edmund **Burke** (1729–1797) and Joseph de **Maistre** (1753–1821), in romanticism and the revolt against reason, and in nostalgia for a vanished past. It bore fruit in the temporary restoration of old regimes in France and elsewhere, and in periodic religious revivals. Yet the continued advance of science and technology in the nineteenth and early twentieth centuries, generally rising living standards and the advance of **democracy** and the common man, seemed to confirm the Enlightenment trust in reason, science and human progress.

The twentieth century in some ways marked the triumph of Enlightenment ideas, with further dramatic scientific advances, and with the further spread of liberal democracy and new international institutions. The Enlightenment had been originally a western world phenomenon. The values of the Enlightenment – **rights**, national **sovereignty**, **freedom** and **equality** – were not initially for export to Asia, Africa and South America. Those of other races and religions, who were commonly subject to western colonial exploitation, were not felt to be the equals of white Europeans. The toleration of variants of Christianity was not extended to other 'heathen' religions. Yet the rapid dismantling of the former European colonial empires in and after the Second World War was accompanied by the recognition of human **rights** unlimited by nationality, race or culture. Documents such as the United Nations Universal Declaration of Human Rights (1948) and the European Convention for the Protection of Human Rights and Fundamental Freedoms (1951) seemed to fulfil the promise of the Enlightenment, extending rights and freedoms beyond national frontiers to all humanity.

BOX 2.3 **from the United Nations Universal Declaration of Human Rights (1948)**

Article 1 All human beings are born free and equal in dignity and worth. They are endowed with reason and conscience and should act towards each other in a spirit of brotherhood.
Article 2. Everyone is entitled to all the rights and freedoms set out in this Declaration, without distinction of any kind, such as race, colour, sex, language, religion, political or other opinion, national or social origin, property, birth or other status.

Further articles provided for a whole range of social and welfare rights beyond those envisaged in the eighteenth century, including 'the right to take part in the government of his country' (article 21), 'the right to social security' (22), 'the right to work', 'free choice of employment' and 'equal pay for equal work' (23), 'the right to rest and leisure' including 'periodic holidays with pay' (24), 'the right to a standard of living adequate for the health of himself and his family, including food, clothing, housing and medical care and necessary social services' (25), and 'the right to education'(26).

Yet the rights that were so solemnly affirmed had little reality for much of the population of the world, who continued to suffer from acute poverty and sometimes starvation, and from a range of preventable diseases. Two world wars and mass exterminations on a scale hitherto unimaginable in the Holocaust of the Jews and other 'ethnic cleansing' provided dramatic continuing evidence of 'man's inhumanity to man'. Modern science had enabled the production of weapons of war and extermination capable of destroying the world. At the same time the industrialization that had promised such a significant advance in living standards also threatened the longer-term survival of the planet through pollution and resource depletion. All this appeared to discredit Enlightenment optimism over the benefits to be derived from human reason, science and progress. It has reawakened old fears over human nature and human motivation.

Thus while we still live in a world substantially shaped by the ideas of the Enlightenment, those ideas have been subject to challenge from a number of directions. From the end of the First World War to the end of the Second, one challenge came from **fascism**, which among other aspects involved a revolt against reason and a denial of a sense of common humanity. More recently the challenge has come from other quarters, particularly intellectually from **postmodernism** (see pages 98–101), and some strands of **feminism** (see pages 101–3). **Greens** have perceived the Enlightenment as too anthropocentric, focused on the needs and interests of humans, rather than other species and the planet. Some moral philosophers, such as Peter **Singer**, have sought to extend the rights proclaimed by thinkers of the Enlightenment to animals. Beyond all this, the revival of religious fundamentalism threatens to return the world to a pre-Enlightenment era of religious wars and massacres (see pages 59–62).

Liberalism, capitalism and democracy (from the late eighteenth century to the present day)

Liberalism, **capitalism** and **democracy** are three terms at the heart of the modern analysis of politics. Each term is distinctive: liberalism is a political creed, capitalism is an economic system and democracy is a form of government. Yet all three had common roots in the Enlightenment and (to many) appeared compatible, as we might assume from their frequent use in combination, such as 'liberal capitalism' or 'liberal democracy', particularly to describe the modern western world. However, at the same time these hybrid terms not only suggest at least the possibility of a different kind of capitalism or another variant of democracy, but also hint at an element of tension between them. Any student of politics has to consider the relationship between liberalism, capitalism and democracy, although first it is important to explore the meaning of each term separately.

Liberalism

Liberalism is a term commonly employed to describe a broad political, economic or philosophic outlook that appears to be widely shared in the modern western world, so much so that it is sometimes described as a dominant or 'hegemonic' **ideology**. Indeed the words 'liberal' and 'liberalism' have become used so broadly and variously as to require some interpretation or qualification, as they are employed in different senses or in different contexts. Yet all these variants of liberalism are ultimately derived from their common origins in the sixteenth-century Reformation, the seventeenth-century scientific revolution, and the eighteenth-century Enlightenment.

> Liberalism is a political creed, capitalism is an economic system and democracy is a form of government. Yet all three had common roots in the Enlightenment and (to many) appeared compatible.

Individualism is the premise they share, the notion that all theorizing about society, economics and politics starts with individual men and women. Society is simply an aggregate of individuals, no more and no less than the sum of its parts. The classical liberal economic theory of Adam **Smith** (1723–1790) and David Ricardo assumes that countless individual consumers and producers, acting independently and in their own rational self-interest, determine the price and output of goods and services, as well as wages, profits, interest and rent. The liberal political theory of James

Mill (1773–1836) and Jeremy **Bentham** (1748–1832) assumed individual citizens would, if free from external pressure, use the vote and other means of political influence rationally and in their own interest.

> *The enhancement of the freedom of the individual seemed to require controls on government.*

The key liberal value, **freedom**, was necessary if the individual was to be able to act in his or her rational self-interest. In the eighteenth century the most obvious obstacle to the free exercise of individual choice was government in some shape or form. The **state** appeared the enemy of freedom. In the political sphere autocratic governments limited freedom of expression and innovation. In the economic sphere governments sought to control trade and industry, imposing all kind of restraints on market forces through direct intervention, duties and taxes. The enhancement of the freedom of the individual seemed to require controls on government. The liberal political programme thus involved limited constitutional government rather than **absolutism**. Government by **consent** would provide a check on wilder government schemes and wars. The slogan 'no taxation without representation', used by the parliamentary opposition to the monarchy in Britain, was later adopted by the American rebels against the British government. It was of course assumed that this would put an effective brake on government taxation and expenditure. Thus there was no apparent contradiction between the liberal political programme and the liberal economic programme. Limited constitutional government would assist laissez-faire ('leave alone') policies.

Capitalism

Liberalism has been closely associated with industrial capitalism, an economic system that emerged over much the same period as liberalism, which indeed is sometimes represented as the ideology of the industrial bourgeoisie. Liberals had always emphasized the sanctity of private **property**, and the freedom of individuals to use and dispose of their property as they saw fit. A key feature of capitalism is production for exchange and profit rather than immediate use by the producers. It assumes private ownership of resources used for production and capital accumulation, and also assumes largely **free markets** for goods and resources. It implies that some have surplus wealth and income to invest in productive resources in pursuit of profit, and thus further wealth, although of course there is an element of risk in such investment. Thus any profits reaped are deemed a reward for enterprise and risk taking.

There can be little doubt that industrial capitalism, over time, facilitated an unprecedented cumulative expansion of productive capacity, national income and living standards in industrializing countries (although some clearly benefited far more than others). The growth of capitalism inevitably also had important social and political consequences. Ownership of capital overtook the ownership of land as the most important route to wealth and influence in society. In all industrializing countries capitalists had increasing political influence, which they used to further their interests as they perceived them. Industrial capitalism also led to the increased concentration of a fast-growing population in expanding urban centres, and the emergence of a spatially concentrated industrial working class with more potential for effective political organization, initially through trades unions and various forms of voluntary bodies or **pressure groups**, subsequently through mass **political parties**. The political geography of industrializing states was transformed, with rapidly developing manufacturing cities acquiring more political weight.

To an extent the content of politics changed also, partly from the increased political influence of these class interests, but also in response to the needs and problems of an industrial society and economy. Thus although there was a continuing presumption in orthodox economics against state intervention, in practice in almost all advanced industrial economies there was an increase in state regulation (e.g. in banking and transport) and in state provision of amenities and services, initially in public health and education, subsequently in old age pensions, sickness and unemployment insurance.

Business (which had earlier benefited from a relaxation of some state controls) was not necessarily opposed to this growth in state intervention. Thus business interests often favoured state services (particularly education, health and family support), which both assisted the creation of a better trained, healthier work force, and transferred some business costs to the taxpayer that might otherwise have to be met out of profits. Even attitudes to free trade varied with changing circumstances. In the mid-nineteenth century this was supported by British business, but opposed by many French, German and American business interests which wanted protection against lower-cost British manufactured goods. Later, in the early twentieth century, faced with increased foreign competition from Germany, the United States and Japan, British businesspeople demanded 'fair trade' (effectively protection) rather than free trade.

Democracy

Industrial capitalism was to flourish under a variety of political regimes, although it appeared particularly compatible with liberal democracy. Today the terms 'liberal' and 'democracy' are commonly combined, but in the early nineteenth century liberalism did not necessarily entail democracy. Many liberals then desired little more than the end of **absolutism** and a greater say for the middle classes in government, through assemblies or parliaments with a rather wider franchise. They wanted reform not **revolution**. They did not seek to extend political power to those without property, whom they feared.

In the early nineteenth century only radical liberals advocated democracy, a political system virtually defunct from the time of the Greeks, until resurrected in a rather different form in modern times. Direct democracy on the ancient Greek model hardly seemed feasible for the geographically extensive states that dominated eighteenth-century Europe. What changed this calculation was the notion of **representative democracy**, government controlled by and accountable to elected representatives of the whole people. The practice of electing representatives had been long familiar in some countries, but election was limited to the few, so that representatives never represented more than a small minority of the people, and moreover commonly only exerted a partial and occasional influence over government. Advocates of representative (or liberal) democracy (such as James Mill and Jeremy **Bentham**) assumed that a government controlled by, and accountable to, a parliament elected by the whole people would have to pursue the interests of 'the greatest happiness of the greatest number'. Thus representative government would be a true democracy.

Yet even the founding fathers of the American Constitution, who freely invoked the name of the people and the notion of popular

> *Advocates of representative (or liberal) democracy assumed that a government controlled by, and accountable to, a parliament elected by the whole people would have to pursue the interests of 'the greatest happiness of the greatest number'.*

sovereignty, sought to put checks and balances in the way of unrestrained people power. James **Madison** (1756–1836), in particular, distinguished between the representative principle that he associated with a republic and a full democracy. 'It may well happen that the public voice, pronounced by the representatives of the people, will be more consonant to the public good than if pronounced by the people themselves, convened for the purpose' (Madison, Hamilton and Jay, no. X, 1987 ed.: 126). However, in practice some of the checks on popular sovereignty, such as the electoral college to choose the president, never operated as the founding fathers envisaged, and the American system of government did rapidly become the first functioning modern representative democracy.

American democracy in the early nineteenth century was an object of some curiosity and wonder in old Europe, largely still ruled by absolute monarchs. The account of this strange new world and novel system of government by a young French aristocrat, Alexis de **Tocqueville** (1805–1859) whose own family had suffered executions and (temporary) dispossession in the French Revolution, became a best seller (*Democracy in America*, two volumes, 1835, 1840). Tocqueville was convinced that in America the sovereignty of the people was a reality. 'The people reign in the American political world like God over the universe' (Tocqueville, 2003: 71). He admired some aspects of American society and politics, particularly the spirit of freedom and equality he discerned, although he was critical of others (especially the treatment of native Americans and black slaves). He also feared the threat of the 'tyranny of the majority' to individual freedom. Yet whatever his personal reservations over American democracy, he was convinced that it represented the future. European states such as France, Britain and Germany would be unable to resist the democratic tide. He plainly concluded that those liberals who sought limited political reform short of full democracy were doomed to disappointment: 'When a nation starts to tamper with electoral qualifications, we can anticipate, sooner or later, their complete abolition …. For after each concession, the strength of democracy increases … and the process can be stopped only when universal suffrage is achieved' (Toqueville, 2003: 70).

Tocqueville presciently predicted the outcome of the electoral reform process in countries like Britain, where initially modest extensions of the franchise led ultimately to granting the vote to working-class males and ultimately women (a development Tocqueville had not foreseen, and would not have approved). He was also well aware that democracy involved a fundamental transformation of politics, which went far beyond constitutions and formal institutions of government to include political parties and other forms of political association, and a free press. 'A new political science is needed for a totally new world' (Tocqueville, 2003: 17).

Democracy and liberalism

Democracy appeared in many ways the logical culmination of liberal political principles – government by **consent**, **freedom**, **equality**, the Enlightenment ideas embodied in formal statements of the **rights** of man or the citizen (see last section). Yet representative democracy seemed to threaten liberal economics, the principle of free markets and laissez-faire. Newly enfranchised citizens, following their own rational self-interest, commonly demanded more interference with **free market** forces rather than less. Thus farmers sought duties on imported grain to keep prices up and maintain income derived from land. Businesses wanted protection from foreign competition. Workers commonly opposed a free market in labour that might depress wage rates. Many voters wanted more public services, such as state education, health or housing, subsidized or free at the point of use. These tensions led to a split among liberals. Some liberals (sometimes called 'social liberals') embraced social reform and effectively abandoned laissez-faire. Such liberals justified state intervention as an expansion of individual **freedom** and **rights**, involving a right to education, work and a 'living wage'. Economic liberals continued to assert that the **free market** was the essence of their creed.

Democracy and capitalism

For many there was a more obvious conflict between democracy and capitalism. Democracy assumed political equality. Capitalism involved massive economic inequality. Conservatives and liberals feared, and socialists hoped, that the political equality implicit in democracy would lead to much greater economic equality. They assumed the many who were relatively poor would use their increased political power to secure a massive redistribution of income and wealth (involving extensive interference with another liberal value, the freedom to acquire, use and bequeath private property without state interference). Democracy thus appeared a potential threat to not only old landed wealth, but the new wealth of the industrial capitalists.

> *Democracy assumed political equality. Capitalism involved massive economic inequality.*

All socialists in the nineteenth and early twentieth centuries assumed that full democracy was incompatible with capitalism, and looked forward to the latter's replacement by a new economic system. Those socialists committed to representative democracy saw it as the first step towards this goal, while others, such as **Marx** and his successors, believed that what they called 'bourgeois democracy' was neither real democracy, nor a threat to capitalism. To many Marxists the failure of parliamentary socialism to transform the economic system and create a more equal society simply confirmed that representative government did not really involve the rule of the people (see next section, on **Marxism**). Others who were not Marxists were also sceptical over popular sovereignty, arguing that behind the façade of parliamentary democracy, elite rule continued (see section on elitism and pluralism, page 80–4).

Threats to liberalism, capitalism and democracy

In the course of the twentieth century, liberalism, capitalism and democracy all appeared under serious threat at one time or another. **Liberalism** for long seemed a political creed of declining appeal and relevance, and political parties that retained the name 'liberal' commonly found themselves squeezed between the mass parties of the **left and right. Capitalism** experienced one serious crisis following the slump precipitated in 1929, and periodic scares that seemed for a time to confirm predictions of its inevitable collapse. Moreover, from the Russian Revolution in 1917 to the fall of the Berlin Wall in 1989, capitalism faced what appeared to be a viable alternative economic system in the centralized command economies of the Soviet Union and its allies. Following the First World War (fought 'to make the world safe for democracy'), liberal democracy also appeared to be under threat from the **right** in the form of traditional authoritarian **dictatorships** and **fascism**, and from the left in the shape of soviet

> *From the Russian revolution in 1917 to the fall of the Berlin wall in 1989, capitalism faced what appeared to be a viable alternative economic system in the centralized command economies of the Soviet Union and its allies.*

communism. Fascist dictators partially legitimized their rule by recourse to the apparently democratic device of the **plebiscite**, while the 'people's democracies' of the USSR, and later eastern Europe, maintained an electoral façade for single-party dictatorships.

The triumph of liberalism, capitalism and democracy?

However, by the end of the twentieth century liberalism, capitalism and democracy had all survived and thrived. Progressive or social liberalism was essentially the dominant element in what came to be called the social democratic or Keynesian consensus in the decades after the Second World War. The capitalist economies of the west flourished in '*les trente glorieuse*' (the 30 glorious years) after the war, to the extent that even socialist political parties now talked of channelling or transforming capitalism rather than abolishing it. Economic liberalism subsequently made a remarkable comeback in the last quarter of the century, so much so that the **free market** is now generally endorsed across the political spectrum. Following the implosion of soviet communism, the only alternative economic system that seemed for a time viable, capitalism appeared now unchallengeable. Moreover, capitalism was now global in scope.

> *By the early twenty-first century liberalism, capitalism and democracy seemed to have merged into a global value system, a dominant or hegemonic ideology to which, following the end of the cold war, there appeared to be no alternative.*

Democracy too has become almost universally approved (although not necessarily so universally practised). The surviving dictatorships in Europe have been transformed into parliamentary democracies. Former European colonies, now independent sovereign states, have largely maintained democratic forms. India remains the largest functioning democratic system. Many of the former **communist** one-party states have been transformed into competitive multi-party representative democracies. Thus by the early twenty-first century liberalism, capitalism and democracy seemed to have merged into a global value system, a dominant or hegemonic ideology to which, following the end of the cold war, there appeared to be no alternative, apart from the political nihilism of **terrorism** inspired by religious fundamentalism.

Continuing tensions

Yet although liberalism, capitalism and democracy have survived and flourished to hold sway over much of the world, there is still some continuing tension between the three terms. The huge disparities in wealth and income under capitalism, even more apparent between nations than within nations now capitalism is global, continue to call into question the assumption of political equality that remains central to democracy. Economic liberals assert that people cannot 'buck the market'. The helplessness of individuals and whole communities in the face of global market forces seems to limit the scope for real democratic change through popularly elected politicians and parties. This is one of the factors that has perhaps contributed to a growing mood of popular frustration, disillusion and apathy towards democratic politics, evident in declining voting figures and party membership. Such disillusion and apathy threatens the active citizen participation that remains at the heart of the democratic ideal.

However if individuals and communities appear effectively helpless in the grip of economic forces they cannot control, this limits the scope not only of democratic politics but of all political action. Others continue to assert that politics can make a real difference to people's lives, and that there are still important political choices to be made by governments and peoples. This is perhaps most obvious on the **environmental** issues that increasingly loom large. It is by no means clear that capitalism and free market economics can, unaided, solve the environmental crises that the world faces. It will take cooperative action by governments with the engaged support of peoples to take the political decisions necessary to address these problems, including resource depletion, environmental pollution and degradation, and global warming. In either case the relationship between economics and politics remains crucial. Indeed, what used to be called 'political economy' in the nineteenth century is very much back in fashion.

The Marxist challenge (from the mid-nineteenth century to the present)

Until 1989 and the fall of the Berlin Wall, the contrast between the liberal democracies of the capitalist west (the 'first world') and the Marxist-Leninist regimes of the former Soviet Union, its allies and satellites (the 'second world') was naturally a major focus for the study of comparative politics. Moreover the 'cold war' between these opposed systems was a key theme in the study of **international relations**. Communism is no longer a realistic challenge to liberal democracy, yet modern students of politics still need to know something of **Marx** and Marxism, as for much of the twentieth century a significant proportion of the world's peoples were subject to regimes inspired by particular interpretations of Marxism. Moreover, Marxist theory and analysis has long been a significant strand in modern social science, and has made an important contribution to the study of politics.

Marx and Engels

Karl **Marx** (1818–1883) and his collaborator Friedrich **Engels** (1820–1895) saw conflicting economic class interests at the heart of politics and historical change. As they wrote at the beginning of the *Communist Manifesto* (1848: in Marx and Engels, 1959), 'The history of all hitherto existing society is the history of class struggle.' Broadly speaking, Marxists argue that political power reflects economic power. Real political power is in the hands of those who own and control the means of production in any society, regardless of whether it is formally an absolute monarchy, a constitutional monarchy or some kind of republic. Thus in the modern industrial capitalist economies that were emerging in the west in the nineteenth century, effective power was in the hands of the bourgeoisie or capitalists, rather than hereditary rulers or the old landed aristocracy on the one hand, or the mass of the people on the other.

> Marxists argue that political power reflects economic power. Real political power is in the hands of those who own and control the means of production in any society.

In assuming the primacy of economic factors, Marx implicitly denied or at least significantly constrained the autonomy of politics. This debate over the role of economic factors in shaping political activities and outcomes continues, and not just among Marxists. It relates back to old arguments in philosophy about free will and determinism, and continuing discussion over the relative importance of **structure and agency** among social scientists and historians. It is an issue that any student of politics has to consider, because it has to do with the nature and scope of the subject.

Yet Marx himself was never a wholehearted economic determinist. He famously argued, 'Philosophers have only interpreted the world in various ways; the point is to change it'

(Marx [1845] in Marx and Engels, 1959). Elsewhere he writes that men make their own history but not in circumstances of their own choosing.

Marx assumed that capitalism would ultimately be destroyed by its own internal contradictions. Competition between capitalists would lead to falling rates of profit, and capitalists would be forced to increase the exploitation of their workers to stay in business. The poverty and hardship (or 'immiseration') of the workers would intensify until they rose in revolution, and capitalism would be replaced by socialism, although Marx said very little about what this revolution would entail, nor about the socialist society that would succeed it. He did indicate that there would have to be a temporary 'dictatorship of the proletariat' to prevent counter-revolution, before the institution of a classless society to be organized on the principle 'from each according to his abilities, to each according to his needs'. In the absence of class conflict the state would 'wither away'. Coercive government of the old kind would no longer be necessary.

Marxism and democracy

In assuming a preponderant if not necessarily determining role for economic forces in politics, Marx denied that true democracy was compatible with capitalism, for how could political power be in the hands of the people when economic power was heavily concentrated? Alternatively, if democracy was a reality and the people did have effective power, they would surely use it to improve their lot and establish a more equal socialist society rather than the existing capitalist society. As capitalism, and accompanying gross inequality, continued to thrive, democracy was not a reality. Thus although Marx certainly considered himself a democrat, he scornfully dismissed the parliaments of his day as 'committees for discussing the common affairs of the bourgeoisie'. In other words they served the interests of industrial capitalists rather than the people as a whole.

One explanation for this in Marx's lifetime was that the British Parliament and most other representative bodies were not elected by anything near a universal franchise. Subsequently, following the extension of the franchise, some followers of Marx in Germany and elsewhere hoped that **socialism** could be achieved peacefully, through the ballot box. Eduard **Bernstein** (1850–1932) was the most prominent of these 'revisionists'. Yet while socialist parties later won elections and formed governments, either innate caution or the constraints of the capitalist economy and the parliamentary political system inhibited their actions, so that they failed to use their control of government to establish a socialist economy and society. Thus the British Marxist Ralph **Miliband** (1924–1994) gloomily concluded in *Parliamentary Socialism* (1972) that the British Labour Party had consistently sacrificed socialism for what he called 'parliamentarism'.

Other Marxists rejected revisionism and continued to deny that what they still called 'bourgeois democracy' was real democracy, even with a universal adult franchise. The argument in part revolves around the ability of voters to perceive their own real interests. It had been a key assumption of advocates of representative democracy that individuals perceive and act on their own rational self-interest. Thus a government elected by, and accountable to, the people would be constrained to act in the interests of the majority. Yet Marx and his followers did not assume that individuals would necessarily be guided by their own rational self-interest. Marx had asserted, 'It is not the consciousness of men that determine their being, but on the contrary, their social being that determines their consciousness' (Marx [1859] in Marx, 1977). In other words, it is our upbringing and social circumstances that shape what we think. Elsewhere he wrote, 'the ruling ideas of every age are the ideas of the ruling class'. Thus in a capitalist society, the workers would share the economic and political outlook of the capitalists.

Lenin and Marxism-Leninism

Other Marxists argued that the workers in advanced industrialized western states had been effectively seduced from revolutionary socialism by improving living standards and imperialism. One of Marx's key predictions, the increasing impoverishment of the working class, had failed to come to pass. The Russian revolutionary Marxist leader, **Lenin** (1870–1924), gave one plausible explanation: imperialism, the 'highest stage of capitalism', involved the transfer of exploitation from the western working class to the subject peoples of the colonies of European powers.

When Lenin seized power in the Bolshevik Revolution of November 1917 he promptly dissolved the newly elected Russian Parliament. Lenin scornfully dismissed what he called 'bourgeois democracy', which only offered a *formal* equality and effectively excluded workers from power. He argued that the Soviet government he had established in Russia was a genuine 'proletarian democracy'. Of course the 'people's democracies' established in the Soviet Union, and subsequently in eastern Europe and elsewhere, involved rejection of some of the fundamental principles of liberal representative democracy. They established centralized one-party dictatorships with no effective competition for power, and with only very limited toleration of dissent and free expression. Under Lenin's successor, Stalin (1879–1953), even this limited toleration of dissent was extinguished, as millions perished in a series of purges that included most of Lenin's leading Bolshevik colleagues. The government of the Soviet Union and its satellites in the post-Second World War era did not indulge in such wholesale murder, but remained ruthless oppressive dictatorships.

However, the Soviet Union also seemed to offer a radical alternative to capitalism in managing the economy. From 1917 until 1989 there were two competing economic models, the communist command economy and western capitalism. For a time it appeared that the ruthless forced industrialization of the previously backward Russian economy by a succession of centrally-imposed five-year plans had enabled the Soviet Union almost to catch up with the west. Jobs of some kind for all contrasted favourably with the rising unemployment and poverty in the west in the 1930s.

> *The Soviet Union also seemed to offer a radical alternative to capitalism in managing the economy.*

After the Second World War there were only two superpowers, the USA and the USSR. In specific fields such as armaments and space exploration the USSR appeared to be competing successfully. Yet in the economic sphere, as in the political sphere, choice was absent or constricted, and the rapid development of heavy industry and arms-related products was at the expense of consumer goods and living standards. Even so it appeared that the soviet economic model was a viable alternative to capitalism. Thus some Marxists in the west swallowed any of the reservations they felt about restrictions on political freedom, and continued to support 'really existing socialism' against the capitalist alternative. Others condemned it as a betrayal of socialism.

It should be emphasized that other variants of Marxism continued to have some influence in the west. These include the revisionist Marxism of **Bernstein** and others, still influential within social democratic and socialist parties that were prepared to work within the framework of parliamentary democracy. There were also various forms of Trotskyism, Titoism in Yugoslavia, and the distinctive euro-communism of the once strong Italian Communist Party, influenced by the important Italian theorist, Antonio **Gramsci** (1891–1937). The 'critical theory' of the Frankfurt school, the existential Marxism of **Sartre** (1905–1980) and the structural Marxism of **Althusser** (1918–1990) and **Poulantzas** (1936–1979) were all influential in the academic study of politics, as well as having a (generally much more limited) impact on political practice (McLellan, 1980).

The continuing relevance of Marx and Marxism

The subsequent implosion of the Soviet empire has substantially destroyed the credibility of the hitherto dominant interpretation of Marx's thought, Marxism-Leninism. Most of those who lived under it have no desire to return to it. Some students might conclude that there is no longer much point in bothering too much with Marx and Marxism. Yet Marx remains a hugely important thinker whose ideas cannot be dismissed because one interpretation of Marxism has apparently been discredited. Marxist theory has to be addressed by any serious student of politics, and indeed any social scientist, including those with no sympathy for any kind of socialism. In some ways the end of soviet-style communism makes it easier to tackle Marxist thought without too many preconceptions.

Why do Marx and Marxism remain relevant? First of all, Marx (and Marxists) still offer a cogent analysis of **capitalism**. While Marx was aware of the tremendous potential for increased production and wealth that industrialization offered, he and Engels were also only too aware of the downside of capitalism. This included both massive inequality and the debilitating effect of the conditions of labour for many industrial workers (the important Marxist concept of 'alienation'). Marx was also prescient on the development of capitalism, anticipating the impact of monopoly and even global capitalism. However he clearly underestimated the resilience and adaptability of capitalism and, **social democrats** would argue, the scope to manage capitalism so as to reduce its destructive capacity through a 'mixed economy'.

Second, Marx emphasized the continuing importance of economic and other external constraints on political action. He, and certainly some of his followers, may have exaggerated the importance of '**structure**' over human '**agency**'. The influence of Marx himself and the political career of Lenin certainly suggest that individuals can change history. Yet we are also only too aware of the constraints under which political leaders and governments operate, particularly perhaps the increased economic and environment impacts of **globalization**.

> *Marx emphasized the continuing importance of economic and other external constraints on political action.*

Third, the Marxist critique still has important implications for the now dominant liberal democratic systems under which most of the world now lives. There are all kinds of important criticisms of particular democracies, relating to electoral systems, the funding of parties and electoral competition, media bias and so on. However it is the Marxist critique that gets to the heart of the matter. Do the people, or can the people, really have effective power in a system where productive resources are controlled by the few? Can political **equality** be a reality without much greater economic equality? Alternatively, if political equality is a reality, why has it not led to significantly greater equality of wealth and income? These are questions that any students of politics need to ponder, even if the answers they finally come up with are not Marxist ones.

BOX 2.4 timechart of key political developments, concepts and thinkers

Period	Events/institutions	Concepts	Thinkers
Ancient Greece (down to 4th c. BC)	Persian wars Peloponnesian war Death of Socrates Rise of Macedon	Law Justice 'Polis' ('city state') Ideal state Democracy Natural law	Pericles Thucydides Socrates Plato Aristotle Stoics
Roman Republic and Roman Empire (down to 5th c. AD)	Growth of Rome Carthaginian wars Civil war Roman empire Rise of Christianity Decline of Rome	Republic Citizenship Roman law Universal empire	Cicero Augustine
Dark ages and Middle Ages (down to 15th c. AD)	Barbarian invasions Schism between Rome and Byzantium Rise of Islam Crusades Church v. state	Feudalism Hereditary monarchy Christendom Papal supremacy Spiritual and temporal power	Averroes Aquinas Marsiglio
Early modern period (late 15th, 16th and 17th centuries)	Renaissance Invention of printing Discovery and colonization of 'New World' Reformation Inquisition Religious wars Dutch Republic Scientific revolution	Protestantism Sovereignty Absolutism Political obligation State of nature Contract Religious toleration	Machiavelli Bodin Grotius Hobbes Spinoza Locke
18th century 'Age of Enlightenment'	Slave trade Beginnings of industrialization and capitalism Dynastic wars American War of Independence French Revolution	Absolute monarchy Separation of powers Enlightenment Rationalism Popular sovereignty Revolution Citizen rights Liberty, equality, fraternity Federalism	Montesquieu Hume Rousseau Smith Kant Paine Jefferson Madison Burke Godwin Wollstonecraft

BOX 2.4 **continued**

Period	Events/institutions	Concepts	Thinkers
19th century	Napoleonic empire Restoration Industrial Revolution Urbanization 1830 and 1848 revolutions Rise of nation states American Civil War Growth of colonial empires	Nationalism Constitutional reform Liberalism Capitalism Conservatism Representative democracy Class Socialism Collectivism Race Imperialism	Bentham Hegel Maistre Owen Tocqueville Marx and Engels Proudhon Mill Green Comte Pareto Nietzsche
20th century	First World War Bolshevik Revolution Votes for women Rise of dictators Economic depression Second World War Cold war Decolonization European Community Fall of Berlin Wall Terrorism	Militarism Pacifism Elitism Pluralism Self-determination Fascism and Nazism Racism Genocide Behaviouralism Feminism Women's rights Patriarchy Neo-liberalism Public choice Neo-conservatism Postmodernism Environmentalism	Michels Lenin Weber Trotsky Gramsci Gandhi Popper Mao Zedong Keynes Hayek De Beauvoir Friedan Dahl Rawls Nozick Buchanan Foucault Lyotard

approaches

Section 2: Theories, models and approaches in modern political science

Elitism and pluralism

We begin the discussion of modern political theories with a review of the long-running debate between elitists and pluralists. Power is what politics is about, it is widely agreed. **Elitism** and **pluralism** involve two contrasting theories or models of power in politics and society. To simplify drastically, elitism suggests that power is narrowly concentrated in the hands of the few, while pluralism suggests that it is relatively widely dispersed.

Classical elitism

What is now generally referred to as classical elitism was advanced by a group of thinkers who flourished in the late nineteenth and early twentieth centuries, Vilfredo **Pareto** (1848–1923), Robert **Michels** (1875–1936) and Gaetano **Mosca** (1858–1941). Mosca ([1896]1939) briefly summarizes the elitist perspective:

> In all societies ... two classes of people appear – a class that rules and a class that is ruled. The first class, always the less numerous, performs all political functions, monopolises power and enjoys the advantages that power brings, whereas the second, the more numerous class, is directed and controlled by the first.

Once this would have appeared a simple truism, hardly worth asserting, but the growth of **representative democracy** and the notion of government by the people provoked these thinkers obstinately to proclaim that power was still effectively in the hands of the few, even in states that were nominally democratic. Elite rule was simply an inescapable fact of human life. This did not mean that particular elites were permanent. As Pareto also observed, history was a 'graveyard of elites'. Yet according to his perspective, although elites are regularly overthrown, they can only be replaced by new elites, never by the rule of the people.

Thus the classical elitists, like Marx, considered the parliamentary democracies of their day to be shams, concealing the continued concentration of power in the hands of a small ruling class or elite. However, there are some crucial differences in their underlying assumptions. For **Marx**, political power reflected economic power, and the elite or ruling class owned and controlled the means of production (see pages 74–5). For the classical elitists the source of the power of the ruling elite might be any attribute, real or imagined, that marked them out from the mass. A more crucial difference was that the classical elitists considered elite rule inevitable, a fact of life, while Marx believed the masses could, and eventually

The classical elitists considered the parliamentary democracies of their day to be shams, concealing the continued concentration of power in the hands of a small ruling class.

would, take power. Classical elitism indeed had at least as many damaging implications for **socialism** as for democracy. According to Michels ([1911] 1962), there was an 'iron law of **oligarchy**' which operated in all organizations, even in those ostensibly committed to democracy, including political parties like the social democrats. Socialism was an impossibility. 'The socialists might conquer but not socialism, which would perish in the moment of its adherents' triumph.' Some would argue this judgement was confirmed by the Bolshevik Revolution, others by the failure of the leaders of social democratic parties to introduce socialism after a victory at the polls.

Mosca allowed for competition between rival elites that might be relatively open and responsive to pressure from the masses (Bottomore, 1966). These ideas were compatible with an elite theory of democracy involving limited competition between political parties, where all the policy initiatives came from the leadership rather than the rank and file, such as that advanced by Joseph **Schumpeter** (1883–1950).

Pluralism

Elitism is contrasted with pluralism. **Pluralism** suggests a diversity or plurality of organizations, interests and values in society. While elitists maintain that power is concentrated in the hands of the few (inevitably, from a classical elitist perspective), pluralists argue that power and influence is widely diffused in modern democratic polities such as the USA. Although these assumptions are highly compatible with **representative democracy**, pluralists emphasize not only, or even largely, occasional participation in the formal electoral process, but the opportunities for ordinary citizens to influence the political process informally, particularly through involvement in pressure group activity.

> *Pluralism suggests a diversity or plurality of organisations, interests and values in society.*

Pluralism is closely linked with mainstream American political science. It grew out of the pioneering group theory of Arthur **Bentley** (1870–1953), who argued, 'All phenomena of government are phenomena of groups pressing one another.' Group competition he saw as the essence of the political process and the science of politics; 'when the groups are adequately stated, everything is stated' (Bentley, [1908]1967). **Pressure group** theory was developed by a succession of leading American political scientists, including David Truman, Nelson Polsby, Charles **Lindblom** (1917–) and above all, Robert **Dahl** (1915–). They and others carried out extensive research into the activities of countless groups, and found evidence of their influence on specific public policies or decisions. There was always a significant normative element to this apparently dispassionate social science. The sovereignty of the people was an axiom difficult to dispute for those who lived and worked in the USA, the cradle of modern democracy. Democracy assumes that power is dispersed. Many American political scientists were intent (perhaps largely unconsciously) on demonstrating that it *was* in fact dispersed, as evidenced by the countless competing groups, all pressing on government.

Thus American pluralists approved of pressure group activity in general. They maintained this pressure group activity aided and improved the democratic process rather than subverting it (as some early critics of pressure groups had argued). In an open democratic society there were ample opportunities for anyone who wanted to defend an interest or promote a cause to organize with others to influence decision makers and the wider public. This, pluralists argued, commonly encouraged those who took a different view to establish opposed groups, leading to a balance of interests (sometimes described as countervailing power). The information and arguments put forward by conflicting interests and causes put more relevant knowledge in the public domain, thus improving the quality of debate and aiding decision making. Pluralists saw this competition for influence between countless groups as the essence of democracy. Governments needed to be responsive to this pressure if they wanted to maintain their popularity and power. Some pluralists implied that governments passively responded to the sum of group pressures, acting as neutral arbiters between conflicting interests in society.

Radical elite theory

Others insisted that the pluralists had a rather rosy view of the prospects for ordinary people to have effective political influence, even in a democracy. Radical elite theorists argued that effective power was far more concentrated than the pluralists maintained. Briefly, critics of pluralism argued that there were massive inequalities in resources and influence between some groups and others, and that the state was far from neutral, but encouraged some interests while effectively excluding others.

As Dunleavy and O'Leary (1987) have observed, a strange thing happened to elitism when it crossed the Atlantic. The old European classical elitists were anti-democratic in outlook. Most American elite theorists were radical political sociologists, influenced to some degree by Marxist ideas. They lamented what they perceived as the concentration of power in what was supposed to be a democratic polity. C. Wright **Mills** (1916–1962), in his classic study of American government and politics, *The Power Elite* (1956), argued that there were close interrelationships and a shared outlook between the US political, military and business elites. There was an essentially similar analysis of the role of the influential role of interlocking elites within western states generally (and the United Kingdom particularly) by the British Marxist, Ralph **Miliband** (1924–1994), who dedicated his own book *The State in Capitalist Society* (1969) to the memory of C. Wright Mills.

However, much of the argument between elitists and pluralists focused not on power at the level of the **nation-state** but on detailed case studies of power and decision making in specific urban **communities**, both in the USA and elsewhere. These studies were suggestive rather than conclusive on the distribution of urban power, and often seemed to confirm the initial assumptions of theorists on both sides. Floyd Hunter (1953) showed that decision making in Atlanta, Georgia was substantially dominated by business interests, while the wider community, and blacks especially had little influence. In marked contrast Robert **Dahl** (1961) concluded that there was no single elite dominating decision making in New Haven, Connecticut, but instead different groups were influential in different policy arenas and political influence was relatively widely dispersed, as the pluralist model suggested. Similar studies of urban power in the UK and France were no more conclusive (see Box 5.2, page 227). Thus some have concluded that such case studies can only be illustrative: they do not prove anything.

Critics of research by Dahl and other pluralists suggested they focused too much on influence on overt decision making. Bachrach and Baratz (1962, 1970) argued that there were two faces of power: the power to influence and make decisions on issues that have arisen for public debate, and the power to deflect potentially dangerous issues from being brought forward for decision. Steven Lukes (1974) has suggested there is a third dimension to power. Power can be exercised more subtly in such a way that issues do not even arise. He cites in support a comparison of the air pollution policies of two apparently similar US steel cities, one of which introduced clean air policies while the other avoided the issue (Crenson, 1971). In the latter, the steel company that provided the main employment in the town successfully kept pollution off the agenda 'without acting or entering into the political arena'. Its reputation alone was long sufficient to prevent the issue coming up for decision.

> *Neopluralists accept that the state is not a neutral referee but an active and often partisan participant in the game.*

Some pluralists, dubbed neopluralists, including Charles **Lindblom**, the economist J. K. **Galbraith** (1908–2006), and even Robert **Dahl** himself in his later work, have made concessions to their critics. Thus neopluralists accept that the state is not a neutral referee but an active and often partisan participant in the game. While continuing to maintain that power and influence is fairly widely dispersed, they acknowledged that some interests, particularly business interests, have considerable practical influence while others may be virtually excluded from the political process.

Corporatism

Pluralism has been compared with another theory of power and decision making, **corporatism**, fashionable in western Europe, particularly around the 1970s (but less so in the USA). Both pluralism and corporatism see groups as important in the political decision-making process. Yet whereas pluralism suggests countless groups in free and open competition to influence government, corporatism suggests a much more constrained policy process in which a few peak or umbrella groups representing the key interests of capital and labour are closely involved with government in a relationship of mutual dependence. To critics, this highly limited form of interest representation involved a bypassing of both parliament and people (Dunleavy and O'Leary, 1987, discuss corporatism under the general heading of **elitism**). However, while modern **Marxists** thought corporatist processes meant the interests of labour were being sacrificed to the interests of **capitalism**, **neoliberals** considered that corporatism involved far too many concessions to producer interests and labour interests in particular. Some neoliberals indeed have criticized not just corporatism, but the wider pluralist influence of groups on the policy process, for example arguing that a combination of client groups dependent on public services, trade unions and business interests have contributed to a malign steady rise in post-war government spending and taxation.

Power and democracy

Thus the long running debate over the effective distribution of power in western political systems has been ultimately inconclusive, although it has generated much important research, and extended and deepened our understanding of the political process. It has also illustrated some of the difficulties in separating positive social science from **normative** political theory. Behind the ongoing debate on how power is actually distributed in modern western political systems, seemingly a question of fact, there are issues around how it *should* be distributed, a question of value. Despite the insistence of early **behaviouralists** (see page 84) that the two issues should be kept separate, they have been, perhaps inevitably, almost inextricably linked in practice. The (largely unspoken) premise behind the radical elitist critique of modern western democracy from those

approaches

like C. Wright Mills and Ralph Miliband is that power should be more widely dispersed than it is. On the other side of the debate, Robert Dahl, a major figure in the behavioural revolution, has never been solely concerned with demonstrating that power is fairly widely dispersed in practice. He has effectively developed a new theory of democracy, that he prefers to call 'polyarchy', based on group politics to which he clearly attaches positive value.

Behaviouralism

Modern political science is closely associated with the **behavioural** revolution that dominated the study of politics in the USA from the 1940s, and became substantially influential elsewhere. The term 'revolution' is hardly too strong to describe the impact of behaviouralism, which might be loosely described as 'out with the old and in with the new'. The behaviouralists rejected much of the traditional study of politics, including normative political theory. They also marginalized the analysis of constitutions, formal public institutions and administrative law. What mattered was not what constitutions, organizational charts and established legal principles suggested *should* happen, but what actually *did* happen: political behaviour, dispassionately measured and assessed. Moreover, these new political scientists were interested in the political behaviour not just of governments, leading politicians and bureaucrats, but of ordinary people as they participated in the political process by voting in elections, forming allegiances to parties and joining all kinds of associations and groups. Thus behaviouralism transformed the focus of the subject.

> *The term 'revolution' is hardly too strong to describe the impact of behaviouralism, which might be loosely described as 'out with the old and in with the new'.*

Methodology

Behaviouralists sought to frame hypotheses or theories that could be tested against the evidence, through the collection and analysis of relevant data, in the manner of other sciences. This required mastery of advanced statistical methods, searching for meaningful correlations between variables to substantiate or reject tentative hypotheses. The methodology was inductive, deriving a general law or principle from a number of observed particular instances. Early behaviouralists believed this approach relied entirely on dispassionate and value-free observation of the evidence, without preconceptions or normative assumptions. However it is now more generally accepted that some initial hunch or idea inevitably guides the search for data.

Thus for example, a researcher might guess that those who are most educated are more likely to vote. To test this tentative hypothesis the research would seek to correlate electoral turnout with levels of education. If a positive link was apparently established, suggesting that the most educated are indeed more likely to vote, this would seem to support the original tentative hypothesis. Others might seek to replicate the research to confirm or refute the findings, perhaps for another time period, or in another country. If this new research leads to contrary conclusions, perhaps suggesting that the least educated are more likely to vote, this would tend to invalidate any general link between turnout and education levels (although it may be possible to refine the original hypothesis to suggest a link in specified circumstances).

The points about replication and possible refutation are crucial. Any scientific research should be capable of being replicated in this way. Karl **Popper** (1902–1994) argued that falsifiability rather than verifiability should be the criteria for a scientific hypothesis ([1934]1959). A scientific hypothesis should be framed in such a way that it could be falsified by the discovery of evidence to the contrary. Countless sightings of white swans cannot prove the hypothesis that all swans are white, but it can be disproved by the discovery of a single black swan. Popper held that theories are unscientific if they are expressed in such broad general terms that it is impossible to test them by seeking empirical evidence that might refute them.

There can be little question that the discipline of politics benefited considerably from the new rigour brought about by the behavioural revolution. There were particularly significant advances in the study of voting, pressure group activity, political culture (see Part V for more on all these) and the whole field of comparative politics (see pages 87–90). The section on elitism and pluralism has already alluded to some of the work of American political scientists on **pressure groups** and community power, which should be included in any account of the seminal literature of the behavioural revolution.

Yet in some respects this work was untypical, as the study of pressure group behaviour and influence was rather less susceptible to methods involving the collection and analysis of statistical data. The examination of the influence of particular individuals and groups on key decisions (or sometimes non-decisions) inevitably involved some essentially subjective judgements. While some case studies of decision making in particular communities were certainly suggestive, they could hardly *prove* that power was relatively dispersed or effectively concentrated. Moreover, it was difficult to *generalize* from the findings in the specific communities. Even if it was true that political influence in New Haven, Connecticut (the focus of Robert Dahl's *Who Governs*, 1961) was dispersed rather than concentrated, this did not necessarily mean that it was similarly dispersed in other American cities, still less elsewhere.

Electoral choice

More central to the behaviouralist approach were the major studies of electoral choice. Voting provided a particularly fertile field for the new political science. **Elections** and voting were central to the theory and practice of modern liberal democracy. Democratic theorists had assumed individuals would cast their vote in accordance with their own rational self-interest. Advances in statistical techniques, coupled with the availability of copious election data, official population statistics and commercial opinion surveys allowed a far more scientific analysis of voting behaviour in practice. While initially, in the 1940s and 1950s, the analysis of data depended on the time-consuming use of punched cards, limiting the scope for examining correlations, the introduction of computers enabled complex multivariate analyses of an ever-expanding quantity of data. Much of the ground-breaking work in election and voting analysis was carried out in the USA. Pioneering studies included *The People's Choice* (Lazarsfeld et al, 1944) and *The American Voter* (Campbell et al, 1960), but the approach was soon imitated in Britain (Butler and Stokes, *Political Change in Britain*, 1969) and other western states.

Most of these early key studies of voting behaviour by American and British political scientists focused on single countries: *The American Voter, Political Change in Britain* (emphasis mine), and were thus not comparative. Some of the analysis of electoral choice and party preference reflected assumptions around specific electoral and party systems that were not typical of other countries. The vast majority of modern democracies do not employ the simple plurality (or 'first past the post') electoral system still used in the USA and (for UK parliamentary elections) in Britain. Nor do they have only two major parties competing for power, as in the USA, and (substantially, until recently) in the United Kingdom. These differences have significant implications for voter behaviour, including whether individuals feel motivated to participate in the process. For those who do vote, the choice of party may be influenced both by the extent of party competition and the electoral rules. The generalizations made about the behaviour of the American voter may thus not apply to the French, German or Italian voter. If we wish to understand voting behaviour in general, rather than in specific political systems, a comparative approach is necessary.

The comparative approach

Those at the forefront of the behavioural revolution fully appreciated that political science must be comparative. Gabriel **Almond** (1911–2002) played a key role in the systematic development of a more scientific and more broadly based study of comparative politics, one of the enduring legacies of the behavioural revolution (see page 87). One problem in comparing politics in different countries, is that each appears to have its own institutions and processes and its own particular political terminology. Even institutions and processes with similar names may have a very different role in other political systems, so that we may not be comparing like with like. Thus it appeared important to develop a universal framework and vocabulary to describe and analyse key elements of the political process everywhere (see the section on comparative politics, page 87–90).

Systems theory

Hugely influential was the systems approach. Systems theory, used in various fields (such as biology) to describe any self-regulating system, was adapted by Talcott **Parsons** (1902–1979) for the study of sociology and by David **Easton** (1917–) for politics. One of the great merits of the systems approach was that it focused on the interrelationship of the political process and the wider economic and social environment, and the interdependence of various parts of the political process.

The basic systems model is very simple. Inputs are fed into the system from the wider environment, converted by the system into outputs that in turn affect the environment, and through a feedback process lead to new inputs. Applied to politics, the inputs are the 'demands' made by people, for example, for jobs, higher living standards, public services, and the 'supports' in the shape of taxes, compliance, participation and so on. These demands and supports are processed by government to produce outputs in the form of laws, decisions and adjudications which in turn affect people, and feed back into fresh demands and supports. Some versions of the model suggest that such institutions as **pressure groups** (articulating demands) and **political parties** (aggregating demands) act as key intermediary 'gatekeepers' between people and government. Others distinguish between the formal outputs of government, and the actual outcomes as they affect people in practice.

Systems theory had a substantial impact on the way politics was studied and explained, yet it has also been subjected to extensive criticism. One objection was that it essentially involved little more than a new description of the political process, and new terminology (or jargon). As a theory it was effectively unfalsifiable (see the arguments of Popper, page 85). Moreover, in focusing on inputs into the political system and outputs from it, the systems model substantially downplayed the role of **government** and the **state**, viewed as a mere conversion mechanism (converting inputs into outputs) or a mysterious 'black box'. Although the systems model purported to provide a framework for the analysis of any political system, some detected an implicit American or western bias. Others argued that it prioritized the maintenance of political stability, and failed to explain system breakdown, crises and **revolutions**. Thus the full systems model has been largely abandoned, although some of the associated key terms are still routinely used, while its essential emphasis on politics as an interactive and interdependent process remains.

Conclusion: the behavioural revolution in retrospect

The behavioural revolution was never dependent on the systems model, but it too has attracted plenty of retrospective criticism. Dedicated to the study of observable political behaviour, it inevitably concentrated on parts of the process that were most easily observed and measured, although not necessarily the most important. Those aspects of politics that are more difficult to quantify were relatively neglected. It also claimed too much for the new political science. Even in those areas where its achievements were most solid, such as the analysis of voting, it has not delivered the definitive explanations enthusiasts had anticipated. Progress in the whole field of comparative politics has also rather disappointed early high hopes (see page 89). Moreover, the behaviouralists were too sweeping in their rejection of older approaches to the study of politics. Political philosophy, the study of institutions, and the analysis of politics using the deductive approach of economics rather than induction have all made a strong comeback, and the study of politics is stronger for the diversity of current approaches. However, it was the behavioural revolution that substantially re-established politics as a major discipline in its own right, with a fast-growing body of theory, and it equipped those researching into politics with an invaluable new toolkit of methods. All modern students of politics owe a substantial debt to behaviouralism.

An important benefit of studying another country's politics is to appreciate that there are other options, other ways of doing things, and to learn to see the politics of one's own country through fresh and perhaps more critical eyes.

Comparative politics

Studying foreign political systems

Anyone who begins the study of the government and politics of any country other than that in which they were brought up is soon struck with a sense of surprise and wonder that 'they do things differently there'. The survival of hereditary **monarchy** seems remarkable to those living in **republics**, **federalism** weird to anyone from a unitary state, multi-party coalitions dangerously unstable to those who are only familiar with a two-party system and single party government. It is sometimes difficult to understand that there are credible alternatives to familiar institutions and practices. An important benefit of studying another country's politics is to appreciate that there are other options, other ways of doing things, and to learn to see the politics of one's own country through fresh and perhaps more critical eyes. Thus both **Montesquieu** and **Tocqueville** drew inspiration from the study of foreign political systems with relevance for politics nearer home.

In examining other systems we inevitably compare and contrast. We learn the possibility of change or reform. Other countries have freedom of information, why cannot we? Other countries have electoral systems that appear fairer than ours; surely we should have a similar system? Sometimes, of course, we discover that there are disadvantages in foreign institutions and practices, and learn to appreciate that there is something to be said for our own. Sometimes we may find features of another political system attractive, but doubt whether they could be easily and successfully transferred into a different context. Such comparisons are commonly the beginning of critical thinking about politics. Indeed, it has often been argued that the study of all politics should be comparative, for how is it possible to make any generalizations about the theory and practice of politics from one political system that may be quite atypical?

The need for a comparative framework

Yet merely studying foreign political systems, although often described as comparative, is not comparative politics as the real practitioners of the subject understand it. The more systematic study of comparative politics requires a comparative framework and methodology, and preferably a much wider range of comparison, identifying similarities and differences between systems and endeavouring to develop plausible hypotheses and test them against the evidence.

The **behavioural** revolution, described in the last section, gave a major impetus to the more systematic study of comparative politics, although the subject was hardly new. **Aristotle**, as we have seen, presided over an apparently wide-ranging study of constitutions. Indeed, much of the work that was genuinely comparative before the middle of the twentieth century similarly focused narrowly on comparative *government*, rather than politics in the broader sense, and on constitutional theory rather than governmental practice. Thus the main emphasis was on the formal institutions of government (executives, legislatures, bureaucracies, judiciaries) and sometimes other institutions or organizations not part of the formal structure of the state, such as political parties.

Those who, like Gabriel **Almond**, were among the leaders of the behavioural revolution in the study of political science, not only stressed the central importance of comparative politics, but sought to transform the whole scope and methodology of the subject. Thus the study of comparative politics moved beyond limited comparisons of a few western political systems to a global approach taking in communist political systems and the politics of developing nations. To provide a suitable broad framework for comparison, the new comparative politics commonly adopted the systems model associated with David **Easton** (see pages 86–7). In line with the behavioural revolution in American political science more generally, the focus also shifted from government and political 'outputs' (decisions, policies, laws) to 'inputs' into the political process from the mass of citizens. Thus there was a new emphasis on studying **political culture**, political socialization, political communication, and all forms of political participation.

The scope of the new comparative politics that emerged in the 1960s was thus extremely ambitious. It was hoped that this

> *The scope of the new comparative politics that emerged in the 1960s was extremely ambitious.*

more extensive and thoroughly comparative research would lead to new sustainable evidence-based generalizations and theories. Some of the new work in the field involved collaborative research by academics from a wide range of countries and universities. One influential work was Almond and Verba's *The Civic Culture* (1963), involving survey-based comparisons between the **political cultures** of five states (the USA, United Kingdom, West Germany, Italy and Mexico). This revealed significant differences in political beliefs and attitudes of respondents from different countries, with implications for the general health of the democratic political process. (For more on this study and on political culture in general, see Part V.)

The difficulties of global comparison

Yet Sidney Verba, one of the standard bearers of the new comparative politics, confessed in 1985 that it 'has been disappointing to some', especially, he suggests, 'in comparison to past aspirations and hopes' (quoted by Peter Mair in Goodin and Klingemann, 1996: 314). One obvious problem with a comprehensive approach to the study of comparative politics is the very scale of the number of states and the wide range of systems. In 1945, there were just 50 members of the United Nations. By 2007, largely as a consequence of former colonies securing political independence, but also because of the break-up of some former large states (such as the old USSR and Yugoslavia), there were no fewer than 192. Most of these states differ massively in size, in social structure, in the level of economic and political development, in the formal structure of government, and in their longevity and stability. Even basic statistical comparisons for key indicators (such as population, national income and growth, unemployment levels, literacy, electoral turnout) are not always reliable. In such circumstances meaningful comparison is often difficult.

One obvious way to bring some order into an increasingly crowded field is through the classification of political systems. Under the influence of the cold war, regimes were commonly classified under three headings, depending on whether they were part of the 'first world' (the liberal democratic and capitalist west), the 'second world' (the alternative communist bloc), or the 'third' or 'developing' world (effectively, the rest of the globe). Needless to say, each 'world' included a wide range of political and economic systems, particularly the third or residual category. This classification, which was always flawed, reflecting normative assumptions, became effectively redundant with the end of the cold war. Some comparative politics specialists were so disoriented by the virtual disappearance of the 'second world' that they talked of a 'death in the family'. Others attempted to design new typologies more suited to an altered reality (including such categories as 'Islamic states'), without establishing any general consensus. Indeed, the collapse of the Soviet bloc has further increased both the number and variety of states, magnifying the problem of effective and meaningful comparison, and developing new 'grand theories' covering the whole range of very varied political systems.

Others might object that this whole approach is too state-centred. Although the behavioural revolution involved a shift in comparative studies from government to politics, and from elite to mass behaviour, it remained essentially focused on sovereign states. Yet any student of politics today soon becomes aware of the growing importance of international organizations (both governmental and non-governmental) and transnational corporations. These, together with the growth of cross-national political identities, attitudes and behaviour, suggest that the framework of independent sovereign nation-states may no longer be entirely adequate for the study of comparative politics in the modern world.

Both the growth in number and type of state regimes and the increasing importance of cross-state political developments make the generation of new grand theories covering the whole field of comparative politics much more difficult. Many comparative specialists no longer try, instead choosing to concentrate more on area studies, such as African politics or Scandinavian politics, or specializing in particular types of regimes, such as parliamentary democracies or military dictatorships, or on key and often problematic processes, such as democratization studies (see Part V). Such a narrower focus may be less ambitious, but more realistic, facilitating more limited but perhaps more meaningful comparisons, and generating some potentially more useful hypotheses, albeit with more restricted applications.

Rational choice (or public choice) theory

Rational choice theory, or public choice theory as it is often called, with specific reference to choice within the public sector, has become extremely influential in the study of politics in the USA and features strongly elsewhere. It is impossible to ignore it, as numerous references throughout this book indicate. Any student of politics needs to consider the challenge posed by rational choice theory. It is based on some plausible assumptions on individual human motivation and behaviour, essentially the pursuit of rational self-interest. The main policy prescriptions derived from these assumptions involve a substantial cutback and reorganization of the role of the modern state.

The influence of economics

While the behavioural revolution in the study of politics drew inspiration from sociology, and used a similar inductive methodology, deriving general theory from a mass of particular instances, rational choice theory employed the essentially deductive methodology of economics. It can be regarded as a return to the political economy approach which was dominant in the nineteenth century. Thus the main thrust of rational choice theory was hardly new. Classical economics from Adam **Smith** onwards had assumed that individuals, both as producers and consumers, pursued their own rational self-interest. Classical economic theory had been similarly largely hostile to state intervention, assuming that free market forces promoted the common good while well-intentioned state intervention would undermine prosperity (Hindmoor, in Hay et al, 2006: 83). Indeed, an ideological presumption against state intervention (the notion of laissez-faire, or 'let be') persisted despite the general growth of state service and expenditure in the nineteenth century.

> *Rational choice theory employed the essentially deductive methodology of economics.*

In the twentieth century the increased influence of a progressive social liberalism and social democracy gave theoretical support to state intervention to correct market failure. Later, the theories of John Maynard **Keynes** (1883–1946) legitimized state management of the macro-economy, and appeared to provide justification for increased government spending in the decades following the Second World War. It was against this prevailing **consensus** that public choice theorists powerfully reinforced the arguments of **neoliberal** economists like **Hayek** and Milton Friedman to reverse the growth of the **state**.

Rational choice, politics and government

While rational choice by business firms and individual producers and consumers has long been a key assumption in classical and neoclassical economic theory, public choice theory extends this assumption to political behaviour and the public sector. A pioneering study by Anthony **Downs** (1930–) applied economic assumptions of rationality to voting and party competition (*An Economic Theory of Democracy*, 1957). James **Buchanan** (1919–) and Gordon **Tullock** (1922–), in their key work which they co-authored, *The Calculus of Consent* (1962), applied similar assumptions of the pursuit of rational self-interest to government and the public sector.

Anthony Downs (*Inside Bureaucracy*, 1967) and William **Niskanen** (1933–) (*Bureaucracy and Representative Government*, 1971) used the same kind of approach to analyse the behaviour of those working in public sector **bureaucracies**. Largely immune from the discipline of the market and from the assumed goal of private sector firms to maximize profits, public sector bureaucrats, they argued, would pursue their own self-interest by maximizing the size of their own 'bureau' (office, agency or department). They would do this by increasing the size and scope of its responsibilities, its workforce and its budget. This would boost the status, income, career prospects and job interest of key bureaucrats. Another American social scientist, Mancur **Olson** (1932–1998) (*The Logic of Collective Action*, 1965), used rational choice theory to explain why special interest groups favouring protection or subsidies against the wider public interest were often more effective in influencing policy makers. Their activities commonly led to an alliance between public sector bureaucrats and client groups to increase state spending and taxation.

Rational choice and public administration

This analysis ran counter to the assumptions of many academics working within the field of public administration and public policy. Some of this work appeared essentially descriptive and atheoretical, taking at face value the claims of politicians and public sector bureaucrats to pursue the wider public interest, or public good, rather than their own self-interest, and assuming a public sector ethic quite distinct from the morality of the private sector. Public choice theory challenged the assumption that public administration was quite distinct from the private sector, and that it operated under very different principles from business firms. Instead, rational choice theorists argued, the pursuit of rational self-interest governed human behaviour in government organizations as it did in private firms, with the only crucial difference being that the state had monopoly powers and most state organizations were not subject to competition and market discipline. In so far as the public have become more cynical about professions to serve the public interest from politicians and state officials, it is partly in response to popularized versions of neoliberal and public choice economics (Hindmoor, in Hay et al, 2006: 93).

> *Rational choice theorists argued that the pursuit of rational self-interest governed human behaviour in government organizations as it did in private firms.*

Much of their analysis seemed only too plausible. It was enthusiastically taken up by New Right politicians (for example Margaret Thatcher and Keith Joseph in Britain, those around Ronald Reagan in the USA) and others critical of the growth of the state and public sector employment and expenditure. Public choice theory provided both an explanation for state growth, and some practical remedies. These remedies included cutting back on government generally, downsizing, privatizing and 'contracting out' some state activities, and exposing others to competition both from the private and voluntary sectors and from within the public sector. Private sector techniques and principles were introduced into public sector management. The development of internal markets or 'quasi-markets' into the delivery of public services, would, it was anticipated, introduce the discipline of competition into the public sector.

Criticism of rational and public choice theory

Those who found public choice theory unpalatable could resort to various different lines of criticism. One obvious response is to deny the basic assumptions on human motivation and behaviour. Thus plenty of examples can be found of human beings not pursuing their own rational self-interest, sacrificing their lives for others or undergoing life-threatening surgery to donate a kidney to help a relative. One obvious issue here is how far such altruistic behaviour is exceptional rather than typical. Moreover, some apparently altruistic activities (donations to charities or other 'good causes') may have a more self-interested motive (public recognition, honours, influence over others). Yet there is still a problem with the core premise of rational or public choice theory. It rests on an admittedly plausible assumption, but one that cannot be proved.

> *Plenty of examples can be found of human beings not pursuing their own rational self-interest, sacrificing their lives for others or undergoing life-threatening surgery to donate a kidney to help a relative.*

Another line of argument is to stress the influence of social conditioning on human behaviour. Thus most people vote, despite the suggestion of **Downs** that voting is irrational, because the chance of an individual vote materially affecting the outcome cannot compensate for the 'costs' (in time and effort). **New institutionalists** (see pages 94–6) stress the importance of institutional cultures in influencing attitudes and behaviour. It is certainly plausible that employees can be socialized into accepting norms of service to others in the armed forces, hospitals and schools, for example, and it is commonly in their self-interest to comply with established norms of behaviour.

One distinctive and influential line of argument (from the British political scientist Patrick Dunleavy, 1991) largely accepts the assumptions of the public choice school on human motivation and behaviour, but questions the conclusions they derive from these assumptions. Thus he argues that self-interested public bureaucrats will not necessarily pursue what **Niskanen** described as bureau maximization, but instead pursue bureau-shaping. From Niskanen's analysis we might assume that senior public sector bureaucrats would strenuously resist cuts in their departmental budgets, workforce and activities, but instead they have often substantially cooperated with and largely apparently accepted major cutbacks and reorganizations of departments, including privatization and contracting out. Dunleavy suggests reasons for this.

Thus senior bureaucrats are rarely directly affected by budget cuts, which commonly involve fringe agencies and activities, and junior staff. It is only the core budget that is of crucial concern to them. Similarly cuts in the departments' total workforce are much more likely to affect unskilled workers, casual workers and outlying activities than senior managers and professionals. While contracting out some services previously provided in-house, such as cleaning and catering, may seriously affect the pay and conditions of manual workers, it can provide increased work and promotion opportunities for accountants and administrators specializing in contract specification and regulation. There may even be the

approaches

chance of a profitable management buy-out. Moreover, some senior managers may prefer to lose direct responsibility for managing awkward unionized manual workers. The same goes for activities, some of which may be so troublesome to manage that senior bureaucrats are only too happy to 'outsource' or transfer them to others. It may be noted that some of the smallest government departments are often among the most prestigious.

A note of caution may also be entered on some public choice remedies and recommendations. Some argue that increased competition within the public sector has been counterproductive, involving additional costs in managing internal markets and contracts with contentious implications for service levels. At the same time, competition has also arguably reduced the scope for cooperation within and between public services. Why should successful institutions want to share the secrets of their success with their leading competitors? Thus critics suggest that the reorganized public sector has lost some of the traditional values of the public sector, including coordination and cooperation between agencies. At the same time the public sector may not always benefit from the presumed discipline of the market, as some institutions simply cannot be allowed to fail.

Yet it seems clear that public choice theory is here to stay. The work of Downs, Buchanan, Niskanen and Olson in particular has transformed ways of thinking about politics and government. No one embarking on the study of politics can afford to ignore the implications of their analysis of political attitudes and behaviour. It has stimulated new thinking throughout the discipline. One consequence has been to refocus on the core activities of government, which had been relatively neglected by behaviouralists, partly because the interaction of leading politicians and public sector bureaucrats was less susceptible to systematic statistical analysis. Public choice theory has restored government and the state to centre stage. This was also true of the new institutionalism, the subject of the next section.

> *Public choice theory has restored government and the state to centre stage.*

From old to new institutionalism

Criticism of the old focus on government institutions

Much of the focus of the older study of politics in the nineteenth century and the first half of the twentieth century was on **constitutions**, public law and the formal institutions of government at every level. Thus constitutions were examined, classified and compared, the relations between levels of government (e.g. federal and state, central and local), analysed, and the structures and hierarchies of government departments and agencies scrutinized. Critics suggested that this focus on the formal structure of government and public administration was too descriptive and insufficiently critical and theoretical. Thus it was perhaps too readily assumed that government operated as constitutional documents and orthodox interpretations suggested it should, or that public officials were selflessly devoted to the service of the national interest or public interest. Nor was sufficient attention paid to politics outside government, and influences on the public policy process.

> *It was perhaps too readily assumed that government operated as constitutional documents and orthodox interpretations suggested it should.*

Much of this changed with the behavioural revolution led by American political scientists in the mid-twentieth century. The new focus was on political behaviour throughout society rather than within government, on political culture and socialization, on voting and forms of political participation, on pressure group organization and influence, on mass political parties at both leadership and grass roots levels. This focus on behaviour and process tended to marginalize work on formal structures of government and the state, such as the organization of central government departments and the structure and reform of local government, which was increasingly confined to public administration specialists. This tendency was reinforced by the then-fashionable systems theory advanced particularly by David **Easton** (see pages 86–7). Here all the emphasis was on the influence of the wider economic and social environment on political systems, in ways which seemed to reduce the state, its institutions and personnel to a passive mechanism for converting political inputs (such as demands from groups and parties) into outputs (or decisions).

The impact of neoliberalism and rational choice theory on the study of politics from the 1970s restored some of the focus on government, as we have seen (page 93), although this focus was essentially critical. The state was viewed as at best a necessary evil and at worst positively malign. The thrust of neoliberal theory was to cut government down to size. Moreover, much of the language, values and assumptions of government and public service was not taken on trust. Rather, neoliberals assumed that state organizations and more particularly their paid employees were motivated by the same individual self-interest as the private sector. In the absence of profits and the sanctions of the free market, they would seek to promote their own bureaucratic empires, thus improving their own job prospects and security, their prestige and status, and incidentally, the interest of their work. Rational choice theorists were concerned with the structure and organization of government, but largely to reform it, to modify its more malign tendencies (as they saw them). Thus they sought to increase competition both within government and between government and the private sector. Some of this might involve disaggregation and decentralization, and pruning excess levels of bureaucracy by cutting out intermediate tiers of government. Yet although rational choice theorists made recommendations about institutions, their main assumptions and focus were on individual motivation – how men and women pursued their rational self-interest within institutional frameworks, which were themselves established and developed by individuals pursuing their own interests.

The new institutionalism

However, over the last two decades, some academics have sought to bring the state and institutions back in to the study of politics, as part of what has been termed a 'new institutionalism'. Theda **Skocpol** (1947–) had re-emphasized the importance of the state and political institutions generally in her study of revolutions (1979), and went on to become one of the editors of an influential collection of essays under the title *Bringing the State Back In* (Evans, Reuschemeyer and Skocpol, 1985). One of the pioneers of the new American political science, Gabriel Almond (1988), noted in an article 'the return of the state' (which from a European perspective had never gone away). Yet it was James March and Johan Olsen in a seminal article (1984) and then a book (1989) who re-established the important of institutions, both state institutions and institutions more generally, and who coined the term 'new institutionalism'.

Thus March and Olsen argued that 'the organization of political life makes a difference'(1984: 734). It cannot all be reduced to individual motivation and behaviour. Political institutions influence the behaviour of individuals by shaping their 'values, norms, interests, identities and beliefs' (March and Olsen, 1989: 17) There are institutional rules of behaviour, 'standard operating procedures and structures that define and defend interests'.

Institutions 'are political actors in their own right' (March and Olsen, 1984: 738). So the new institutionalism re-emphasized the importance of the institutional context in which politics takes place.

What exactly was new about the new institutionalism? It was more analytical and theoretical, and less descriptive, than the old institutionalism. However, it is only fair to point out that it also involved a partial reappraisal of the old institutionalism, which was never as purely descriptive and atheoretical as some of its critics suggested. Thus Rhodes (1997: 63–83) has mounted a vigorous defence of much of older institutional approaches. He praises particularly the study of comparative government by the American, Herman Finer (1932), and the work of British writers on public administration, such as William Robson (1928, 1948, 1960). However, Rhodes admits that Robson displayed 'two of the institutional approaches' defects: a mistrust of theory and a reformism bordering on the polemic'.

The new institutionalism recognized the importance of theory and sought to explain rather than reform institutions. Vivian Lowndes (in Marsh and Stoker, 2002: 97–101) suggests that the new institutionalism involved a shift from a focus on organizational structures to the institutional rules or norms that guide and constrain the behaviour of individuals. There was also, she argues, a more informal conception of institutions, a focus on 'informal conventions as well as formal rules'. There was a more dynamic view of institutions that might evolve incrementally over time. There was also a concern to analyse the interplay of societal and institutional values. Finally, the new institutionalists addressed the relationship between specific political institutions and the political and social system as a whole of which they are a part. Thus institutions are 'differentiated' rather than simply integral parts of the state or political system, but are not independent entities, in that they are inevitably embedded in a specific locality and a specific historical time. As another commentator has observed:

> Institutionalism is characterized, unremarkably perhaps, by its emphasis upon the institutional context in which political events occur and for the outcomes and effects they generate. In contrast to ... behaviouralist and rational choice orthodoxies it emphasizes the extent to which political conduct is shaped by the institutional landscape in which it occurs, the importance of the historical legacies bequeathed from the past to the present.
>
> (Schmidt, in Hay et al, 2006: 98)

Varieties of the new institutionalism

However, the new institutionalism now covers a wider range of distinctive strands or strains. Guy Peters (in Goodin and Klingemann, 1996: 207–13) distinguishes between five types of institutionalism (normative, rational choice, historical, social and structural), expanded to seven by the same writers in 1999. Vivien Schmidt (in Hay et al, 2006: 102–14) distinguishes four distinctive strands to the new institutionalism: rational choice institutionalism, historical institutionalism, sociological institutionalism and discursive institutionalism, which overlaps with Guy Peters' typology. However, in illustrating these distinctive strands she acknowledges that there are extensive mutual influences between the tendencies and differences of emphasis within them.

Rational choice institutionalism is perhaps the most surprising and interesting among these different types or strains. March and Olsen had been concerned to demonstrate that collective political action cannot be reduced to individual behaviour. They showed how the development of specific institutional structures and processes over time produce shared organizational cultures that shape the ideas, attitudes and behaviour of those who work within them, influencing the way specific issues are perceived and tackled. This seems incompatible with the individualist assumptions behind rational choice theory. Yet some rational choice theorists found the institutional context was helpful in accounting for differences in policy outcomes between organizations. Thus they accept that institutions can make a difference. Yet rational choice institutionalists still focus essentially on individual motivations and behaviour, bounded to a degree by institutional influences and constraints.

So the study of institutions is very much back in fashion. Compared with the old institutionalism, the new institutionalism is concerned not just with public administration but with all societal institutions that are important in the political process, including parties, pressure groups and social movements. The new institutionalism is also more theoretical, placing specific institutions within a broader analysis of power in state and society, derived in part from variants of Marxism. Unlike the old public administration, which was sometimes perceived as an isolated and self-contained sub-discipline, the new institutionalism is more engaged with issues that are central to the study of politics.

Political philosophy

Nearly all the writings on politics, from the ancient Greeks to the nineteenth century, that are still read today come under the general heading of political theory or political philosophy. Yet by the middle of the twentieth century political philosophy seemed at best marginalized, at worst no longer a legitimate field of enquiry. The rise of logical positivism to dominance in twentieth-century philosophy meant that normative statements, statements of value rather than statements of fact, were no longer regarded as knowledge but merely as expressions of feeling. Within the discipline of politics the behavioural revolution had shifted the focus of enquiry to the study of political behaviour, politics as it was practised, rather than as it should be practised. The age-old questions about the ideal state, justice, freedom, political obligation and rights were apparently consigned to the dustbin In 1956 Peter Laslett famously pronounced that political

> By the middle of the twentieth century political philosophy seemed at best marginalized, at worst no longer a legitimate field of enquiry.

philosophy was dead. To others it appeared at best moribund, for it was widely reckoned that the 1950s and 1960s were relatively barren in original work in moral and political philosophy, although new commentaries on classic texts continued to appear.

Rawls and the revival of political philosophy

It is argued by Brian **Barry** (1936–) (e.g. in Goodin and Klingemann, 1996) and others that it was the publication of John Rawls' *A Theory of Justice* in 1971 (see pages 97, 201) that successfully revived political philosophy, although not everyone agrees. Bhikhu Parekh (in Goodin and Klingemann, 1996) strenuously maintains that the previous decades were far less barren than suggested, pointing to the work of **Oakeshott**, **Arendt**, **Popper**, **Berlin** and many others published in this period. He has a point, although Parekh's argument should perhaps be understood in the light of his own criticism of Rawls, and admiration for Oakeshott. However, it should also be acknowledged that both the 'death' and the subsequent 'revival' of political philosophy was substantially an Anglo-Saxon phenomenon. On the European continent there was a ferment of ideas throughout the post-war period. Despite increased disillusion with orthodox soviet **Marxism-Leninism**, varieties of western Marxism flourished, including **Sartre's** existential Marxism, the structural Marxism of **Althusser** and **Poulantzas**, and the critical theory of the Frankfurt school, with influential work from **Adorno**, **Marcuse**, and subsequently **Habermas**. Other ideas, later to be grouped under the heading 'postmodernism', were already beginning to make an impact (from theorists such as **Foucault**).

> *Whatever the ultimate judgement of Rawls' work, it is difficult to deny the impact that it had on the study of political philosophy.*

However, whatever the ultimate judgement of Rawls' work, it is difficult to deny the impact that it had on the study of political philosophy, particularly in the USA and Britain. To admirers, *A Theory of Justice* was an original work in the great tradition of moral and political philosophy, which could stand alongside the classic texts of the past. Indeed, Rawls consciously connected with these works. His 'original position' and 'veil of ignorance' was a subtle reworking of the 'state of nature' and ensuing 'social contract' employed by **Hobbes** and **Locke**. His book also had considerable influence on thoughtful politicians on the centre left, for Rawls apparently provided strong theoretical support for the kind of social redistribution favoured by progressive liberals and social democrats.

Communitarians, neoliberals and others

At the same time Rawls' work demanded a response from those opposed to his assumptions or his conclusions. One set of critics rejected his individualist assumptions. Those thinkers described as **communitarians** (e.g. **MacIntyre**, **Taylor**, **Sandel** and **Walzer**) objected that Rawls conceived of individuals as isolated self-interested rational calculators, cut off from the social communities to which they belonged and which shaped their values and behaviour. The communitarians instead emphasized the reciprocal ties and mutual sympathies and obligations between human beings and the communities to which they belonged.

There were plenty of others who shared Rawls' individualist assumptions but opposed his conclusions, including free market neoliberals and rational choice theorists (see pages 90–1), although as these were primarily economists rather than philosophers they took less notice of his work. Thus **Hayek** had already supplied his own arguments against distributive justice in *The Road to Serfdom* (1944), well before the publication of *A Theory of Justice*. The main attack from a philosopher came from the extreme libertarian anarchist, Robert **Nozick**, who worked in the same philosophy department at Harvard University as Rawls. In *Anarchy, State and Utopia* (1974), Nozick advanced a labour theory of inviolable individual property rights derived from that of John **Locke**, which effectively ruled out any redistribution of income and wealth, and any notion of distributive justice of the kind favoured by Rawls. While Rawls provided a justification for state intervention of the kind favoured by social democrats, Nozick's radical individualism ruled out such a role for the state.

New perspectives in political philosophy

In the last quarter of the twentieth century Anglo-American political philosophy began to come to terms with some of the very different ideas emanating from the European

approaches

continent and particularly France. Post-structuralism and **postmodernism** (see next section) emerged substantially among disillusioned former Marxists. As works of leading thinkers associated with postmodernism were translated into English, they had an increasing influence on American academics, feeding into particularly **feminist** theory and theories of **international relations** (see pages 101–3, 103–7). Arguments over military action in various circumstances revived old debates over the notion of a just war, and the moral case for humanitarian intervention. Thus moral and political philosophy appeared more relevant than ever as the twentieth century drew to an end and the twenty-first began.

There has also been a notable revival of the long controversy surrounding human rights, for example by the British legal theorist H. L. A. Hart and the American legal and political theorist Ronald **Dworkin** (1931–). Later, clashes between cultures, and the growing importance of 'identity politics', reopened the issue of universal human **rights**, which had been apparently settled by the widespread consensus over such documents as the United Nations Universal Declaration of Human Rights (1948) and the European Convention on Human Rights. Will **Kymlicka** (1933–) has championed the group rights of minority communities, particularly indigenous peoples. Bikhu Parekh (among others) has argued that there is a 'distinctly liberal bias' in the UN Declaration, which includes rights that 'cannot claim universal validity'. Parekh (2000) maintains that these apparently 'universal values' might 'come into conflict with the freely-accepted central values of a cultural community,' such as, for example, the Asian values of 'social harmony, respect for authority, orderly society, a united and extended family and a sense of filial piety'. The liberal philosopher Brian **Barry** has strongly contended that such an approach 'is liable to be harmful to women and children in minority communities and to those within them who deviate from prevailing norms' (2001b). Thus cultural norms might be employed to trump universal human rights including women's rights, gay rights and even rights to freedom of speech (see the discussion of multi-culturalism in Part V, page 248–52).

An even more contentious debate over rights has been opened up by the attempt of Peter **Singer** (1946–) and others to extend them from humans to animals. Some moral philosophers are vegetarians. Much of the moral case for vegetarianism revolves around the exploitation of animals and the denial of their rights. This widening of concerns beyond the immediate interests of humankind might be seen as part of a wider environmentalism. Growing concerns over resource depletion and irreversible environmental pollution have made some perhaps surprising converts. Thus Brian Barry (1977) has vigorously argued the case for 'justice between generations'. He maintains 'those alive at any time are custodians rather than owners of the planet'. They 'ought to pass it on in at least no worse shape than they found it in'. He confesses that he feels 'great intellectual discomfort in moving outside a framework in which ethical principles are related to human interests'. However he concludes 'these are the terms in which we have to start thinking'. The concerns raised by Barry now seem even more urgent. The moral case for moving away from relating ethical principles solely to human interests have been strongly urged by leading ecologists like James **Lovelock** (1919–) and contemporary moral and political philosophers such as Onora O'Neill.

Postmodernism

Despite the fact that none of the leading individuals associated with **postmodernism** were primarily political scientists or political philosophers, this intellectual movement has had a considerable impact on some aspects of the study of politics. As postmodernism was more an anti-theory than a theory, and involved scepticism towards all forms of knowledge and all kinds of science, including social science, its main implications might be seen as essentially negative towards mainstream political theory and modern political science. Indeed, the postmodernists' 'incredulity towards meta-narratives' (Lyotard) involved a pronounced scepticism towards not only major political perspectives, such as liberalism and Marxism, but also the claimed positivism and objectivity of modern behaviouralists and rational choice theorists alike. Many political scientists understandably rejected this extreme scepticism that apparently undermined the legitimacy of their own search for knowledge and truth in social and political relations.

Even so, it is possible to argue that postmodernism has had an important and generally salutary effect on the study of politics. Thus Hay has persuasively argued that postmodernism 'is perhaps best seen as a heightened sensitivity to the opinions and world views of others – a respect for others and other perspectives' (2002: 226). Postmodernism rejects any single dominant world view. It suggests that the world can be seen from many different perspectives, all of which should be equally respected, and none of which should be granted privileged status. This moral relativism that demands respect for 'the other' and those who are 'different' explains some of the appeal of postmodernist ideas to minorities of all kinds, and those who feel marginalized by mainstream orthodox ideas and assumptions. Thus postmodernism has appealed to some radical feminists, to ethnic and religious minorities, and to all those considered deviant or abnormal by prevailing social norms.

Some of the most persuasive postmodernist analysis is of the relationship between knowledge, language and power. Foucault argues that knowledge, and the language used to describe and explore knowledge, reflects power. There is, he suggests, no such thing as objective, impartial knowledge. Rather, power relations underpin language to establish what he calls 'power-knowledge regimes'. Defining and labelling is a source of power. From Foucault's perspective, more recent methods of defining, analysing and treating social deviance (including activities labelled as mad, criminal or 'unnatural') did not necessarily involve progress but reflected different (and perhaps more effective) forms of social control. The labels used to describe deviance, and social relations more generally, are not neutral, but reflect social hierarchy and power.

Defining and labelling is a source of power.

Some radical **feminists** have utilized this approach, and applied it to the way in which the language employed in mainstream history, literature and politics reflected gender power relations. This was most obviously demonstrated in the way that masculine terms were routinely treated as the norm. While such terms as 'he', 'man', 'chairman' and 'mankind' might be claimed to be useful shorthand terms in which female equivalents were tacitly understood rather than deliberately excluded, the language reflects a world in which male is the norm, female the exception, and male by implication superior and female inferior. The dominant male discourse marginalizes the role of women. Those feminists who sought to replace a gender-loaded term such a 'chairman' with a more gender-neutral term (such as 'chair' or 'chairperson') were not thus indulging in 'political correctness gone mad' (as some of their critics alleged), but making an important point of principle. Moreover, in so far as a gender-neutral term removes the implicit assumption of traditional language that the holder of the post would normally be male, the symbolic change may assist a more substantial change. As language reflects power relations, a change in language may help to transform power relations. Some feminists, such as Mary Daly, have gone further, attempting to devise a whole new feminist discourse to replace the traditional male discourse, and to accommodate different female ways of thinking in place of male reason.

The connection asserted by postmodernists of the link between language and domination has also been found useful by other marginalized perspectives. Thus Edward **Said** (1935–2003) in *Orientalism* (1978) argues that western ideas and values are presented in terminology that implies they are the norm, while the 'oriental' is described in such a way as to suggest deviance and inferiority. Here western terminology and analysis legitimizes the dominance of the rational enlightened western world over the 'inferior' and 'unenlightened' orient, perpetuating colonial attitudes and post-colonial western power. Said's work is a useful corrective to blinkered western perspectives. Postmodernism usefully challenges the casual assumption that some cultures are superior or more advanced than others.

Although the influence of postmodernism on mainstream political science has been generally relatively marginal, its impact on the study of **international relations** has been more marked latterly, with a number of writers questioning long-held assumptions, concepts and theories. Richard Ashley (1988) used Derrida's method of deconstruction to re-examine the concepts of **anarchy** and **sovereignty** in international relations. It has long been argued (see page 104) that the prevailing condition in international relations is one of anarchy, in which independent sovereign states pursuing their own interests are the only actors that really matter. This implies a fundamental contrast between two mutually exclusive conditions, anarchy (violent, unstable and illegitimate) and sovereignty (peaceful, stable, legitimate). Ashley suggests the terms are not opposites, nor necessarily mutually exclusive. Other writers have argued that the ideal of the homogenous sovereign **nation-state** associated with the modern understanding of sovereignty is part of the problem in modern international relations rather than the solution. Postmodernist ideas have assisted the growing weight attached to agencies and movements operating outside and across state boundaries in international relations.

Thus postmodernism has led to a generally beneficial re-examination of some long-held assumptions and attitudes, to more humility in claims to knowledge and truth, and to more respect for alternative views. Yet its numerous critics make a number of reasonable points. A common criticism is that much of the writing of postmodernist thinkers is difficult and almost impenetrable. It is thus alleged that leading postmodernists do not express their ideas in clear enough terms to enable others to understand them or seek to refute them. Thus they fail **Popper's** criteria of falsifiability. Sometimes postmodernists have pontificated in areas they do no know enough about, such as the physical sciences and mathematics, infuriating those working in these areas and opening themselves not only to criticism but to ridicule (see for example Box 2.5 on the Sokal affair).

Another criticism is that postmodernism is essentially negative, devoted to debunking, to deconstruction; postmodernists do not put forward constructive alternatives for others to criticize. Indeed, although most of the postmodernists began on the left politically and some continued to support progressive causes, their extreme scepticism and relativism have ultimately conservative implications. If all narratives or discourses have equal validity (or invalidity), why should we prefer one over another? It may seem laudable to respect other world-views, and other cultures, to regard them as different, rather than inferior, but taken to extremes this implies the acceptance of cultures tolerating slavery and the subordination of women. A literal interpretation of postmodernism denies us the capacity

BOX 2.5 **the Sokal affair**

Alan Sokal, a physics professor irritated by postmodernist rejection of scientific method, wrote a spoof article applying postmodernist ideas to science and mathematics, with appropriate postmodernist terminology and quotations from leading postmodernist thinkers, but also littered with glaring scientific howlers. The spoof article was accepted and published by a prestigious American postmodernist academic journal, *Social Text*, in 1996. A week later Sokal revealed the hoax and his motives in an essay for another magazine. The story received world-wide publicity and was a considerable embarrassment not only for the editors of *Social Text*, one of whom insisted the article's argument was still valid, despite its being repudiated by its author, but also for postmodernists generally. Sokal, with Jean Bricmont, went on to challenge the postmodernist 'attack on science' in the book *Intellectual Impostors* (1998).

to challenge what we see as injustice in the world and rules out the possibility of progress. Effectively it renders us political eunuchs.

Feminist approaches to the study of politics

Feminist theory is clearly important in its own right, but it will be argued here that one key strand in feminist thought, modern radical feminism, has much wider implications for politics, for its scope, its practice and its academic study. The conventional analysis of feminism distinguishes between two periods or 'waves' of feminism, the first culminating in the successful achievement of the vote and legal equality in the early part of the twentieth century, and the second, from around 1970 onwards, focusing on the continued discrimination against women. The conventional analysis also distinguishes between three main types of feminism, **liberal**, **Marxist** (or **socialist**) and radical. It will be argued here that it was only second-wave radical feminism that offered a really distinctive political theory and feminist contribution to the study of politics.

> The conventional analysis also distinguishes between three main types of feminism, liberal, Marxist and radical.

This is not to underestimate the real achievement of other feminists. The liberal feminism of Mary **Wollstonecraft** (1759–1797) and John Stuart **Mill** (1806–1873) was ultimately successful in securing formal political and legal equality for women. Yet it substantially involved applying established liberal principles to the position of women rather than developing a distinctive new theory. Although Mill wrote that it was impossible to know the real nature of women in a society where they had been conditioned to accept a subordinate role, he tacitly assumed women would be able to compete on equal terms because, in important respects, women were much the same as men. Similarly, some feminists in the second half of the twentieth century applied Marxist theory to the condition of women in imaginative ways, and with particular relevance to the role of women in the workplace and family. Yet ultimately Marxist feminism, like liberal feminism, was derivative rather than essentially new, and neither 'capitalism' nor 'class' were particularly useful concepts in explaining the continued subordination of women almost everywhere and at almost every level.

Radical feminists sought to explain the continued inequality of women despite the achievement of formal political and legal equality. In doing so, they significantly enlarged the scope of politics, and not only turned feminism itself into a major field of political study but also opened up the prospect of a distinctive feminist contribution to other parts of the discipline. It is hardly possible any longer to ignore feminism in the study of politics. For radical feminists, women's oppression was not just the result of an inadequate political and legal system, or a by-product of capitalism, but was due simply to men, and their domination in almost every known society. For radical feminists it was the sex war rather than the class war that was fundamental. The term used to dignify this simple but far-reaching assumption was 'patriarchy' (literally rule of the father).

Radical feminists did not focus principally on the high politics of government and parliament and the public sphere (although they did point to the substantial under-representation of women in formal political roles, the professions and company boardrooms). Instead they focused on ordinary everyday life, the experience of being a woman in the workplace, in the home and the bedroom. 'The personal is political' was not a trite slogan but an accurate description of the essence of the radical feminist approach, involving a massive extension of the political sphere. Personal relations between men and women, the role of women in the home and in nurturing, the physical and sexual abuse of women, and the harassment of women in the workplace, became legitimate political issues. Feminists still focused on **power**, but power throughout society, not just or even primarily power in government or the state.

A significant forerunner of radical feminism was the French writer Simone **de Beauvoir** (1908–1986), whose book *The Second Sex* (1949) 'was for a generation of women the only available feminist text' (Bryson, 1992: 149), and which anticipated at least some of the concerns of a later generation of feminists. Around 1970 a number of new feminists texts were published, including Kate **Millett's** (1934–) *Sexual Politics* (1970), Germaine **Greer's** (1939–) *The Female Eunuch* (1970), Eva Figes' *Patriarchal Attitudes* (1970), and Shulamith Firestone's *The Dialectic of Sex* (1970). What these books had in common was a concern with the biology and sexuality of women. They were less concerned with the discrimination against women in the public sphere, and more interested in the everyday relations between men and women in the home, family and bedroom. They illustrated their themes of female exploitation with examples from literature and popular culture.

Power has long been seen as central to the study of politics. A significant concern of most radical feminists was male sexual power. Andrea **Dworkin** (1946–2005) and Catharine **MacKinnon** (1946–) linked the harassment and sexual abuse of women with the pornography industry, which they regarded as inherently degrading to women, as well as legitimizing violent and invasive sexual relations. Rape was perceived by the radicals as not a highly aberrant form of male behaviour, but as Susan Brownmiller argued 'nothing more or less than a conscious process of intimidation by which all men keep all women in a state of fear (*Against Our Will*, 1977: 15). Sexual dominance was at the heart of male power. Other feminists took up the link between language and power explored by **Foucault** and post-modernist thinkers. Thus Dale Spender (*Man Made Language*, 1985) has argued that language was fashioned by men and reflects male dominance, not least in the regular use of male terms such as 'he', 'his', 'man' and 'chairman'. Although these are conventionally interpreted to include the female equivalent, the use of such terms reinforces the notion that 'male' is the norm.

Much of this suggests that the radicals did not think that women were much the same as men. Perhaps the way in which some radical feminist approaches have departed most from previous variants of feminism is in their insistence that women are different from men, mentally and psychologically, and not just biologically. Many radical feminists have been prepared to assert women's difference (and superiority in some respects). From this perspective, competition and violent aggression are features of male nature rather than human nature. There is now some support for the proponents of female difference from other social sciences and the physical sciences. Thus the role of genes (including male and female genes) in influencing behaviour is increasingly recognized, as well as the importance of testosterone levels in explaining some masculine behaviour.

If male and female natures are significantly different (allowing of course for considerable differences within both sexes and overlap between them), then the implications are considerable. It clearly has implications for relations between the sexes, including physical relations. It may have implications for skills and roles in society that are not always comfortable for feminists. Perhaps women are, after all better at nurturing. It is another dimension to the 'same–difference' debate among modern feminists.

There are also implications for the wider study of politics. There has been a natural tendency for many women political scientists to focus on feminism as a rapidly expanding area of study, with obvious relevance to their own lives and beliefs. It is one field of the discipline where women very substantially dominate (although here arguably there is a case for rather more dialogue with men). Yet some women political scientists, while commonly retaining an interest in and involvement with feminism, have chosen to work largely within other, still largely male-dominated, fields, such as voting and political participation, public administration and policy, moral philosophy, state theory and **international relations**. In some surveys of these fields of study within the discipline of politics, there is an acknowledgement of the 'feminist contribution' (sometimes in separate chapters or sections).

> *If women do really hold different values and think differently, as many radical feminists maintain, they may bring distinctive and fresh insights to particular subjects.*

In certain respects the notion of a specific feminist contribution to a range of fields of study or sub-disciplines appears artificial. We might anticipate that as more women work alongside men in these fields there will be no need to distinguish between contributions by gender. Indeed there may be as much diversity among female political scientists as among their male counterparts. Yet if women do really hold different values and think differently, as many radical feminists maintain, they may bring distinctive and fresh insights to particular subjects. It may be noted, for example, that relatively few of the increasing number of women political scientists working on international relations belong to the **realist** school that has dominated the discipline until recently. It is certainly possible that the involvement of more women political scientists (who may or may not describe themselves as feminists) in many more areas within the discipline will have a distinctive impact on the direction of research, scholarship and theory.

International relations

Most of the various approaches to the study of politics discussed under previous sub-headings have focused on politics within the state. Even comparative politics has substantially involved comparing the internal political structures and processes of independent sovereign states across the world, rather than the politics of relations between states. Inter-state politics, or **international relations**, has long been considered quite different from intra-state politics, so much so that it has almost come to be regarded as a separate discipline. More recently, however, the connections between domestic and international politics have been reaffirmed.

Development of the study of international relations – the liberal approach

The academic study of international relations took off only with the First World War and its aftermath, although a number of earlier political thinkers, notably perhaps Hugo **Grotius** (1583–1645), Baruch **Spinoza** (1632–1697) and Immanuel **Kant** (1724–1804), contributed significantly to the stock of ideas. Before the First World War the conduct of international relations revolved around concepts such as national **sovereignty**, national interest and the balance of power. The whole system of relations between independent sovereign states appeared to be essentially one of **anarchy**, with no legitimate and effective international authority to arbitrate over disputes between states to prevent recourse to war. The unprecedented slaughter of the First World War was a catalyst for stimulating new ways of thinking of international relations, and applying liberal principles to the management of international affairs, commonly described as 'liberal internationalism'.

The Fourteen Points announced by the US President, Woodrow Wilson, in January 1918 provided a programme for a liberal approach to international relations. Wilson had taken the USA into war, but saw it as 'a war to end war'. Wilson's programme included national self-determination, on the assumption that a world of democratic nation states would be the best guarantee of future peace. The demand for 'open covenants openly arrived at' reflected the view that secret diplomacy had effectively committed states to war in support of allies, bypassing any attempts at effective democratic control by representative assemblies. Most important of all was to be a new international body, the League of Nations, to provide 'collective security' for all states. It was hoped this would remove the need for individual states to provide for their own security and protection through such traditional means as defence spending, promoting military alliances and maintaining a balance of power. Thus there would be a wholly new system of international relations in which international order would replace anarchy and international law would banish war.

The realist theory of international relations

If the liberal or idealist approach to international relations was articulated in response to the horrors of the First World War, the alternative realist perspective was the direct consequence of the apparent failure of liberal international relations with the breakdown of peace and collective security in the 1930s. It was this that provoked the British historian E. H. **Carr** (1892–1982) (ironically then the Woodrow Wilson Professor of International Relations) to write *The Twenty Years Crisis* (1939), reviewing the developments that had brought nations to the brink of another world war. Against what he regarded as the 'utopianism of current political thought' he quoted with approval the realist philosophy of **Machiavelli**. Carr argued that there was no natural harmony of interest between nations. Statesmen pursued national interests, using the power at their disposal, although they sometimes cloaked their real aims in a more universal moral language.

The key figure in the development of a realist theory of international relations after the Second World War was Hans J. **Morgenthau** (1904–1980), a German Jewish émigré who escaped from Hitler's Germany to settle in the USA. His key work was *Politics Among*

Nations: The struggle for power and peace (1948). He argued that international relations essentially involves 'states, pursuing interests defined in term of power' (Brown, 2005: 30). States were not the only actors in the international sphere (Morgenthau conceded that other bodies such as international governmental and non-governmental organizations could have an influence), but international sovereign states remained by far the most important. Thus the realist perspective is 'state-centred'. States act in accordance with their interests, rather than altruistically. In pursuit of their interests they have to rely substantially on their own resources, or self-help. This realist perspective was articulated against the backdrop of the cold war between the two 'super-powers', the USA and the USSR, and their respective allies. Peace and security could not be preserved by promises and agreement, but only by the realistic threat of force, backed up by strong military capability and alliances. Aggression would effectively be prevented by the threat of massive retaliation from the escalating stockpiles of nuclear weapons, involving 'mutually assured destruction'.

Both Carr and Morgenthau considered their realist analysis of international relations more scientific than the liberal, idealist or 'utopian' alternative. However, both the behavioural revolution in American political science (see pages 84–7) and the subsequent influence of the rational choice school on the discipline of politics (see pages 90–3) has led to the introduction of a rather more rigorous scientific methodology in the study of international relations. Some approaches showed greater awareness of the importance of non-state actors and the importance of interdependence between states, for example as in the volume edited by Robert **Keohane** (1941–) and Joseph Nye, *Transnational Relations and World Politics* (1971). Yet the realist perspective remained dominant. When there was a shift in emphasis it took the form of a modified realism, or 'neorealism', as it has been termed.

Neorealism

The key text associated with neorealism is Kenneth Waltz's *Theory of International Relations* (1979). **Waltz** (1924–) argues that there are only two kinds of international system possible, a hierarchical system or an anarchical system, and anarchy still prevails in international relations, despite the increased role of international institutions of various kinds as well as non-governmental organizations and transnational corporations. Thus his approach remains state-centred. While he does not assume that states are necessarily aggressive in the pursuit of national interests, they are concerned to preserve their security, viewing other states as potential threats, and adjusting their policies to the changing international situation. The key to their peace and security is the maintenance of a stable balance of power (a concept familiar to international diplomacy before 1914). Waltz saw the bipolar balance of power between the USA and the USSR and their respective allies as a fairly stable system, arguing that bipolar systems are more easily managed. He drew on neoclassical economics and **rational choice theory** to explain the behaviour of the main protagonists in the international system, comparing it to the role of leading firms in oligopolistic markets, and regulating competition. Brown (2005: 44) suggests that it is 'this economic analogy that might be said to justify the 'neo' in 'neorealism' … offering a "rational choice" version of the balance of power'.

> Waltz argues that there are only two kinds of international system possible, a hierarchical system or an anarchical system.

The impact of the end of the cold war and globalization on international relations

The end of the cold war had major implications for both the practice and theory of international relations. The world had changed. The bipolar balance of power described by Waltz no longer existed. Instead there was just one surviving super-power, the USA. Some optimists hoped that the end of the cold war would lead to a 'new world order' and 'a peace dividend' as spending on armaments was diverted to other uses. Instead, new threats arose from nationalist and ethnic conflicts, leading to civil wars, wars of liberation and in some cases ethnic cleansing and genocide, while religious fundamentalism fuelled the growth of terrorism, culminating a series of atrocities around the world. The 'war on terror' became the new dominant narrative of western diplomacy. These massive changes in the real world inevitably had considerable implications for the study of international relations. While the abrupt end of the cold war could be viewed as a victory for tough diplomacy and western defence policies that reflected a realist perspective, it had not been expected or predicted, and this was the cause of some anguished reassessment within the profession. The altered reality of the post-cold war world assisted a new diversity of approaches in the study of international relations.

> The bipolar balance of power no longer existed. Instead there was just one surviving super-power, the USA.

Thus the hitherto dominant realist or neorealist view of international relations was increasingly challenged from a variety of perspectives, loosely grouped under the heading 'neoliberal', although that rather exaggerates both the connection with older liberal idealism, and the difference from neorealism. Some neoliberals draw on rational choice theory, like Waltz, but give greater emphasis to the scope for cooperative behaviour between states.

Constructivists, hostile to rational choice theory, emphasize rather the importance of social factors in international relations, the acceptance of norms and rules of the game that influence the actors' behaviour. Particularly they have suggested that identity is important in international relations as in other spheres of politics, with feelings of shared identities often having considerable significance for the conduct of foreign policy (Wendt, 1987). Alexander **Wendt** (1958–) went on to outline his own *Social Theory of International Politics* (1999).

There is also more acknowledgement of the two-way relationship between domestic politics and the politics of international relations. Thus it is more widely accepted that there is not a single view of the national interest in international relations, and the balance between contending views can change to affect foreign policy (which can in turn have a major impact on domestic politics, as Vietnam, and later Iraq, demonstrate). The so-called English school has conceptualized a 'society of states' or 'international society' in which states accept norms of behaviour (**Bull**, 2002).

Globalization and neoliberalism

Yet these perspectives remain essentially state-centred. Other theorists argue that the nation-state is obsolete in a world of global capital, global communications and increasingly influential international organizations and transnational corporations, suggesting the need for rethinking the international system. Among radical thinkers, more closely aligned with strands of pre-war liberal idealism are the theorists of cosmopolitan democracy (Held, 1995; Linklater 1998). Although existing international institutions remain effectively dominated by the great powers, radicals suggest the possibility of a new international order accountable to the world community rather than states. Less optimistic perspectives of the post-cold war world point to threats from rogue states, failed states and terrorist organizations transcending state boundaries.

Radically different assumptions over the conduct of international relations can sometimes lead to similar conclusions on specific issues. **Realist** neoconservatives emphasize the need for effective force, pre-emptive strikes and regime change to preserve national security, while some **liberals** press the case for 'humanitarian intervention' to prevent genocide. However, both are prepared these very different-sounding arguments to justify interference on occasion with the internal affairs of independent sovereign states, in contravention of established principles of international diplomacy from the Treaty of Westphalia (1648) onwards. There are no easy answers. Recent history underlines the perils of both non-intervention (Rwanda, Bosnia, Dafur) and intervention (Afghanistan, Iraq), and the difficulty in determining nationally and internationally agreed criteria for action.

Yet all these developments only serve to emphasize the importance of the study of international relations. Its theory has evolved in response to some dramatic shifts in international politics over the last century or so. It began, and still largely remains, an American discipline, influenced by developments in American political science and the social sciences generally, although it has increasingly attracted the interest of scholars around the world. While it has been widely regarded as a separate field of study, related to, but distinct from, the associated discipline of politics, more recently there has been a growing mutual influence between international relations and its 'parent' discipline. Mainstream political scientists and international relations specialists have drawn inspiration from each others' work, and a growing number have crossed discipline boundaries to bring new insights into both.

> *Other theorists argue that the nation-state is obsolete in a world of global capital, global communications and increasingly influential international organizations and trans-national corporations.*

Conclusion: the state of the discipline today

A range of theories, models and approaches to the study of politics over the last 50 to 100 years has now been reviewed. Where does this leave the study of politics today? Contemporary political science has been shaped to a substantial degree by two 'revolutions' in the discipline, the behavioural revolution, most influential from the 1940s to the 1960s, and rational choice theory, particularly important from the 1970s onwards. While both involved a scientific approach, behaviouralism assumed an essential inductive methodology, and rational choice depended on the deductive logic of economics. Both have had wide-ranging implications for the whole discipline: for its focus, theoretical assumptions and research. Yet neither has become totally and exclusively accepted as the right way to study politics. Both have attracted critics that have questioned their assumptions and methodology. Nor has either approach ever altogether succeeded in displacing other ways of studying politics, such as political philosophy, which now enjoys a new lease of life. Some other older and apparently discredited approaches have experienced a revival, sometimes in a novel guise, such as the new institutionalism.

> *Contemporary political science has been shaped to a substantial degree by two 'revolutions' in the discipline, the behavioural revolution and rational choice theory.*

If we turn to some more specific problems and specialist areas, there is often some disappointment expressed, reflecting a sense of promise unfulfilled. Thus we are perhaps no nearer today than we were in the mid-twentieth century to answering the question whether political power is highly concentrated in modern western systems, as elitists argued, or relatively dispersed as pluralists claimed. While far more is known about voting now than when its detailed analysis began, there is still no clear consensus on why people vote as they do. The study of comparative politics has not succeeded in producing a satisfactory global conceptual framework for analysis; instead there has been what might appear a retreat to specific problems and to more limited areas studies. In the study of international relations, a broad consensus around the dominant realist or neorealist perspective has dissolved into a bewildering range of conflicting theories and models. Old problems seem little nearer a solution, while a host of new problems present themselves.

Yet this diversity in approaches to the study of politics should be welcomed rather than regretted. If there was a single theory that explained people's political behaviour everywhere in all circumstances, it would make politics a very boring subject. Controversy is integral both to the practice of politics and to its study. Those in search of definitive answers had better choose something else. The fascination in the study of politics is in grappling anew with issues and problems that have baffled the greatest minds for hundreds and sometimes thousands of years. Politics is about people in all their infinite variety. Its study is complex and messy because people are complex and messy.

concepts

introduction to part III:
key political terms and concepts

This part of the book explores some of the key terms and concepts that students of politics may encounter in their reading and research. Terms are defined, and, where appropriate, their application and significance are discussed. Politics students should appreciate that some terms that are used in everyday speech have a more specialized meanings when used by political philosophers or political scientists. While the definition of some terms is reasonably straightforward, and relatively widely agreed, you will find others have acquired distinctive meanings in different contexts. There are some important terms and concepts that are extremely controversial. They are essentially contested concepts. In other words, there are competing interpretations, sometimes reflecting very different political perspectives. Some of these terms and concepts are examined in rather more depth. Some concepts have become so central to the modern study of politics that they are necessarily explored further at some length in other parts of this book There are appropriate cross-references, as required.

finding your way around Part III

While entries are of course arranged in alphabetical order, you may not always find a term or concept that you are looking for under the appropriate letter. Thus some contrasting terms that are linked in academic discussion (such as 'structure and agency' or 'nationalization and privatization') are discussed together, with appropriate cross-references. Other closely associated terms (such as 'nation, nation-state and nationalism' or 'environmentalism, ecologism and green thinking') are also discussed in a single entry, with cross-references. Wherever in the course of discussion of a particular term other terms or concepts are mentioned that have a separate entry in this part of the book, these are printed in **bold**. Wherever political thinkers and political scientists who are mentioned in this part of book, Part III, have entries in Part IV, 'Key thinkers', these names are printed in **bold brown type** (for full details of cross referencing see p. xiv). Where terms and concepts are discussed further in other parts of the book, cross-references are given (in brackets). I have also sometimes indicated some key texts, with Harvard referencing. The full details of these can be found in the bibliography at the end of Part VII.

Absolutism

The doctrine (associated with **Bodin** and **Hobbes**) that the power of the sovereign in a state should be absolute or unlimited. While the term absolutism can be applied to any system of government where the power of the sovereign body is theoretically unlimited, it is most commonly used to describe the 'absolute monarchies' of continental Europe in the early modern period (particularly the eighteenth century). The saying attributed to King Louis XIV of France, *'L'état, c'est moi'* ('the state – that's me') encapsulates the notion of an absolute ruler, responsible and accountable to no one. (Yet no ruler in practice has absolute power, as they are constrained by circumstances outside their control.) Some eighteenth-century thinkers (such as **Voltaire**) were inclined to defend absolutism, as a few of these absolutist monarchs were patrons of the arts and philosophy and appeared to take their responsibilities seriously (and have been described as 'benevolent' or 'enlightened' despots).

Accountability

The notion that those who have an office or position are **accountable** or answerable to others for their behaviour. Thus in a parliamentary **democracy**, state officials are accountable to ministers, ministers to a **legislature** or parliament, parliament to electors. The terms 'accountability' and 'responsibility' are often used in the same sense, although strictly speaking accountability flows upwards, and responsibility downwards. Thus officials are *accountable to* ministers who are *responsible for* their officials. Accountability may involve a formal requirement to render an oral or written account, for example to answer questions and/or submit written reports to a parliament or legislative assembly. Thus those responsible for a particular action (or inaction) can be called to account.

Agency

See under **Structure and agency**.

Anarchy and anarchism

Anarchy (literally 'no rule') is commonly used as a synonym for chaos and a complete breakdown of law and order, as may happen for example in the midst of **revolution** or civil war. Mainstream political theory suggests that a **state** of some kind is necessary to prevent anarchy. **Anarchism** is a political ideology that suggests that states are neither necessary nor desirable. Although the term 'anarchist' is pejoratively linked with destructive bomb-throwing nihilists, anarchist thinkers (e.g. **Godwin**, **Proudhon**, **Bakunin**, **Kropotkin**) argue that states are inevitably oppressive and limit freedom. Humans are not naturally aggressive and competitive, but social and cooperative, and would realize their true nature in voluntary association in stateless societies. This anarchist vision is attractive, although critics suggest it is unrealistic. Nevertheless, anarchism has had a strong following in some countries (such as Spain, Italy and Russia for a time), with anarchist political parties attracting significant support. Many anarchists are also pacifists, but in the Spanish Civil War (1936–9), most anarchists concluded that defeating Franco was the immediate problem, and not only fought on the side of the Republic but even participated in the government. (There was for a time an anarchist Minister of Justice.)

Anarchism is usually located on the far **left** of the political spectrum, and indeed anarchism is associated with a strand of **socialism**. There was an element of anarchist thinking in **Marx**, who quarrelled with the anarchism of **Bakunin** in the International Working Men's Association, but who also famously suggested the state would ultimately 'wither away' following a successful communist revolution. Yet while many anarchists have been against the private ownership of property, the label 'anarcho-capitalism' has been given to some neoliberals who seek to limit the role of the state to a minimum, particularly in the economic sphere.

Aristocracy

Aristocracy (a term derived from Greek) means literally 'rule of the best', although over time it has come to mean an elite group or **class** whose status depends on hereditary descent, normally combined with possession of extensive landed **property**. (In practice, however, successful merchants or manufacturers were often able to buy their way into this ancient landed aristocracy.) Once this hereditary aristocracy constituted the effective ruling class in many states (such as eighteenth-century Britain or Germany). However, today an aristocrat is, in common parlance, a person with an aristocratic title, such as duke or baron. Some such titles are ancient and inherited, while others are recently bestowed, sometimes in honour of

concepts

distinguished achievements, sometimes in recognition of the person's wealth or influence, sometimes, allegedly, in return for money or political favours. Although aristocratic status remains a source of influence and even power in some modern states claiming to be democratic (such as Britain), the aristocracy in general are no longer *the* ruling class. Some thinkers in the past defended the principle of aristocracy (e.g. **Burke**, Coleridge), but only eccentric mavericks do so still.

Authority

Authority is a power that is (willingly or reluctantly) acknowledged and accepted by those over whom it is exercised. Thus authority might be regarded as lawful or legitimate **power**.

Max **Weber**, the German sociologist, distinguished between three main types or sources of authority: traditional, charismatic and legal-rational. Traditional authority rests on long-established usage or custom – such as the authority of a tribal chief or hereditary monarch. Charismatic authority derives from the compelling personal qualities or behaviour of an individual – for example the authority exercised by Napoleon or Hitler, or more positively, Mahatma **Gandhi**, Martin Luther **King** or Nelson Mandela. Legal-rational authority is authority based on formal rules. Thus the authority of elected politicians or appointed government officials may be accepted and obeyed, not because of custom or personal qualities but because it is acknowledged that they legitimately hold their office under accepted rules and procedures. It is essentially the office or post rather than person who occupies the post that is obeyed. Weber considered that legal-rational authority is the characteristic form of authority in the modern world. Both modern bureaucracy and representative democracy involve legal-rational authority. Note that Weber's three types of authority are not necessarily mutually exclusive. Thus an elected politician (legal-rational authority) may have some charismatic authority, and if he or she occupies an ancient post, an element of traditional authority also. Note also that while charismatic authority may be willingly acknowledged and accepted, it may have little or nothing to do with formal **legitimacy**.

Behaviouralism

Behaviouralism is an approach to the study of politics and other social sciences that focuses on

the observable individual and social behaviour of humans. Behaviouralism was influenced by the methodology of the natural sciences, and by positivism in philosophy. Both implied the rejection of normative approaches, and the adoption of a more rigorous scientific methodology, involving the collection and analysis of (largely) quantitative data. The behavioural revolution in the social sciences that developed in the USA from the 1940s onwards marginalized or rejected older approaches to the study of politics that focused on the study of political ideas or political institutions. While early behaviouralists assumed the need for a purely inductive approach, modern neo-behaviouralists acknowledge that some preliminary hunch or hypothesis to be tested normally guides the collection of data. (For more on behaviouralism, see Part II, Section 2.)

Bourgeoisie

The **bourgeoisie** was once simply a name for town dwellers in France. Later it came to be applied to well-to-do merchants, a rising 'middle **class**', whose wealth was coveted but whose social pretensions were mocked by landed **aristocrats** and squires. **Marx** used the term bourgeoisie to refer specifically to the owners of **capital** in an industrial society. He also used the term 'petty bourgeoisie' (in French '*petit bourgeoisie*') to describe the 'middle class' of small employers, shopkeepers, professionals and others between the **capitalists** and the workers, although he did not use the term very precisely or consistently. Today the term 'bourgeoisie' is still employed by **Marxists** to mean the capitalist class, but is more commonly used to describe an (undifferentiated) middle class. The adjective 'bourgeois' is often used in a disparaging way to describe conventional middle-class values, tastes and attitudes.

Bureaucracy

Bureaucracy was a term coined (originally in France) to mean **government** by permanent officials, and from the start had pejorative (or hostile and critical) connotations. It is still commonly used in the same sense today. Thus to describe someone as a bureaucrat is to disparage them. Bureaucratic behaviour is a byword for officious, inflexible and insensitive treatment of people by the letter of rules and regulations. It is commonly associated particularly with the **state**, and with public officials.

The German sociologist Max **Weber** employed the term bureaucracy in a more neutral or even positive way. For him, bureaucracy was an efficient and effective means of running any modern large organization in either the public or private sector. It involved recruitment and promotion of officials by merit and qualifications rather than by patronage, a clear chain of responsibility and **accountability** in hierarchical organizations, and decisions made impartially in accordance with written rules rather than through personal favours or bribery. Bureaucracy was thus both more efficient and fairer than traditional forms of organization. Weber was well aware that bureaucracy (rule by permanent officials) might be more of a reality than representative **democracy** (rule by the people's elected representatives) in the modern state, but bureaucracy and democracy both involved what he characterized as legal-rational authority, and were compatible.

Many critics since have suggested that behind the façade of democracy in modern states lies the reality of bureaucracy, and that powerful permanent state officials have more influence on key decisions than the elected ministers whom they serve. Some political scientists have researched the recruitment, personal connections and attitudes of leading state officials, in attempts to assess their real influence on the political process.

Economists of the **rational choice** school took a different line. They applied the assumption of the pursuit of rational self-interest to the behaviour of state bureaucrats, suggesting that public officials would pursue their own interest rather than the public interest. Thus William **Niskanen** and others argued that state bureaucrats had a vested interest in the expansion of their own departments, leading to increased public spending (and taxation). This interest they shared with those dependent on state services, thus leading to bureaucratic and electoral pressure for the endless growth of public expenditure. This analysis was a key element in **New Right** thinking in the USA and Europe, leading to measures to cut back the state, increase competition and pursue **privatization**. Cuts in the size of the public sector bureaucracy in many countries and the privatization of public services might suggest that state bureaucrats are less powerful and less capable of defending their own interests than is sometimes imagined.

Capitalism

Capitalism is a term used to describe a largely **free market** economy where the means of production are privately owned and controlled by the relative few, who employ the bulk of the working population as wage labourers to produce and purchase the goods and services required for their own subsistence. Capitalism accompanied by industrialization rapidly superseded the feudal and agrarian economies of first western Europe and subsequently much of the rest of the world. Capitalism was extensively analysed by **Marx and Engels**, and subsequently their followers. While Marx was aware of the unprecedented productive capacity of the capitalist system, he argued it would ultimately be destroyed by its own internal contradictions, as competition would force the capitalists to intensify the exploitation of the industrial workers until they were driven to **revolution**. Marx assumed that political **power** reflected economic power. Thus a society and economy where wealth and income were concentrated in the hand of the few could never become a genuine **democracy**. He did not however sketch out in any detail the **socialist** or **communist** society and economy that would replace capitalism.

In practice, capitalism has been more adaptable and resilient than Marx predicted. While it is certainly arguable that inequality widened under capitalism, the appeal of revolution declined as the living standards of European industrial workers rose rather than fell (**Lenin** among others argued this was a consequence of imperialism and the increased exploitation of colonies). Capitalism also survived the emergence of a rival socialist command economy, first in Russia and later in eastern Europe, China and elsewhere, and the ensuing 'cold war' between the two systems. Although state **collectivism** may have promoted industrialization, it could not ultimately compete effectively with free market capitalism in delivering the goods and services demanded by consumers. The cold war ended with the collapse of communism in the former Soviet Union and eastern Europe, and its transformation through market reforms elsewhere.

Capitalism is now seen as a **global** phenomenon, transcending political borders. Global capitalism still provokes much hostility, particularly for its impact on the environment and for its contribution to widening the gulf between rich and poor nations. Yet despite noisy demonstrations against capitalism there no longer appears a viable alternative. Attention has focused more on rival versions of capitalism, most notably American (or Anglo-American) free market capitalism, and the social market capitalism, sometimes referred to as Rhineland or German capitalism, involving more partnership between business and trade unions, more state regulation of labour markets and more generous welfare services. A third model is East Asian capitalism, of which Japan has long been the standard bearer. This involves an emphasis on cooperation as well as competition, active state guidance, and a more paternalist relationship between business firms and their employees. However, the recent economic difficulties of both post-unification Germany and Japan have perhaps dimmed the appeal of these alternatives. Yet critics of American capitalism can still point to successful economies, particularly in Scandinavia, that continue to prosper despite generous welfare provision and relatively high tax rates.

Christian democracy

Christian democracy has been an important and sometimes dominant ideology in the party systems in Western Europe (such as Germany, Italy, France, Belgium, the Netherlands and Austria) in the post Second World War period. It has also had some impact in South America. Formerly the Roman Catholic church in particular had appeared hostile to **democracy** and reform. After 1945 reformed Catholic and cross-denominational parties became fully engaged in **electoral** competition, economic management and welfare reform, adopting a moderate state interventionist approach, involving what has been called liberal or democratic **corporatism**. A similar centre or centre-right approach has been evident in the European Peoples' Party in the European Parliament.

Citizen and citizenship

A **citizen** is a member of a **state**, who by virtue of **citizenship** has both rights and obligations. The term 'citizen' implies active involvement in the state, as compared with the term 'subject' that suggests passive obedience to a sovereign. As such, the term has become closely bound up with the **republican** tradition, and was used by the American and French Republics following their revolutions towards the end of the eighteenth

century. In contemporary politics, citizenship had become a key concept across the ideological spectrum, although the term is used in different senses, implying very different underlying assumptions and implications. Those who advocate participative **democracy** stress the political rights and duties of the citizen. **Neoliberals** emphasize the freedom of individual citizens to make their own choices without interference from the state and other citizens. **Social democrats** by contrast emphasize the economic and social rights of the citizen in a modern welfare state. Communitarian thinkers (e.g. **MacIntyre**, **Sandel**, **Taylor**, **Walzer**) stress the obligations of citizens to the community.

Civil disobedience

Civil disobedience involves deliberate and open disobedience of the **state**, and is generally justified on moral grounds by those who use this political strategy. The term was first used by the American Henry David **Thoreau** in the mid-nineteenth century to justify disobedience to a government that upheld the institution of slavery. Peaceful civil disobedience was later extensively used by **Gandhi** in his ultimately successful campaign to promote the independence of India from British colonial rule, and by Martin Luther **King** as leader of the civil **rights** movement to end discrimination against American Blacks. Non-violent campaigns are less likely to be successful against a powerful and ruthless government. Peaceful civil disobedience was tried for years unsuccessfully against the apartheid regime in South Africa, and Nelson Mandela among others advocated the switch to armed struggle that was to lead to his long imprisonment on Robben Island.

Civil society

Particularly in liberal thought, the term **civil society** is distinguished from the **state** to describe the 'private sphere' of business, voluntary bodies, interest groups, churches, clubs and families. Thus **liberals** generally argued that the state should not interfere with the **freedom** of autonomous individuals and organizations in civil society. The liberal defence of civil society was contrasted with **totalitarianism**, involving no limits to the **authority** of the state and the effective abolition of the private, independent realm of civil society.

Yet from other perspectives the clear separation of the state and civil society can allow the perpetuation of injustice, discrimination and even violence against individuals and minorities, and irreparable damage to the **environment**. **Socialists** and trade unionists have sought state intervention to ensure health and safety at work, protect workers from unfair dismissal or bullying, and provide a legal minimum wage, thus limiting the freedom of employers to manage their businesses as they saw fit. **Green** activists have campaigned for greater controls over the freedom of individuals and businesses to pollute the environment. **Feminists**, proclaiming 'the personal is political', have sought increased state intervention to protect women from violence within the domestic sphere. Many modern liberals have campaigned vigorously for laws against discrimination on grounds of **race** or **gender**, thus preventing landlords and private clubs from exercising their freedom to exclude whoever they choose from their premises. While many oppose what they see as unwarranted interference with the freedom of the individual by the 'nanny state', extensive state intervention is advocated and defended for a whole range of reasons. Thus the notion of 'civil society' as a sacrosanct sphere, free from state interference, is contested. However, many would argue that a flourishing civil society is necessary for a healthy **democracy**. (See also **social capital**.)

Class

Economic or social **class** has been a key concept in modern political analysis, although some now argue that it is of declining significance. For Karl **Marx** politics was all about the struggle between conflicting class interests. Under **capitalism** there were only two classes that mattered, and their economic interests were diametrically opposed and irreconcilable. These classes were those who owned and controlled the means of production, the **bourgeoisie,** and those who owned only their labour and were forced to sell it on disadvantageous terms to survive, the industrial working class or proletariat. Marx acknowledged that there were other classes, including the old landowning **aristocracy**, the petty bourgeoisie of professionals, and small business owners, and the peasantry, but all these were of declining significance and in process of being absorbed into the two important classes.

Conventional analysis of class involves distinguishing between an upper, middle and lower or working class, sometimes with intermediate groups, such as 'upper middle' or 'lower middle'. The upper class may be identified with the traditional landed aristocracy and/or with those who are sufficiently wealthy not to depend on their labour for their income. The 'middle class' is a broad category covering a wide range of income and wealth that includes not only business owners (Marx's bourgeoisie) and shopkeepers, but professionals and all 'white collar' workers (or those who work with their brains rather than their hands). The working class includes all 'blue collar' or manual workers and their dependants, but may be further subdivided between skilled, semi-skilled and unskilled.

Although these categories are imprecise and unscientific they still have some significance for students of politics, not least because many people are prepared to define themselves in these terms. Such subjective assessments of an individual's class may be important for political attitudes and behaviour (including particularly party allegiance and voting).

Others such as advertisers, government statisticians and social scientists have sought a more practical classification of social divisions for their own purposes. Thus advertisers need to know not only newspaper and magazine circulation figures, and television viewing figures, but something about the social class and purchasing power of each audience. Government statisticians seek to break down the population into employment categories for a number of purposes, such as assessing the impact of government policies on particular sections of the population. Social scientists may use the categories devised by advertisers or official government statisticians, or devise their own. Whatever classification they use, they generally find significant correlations between particular social or occupational groups and political attitudes and behaviour. Thus in some countries there is marked correlation between social class and voting, while other analysis may show that a disproportionate number of elected representatives and appointed state officials come from a highly selective class background.

Yet class may be of declining political significance. This may be partly because of economic change, including the decline of mining and manufacturing and with it the old manual working class, and the rise of service industries. It also partly reflects changing attitudes to class, including a diminished class consciousness partly down to increased affluence, partly because of the growth of new divisions within and across class divisions. Thus other social divisions, including age, **gender**, nation, religion and **ethnicity**, always important in some countries, may now be of increasing political significance even in those countries where class divisions once dominated the political system. Some argue that the politics of identity have increasingly replaced the politics of class. Yet class remains important to an understanding of politics both within and between societies.

Collectivism

Collectivism emphasizes the importance of pursuing the interests of the whole of society or the whole community rather than individual self-interest. This, it is assumed, will be promoted by the active intervention of the **state** and state planning on behalf of the community. Thus collectivism rejects leaving the distribution of goods and services to **free market** forces. The growth of the state, of state services and state expenditure, is commonly seen to involve the growth of collectivism.

Collectivism is commonly associated with the **left** of the political spectrum, and **individualism** and the free market with the **right**, but the relationship of specific creeds to collectivism is more complex. **Socialists** and **communists** on the left favour collectivism, but so do fascists on the far right, while classical **liberals** and **neoliberals** deplore it. On the moderate right, European **conservatives** and **Christian democrats** have often supported state **welfare** provision and some intervention in the management of the economy, while maintaining general support for private enterprise.

Communism

Communism in the broadest sense means the common ownership of wealth, and an absence of private property. Thus **Plato** in *The Republic* advocated common ownership for the guardians of his ideal state, to ensure they pursued the interest of the community as a whole rather than their own private interests. Thomas More (1478–1535) similarly envisaged common ownership in his *Utopia*. The 'Diggers' attempted to establish a communist colony in 1649–50, following the English Civil War. Various early communists, **socialists** and **anarchists** in many countries advocated the abolition

of private ownership. However, today communism is largely associated with the theories of Karl **Marx** and his followers, and the political systems established in the Soviet Union, China and other states under the broad heading of **Marxism-Leninism**.

Communism is often distinguished from democratic socialism and **social democracy**, although the relationship between these terms is complex and contentious (see **socialism**). Marx and his nineteenth-century followers used the terms communism, socialism and social democracy almost interchangeably. **Lenin**, drawing on and developing a distinction by Marx in *The Critique of the Gotha Programme*, treated socialism as a transitional phase leading ultimately to the final institution of communism. Marxist socialists in the west commonly referred to the socialism of the Soviet Union and its satellites as admittedly imperfect but nevertheless 'really existing socialism', to be defended against the alternative liberal **capitalism** of the United States and 'the west' more generally. Other democratic socialists and social democrats in the west distinguished sharply between their own socialism and what they regarded as a perverted interpretation of socialism in communist states, involving one-party **dictatorship**, centralized **state** control of the economy, and the denial of individual freedom. Some communist parties in western Europe, notably in Italy, pursued their own distinctive version of euro-communism, which accepted parliamentary democracy and cooperation with other parties of the **left** and centre in a multi-party system.

For much of the twentieth century communism of the Marxist-Leninist form appeared a viable alternative to western liberal **capitalism**, and following the Second World War the two systems confronted each other in the cold war. The fall of the Berlin Wall in 1989, followed swiftly by the collapse of communist regimes in eastern Europe and the implosion of the Soviet Union itself, ended the cold war and the perceived communist threat to the west, where some former communist parties renamed themselves. Although communist regimes survived elsewhere in the world, in the case of China particularly there has been a marked transformation of the management of the economy, involving an acceptance of **free markets** and private ownership, although this has not been accompanied by political liberalization. There have been similar if less dramatic economic changes in Cuba and Vietnam, but not in North Korea.

Community and communitarianism

A **community** may be defined as any group of people who have something in common, perhaps who are interrelated or who feel a sense of a common identity. It is generally but not exclusively related to specific geographical localities, particularly small face-to-face local communities, although the term 'community' is also freely linked with much larger geographical areas not involving face-to-face contact, such as the 'national community', the 'European community' and even the 'international community'. Yet the word is also sometimes used in a sense that transcends a physical location, as in the 'business community', 'academic community', 'professional communities' or 'Muslim community'. Here it implies common endeavours, perhaps entailing a common outlook, common interests or common values.

It may be clear from the above examples that the term 'community' is used extensively, with little precision, and carries some strong normative associations. 'Community' is widely perceived as 'good'. It is a word freely employed by politicians across the political spectrum. It is also often used as an all-purpose warm sanitizing term to encourage the acceptance of particular institutions and policies. (British examples include 'community care' 'community hospitals' 'community policing' and even the 'Community Charge', the official name for an unpopular local government tax, that has since been abolished.)

'Community' sometimes implies more uniformity of attitudes and behaviour than exist in practice. Thus within the 'Muslim community', the 'Jewish community' or the 'Christian community' there are deep divisions of opinion and behaviour. There are similar differences within the 'business community' and the 'academic community'. Even small local communities can be deeply divided. The 'national community' commonly comprises numerous subcultures, often involving considerable mutual antipathy. Some would argue that the concept of an 'international community' is virtually meaningless, and in practice is employed to describe the views or interests of the governments of the most powerful states or international business.

At another level 'community' and community **rights** and interests are commonly contrasted with the emphasis of **liberals** on the rights and interests of the individual. **Communitarianism** is a political philosophy that emphasizes the importance of the common good, common values, common interests and the reciprocal rights and duties bound up with membership of a community, compared with the atomized individualism and pursuit of self-interest associated with classical liberalism. Leading communitarian thinkers include Alisdair **MacIntyre**, Michael **Sandel**, Michael **Walzer** and Charles **Taylor**. The ideas have been popularized by Amitae Etzioni. They have been taken up by some **social democrats**, '**third way**' thinkers and **conservatives**. They have also influenced the approach of some modern scientists, including the ideas of Robert **Putnam** and his emphasis on the importance of **social capital.**

Although communitarianism has attracted some interest and support from the **left** and centre of the political spectrum, some critics have discerned an inherent conservative or authoritarian bias in the communitarian emphasis on the individual's **obligations** and duties, at the expense of individual rights and entitlements, which in practice involve bolstering traditional social structures and moral codes.

Consensus

Consensus means agreement or compromise. While politics is often seen in terms of conflicting interests and sharp disagreement over values and goals, some see it involving more the pursuit of compromise and the establishment of a broad consensus over values and procedures and often also over specific policies. Thus political leaders may seek to build a consensus through persuasion, bargaining and compromise. Politicians and parties may also try to ascertain what is the public consensus (or what most people think) and adapt their programme accordingly. Thus they will seek to occupy the 'middle ground'.

It has often been argued that the earlier politics of sharp ideological conflict gave way to the politics of consensus in the period after the Second World War. This consensus has been variously described – as a **social democratic** consensus in Europe generally, or as the Keynes–Beveridge consensus in the United Kingdom (from the names of the economist John Maynard **Keynes** and the welfare reformer William **Beveridge**). As these descriptions imply, there appeared to be a broad consensus in favour of state **welfare** provision and government macro-economic management, with often some state ownership of

concepts

industry in what was seen as a mixed economy. However, there was always some disagreement over the extent of consensus (a societal or just an elite consensus?), and even over its reality. Subsequently it appeared that consensus politics had widely broken down, with the reappearance of sharp ideological divisions from the late 1960s and the 1970s onwards, although periodically observers have identified the emergence of a new consensus.

Inevitably there are those who do not share in the consensus or feel excluded from it. Left-wing **socialists** deplore the abandonment or watering down of socialist commitments by party leaders pursuing consensus and power. Similarly, the **New Right** rejected the main planks of the post-war consensus, and sought to destroy it. The British **Conservative** Prime Minister Margaret Thatcher, charged with abandoning consensus politics, responded that she was a conviction politician. 'For me, consensus seems to be the process of abandoning all beliefs, principles, values and policies.'

Consent

Consent, or agreement, is a key **liberal democratic** concept. Liberals from John **Locke** onwards have argued that only the consent of the governed can provide governments with **legitimacy**. Similarly, it is maintained that consent is the basis of an **obligation** to obey laws and government; citizens should obey laws to which they have consented, either in person or through their own elected representatives.

There are practical problems with the notion of government by consent. Most citizens could reasonably object that they have not personally consented to government. Locke, rather unsatisfactorily, argued that government rested on their *tacit* consent. By staying in a country when it was possible to leave, the citizen was giving tacit consent to obeying the government and laws of the country. Yet, as David **Hume** and others have objected, leaving a country is commonly not a realistic option for most people.

Liberals have tended to assume that individuals are rational calculators and the best judge of their own interests, but some would argue that people's ideas can be moulded and manipulated. Thus consent can be engineered by government or by dominant interests. **Dictators** have sometimes legitimized their rule by **plebiscites**, often held under conditions in which the expression of contrary views was not permitted, and sometimes involving blatant intimidation. Even in representative democracies public debate may be weighted in the government's favour by various means, and the appearance of popular consent may not involve a properly informed consent.

In many countries popular consent, through a **referendum** or plebiscite, is required for constitutional change, and sometimes for other changes in the law or in the system of taxation. In some countries the express consent of the **legislature** may be required for some **executive** actions and appointments. Thus in the USA the 'Advice and Consent' of the Senate is required for treaties and the appointment of ambassadors, ministers and members of the Supreme Court.

Consent may also be an important issue in **judicial** decisions and penalties. Consent does not necessarily excuse, but it may mitigate an offence. There are particularly difficult issues surrounding sexual relations. Sexual relations between consenting adults in private is no longer generally regarded as a matter for the law in modern liberal democracies. However, sexual relations with someone under age (commonly 16) is widely treated as a crime even if there is consent. Sex without consent is rape, normally punishable by a long prison sentence, *if proved*. The problem here is that those accused generally claim that express or tacit consent was given, and in the almost invariable absence of witnesses it is difficult to prove rape. Rape, and other forms of violence against women, have been a key concern of radical **feminists**.

Conservatism

As the name implies, **conservatism** as a political doctrine or ideology means conserving, keeping things as they are. Historically, conservatives have been suspicious of change, hostile to the new ideas associated with the Enlightenment (see pages 63–8), industrialization, constitutional reform and above all **revolution**. Conservative thinkers such as **Burke** and **Oakeshott** have emphasized the limitations of human reason and rational plans for change, preferring the known to the unknown, and practical experience to intellectual speculation. 'If it ain't broke, don't fix it' is a familiar expression of conservative **pragmatism**. However, in practice conservatives have often embraced limited or gradual reform as the best means of maintaining stability. While conservatives were initially hostile to representative **democracy**, they ultimately embraced it, once it appeared clear that it did not necessarily involve social revolution nor a substantial threat to existing **property**. They have nevertheless continued to emphasize the need for strong **leadership**, with limited potential for democratic participation in politics beyond voting.

Traditional conservatism has been critical of the **liberal** emphasis on the freedom of the individual and self-help and self-reliance within an environment of **free market** forces. Instead conservatism has emphasized a more organic view of human society, with humans locked in ties of mutual **obligation** and dependence. Conservatives have generally tended to a pessimistic view of **human nature**, as inherently selfish, acquisitive, aggressive or (in religious terms) sinful, requiring a strong **state**, effective leadership and authority to maintain law and order. Conservatives have also largely defended inequality and the existing property rights, particularly landed property, against the demands of **socialists** for greater **equality**, redistribution and social **justice**. Instead, conservatives have emphasized the need for the propertied classes and ultimately the state to acknowledge a proper responsibility towards the deserving poor. However in the late twentieth century a **New Right** combined elements of traditional conservatism with the free market, minimal state convictions of **neoliberals**. In the international sphere conservatives have generally vigorously defended what they perceived as national interests.

Although the appeal of overt conservatism generally declined in the twentieth century, it long continued to thrive in Britain, partly because British Conservatives embraced social reform, but partly also because **nationalism** and even **imperialism** seem to have won votes across social classes. In the USA neo-conservatives (or 'neo-cons') who asserted national interest and realism in **international relations** became particularly influential in US administrations in the late twentieth and early twenty-first centuries.

Constitution

In the study of politics a **constitution** is simply a set of basic principles, rules and processes for the government of any state. Today these are normally set out in a single authoritative document,

following the celebrated American Constitution (1787 onwards). Thus constitutions may contain some statement of fundamental principles perhaps containing a declaration of human or citizens' **rights**. It will normally involve rules governing the relationship of the various parts and levels of **government**, for example between the **executive**, **legislature** and **judiciary** and, in a **federal** government, between federal and state institutions.

Britain, almost alone among modern states, does not have such a written constitution, in the sense of a single authoritative document, although parts of the British system of government are contained in authoritative written sources, so that the British constitution is better described as 'uncodified'. Written constitutions can inspire reverence and confer **legitimacy** on a system of government, although they are not always a reliable guide to political practice. Over time, all written constitutions require supplementing with conventions or accepted usages, while some parts of a constitution may fall into disuse. Thus even parts of the US Constitution (notably the electoral college for choosing a president) are virtually defunct. In the last analysis a constitution offers little protection against individuals or groups who have acquired effective **power** and do not scruple to use it as they see fit. Thus the model constitution of the Soviet Union 1936 bore very little resemblance with the actual practice of government under Stalin, while the model constitution of the German Weimar Republic established after the First World War could not prevent the rise of the Nazi dictatorship.

Most constitutions contain provisions for amendment. Some are relatively flexible, and thus fairly easily modified, while others are much more inflexible, with all kinds of built-in safeguards designed to provide checks against hasty ill-considered change. Thus a constitutional amendment commonly requires more than a simple majority in a representative assembly, but often a two-thirds or three-quarters majority (in both houses in a bicameral system), with sometimes additional provision for popular approval in a **referendum.** (There is provision for referendums on constitutional changes in, for example, Australia, France, Japan, Spain and Switzerland.) The United Kingdom's unwritten constitution appears extremely flexible, requiring only a simple majority in Parliament, and effectively the House of Commons.

Even so, a number of constitutional reforms have been additionally legitimated by referendums (in theory only advisable, but in practice binding). Federal systems will also require the approval of all or most of the states within the federation. Thus amendments to the US Constitution require a two-thirds majority in both houses of Congress and the agreement of three-quarters of the states in their own legislative assemblies. Despite these hurdles a number of important constitutional amendments have been passed, from the first ten adopted in 1791 (and known as the Bill of Rights), down to the present day.

Constructivism

Constructivism is the notion that knowledge does not necessarily reflect some external reality but is socially 'constructed', in other words reflects the particular social and cultural context from which it comes. There is a clear affinity between constructivism and **postmodernism**. Both are relativist theories. A constructivist perspective can be and has been applied to many disciplines (for example, education, psychology, sociology and cultural studies).

Within political science constuctivism has been particularly applied to the study of **international relations**, most notably by Alexander **Wendt**. In a key article, 'Anarchy is what states make of it: the social construction of power politics' (1992), Wendt showed that some central concepts in international relations were socially constructed rather than simply reflecting some objective reality. He applied the argument more systematically in his book *Social Theory of International Politics* (1999), where he emphasized the importance of identity and norms in international relations. There are now many international relations scholars applying constructivism in various ways. Some argue that the concept has become blurred as a consequence (Brown with Ainley, 2005: 48–50).

Corporatism

Corporatism involves incorporating major organized socio-economic interests into the process of **government**. What is now sometimes described as liberal corporatism or societal corporatism is generally distinguished from the state corporatism associated particularly with Mussolini's fascist **state**. Mussolini introduced a Chamber of Corporations involving the functional representation of major economic interests rather than the

representation of individual voters through electoral areas (or constituencies). The dictators Salazar (in Portugal) and Franco (in Spain) pursued a variant of this fascist corporatism.

A liberal form of corporatism has been pursued in some democracies in western Europe in the post-war period, particularly Austria but also to some extent in Germany and Sweden, and for a time Britain, where a modified version of corporatism was sometimes described as tripartism (decision-making by government, business and trades unions).

Corporatism stimulated the growth of a formidable academic literature in Europe (less so in the USA). For some, corporatism involved partnership, cooperation and consensus politics, all deemed beneficial. Corporatism was hailed as an improved system of decision making and by some even as a new economic system. Although, like pluralism, corporatism assumed the representation of interests, corporatism involved the interaction and collaboration of a relatively few 'umbrella' or 'peak' groups rather than the countless multitude of freely competing groups of pluralist theory. (Philippe Schmitter provided an influential distinction of corporatism from **pluralism**.)

Corporatism has been criticized by both the **left** and the **right**. **Marxists** saw it as an attempt to reconcile conflicting interests of bosses and workers that were irreconcilable in a capitalist system. Some perceived it as the response of **capitalism** to falling profits. Thus incomes policies involved restraining wage increases to the benefit of business owners at the expense of workers. The **New Right** by contrast considered that corporatism conceded too much influence to producer groups and particularly trade unions, at the expense of consumers and taxpayers. For others, corporatism involved the bypassing of parliamentary **democracy**, a top-down process involving ministers, trade union bosses and major employers, and ignoring both the shop floor and small businesses as well as consumer interests generally. In Britain corporatism was not deemed a success and was abandoned by the incoming Thatcher government of 1979, and has not been revived since, although some saw echoes of corporatism in Blair's early interest in stakeholding. Other European states have had a more fruitful experience of corporatism over a longer period, and have viewed it more favourably. Some of the processes and institutions of the European Union have sometimes been

concepts

described as corporatist (one reason for Margaret Thatcher's disenchantment with Europe).

Corruption

Corruption in general terms means physical and particularly moral decay. In politics it refers to the illicit purchase of influence or favours from politicians or state officials. Thus an offence may be overlooked in return for a bribe, a government post or contract may be secured by financial or other inducements, inside information may be misused for private gain, votes may be bought. In some political systems, corruption appears to be endemic; in others it is assumed to be rare, although some critics suggest that the occasional case in which corruption is found is only the tip of the iceberg. While it may be impossible to eliminate corruption, appropriate rules and procedures may limit its extent, although the best safeguard is a political **culture** in which all forms of corruption are regarded as unacceptable.

Culture and political culture

Culture in general terms is the attitudes, beliefs and values acquired as a consequence of living in a specific human society, as opposed to inborn human nature. Within a state there may appear to be a common national culture, although there may be distinctive regional subcultures, or other minority cultures, perhaps based on a distinctive religion, language or ethnic background. Sometimes a distinction is drawn between 'high' and 'low' culture, or 'elite' and 'mass' (or 'popular') culture, although sometimes the term 'culture' is narrowly identified with the 'high' culture of an educate elite (and perhaps rejected and disparaged by those who do not share this high culture).

Political culture refers to the attitudes, beliefs and values of people that affect their political behaviour. Thus some political communities may appear to be relatively deferential towards authority and officialdom, others much more resistant. Some political cultures may favour active engagement in the political process, while others might incline to political apathy. There may be big differences between political cultures over attitudes to such values as **freedom**, **equality, social justice** or **toleration**.

Political culture may have a crucial influence on political behaviour. Thus it has been argued that **democracy** may only thrive within a suitable political culture.

In a celebrated work Gabriel **Almond** and Sidney Verba (1963) subjected a range of five national political cultures to comparative analysis. They suggested that what they called a 'civic culture' (a blend of aspects of the US and UK political cultures) was most compatible with representative democracy. Their work was hugely influential but also attracted criticism (because of its neglect of divergent subcultures within nations, for example). Because the concept of political culture seemed difficult to operationalize, it subsequently somewhat fell from favour. However, more recently interest in it has revived. Ronald **Inglehart** (1971, 1990) has detected a significant shift among the younger generation in **post-industrial** societies towards 'post-material' values, with significant political implications. The work of Robert **Putnam** on **social capital** also seems to belong under the broad heading of political culture. Moreover, those researching **democratization** have rediscovered the importance of political culture for consolidating and stabilizing new democracies. (See Part V for more on political culture and democratization.)

Decentralization

Decentralization within a state normally involves the transfer of power downwards from central **government** to regional or local institutions. Sometimes a distinction is drawn between political decentralization, involving a transfer of power to elected regional or local authorities, and administrative decentralization. This may involve the transfer of government departments and offices from the state capital to the regions, although the term is sometimes used to mean the delegation of authority to front line staff.

Decentralization is widely assumed to be beneficial. Thus governments often promise to decentralize, and give more power to local people over their own lives, or more authority to 'front line' workers (although sometimes such promised decentralization can seem more cosmetic than real, as governments may be reluctant to relinquish real power). Yet decentralization, even if it is genuine, can have a downside. Where real discretion is given to local politicians or officials, one inescapable consequence is variations in decisions and service levels. Thus effective decentralization can detract from the ideal of social **justice**, that all state citizens in the same circumstances should be treated equally. Indeed, one consequence of decentralized decision making is the growth of complaints about a 'postcode lottery', where the level of service or even the availability of a service depends on where people live. Those who argue for increased local democracy argue that local communities should be able to determine the level of service they require, although it is debatable how far they should be able to opt out of services that the state or national community deems necessary. (See also **devolution**.)

Democracy

Democracy means government by the people, or in Abraham Lincoln's slightly expanded formula, 'government of the people, by the people, for the people'. A form of democracy existed in ancient Athens in the fifth century BC. Athenian democracy excluded women, resident foreigners and slaves, but it also, more positively, involved direct citizen participation in **government**. This system of direct democracy was memorably eulogized in words put into the mouth of the great Athenian statesman **Pericles** by the historian Thucydides, although that same democracy also subsequently tried and executed **Socrates**, whose celebrated pupil **Plato** later castigated democracy as the rule of the ignorant.

Such direct democracy, feasible for small city states, was scarcely practical for the more extensive empires and states of later centuries. Thus until the late eighteenth century democracy scarcely existed anywhere, and was widely perceived as undesirable as well as impractical. Even those who, like **Rousseau**, advocated democracy, were extremely pessimistic over its prospects. The democracy that emerged in the nineteenth century and became the system widely, almost universally, approved by the end of the twentieth century was representative democracy, government not by the people themselves but by the elected representatives of the people. Representative democracy was advocated by such thinkers as Tom **Paine** and Jeremy **Bentham**, and substantially implemented in the newly independent USA, whose democracy was fully and generally sympathetically described by the French aristocrat Alexis de **Tocqueville**, although he raised some concerns over the potential 'tyranny of the majority'. In leading western countries the vote was extended to almost all adult men in the course of the nineteenth century and to women in the early twentieth century.

Not everyone accepted that the right to vote

meant that real **power** was effectively transferred from the few to the many. Marxists continued to argue that even in parliamentary systems, political power reflected economic power, which remained highly concentrated. Classical elitists, such as **Pareto**, **Mosca** and **Michels** argued that power was still held by the few, and ridiculed the notion of rule by the people, while pluralist thinkers countered that power was effectively dispersed, substantially through the activities of countless interest groups competing for influence. Joseph **Schumpeter** (1943) subsequently attempted to redefine democracy as a limited choice between alternatives promoted by political leaders, in an approach described by David Held (2006) as 'competitive elitism'. Others, from John Stuart **Mill** to Carole **Pateman**, have advocated a more participatory democracy and active citizenship that goes well beyond just registering a vote in infrequent elections. One apparent means of giving more direct power to the people is through using a **referendum** (used quite often in some democracies like Switzerland), **plebiscite** or initiative (in some US states).

Despite such criticisms and despite periodic challenges from other versions of democracy (such as the one-party 'people's democracies' of the **communist** world before the fall of the Berlin Wall, or 'plebiscitory democracies' often associated with charismatic leaders), western-style 'representative' or 'parliamentary' democracy has become the generally approved model. This suggests the necessary conditions for democracy are regular, free and fair elections, contested by competing parties and individual candidates. These conditions are not always met. In some countries elections are patently rigged, party competition limited or absent, and voters denied an effective choice. In most other countries the electoral process is properly administered, although there may be some scope for arguing over electoral systems, or the fairness of the competition between candidates and parties, with very unequal resources.

Such a concentration on the mechanics of elections implies that democracy is all about process, although it is also widely assumed that democracy entails some core values, such as individual **freedom** (including freedom of expression), **toleration** of dissent and minority opinions, political and legal **equality**. Yet if democracy means simply the rule of the people or the rule of the majority of the people, it does not necessarily follow that the majority will tolerate the views and behaviour of minorities.

However, the core issue surrounding democracy remains the reality or otherwise of the power of the people. Key questions remain. How much real power do elections give to the people? Are voters able to recognize their own real interests, or are they effectively told what to think by the media and the whole process of political socialization? Do elected representatives of the people really control the government and key decisions, or is it appointed **bureaucrats**, or big business, or any other minority interest? Is power in practice relatively dispersed in states and communities, as **pluralists** argue or does it remain highly concentrated, as elite theorists and **Marxists** assert?

It may further be questioned how much real power any state government, elected or otherwise, really possesses to shape events in an era of **globalization**. For some the only answer to the power of global capital and global markets is some form of global democracy. For others, this remains an impossible pipe dream. The debates around democracy remain central, but unresolved.

Democratization

Democratization is the process of extending and consolidating **democracy**. Samuel **Huntington** (1991) has identified three main periods or 'waves' of democratization (with intervening 'reverse waves') over the last century or so. While most countries and most peoples now live under systems that are described as democratic, 'new democracies' have not always been successfully consolidated and stabilized. There are continuing questions over the extent to which many 'new' and some 'mature' democracies fulfil the basic criteria of a liberal representative democracy. The term 'illiberal democracies' is sometimes applied to these political systems.

Devolution

Devolution involves the delegation of powers by an upper level of government to a lower level. Unlike **federalism**, devolution does not involve any transfer or division of **sovereignty**. Devolution was the term used to describe the proposed transfer of powers by the UK government to representative assemblies in Scotland and Wales in the 1970s, while maintaining the sovereignty of the Westminster Parliament. The same word was used to describe the eventual establishment of the Scottish Parliament, Welsh Assembly and (more intermittently) a Northern Ireland Assembly in 1998, and (so far abortive) attempts to introduce elected assemblies for English regions. Devolution is an appropriate term to describe the introduction of regional political institutions in other unitary states (such as Spain) wishing to avoid a fully federal system. One motive for introducing regional devolution is to satisfy peripheral nationalist pressures within a state. However, **nationalism** normally involves demands for sovereign independence rather than simply more autonomy, and it is questionable whether devolution will satisfy the national sentiment of (for example) many Scots, Basques or Corsicans. Thus some critics fear (while others hope) that devolution involves a slippery slope towards the disintegration of states like the United Kingdom or Spain.

In theory, as sovereignty is not transferred, **power** devolved is power that might be recalled. Indeed the UK government has several times suspended devolved institutions and resumed direct rule in Northern Ireland. However, it would appear politically difficult if not impossible for the UK government to reverse devolution in Scotland and Wales (except in the unlikely event of this becoming the settled preference of Scots and Welsh). Indeed all the pressures are the other way, to devolve more powers. Thus some argue that Britain is already a quasi-federal state, and the sovereignty of the Westminster Parliament effectively dead. (See also **decentralization**.)

Dictators and dictatorship

Dictatorship is today a term used to describe the absolute rule of a single individual, who has seized **power** (generally unlawfully) and exercises it unconstrained by constitutional or other checks. The term originated in the time of the Roman Republic, when, however, dictatorial powers were initially granted only for a limited period to deal with a specific emergency, and the dictator could be called to account subsequently. Since then the term has been more commonly used for those who have taken power by force of arms. In the twentieth century, some of the most notorious rulers widely described as dictators, such as Mussolini, Hitler and Stalin, owed their position not to the support of the army but to their effective exploitation of modern mass communication to win and retain substantial popular support. This

concepts

arguably enabled them to exercise power more extensively and completely than dictators in the past (see **totalitarianism**).

The term 'dictatorship of the proletariat' was coined by **Marx** to suggest the need for a temporary period of class rule after a socialist revolution to prevent counter-revolution. The term was later used by **Lenin** to justify his own concept of democratic centralism, and subsequently, after the Bolshevik revolution, the exclusion of other parties from the political system.

Ecology, ecologism

See **environmentalism**.

Elections and electoral systems

Elections have become the generally approved method of selecting political **leaders** and **governments** over most of the world. Conditions for representative **democracy** include votes by secret ballot for all adults in regular, free and fair elections. These conditions have not always been met everywhere, and it is alleged that in some countries elections are rigged to favour particular individuals or parties. Broadly speaking, most mature democracies are free of the grosser forms of electoral malpractice.

However, the particular **electoral system** adopted can have an appreciable impact on the outcome in terms of translating the proportion of votes for individual candidates and political parties into numbers of seats in representative assemblies and control of government. In single member, simple plurality (or 'first past the post') systems (such as in UK parliamentary elections and in the USA), the candidate with more votes than any rival wins, regardless of whether they have a majority of the overall vote. In majoritarian systems (such as France), an alternative vote or two-ballot system ensures that those individuals who win posts or seats have a majority of votes. However, such systems do not ensure there is a roughly proportionate relationship between the percentage of votes won by a party and seats gained in assemblies or parliaments. Proportional systems (such as Israel, Germany, Scotland) can secure a more or less proportionate relationship between votes gained and seats won by a party, and advocates claim they are fairer and more democratic. However, critics argue that proportional representation can lead to multiparty systems and weak coalition government.

Electoral systems not only remain acutely controversial; there is increasing evidence that different systems can appreciably affect the behaviour of voters, as shown for example by various forms of tactical voting (see Part V).

Elites and elitism

An **elite** is any small group in society that by virtue of some attributes or qualities (real or imagined) has prestige, political influence and **power** beyond its numerical strength. An elite group in practice may be a priesthood, a traditional hereditary landed **aristocracy**, a military caste who have acquired power and prestige through their control of weapons, organization and expertise, a business elite who have acquired wealth and influence through trade or manufacturing, or a **meritocracy**, whose influence is based on education and formal qualifications.

Elitism is the belief that political power is effectively concentrated in the hands of elites, or a single elite, even if it is formally controlled by, or accountable to, the whole people, or the majority of the people. Thus real power, even in a state that is supposed to be **democratic**, is effectively in the hands of the few rather than the many. For some elite theorists, such as **Pareto**, elitism is not only an inescapable fact of political life, but is also a normative principle; power should be in the hands of the few. For radical elite theorists (such as C. Wright **Mills**) the concentration of power in the hands of elites in modern democracies is to be deplored rather than celebrated. (See also the discussion of elitism and pluralism in Part II, Section 2, pages 80–4).

Empiricism

Empiricism is the philosophic and scientific doctrine that all knowledge is derived from the direct experience of the senses. Theories and hypotheses require testing by repeated observation and experiment. **Locke**, Berkeley and **Hume** were three key figures in what is known as the British empirical tradition. The empirical approach underpinned the subsequent development of positivism, **behaviouralism** and modern western political science.

Empiricism is often linked with induction or inductive reasoning – inferring a general rule from a number of particular instances – as opposed to deduction, deriving logical conclusions from initial assumptions. Empiricism is also sometimes asso-

concepts

ciated with **pragmatism**, which emphasizes the importance of practical application ('what matters is what works') rather than relying on abstract theory.

Empiricism has been criticized by all those who argue that we can not make much sense of the world purely from subjective observation and experience of a tiny part of social relations that are intricately interconnected.

Environmentalism, ecologism and green thinking

Environmentalism is one of the labels (other labels include **ecologism** and **green thinking**) used to describe the political outlook or **ideology** that places a special priority on the protection of the environment. Although the roots of environmentalism can be traced back a long way, it is essentially a new ideology that has only acquired any political significance over the last half century or so. It has articulated a number of more specific concerns (over, for example, population growth, resource and energy conservation, environmental pollution, and animal rights) and woven these into a coherent and distinctive political philosophy. Greens place the environment at the centre of their political philosophy; they are ecocentric. Mainstream ideologies are anthropocentric. They focus on the presumed interests, needs or rights of humankind, or a particular section of human society – such as a particular class, race, nation, religious affiliation or **gender**. Environmentalists focus instead on the planet.

The environmental movement has already spawned a number of influential green **pressure groups** (such as Friends of the Earth and Greenpeace), and green parties. These have had considerable success in alerting people to the dangers of specific problems such as unrestricted population growth, depletion of non-renewable energy sources, irreversible pollution of the environment and climate change. Some of this has impacted on mainstream ideologies and parties, to the extent that these have acquired a greenish tinge and incorporated some green policy proposals. Yet green parties and pressure groups, while welcoming some of these initiatives, have generally dismissed them as too little, too late.

Green parties have won some electoral support, most notably in Germany, where until 2005 the Green Party was a junior partner in a coalition government. Elsewhere they have had less impact.

They have a difficult message to sell, a message that is at odds with prevailing political assumptions over the pursuit of material self-interest. There are some internal differences among greens over the compatibility of environmental preservation with economic growth and living standards. However, most seem to assume some restrictions on growth at least, and many greens concede that it will involve what most people would see as a reduction in their standard of living, with less air travel and less car use. Most political parties promise to make people or a section of the people better off. Greens in effect are promising to make them materially worse off, to prevent a catastrophe others think may not happen, or at least will not affect them in the foreseeable future, if at all. Environmentalists express concerns for interests that have no vote and no voice, for generations yet unborn, for other species, for Planet Earth, and the future of the planet. There is no way in which these interests can be taken into account in the current economic and political market place, unless humans show more altruism than most perspectives on politics assume.

Equality

'Liberty, **equality** and fraternity' was the celebrated slogan of the French Revolution. There was some potential for conflict between these principles, particularly between liberty and equality. Thus increasing equality might entail some restraint on individual **freedom**, while increasing freedom might lead to more inequality. Separately, each of these principles was problematic, but equality has been the most contested.

It had long been argued by some political thinkers (including **Hobbes**) that all men were equal in their original state, or state of nature. Religious texts suggested that all were equal in the sight of God. **Liberals** went on to argue that all men (and later women) were, or should be, equal before the law, and some went to demand equal political rights, the right to vote and stand for election. Yet formal legal and political equality have not ensured that everyone in practice is treated equally before the law, and certainly has not entailed equal political influence. Thus women have long had the same rights as men to vote and stand for political office, but they remain substantially under-represented in elected assemblies and government almost everywhere.

Both **conservatives** and liberals stress

equality of opportunity, rather than equality of outcome. Indeed they defend substantial inequality of outcome, as they argue this provides incentives and rewards for effort and initiative. Equality of opportunity amounts to the opportunity to become unequal. The result in theory should be a **meritocracy**: those who deserve to succeed will do so. Yet in practice this is a race in which the competitors do not start equal. Conservatives stress the right to bequeath and inherit property, and commonly criticize inheritance taxes. They also defend the right of parents to purchase a better education for their children. Yet these are advantages that in theory could be removed. It would, however, be virtually impossible to eliminate all the advantages of nature and nurture that ensure some children have a far better chance of success than others.

While conservatives and liberals defend inequality, **socialists** argue for equality and social **justice**. Indeed, equality is perhaps the term most associated with socialism. Socialists point to the massive inequality existing in almost all societies, and advocate a substantial redistribution of income and wealth, through either **revolution**, or more gradual reform. Yet while a few socialists and **anarchists** have championed the total abolition of private **property**, and the equal rights of all to the fruits of the earth, most socialists and **social democrats** have argued for not **communism**, or absolute equality, but greater equality. As critics such as **Hayek** have observed, absolute equality at least provides a clear criterion for the socialist planner, while the goal of 'greater equality' provides no practical guidance for distributing income.

How far socialists have succeeded in their aim of making society more equal is debatable. Socialist revolutions have commonly involved a substantial redistribution of income and wealth, although critics suggest they have created new forms of inequality. The evolutionary social democratic route appeared to achieve some more modest redistribution over time through the tax and benefits system, particularly in the decades immediately following the Second World War, but progress towards a more equal society under recent social democratic governments seems at most to have been marginal.

Radical critics today place more emphasis on **global** inequality, the massive differences in living standards between societies rather than within

them. While such differences existed in the past, they are now far better documented and far more publicized. The consequences of this inequality are more dramatic. In many countries people suffer from absolute rather relative poverty, lacking basic necessities. This global inequality involves the danger of further humanitarian disasters, as well as threats to peace and the **environment**. Yet tackling global inequality seems immeasurably more difficult than tackling inequality within countries.

Ethnicity and ethnic minorities

The definition of **ethnicity**, and how far it can be distinguished from terms such as **nation**, **community** and (most contentious of all) **race**, is problematic. The term 'race' long involved the now totally discredited notion of biological differences among humans. The term 'ethnicity' refers not to biological but to cultural differences between communities, relating to their origins and development over time, involving distinctive language, beliefs, customs and traditions. Thus Jews may be considered to constitute an ethnic group, and a distinctive ethnic minority in many states (and an ethnic majority in the state of Israel). Other minority religious groups or those speaking a different language may be regarded as an ethnic minority (such as the Basques in Spain and the Christians in the Lebanon).

Commonly an immigrant minority might be considered a distinctive ethnic group. Thus Italians, Poles or Greeks living in the USA or Britain might be regarded as **ethnic minorities**, although the term is more commonly applied to those who are black or Asian. Thus an ethnic group may be defined by others, but it may also be defined by its own members, who may passionately assert their own distinctive identity. Such an ethnic identity may be compatible with loyalty to the **state**, particularly a **multicultural** state. Hyphenated or multiple identities (such as Irish-American, Muslim-British) might be regarded as an increasingly common phenomenon in the modern world. However, distinctive ethnic groups that dominate a particular geographical area may indeed regard themselves as a separate nation and demand political independence (although this is not an option for more widely dispersed ethnic minorities).

'Ethnicity' and more particularly the term 'ethnic minorities' are sometimes employed by racists as code words for people of different skin colour, or race. The 'problem' of ethnic minorities is often essentially the problem of the ethnic majority that consciously or unconsciously discriminates against minorities, and fails to treat them as equals.

Executive

In the study of politics the **executive** is the branch of the state responsible for day to day **government**. Thus it administers laws, and determines and executes policy, including responsibility for defence and foreign relations. The executive functions of the state are distinguished from the **legislative** or law making functions, and from the **judicial,** or law adjudicating functions under the influential ideal of the '**separation of powers**'. In many countries the separation of powers is imperfect in practice, and in some **dictatorships** and **totalitarian** systems it does not exist even in theory.

In **democracies** the executive is normally either directly elected, or emerges from, and is responsible to, an elected parliament or assembly. The executive can be a single person (who may be called president), but it can also be a committee or cabinet (a plural executive), perhaps headed by a leading minister or prime minister, but in theory involving 'collective responsibility' for policy.

Generally, the form of the executive and its **powers** (and limitations to those powers) are spelled out in a state's **constitution**. Thus the US Constitution vests executive power in the president, describes how the president is elected, and the limits to the president's term of office, and sets out the president's most important functions. The US President is both the formal head of state and holds real executive power. In many other countries (such as the Netherlands, Sweden, Spain, Germany, Ireland, Italy) the role of formal head of state (sometimes a constitutional monarch, sometimes a directly or indirectly elected president) is separated from the effective executive. Thus the head of state does not control the government. France (under the constitution of the Fifth French Republic) unusually has what is sometimes described as a dual executive, with a directly elected president with real powers (particularly in foreign affairs), and a parliamentary executive headed by a prime minister. In Britain, which lacks a written constitution, the executive is generally identified with the Cabinet, but the growth of prime ministerial power suggests to some critics a quasi-presidential system, while others define a broader 'core executive', covering the Cabinet, junior ministers and leading civil servants and advisers.

Fascism

Fascism is the name of a political **ideology** that had antecedents but essentially developed in Italy at the end of the First World War, and spread to other countries, particularly in Europe and South America. The name 'fascism' was derived from the 'fasces', the bundle of rods carried as a symbol of authority by the lictors in ancient Rome. The name and symbol was adopted by the former socialist Benito Mussolini, whose fascist party came to power following the so-called 'March on Rome' in 1922, amid the confused state of parliamentary democracy in post-war Italy. Mussolini soon established a one-party state, with himself as 'Duce' or leader. His fascist state appeared to restore order, achieved some initial success in foreign policy and economic policy, and won some admiration and imitation abroad.

Fascism was presented as a new and distinctive political philosophy, offering a 'middle way' between **capitalism** and revolutionary **socialism**. As such it appealed particularly to those classes in society apparently threatened on the one hand by big business, and on the other by militant trade unionism and socialism, particularly the lower middle classes and peasants. Mussolini made much of his brand of '**corporatism**', involving the functional rather than the territorial representation of interests. This combined employers and workers (whose old free trade unions were banned). He also emphasized total allegiance to the state (see **totalitarianism**). More obvious elements of fascism included aggressive **nationalism**, **militarism** and **dictatorship**. Mussolini sought to build a new 'Roman empire' with himself at its head. This culminated in the Italian invasion of Abyssinia and the alliance with Hitler's Nazi Germany.

Among scholars there is some disagreement over how far Nazism can be distinguished from fascism. Nazism shared many of the characteristics of fascism, but added virulent **racism** and particularly anti-Semitism, initially not shared by Mussolini but subsequently imitated by him. Thus Nazism and fascism became in effect a single creed, diametrically opposed to **liberalism** and **democracy.** Fascist and quasi-fascist movements appeared in many other countries, although in Europe these mostly only came to power briefly as a result of external pressure or occupation. Even so, liberal democracy seemed in general retreat between the wars, and the main threat came from the fascist **right** rather than from the **communist left**.

There is further debate over whether fascism in some shape or form survived its defeat in 1945. Certainly quasi-fascist regimes survived for a time in Spain and Portugal, and periodically flourished in South America. Subsequently 'neo-fascist' movements have won some significant support in several countries more recently – in Italy, Germany and France. These place an emphasis on some familiar fascist ideas – including the cult of **leadership** and extreme nationalism. However, little remains of Mussolini's own conception of fascism, which has become little more than a generalized term of political abuse. The core element of the various neo-Nazi and neo-fascist movements, and the only element which remains significant is racism, sometimes still directed against Jews but more often against blacks and Asians, and against immigration in general.

Federalism

Federalism involves the division of supreme **power** or **sovereignty** in a **state** between two or more levels of **government**, each of which is (in theory) supreme in its own sphere. Commonly there is a federal government responsible for the interests of the federation as a whole, and in addition governments for each of the states that belong to the federation. Thus a federal system virtually requires a written **constitution** laying down the powers and responsibilities of each level of government. For example, in the US Constitution the powers of the federal institutions are outlined, reserving all other functions to the constituent states and the people. In practice there are commonly ambiguities and tensions over respective responsibilities. In many federal systems it appears over time that more power accrues to the federal government at the expense of the states. In some others the federal authority is relatively weak and the states operate as virtually independent sovereign states.

Federalism is an attractive solution where close cooperation between states or peoples is needed for their mutual defence or to yield economies of scale in production and trade, but where religious,

linguistic or other cultural divisions between peoples render closer union impractical, and potentially damaging for minorities. (Examples include Switzerland, Canada, Belgium and Germany.) In many countries today there are pressures to devolve more power or allow more autonomy to regions, and where these are conceded a 'quasi-federal' system may develop (examples include Spain and the United Kingdom). The term federalism is also often applied to the European Union, in a way that appears unproblematic to member states used to federal arrangements within their own countries, but appears threatening to the United Kingdom. (See also **devolution**.)

Feminism

Feminists seek women's liberation from male domination or **patriarchy**. Like other **ideologies** feminism involves a critique, an ideal and a programme. The critique contains an analysis of the discrimination and injustices suffered by women in existing society. The ideal is **justice** for women, generally but not exclusively interpreted to mean full equality between the sexes. The practical programme has included action to secure for women political and legal **rights**, **equality** in the economic sphere, the elimination of sexual discrimination in education and the workplace, a more equitable division of domestic and child-rearing duties, and protection against physical and sexual violence.

Literature on feminism commonly refers to two main 'waves' of feminism. The first wave extended roughly from the late eighteenth century to the 1920s, culminating in many western states with the extension of legal and political rights to women, including particularly the right to vote. The second wave of feminism, from the 1960s onwards, focused on the continuing discrimination still suffered by women in practice despite their formal legal and political equality. The literature also distinguishes between three main types of feminism: **liberal** feminism, **Marxist** (or **socialist**) feminism, and radical feminism.

Early liberal feminists, such as Mary **Wollstonecraft**, Elizabeth Cady Stanton and John Stuart **Mill**, applied liberal theory by extending the 'rights of man' to women, demanding their full equality. Liberal feminists were ultimately successful in securing formal legal rights for women, and some practical advances, particularly for a minority of educated middle-class women enabled them to compete in a man's world. They have been criticized for accepting essentially male values, and concentrating on the 'public sphere' of law, politics and employment, while largely neglecting women's role in the private world of home and family, to many feminists the very centre of women's exploitation and subordination.

Socialist feminists such as Juliet Mitchell and Michelle Barrett employed Marxist methodology to explain the subordination of women in modern capitalist society. The unpaid domestic labour performed by women was related to the requirements of **capitalism**. As part of the paid workforce women could also be used as an 'industrial reserve army of labour' to swell the ranks of workers in times of boom and to undercut the wages of male workers. It followed that the emancipation of women could only be achieved with the abolition of capitalism and the **bourgeois** relations between the sexes associated with capitalism. Socialist feminists sought to reverse the inequality and discrimination women faced in work, campaigning to involve women in trade unions, and to secure the provision of nurseries and workplace creches. Some advocated wages for housework. Socialist feminists have been criticized for assuming women's exploitation was a function of capitalism, and that therefore the **gender** issue was secondary to the class issue, and for their relative neglect of the domestic sphere.

Radical feminists such as Kate **Millett**, Germaine **Greer**, Eva Figes, Catharine **MacKinnon** and Mary Daly focused on the concept of patriarchy to argue that the problem for women was not essentially an inadequate political and legal framework, nor capitalism, but simply men and male **power**. For radicals it was the sex war rather than the class war that was fundamental. At its heart were the everyday relations between men and women in the home, family and bedroom. This involved not so much a retreat from politics as a deliberate widening of the political sphere, as implied in the radical feminist slogan 'The personal is political.' A key target was violence against women, particularly rape, including rape within marriage, and pornography, which appeared to legitimize the degradation of women. Influenced by **postmodernism**, some radicals argued strongly that language and literature reflected an orthodox 'malestream' discourse that diminishes women. Radical campaigns changed attitudes and significantly influenced the portrayal of women in the media, although some women were alienated by their criticisms of traditional feminine tastes, the family and motherhood. Radical feminists have also sometimes been accused of universalizing their own circumstances as typical of women everywhere, overlooking the very different needs and problems of women from different cultures.

Among the diverse strands of modern feminism may be included such categories as black feminism, eco-feminism, linking **environmentalism** with the caring, nurturing role of women, and the so-called new feminism, articulated by Natasha Walter (1999) among others. She criticizes the radicals for reinforcing the hostile stereotype of feminists as lesbian man-haters, and for rejecting much that ordinary women enjoy, such as jewellery, fashionable clothes and make-up, which Walter argues can help to make women feel good and thus empower them. Feminism has also provoked something of a backlash, even among a few women. Post-feminism is a label that implies the main objectives of the movement have been achieved, a verdict that feminists of all varieties would emphatically deny.

Freedom or liberty

Freedom, or **liberty**, has long been a key political concept, and an inspiring political ideal. 'Give me liberty or give me death!' the American revolutionary Patrick Henry declaimed in 1775. In contrast to the unfree slave or serf, a free citizen appears to have control over his or her own life. State **constitutions** and international charters of human **rights** spell out specific freedoms, commonly including freedom of speech, freedom of religion, and freedom to own, obtain and dispose of property. Yet some freedoms imply restraints on others. 'Freedom from fear' involves a framework of law and order that clearly limits the freedom of those who seek to intimidate or rob their fellows. Thus liberty is not licence to do as one pleases, regardless of harm to others. **Liberals** and **socialists** tend to an optimistic view of the capacity of humans to pursue their interests rationally and peacefully with only limited external control. However, **conservatives** have more generally assumed that most humans are inherently quarrelsome, and governed by the passions rather than reason, and thus require strong **government** and **law**, vigorously enforced, to keep them in order.

Isaiah **Berlin** famously distinguished between two kinds of liberty: negative, involving essentially freedom from external control, and positive, involving freedom to enjoy something worth enjoying and fulfil personal potential. Older liberals like Herbert **Spencer** and **neoliberals** like **Hayek** have championed the freedom of the individual from interference or oppression (including government oppression). However, progressive or 'New' liberals such as T. H. **Green** and Leonard **Hobhouse**, as well as socialists and **social democrats**, supported the notion of positive freedom to enjoy the benefits of employment, housing, health and especially education to enable people to develop their true potential. Yet of course the freedom of all to enjoy these benefits entails increased state intervention and interference with the freedom of the individual. At the very least a heavier burden of taxation reduces the freedom of individuals to choose what to do with their own money.

Although liberals assume that freedom is highly desirable, some thinkers also suggested that freedom creates uncertainty and anxiety. Similarly, Theodore **Adorno** described the 'authoritarian personality' of those who prefer a framework of leadership, order and obedience, without freedom of choice. Such notions may help to explain why millions appeared willing to surrender democratic freedoms to follow without question leaders such as Mussolini and Hitler.

Free market

A **free market** is a market free from interference by **state governments**, or by monopoly powers. Thus the free market assumes unrestrained competition. For **liberals** and **neoliberals** only a free market is compatible with economic efficiency and growth, but it is also seen as a key element of individual **freedom**. **Conservatives** have sometimes been prepared to justify interference with the free market to protect some interests or preserve social harmony and stability, for example advocating protection and 'fair trade' rather 'free trade'. Socialists have commonly sought to interfere with free market forces to secure objectives such as full employment, greater **equality** and social **justice**, although they have also argued that state planning is more efficient. They would also argue that state provision of services can enlarge freedom.

Gender

Although the terms **gender** and sex are often used interchangeably, most **feminists** make a clear distinction between them. While 'sex' refers to the physical or biological differences between men and women, 'gender' describes the socially and culturally conditioned roles of men and women. Thus assumptions about men and women's different nature, aptitudes, potential, rights and duties are part of socially conditioned expectations of different gender roles, rather than biologically determined. The inferior position of women compared with men in many fields of employment and in politics is a consequence of assumed gender differences rather than real biological differences. Similarly, it is argued that women's considerably greater burden in child rearing and caring for elderly or infirm relatives arises from socially conditioned expectations of gender roles rather than biological differences. For many feminists, gender is the most fundamental social and political division, more important than social class or ethnicity. Thus feminists seek gender **equality**.

Yet while most feminists deny that there are any socially or politically significant differences between men and women, and that the two sexes are substantially similar, some feminists are prepared to assert that women are different, not just physically but mentally. They argue women may be less aggressive, more cooperative than men, more sharing and caring (with implications for the social and political roles). Some leading male political theorists (for example **Plato**, **Rousseau** and **Mill**) have speculated on male and female nature. The same/difference debate among feminists has brought a new dimension to this ancient debate.

Globalization

Globalization has become an extremely important but contentious concept in the study of politics. It refers to the increasing impact of global trends and pressures on the lives of everyone, transcending **state** borders (and some would even argue, making the **nation-state** obsolete) and creating a globalized economy and culture. Important manifestations of globalization include increasing global communications (creating what Marshall McLuhan described as a 'global village'), expanding international trade and investment, and the increased recognition of the global impact of **environmental** pollution and the exploitation of scarce resources. The growing **power** and influence of trans-national corporations (TNCs) and a range of **non-government organizations (NGOs)** and international institutions appear to have significant implications for the politics of the nation-

concepts

state. Global **terrorism** is the latest manifestation of the globalization of politics.

Globalization may have intensified more recently, and its effects may be more widely recognized, but it is not entirely new. National economies have long been subject to events and trends in the wider world over which state governments have little or no control. Governments have often in the past found it difficult to resist the impact of political developments outside their borders. Yet if globalization is not new, its impact has increased and it has become more evident, particularly perhaps following the end of the cold war and the apparent victory of the values of **liberal capitalism**, to which there no longer appears a viable alternative.

While some argue that the politics of the nation-state is effectively obsolete, as state governments are increasingly subject to global forces they cannot control, others suggest the impact of globalization has been exaggerated. Nation-states retain considerable **power** and significant autonomy. Global **capitalism** has not obliged states to abandon **welfare** provision, nor significant economic regulation. International institutions are created by states, and can only succeed if states continue to support them. Large and powerful states can ignore them. NGOs may influence opinions, but have little power or authority unless state governments choose to acknowledge them.

Yet there are massive global problems that require cooperation on a global scale if they are to be tackled effectively. Such problems include global warming and other actual or potential environmental threats, global poverty and inequality, nuclear proliferation, global terrorism, as well as the more long-standing threats of famine, disease and war. Yet effective international cooperation and strong international institutions are not created by the existence of a need for them. There has been some resurgence of interest in notions of world government and global **democracy**, but although these may be desirable ideals, they seem a long way from current reality.

Government and governance

To govern is to exercise control over others, and some form of **government** can be identified in any organization. In the study of politics the term is particularly applied to the formal institutions for maintaining public order and making, executing and adjudicating on **laws** in any state. Yet in popular usage the term 'government' is used more narrowly to mean only the **executive**, while 'the government' is used to describe those individuals who constitute the executive at any particular time. Both terms are most commonly used to describe the national or central government, but it is accepted that government may take place at various levels within a **state**, such as **federal**, state, regional and local government.

The need for government of some kind is widely acknowledged (although not by **anarchists**), but there is considerable disagreement over both the scope of government (extensive or strictly limited) and the form of government. The government of states can take many forms. Greek thinkers identified three main types; the rule of one (monarchy), rule of the few (oligarchy), and rule of the people (**democracy**), with many sub-variants. Government may be characterized as legitimate or illegitimate, constitutional or unconstitutional, limited or absolute. Key **liberal** concepts implying legitimate, and limited (or constitutional) government include the notion of government by **consent**, and the **separation of** (executive, **legislative** and **judicial**) **powers**.

Governance has sometimes been used simply as a synonym for government, but it has become a fashionable term to describe the process of governing, rather than the institutions of government (Osborne and Gaebler, 1992). Governance blurs the distinctions between governors and governed, the public and private sectors, the state and civil society, because we are all more or less involved in that process. It implies the delegation, decentralization and fragmentation of power rather than the concentration of sovereign authority in the hands of a single national government within a unitary state. The term 'governance' is compatible with partnerships, networks and other forms of collaborative activity rather than the unified chain of command and control associated with much traditional government. The term 'multi-level governance' suggests that these processes can and perhaps should take place at different levels.

Green thinking

See **environmentalism**.

Hegemony

The term **hegemony** has been used to describe any form of dominant influence, for example of one state over another. **Marxists**, following Antonio

Gramsci, have used the term more specifically to describe the ascendancy one **class** may acquire over other classes, not just from its ownership and control of economic resources, but though the permeation of the dominant **culture** and **ideology** throughout society. Thus subordinate classes accept the perspective of the dominant class and regard it as their own. This cultural and intellectual hegemony allows the dominant class to rule by apparent **consent** rather than coercion.

Human nature

Human nature refers to the inborn characteristics of human beings, as opposed to those produced by upbringing, education and social conditioning. Thus 'nature' is contrasted with 'nurture'. Underpinning most perspectives on politics are sometimes implicit, but often explicit, assumptions about human nature. Thus **Aristotle** assumed that men were by nature social and political animals, and the **state** (or political community) also exists by nature. However, many later political thinkers posited a (historical or hypothetical) 'state of nature' before the emergence of society or **government**. **Hobbes** reckoned that humans were aggressively competitive, and hypothesized an original 'state of nature' involving a war of every man against every man. **Rousseau**, by contrast, viewed the 'state of nature' with some regrets. His 'noble savage' was free from social and political constraints and was capable of pity and sympathy for his fellow creatures.

Assumptions about human nature underpin ideological perspectives. **Liberals** see humans as self-interested and competitive but also rational and enlightened. They assume that the pursuit of enlightened self-interest by individuals will promote the greatest common good (an assumption shared by modern **rational choice** theorists). **Conservatives** are more sceptical over the capacity of most humans to be guided by reason, rather than passion or emotion, and commonly perceive a need for **authority** and strong government to control the evil streak (or original sin from a religious perspective) in humanity. Yet, in marked contrast to liberal individualism, conservatives also emphasize the family, **community** and national ties that bind people together in mutual dependence and solidarity. **Socialists** similarly stress the social nature of humankind, rejecting liberal individualism, but are more optimistic than conservatives over the human capacity for fruitful cooperation

for the common good. Selfish competitive behaviour is seen as the product of **capitalism** rather than a universal human characteristic. **Anarchists** optimistically assume that humans could live together peacefully and cooperatively without the coercive and corrupting role of government. **Fascists** make some fairly cynical assumptions about the pliability of ordinary human beings, and the potential for their manipulation.

Many older writers commonly referred to the nature of 'man', either ignoring women or tacitly assuming that male and female natures were fundamentally similar. Yet some political theorists did suggest that women's nature was markedly different from men's. Indeed, this assumed difference between the sexes was commonly used to justify refusing women political and other rights. To counter such arguments used in his own day, John Stuart **Mill** maintained that 'what is now called the nature of women is an eminently artificial thing – the result of forced repression in some directions, unnatural stimulation in others' (Mill [1869] 1988: 22). Yet while liberal **feminists** tacitly assumed there were no significant differences between male and female nature, some modern radical feminists have been more ready to assert that aggression and violence are essentially male characteristics, while women are naturally more caring and sharing (see also **gender**).

Idealism

Idealism in philosophy and political theory is contrasted with **materialism**, **empiricism**, and particularly in **international relations** theory, with **realism**.

Plato argued that knowledge involved understanding perfect unchanging ideals or forms, rather than the imperfect transient world of our sense perception. Thus his ideal state, explored in *The Republic*, was for Plato more 'real' than actual imperfect states, subject to constant change and decay. **Kant** and **Hegel** similarly denied the empiricist claim that real knowledge of the world could only be derived from experience, assuming instead that there were eternal values and ideals that could be validated by human consciousness.

In politics idealism is associated with the pursuit of abstract ideals or principles, and is contrasted with **pragmatism**. Some argue that politicians and parties should be guided by clear ideals and principles, rather than a pragmatic concern to follow public opinion and/or their own interests.

concepts

However policies are sometimes castigated for being 'too idealistic' or 'unrealistic'. In international relations the label 'idealist' has been attached to those **liberals** who had sought to end war and promote international harmony through the development of international law, collective security and the establishment of international institutions. To 'realists' like E. H. **Carr** and Hans **Morgenthau** this involved a naïve neglect of the reality of international **anarchy**, conflicting national interests and **power**. The failure of international **law** and institutions to prevent aggression and ultimately war in the 1930s appeared to validate their criticism of idealism in international relations, although more recently idealist theories of international relations have enjoyed a partial comeback.

Ideology

The term **ideology** is problematic and contested. Ideology may be loosely defined as any system of ideas directing political action. The key words here are 'system' and 'action'. An ideology involves firstly an interconnected set of ideas that forms a perspective on the world – what the Germans call *Weltanshauung* (world outlook). Second, ideologies have implications for political behaviour – they are 'action-oriented'. Political ideologies normally contain three key elements: an analysis of existing social and political arrangements, a political ideal or vision of the future (which for some might involve a return to the past!) and a strategy for realizing that ideal. However, the balance between these three elements inevitably depends on the extent of satisfaction with the current state of affairs and of optimism over the possibility of change.

Karl **Marx** commonly employed the term ideology in a pejorative (or negative) sense, identifying it with illusion. Because, he argued, the prevailing ideas in any society will reflect the interests of the dominant **class** (through for example its control of education and the mass media), it follows that subordinate classes will not recognize their own exploitation, but will hold a distorted view of their own interests. This 'false consciousness' he described as ideology. Much of the prevailing wisdom of his own day, including classical economics and conventional **bourgeois** morality, Marx considered ideological rather than scientific. His own method, he considered, involved science rather than ideology.

Much of modern American political science takes a diametrically opposed view. For them, **Marxism**, along with other 'isms', was dogmatic, unscientific and 'ideological' compared with their own detached value-free, rigorous empirical research. Ideology was particularly identified with 'closed' totalitarian systems of thought. Daniel **Bell** (1960) proclaimed 'the end of ideology'. **Conservatives** and **liberals** denied that their own political creed was ideological. Some critics suggested that that western politics was characterized not by the end of ideology, but the dominance of a particular ideology, pluralist liberal **democracy** or **capitalism**. Indeed many commentators identified an ideological **consensus** in the west, based on Keynesian economics and **welfare** reform, sometimes identified as a **social democratic** consensus. This consensus (if it ever really existed), was challenged by new ideological perspectives (such as **feminism** and **environmentalism**) and the revival of an old one (**neoliberalism**). The end of the cold war and the break-up of the Soviet empire seemed to some to mark the victory of liberal capitalism, although it soon became apparent that new political divisions based on **culture**, **ethnicity** and religion were replacing the old cold war split between **communism** and capitalism.

Today most (but by no means all) commentators seem to prefer a more neutral non-pejorative understanding of ideology. Thus liberalism, conservatism, **socialism**, **nationalism**, feminism and environmentalism all commonly figure in surveys of political ideologies, sometimes alongside other older or more recent political doctrines. It is also generally accepted that ideologies may be expressed at various levels and with different degrees of sophistication; for example by political thinkers, practising politicians, the media and the wider public. Thus at the popular level ideologies may be expressed in terms of images and slogans.

Imperialism

Imperialism, the development of empire, involves the expansion of the state beyond its boundaries to secure domination over other countries and peoples. Empires have been established throughout history – notable examples being the Egyptian, Chinese, Persian, Alexandrian and Roman empires of ancient times. More recently, from the sixteenth to the nineteenth centuries European states, such as Spain, Portugal, Britain, France and the Netherlands acquired colonial empires in other continents, and relative newcomers Germany and Italy became involved in the 'scramble for Africa' in the late nineteenth century. While some authors distinguish between imperialism and colonialism, the European empires established from the sixteenth to the nineteenth centuries were all essentially colonial empires.

The case for imperialism was variously advanced. **States** commonly justified their own imperialism as a civilizing mission, spreading the benefits of Christianity and western **law** and **culture** to 'heathen' native peoples – the 'white man's burden' in the poet Rudyard Kipling's words. Others saw it as a competitive struggle for **power** and influence in the world; thus if the opportunities for imperial expansion were neglected, other states would seize them, in what was perceived as a kind of Darwinian contest for the survival of the fittest. Imperialism could also be seen as an extension of **nationalism**, validating the claims of superiority made for the nation. An additional advantage for ruling **elites** was that both nationalism and imperialism appeared useful in diverting the working classes away from **revolutionary socialism**.

Others again argued that the motive for imperialism was essentially economic, part of the industrializing nations' search for captive sources of raw materials and markets for finished goods. **Lenin** argued, in *Imperialism as the Highest Stage of Capitalism*, that imperialism was an economic necessity for **capitalist** states. Exploitation of colonies enabled imperial powers to postpone the increasing poverty of their own working **class** that would otherwise spark **revolution.** Not everyone, however, agrees that colonies were invariably to the economic advantage of the imperial powers. Indeed some colonies appeared an economic burden, and it has been argued that empire was more of a political distraction and a drain on resources than a benefit.

From the perspective of the colonized there was a glaring inconsistency between the **liberal** ideals preached by their colonial masters and imperial practice. They were treated as subject peoples rather than equal citizens within an imperial state. Colonial subjects used the language of their conquerors to demand their own **freedom** and self-determination. In the course of the twentieth century empire increasingly appeared an anachronism. When Mussolini's Italian **fascist** government invaded Abyssinia in 1936, it was only doing what other European powers had done

in the nineteenth century, but the aggression was almost universally condemned. The remaining European empires were rapidly liquidated in the decades following the Second World War, which had reduced the power and prestige of the old colonial powers. Apart from a few tiny anachronistic survivals, the age of empire, at least in its traditional form, appears over.

However, although imperialism and colonialism have become pejorative (or derogatory) terms, some argue that the relationship today between the economically developed states and the developing world is a profoundly unequal one, amounting to economic and cultural exploitation without direct political control, which is sometimes described as neo-colonialism or neo-imperialism.

Incrementalism

Incrementalism is a model or theory of policy making that suggests that most policy involves a limited choice between relatively few options and only a small (or incremental) change from past policy. It is associated particularly with Charles **Lindblom**, who developed his incremental model in opposition to the rational model of decision making linked with Herbert **Simon**. In Lindblom's hands incrementalism was both a descriptive and prescriptive model of the policy-making process. He thought not only that most policy was made incrementally, but that policy was better for being made in this way. Provocatively, he described it as 'the science of muddling through'. Incrementalism avoids the potential risks of radical reform. It also assumes accommodation and compromise between different interests, a process Lindblom described as 'partisan mutual adjustment'. His understanding of incrementalism is thus linked with **pluralism**. Incrementalism also has obvious affinities with the cautious approach to reform associated with **conservatism**, the gradualism of Fabian **socialism** of Beatrice and Sidney **Webb** and the 'piece-meal social engineering' recommended by Karl **Popper**.

Critics have argued that while incrementalism offers a realistic description of much policy making, particularly the budgetary process, it does not explain sharp switches, as sometimes demonstrated in foreign policy. As a prescriptive model, incrementalism has been criticized for its in-built **conservative** bias, when radical change might sometimes be required. Other theorists, such as Amitai Etzioni and Yehezkal Dror, have recommended more complex models of decision making, drawing on the insights of both Simon and Lindblom.

Individualism

Individualism involves an assumption of the prime importance of individuals over any social group. Society is seen as no more than an aggregate of individuals. All theorizing about politics and society begins with the individual, and the rights and freedom of the individual are seen as paramount. The former British Prime Minister Margaret Thatcher expressed an extreme form of individualism in her much-quoted (and frequently misquoted) remark, 'There is no such thing as society. There are individual men and women, and there are families.'

Individualism is a key concept in classical **liberalism** and most forms of modern liberalism. It also underpins the social contract theory of **Hobbes** and **Locke**, the **utilitarianism** of Jeremy **Bentham**, and much modern economics, including **rational choice** theory. Traditional **conservatism** by contrast commonly involved a more organic conception of society, over and above the individuals who at any one time constitute society. **Socialism** assumes both the importance of social pressures on individual consciousness and behaviour, and the need to consider the interests and welfare of wider society, and not just the self-interest of individuals.

Institutionalism and new institutionalism

In the study of politics and (especially) public administration, traditional **institutionalism** involved a focus on the formal organizations involved in **government** and the **state**. From a **behaviouralist** perspective this approach was too descriptive and atheoretical, and involved an often uncritical acceptance of the letter of the **law** and the **constitution** in defining the role of government institutions. in the political process. However, critics thought the behaviouralists underestimated the role of institutions in the political process. March and Olsen (1984, 1989) coined the term **new institutionalism**. This took a broader view of institutions, to include organizations outside government, social institutions and informal organizational networks. Institutions of all kinds involved norms, rules and 'standard operating procedures' that were internalized by those who worked within them, and thus influenced their behaviour. The

new institutionalism has influenced not just the study of public administration and public policy, but mainstream political science, including (to a degree) **rational choice** theory and **international relations**.(See also Part II, Section 2 on the new institutionalism, pages 93–6).

International law

International law is commonly divided into public international law, involving rules governing the relations between **states**, and private international law, involving the adjudication of disputes between **non-governmental organizations (NGOs)** from different states. It is public international law that has attracted more interest by political theorists and writers on **international relations**, although private international law is of growing importance in an era of increasing **globalization**.

The problem for international law, as compared with state law, has long been the absence of a generally acknowledged international body to make **law** or enforce it. Thus the 'rules' governing relations between states have commonly amounted to little more than descriptions of practice on the one hand or pious expectations on the other.

Hugo **Grotius** (1583–1645) is widely considered to have laid the foundations for the study of international law. He sought to derive not only state law but law governing relations between states from a universal natural law. Rather less ambitiously, he argued that states should uphold treaty obligations freely entered into. It is such treaties and other agreements between states that constitute the substantive body of international law. These initially involved agreements between a few (two or more) sovereign states, but over the last century or so at least some of these agreements were international in scope.

A number of international organizations were established whose **authority** to make law was widely but not universally acknowledged, but whose **power** to enforce this law, particularly against powerful states, often appeared defective. Thus while liberal theorists of international relations championed the growth of international institutions and international law, the failure of international institutions and agreements between the wars rendered convincing the **realist** counter-assertion that international relations involved states pursuing interests, defined in terms of power. According to this realist perspective, **liberal idealist** notions of international justice and international law were a chimera. Relations between sovereign states necessarily involve a Hobbesian state of **anarchy**.

A number of factors have nevertheless have led to renewed interest in extending and strengthening international law. These include the growth of trans-national corporations (TNCs) and non-governmental organizations (NGOs) and the erosion of state sovereignty by **globalizing** trends, continuing threats to peace both from states and from non-state organizations, a series of humanitarian disasters, major trade concerns, and rising worries about irreversible damage to the **environment.** There is no longer a balance of power to provide a framework of order and security. The world has become less predictable and safe, and there appears to be more willingness to pursue and abide by international agreements, although enforcement remains a major problem.

International relations

International relations is sometimes regarded as a separate discipline, more usually as a very important specialist subdiscipline within political science. It involves the political interrelationships of **states** (and increasingly a number of non-state institutions). A number of older writers, including **Thucydides**, **Machiavelli**, **Grotius**, **Spinoza** and **Kant**, had much of interest to say on the political relations between states and issues of diplomacy, peace and war. However, international relations only became more systematically studied in the twentieth century, initially as part of a sustained initiative to apply **liberal** principles and the notion of **international law** and collective security to inter-state relations. It was widely hoped that this would make war redundant.

The events leading up to the Second World War marked the failure of this liberal international relations. Following the work of E. H. **Carr** (1939) and Hans **Morgenthau** (1948), a rival **realist** theory of international relations gained widespread acceptance in the cold war era, suggesting that states use their resources to pursue their interests. Some critics suggested that mainstream international relations theory was too state-centred, neglecting the influence of international institutions and other **non-government organizations (NGOs)**. It also neglected the influence of domestic politics on foreign and defence policy. **Waltz** (1979) developed a theory of international relations (dubbed 'neo-realism') that took some notice of other influ-

ences. However, the sudden end of the cold war (which scholars had not predicted) has led to a wider range of theories, including the **constructivist** approach of Alexander **Wendt** and others, and a revival of liberal international relations. (See also Part II, Section 2 on international relations, pages 103–7.)

Judiciary

The **judiciary** is the part of the **state** that deals with legal disputes: both criminal prosecutions, normally brought by the state, and civil cases involving disputes between private citizens or organizations. The judiciary consists of a body of judges, whose detailed organization and functions may differ from state to state. However, commonly there is a hierarchy of judges dealing with different levels of courts, with the highest level dealing with the most important cases, often including **constitutional** issues, and appeals from inferior courts. Increasingly, however, state judicial systems are subject to some degree to the decisions of supranational courts, such as European Court of Justice, the European Court of Human Rights and the International Court of Justice.

Important issues surrounding the judiciary are judicial independence and neutrality, recruitment, bias, and judicial powers, relating especially to the constitution, **legislation** and judicial review of **executive** action. One key issue is judicial independence. This may be regarded as part of the principle of the **separation of powers**, although even those **liberal democracies** where the executive and legislative functions of the state are interdependent and not separate normally proclaim the independence and political neutrality of their judiciary. To reinforce the principle of judicial independence, recruitment is restricted to those with appropriate professional legal qualifications and experience, and there is normally security of tenure (sometimes appointments are for life, sometimes to a relatively late retirement age). Thus it is very difficult to get rid of judges, and influence their decisions, except in 'totalitarian' **dictatorships**, where the judiciary is controlled by the regime.

The judiciary in theory adjudicates on the law rather than makes the law, which is the function of the **legislature** (although the executive may in practice take the dominant role). However, judges inevitably have some discretion in interpreting the law. In common law systems where past court decisions constitute a body of case law that guides subsequent judgements, judges may be effectively making rather than just declaring or interpreting the law.

In some states the highest judges are guardians of the constitution. Thus the Supreme Court of the USA, and similar supreme courts or high courts in other states, can declare laws passed by the legislature or decisions of the executive to be unconstitutional and null and void. The judges have no such power to strike out laws in states where parliament is sovereign. However, even in the United Kingdom, where parliamentary sovereignty is still officially regarded as a key principle of the unwritten constitution, judges may declare a law to be apparently inconsistent with the European Convention on Human Rights, with fast track procedures for its parliamentary amendment.

Even in those states where judges have no power to strike out unconstitutional law there is commonly provision for judicial review of decisions and actions by the executive. Citizens who are aggrieved by a particular action of a minister or government department of other public body may be able to appeal to the courts for a judicial review of the decision.

If the judiciary is normally free from executive control in liberal democracies, this does not necessarily mean that the judiciary is free from political bias. In most countries senior judges are predominantly male, elderly, and come from a relatively narrow social background, and this inevitably (if only subconsciously) influences their outlook and their judgement. Thus it is sometimes alleged that they may be unduly lenient in dealing with white collar crime or male rapists, and they may be too inclined to trust the word of those in **authority** and the police. Some argue that the judiciary has an in-built **conservative** (with a small 'c') bias, and is out of touch with modern values and modern life. This raises issues over the recruitment of the judiciary. In some countries there are pressures to recruit particularly more women, and members of **ethnic minorities** in an attempt to make the judiciary more socially **representative**.

Justice

The term **justice** is used in a range of different but overlapping senses. **Aristotle** distinguished between 'distributive justice', the proper distribution of goods within a **community**, and 'commutative justice', the treatment of individuals in respect of their behaviour towards each other and the community, commonly involving punishment (criminal justice). Both involve notions of fairness or justice; income and wealth should be distributed fairly or justly, those accused of crimes or civil wrongs should be treated fairly or justly according to their deserts. Yet criminal justice essentially requires fairness in procedures (a fair trial), while distributive justice (sometimes called economic or social justice), involves more difficult and questionable assumptions over what constitutes 'fairness' or a just distribution of scarce resources. It is distributive (or economic, or social) justice that has more exercised political theorists, moral philosophers and economists.

Distributive justice has commonly been linked with some notion of **equality. Aristotle** argued that equals should be treated equally, incidentally justifying the unequal treatment of inferiors (including, on his assumptions, women and slaves). **Liberal** theory asserted the equality of man and, originally, equal **rights** to the fruits of the earth, and had some problems in explaining and justifying substantial differences in income and wealth in practice. **Locke** justified unequal **property** rights in terms of individual labour mixed with natural resources. Subsequently, liberals emphasized equality of opportunity rather than outcome (and some later extended this principle of equality of opportunity to women as well as men). **Marx** used the labour theory of value derived from **Locke** and Ricardo to denounce the exploitation of workers, demanding initially 'from each according to his ability, to each according to his work', but ultimately 'from each according to his ability, to each according to his needs'. **Socialism** in all its variants involves some assumptions about redistribution. While a few socialists argued for the abolition of all private property and a form of primitive **communism**, most demanded simply 'more equality' rather than complete equality of outcome (a compromise which, while understandable, poses obvious theoretical and practical problems). Many progressive (or social liberals) and modern **social democrats** enthusiastically endorsed the influential theory of justice as fairness, expounded by John **Rawls**, which appeared to offer a way out of these difficulties. However, **conservative** thinkers from Edmund **Burke** to Michael **Oakeshott** have defended inequality, while both the **neoliberal** Friedrich **Hayek** and Robert

concepts

Nozick have denounced the very principle of distributive justice.

Law and the rule of law

Laws are public rules, today normally made by the **state** through a recognized legal process. They take precedence over other rules. They are compulsory, and supported by penal sanctions, but also widely accepted as binding by state subjects. It is generally conceded that it is better to be ruled by consistent and impersonally executed laws rather than the arbitrary decisions of human rulers. This is a key element of the **rule of law**. Rulers are bound to uphold the law. No one, not princes, nor politicians nor public officials is above or outside the law. **Government** actions without legal **authority** can be challenged in the courts. The **judiciary** is supposed to be independent of the **executive** and impartial in its adjudication. The rule of law also generally held to embody key principles such as natural **justice**, fairness, and reasonableness.

Yet there have often been cases when individuals or groups have felt strongly that a particular law is unjust, to the extent that they feel may justified in defying it (see, for example, **civil disobedience**). Those who defy the law of the state may claim that it is against a higher law, such as the eternal law of nature or the law of God. From the **Stoics** and medieval Christian theologians onwards, some have maintained that human law should be derived from natural law or divine law (with the implication that it is human law that should give way if there is a clash). One obvious problem is that there is far from universal agreement over what is natural law. **Bentham** attacked the whole notion of natural law and the associated idea of natural **rights**. Since then there has been a strong tradition of 'positive law', which suggests that laws are simply the command of the sovereign. However, the return to fashion of the language of rights (if now universal human rights rather than natural rights), and the incorporation of such rights into law, suggest that the natural law tradition is far from dead. The modern American legal and political philosopher Ronald **Dworkin** has championed natural law and natural rights.

The broader relationship between law and morality remains contentious. Some (such as Patrick Devlin) have continued to maintain that state law should uphold public morality. However, many modern jurists (such as H. L. A. Hart) would deny that it is the role of the state, and the state's laws, to enforce public morality, following the arguments of **Mill** that the only justification for interfering with the freedom of the individual is to prevent harm to others.

Leadership

Leadership implies a natural rather than imposed **authority**, derived from qualities that make the leader willingly followed and obeyed, for a leader requires others to be led. While leadership is commonly highly prized not only in politics but also in many other spheres (such as business, the armed forces and schools), criticism is levelled at those who are 'easily led' or 'led astray'. Such criticism suggests a culpable lack of independence and self-reliance on the part of the led, and implies also that leadership may be malign as well as beneficial. This is particularly evident with political leadership. While **Pericles**, Lincoln, **Gandhi** and Churchill are commonly cited as positive role models, other 'strong leaders' such as Hitler and Stalin are now widely execrated, and those who obediently followed them condemned.

Thus attitudes to leadership vary considerably. In **fascist ideology** the leader was viewed as a kind of superman, the *duce* or *Führer*, inspiring an almost religious devotion among his followers. **Communist** leaders were similarly elevated to a quasi-divine role, their images placed everywhere in life, and even in death their bodies embalmed for the faithful to file past. **Nationalist** leaders have sometimes inspired a similar reverence. Such leaders commonly 'emerge' and may be effectively self-appointed, although personal charisma (see **authority**) as well as **power** may secure willing followers who provide a kind of **legitimacy** for their leadership.

Democratic norms require that political leaders should be chosen by and accountable to, and ultimately removable by, those they lead. There may be a preference for **collective** rather than individual leadership. **Conservatives** who assume a natural hierarchy and inequality in human society tend to revere strong leaders, but those with more egalitarian assumptions regard leadership with greater ambivalence. Thus leaders should not be too powerful. Democratic **socialists**, while reluctantly recognizing the need for effective leaders, not least in winning power, have sought to constrain them, recurrently fearing betrayal or the sell-out of party principles. Radical social

concepts

movements, such as the women's movement, the peace movement and the green movement, have commonly avoided identifying leadership roles. For **anarchists** the whole notion of leadership is inimical to everything they believe in (although even so, some anarchists have clearly had a personal charisma that inspired a following).

Left and right

The labels **left** and **right** are still widely used to classify **ideologies**, **political parties** and intra-party factions, and to describe the position of individual thinkers and politicians. The terms derive from the seating positions in representative assemblies following the 1789 French Revolution. Today, on the conventional left–right political spectrum **communists** are placed on the far left, **socialists** on the left, **conservatives** on the right and **fascists** on the far right. **Liberals** are generally located somewhere in the centre, although the term 'liberal' today covers a wide range. Some Liberal parties on the European continent are more to the right, while many British Liberal Democrats see themselves as left or centre-left. In the USA the label 'liberal' is (sometimes pejoratively) attached to radical (usually Democrat) politicians who support **welfare** reforms and champion leftist causes.

left-right, conventional scale

far left   left   centre right   far right

⟵──────────────────────────⟶

communists socialists liberals conservatives fascists

Other ideologies are more difficult to place. **Nationalism** is today more commonly associated with the right, although in different times and places it has been linked with ideas and parties from across the ideological spectrum. **Green thinking** is generally linked with the left, although Greens themselves often claim to be off the scale – 'not left, not right, but forward'. **Anarchism** was usually regarded as far left, although some extreme **free market** thinkers described as anarcho-capitalists are associated with the right. **Feminism**, like green thinking, cuts across the left–right spectrum, although most feminists have been linked with the left.

If degrees of 'left' and 'right' can be marked on a scale, it is by no means clear what that scale is measuring. Attitudes to change? Attitudes to authority? Attitudes to **capitalism** and the **free market**? None of these seems to fit closely the way in which the terms 'left' and 'right' are actually used. Consequently, some argue that the terms are confusing and should be abandoned. Others have suggested a more complex two-dimensional system of classifying political ideas, with attitudes to authority on the vertical axis and attitudes to change on the horizontal axis (Eysenck, 1957). Whatever the merits of such more complex systems of classification of political attitudes, it is unlikely that they will ever displace the more familiar language of left and right.

Legislation and legislature

A **legislature** is in theory a **state** institution responsible for law making (or **legislation**). Legislation is one of the three main functions of the state – the others being the **executive** function (essentially governing and administering the **law**) and the **judicial** function (adjudicating). According to the doctrine of the **separation of powers** these three functions should be entrusted to different institutions. In many countries a directly elected parliament or assembly is primarily responsible for legislation, and these bodies are commonly described as legislatures or legislative assemblies. However, it is widely argued that executives have gained in power at the expense of legislatures. In practice, the executive (particularly where it is a parliamentary executive, drawn from and dominating the legislature) is often the main source of legislative proposals, and the role of many parliaments or assemblies involves more deliberation and discussion than the initiation of laws. (This is perhaps particularly true of the European Parliament within the European Union, although it has acquired more influence over legislation in recent years.) Arguably also, particularly in countries with a common law tradition, the **judiciary** has a key role in making and not just adjudicating on the law. Thus although legislatures may be involved in making the law, they are not the sole or even the main source of new law.

Legitimacy

Legitimacy is a term that can be used in a literal sense to mean lawfulness. Thus a **government** or an order or a ministerial act may be considered legitimate if derived from law or exercised under lawful **authority**. Lawyers distinguish between *de jure* authority which one is legally obliged to obey, and *de facto* **power** which is not lawful (although it may be prudential to obey or acknowledge it). Sometimes a government in exile is recognized as the legitimate government, even if another government wields effective power over the territory. Yet commonly a claim to legitimacy can not long survive effective loss of power, while a *de facto* government over time gains recognition and legitimacy.

For political theorists issues of legitimacy are bound up with the grounds of political obligation – why should I obey the state? Some asserted the ruler's authority was derived from God, others assumed an original contract between people and government. Today, in the west it is widely argued that only governments deriving their authority from free and fair elections are fully legitimate.

Quite apart from these legal and philosophical arguments, popular acceptance of legitimacy is in practice very important for national unity and the maintenance of law and order, as can be plainly seen where the majority or a sizeable minority do not accept a regime's legitimacy. Thus in Northern Ireland much of the large Catholic minority never accepted the division of Ireland and the legitimacy of the government of Northern Ireland, nor the authority of the police. In many other parts of the world (for example Sri Lanka, Chechnya, Palestine, Ethiopia, Afghanistan and Iraq) there has been long-running violence and sometimes full civil war arising from the rejection of the governing regime's legitimacy by a substantial section of its inhabitants.

Sociologists from Max **Weber** onwards have been more interested in how a popular belief in legitimacy arises – why do people in practice regard some power as legitimate? Weber distinguished between three main types (or causes) of authority: traditional, charismatic and legal-rational. While the first and third might be acknowledged by lawyers, charismatic authority on its own has no legal basis, although it may be widely acknowledged without coercion.

Liberalism

Liberalism is sometimes viewed as the dominant or **hegemonic ideology** of the modern western world. Indeed most other western ideologies, including **socialism** and some versions of **conservatism**, might be regarded as 'variants of liberalism'.

Like all ideologies, liberalism has evolved over a long period and has varied considerably over time and space. Although the term 'liberalism' was not coined until the nineteenth century, its roots can be traced back much further. It drew inspiration from the religious reformations of the sixteenth century, the seventeenth-century scientific revolution, and the eighteenth-century Enlightenment. It was however, industrialization from the late eighteenth century onwards that transformed economic and social relations and created new **class** interests with a commitment to a liberal political programme of reform. From a **Marxist** perspective liberalism was the political creed reflecting the class interests of the rising **bourgeoisie**, the owners of capital, as against the interests of absolute **monarchy** and the old landed **aristocracy** on the one hand and the industrial workers on the other. However, liberalism also received considerable support from the professions, shopkeepers and skilled workers. The form its political programme took varied somewhat according to local circumstances, but it generally included constitutional reform, religious toleration, national self-determination, free trade and **free markets**.

Key linked liberal concepts include **freedom**, **individualism**, **rationalism**, **toleration** and the free market. For the liberal, individual human beings, rather than nations, races or classes, are the starting point for any theorizing about society, politics or economics. Society is seen as an aggregate of individuals, who should be free to pursue their own rational self-interest. No one else, not rulers, nor priests or civil servants, are capable of determining the individual's interest for him or her. Individuals should concede a similar freedom to others to pursue their own economic, political and religious interests in their own way.

In the early nineteenth century liberalism was widely perceived as a **revolutionary** creed posing a threat to states and governments almost everywhere. Liberals commonly demanded freedom from state tyranny and oppression. As they also favoured economic freedom, free trade and free markets, they also opposed government intervention in the economy, which was commonly exercised to protect domestic agriculture and industry. Yet in the course of the nineteenth century and into the twentieth century some liberals, such as the New Liberals in Britain, increasingly favoured more state intervention to provide education and health and unemployment insurance. The extension of the franchise, substantially the result of liberal pressure, and the growing acceptance of representative **democracy**, helped transform liberal attitudes to the **state**. Yet elsewhere in Europe some traditional liberals retained a dogmatic attachment to the free market. More recently the revival of free-market ideas has been associated with what has been described as **neoliberalism** (a creed diametrically opposed to the interventionist New Liberalism of the early twentieth-century British Liberal leadership).

Today there is no longer any clear agreement over what the terms 'liberal' and 'liberalism' mean. Liberals are generally placed somewhere in the centre of the left–right political spectrum, and this is still reasonably accurate in terms of some liberals. Yet in the USA the term 'liberal' has been widely used as a derogatory term for those who are perceived to be 'soft' on **communism**, **terrorism**, and law and order, and who favour socialized medicine. Thus in American terms a liberal is on the left of the political spectrum. Some European liberals, such as the British Liberal Democrats, see themselves as progressive or centre-left. Others like the Free Democrats in Germany might be more accurately described as centre right, while other liberals are further to the right than European **Christian democrats** or the UK Conservative Party. Such diverse thinkers as **Keynes**, **Hayek** and **Rawls** have all described themselves as liberals. Any discussion of liberalism today requires some definition of terms and the use of a number of hybrid labels such as 'economic liberal' or 'social liberal' to differentiate between conflicting interpretations of the creed.

Liberty

See **freedom** and also **liberalism**.

Mandate

A **mandate** is an instruction or command that has to be obeyed. Thus a delegate to a conference or assembly may say that he or she has been 'mandated' by the members they represent to vote in a particular way. The concept of the mandate is more specifically used in politics today by elected **governments**, to argue that they have a popular mandate, an endorsement from the people, to implement specific policies in their **party** election manifesto. Opposition parties may sometimes argue that the government has no mandate for policy proposals that were not foreshadowed in the manifesto. Governing parties may however argue that they have a more general mandate from the electorate to govern.

Although the concept of an electoral mandate is still widely employed, there are a number of obvious problems with it. Party manifestos are commonly long on general aims and short on specific commitments. Few voters read them, and many may be ignorant of the details of the party programme. Voters cannot discriminate between particular policy pledges – agreeing with some and rejecting others – but have to accept the whole package. Thus even if most voters have preferred a party to its main competitors, this does not mean they have necessarily endorsed its whole programme.

Often a party may be elected in spite of, rather than because of, specific policy commitments. In practice, circumstances may change after the election, justifying a government in acting contrary to a specific manifesto pledge, or new circumstances arise that could not be foreseen at the time of the election, and governments may have to devise policies in areas ignored in the manifesto.

The notion of a mandate is more difficult to apply in multi-party systems commonly involving coalition government. To form a government, parties have to bargain and compromise, and are sometimes obliged to jettison key elements in their programme to reach agreement with potential partners in government. Such bargaining commonly follows an election, and is a process from which voters are thus effectively excluded. Thus it may be difficult for such a coalition government to claim an electoral mandate, although this does not necessarily restrict its freedom of action.

Marxism and Marxism-Leninism

Marxism is a term that clearly involves the ideas of Karl **Marx**, elaborated over a lifetime, and also as interpreted during his life and after his death by his close collaborator, Friedrich **Engels**. It is a term that more broadly encompasses the ideas of the numerous and diverse followers of Marx, and movements inspire by Marx in the nineteenth and twentieth centuries. How far Marx himself would have endorsed these ideas and movements is contentious, and clearly unknowable on developments after his death, although Engels reported that Marx observed of French 'Marxists' in the 1870s, 'All I know is that I am not a Marxist' (Engels, 1890, in Marx and Engels, 1959: 396).

There were many variants of Marxism around the world, including the western world. The most influential was **Marxism-Leninism**. This involved the interpretation of Marx's ideas by the Russian Bolshevik leader, **Lenin**, both before and during the Bolshevik Revolution, and the subsequent practice of the government of the Soviet Union by Lenin himself, and his successor, Stalin. It became the orthodoxy of **communist** parties around the world, and a model to be followed by communist regimes that came to power after the Second World War, although some of these pursued a distinctive path ('Titoism' in the former Yugoslavia, 'Maoism' in China). Broadly speaking, Marxism-Leninism in practice involved one party **dictatorship** and extensive **state** control of the economy.

Some western Marxists substantially endorsed Marxism-Leninism and what they regarded as 'really existing **socialism**' in Soviet Russia and eastern Europe, although some who continued to revere Lenin rejected Stalinism. Others followed the ideas of Stalin's defeated rival **Trotsky**. Others again followed the ideas of **Bernstein** and subsequently **Kautsky**, and endorsed a parliamentary route to **socialism**, which was denounced by Marxist-Leninists as 'revisionism'. The Italian Communist Party, influenced by the ideas of **Gramsci**, and operating in a liberal parliamentary system, pursued its own version of 'euro-communism'. There were also influential academic strands of Marxism, particularly the critical theory of the Frankfurt school (**Adorno**, **Marcuse**, **Habermas**, although some of these effectively moved away from Marxism), the existential Marxism of **Sartre** and French structuralist Marxism (**Althusser**, **Poulantzas**).

Mass media

The term **mass media** refers to all those forms of communication where large numbers of people are exposed to an identical message. They include the print media (newspapers, magazines and books) and the electronic media: film, radio, television and increasingly the internet (sometimes referred to as the new media).

The 1960s media guru Marshall McLuhan argued that 'the medium is the message', implying that each medium of communication has its own characteristics that shape the message that is received. Thus television is primarily a visual medium, and the main message is conveyed by the pictures. Radio, although an oral/aural medium, abhors silence, so that in interviews and debates prompt short answers work best – there

is no time for considered reflection. Print can deal with serious ideas more appropriately, although tabloid journalism deals in headlines, slogans and pictures.

A free and diverse media expressing a range of political views is widely seen as an essential precondition of a pluralist **democracy**. Media control and media bias are major concerns of political analysts. The concentration of newspaper empires and television channels in the hands of a few **powerful** media magnates (such as Rupert Murdoch or Silvio Berlusconi) is a particular concern. The control of editors and journalists by media owners is another. Some argue that the internet offers more scope for the expression of a wide range of views and real debate, but its impact on politics, although of growing significance, is still essentially peripheral compared with the press and mainstream television. Some television channels and some newspapers exhibit a strong and persistent political bias.

Does media bias matter? Some argue that people do not expose themselves to messages they do not agree with, or filter out or reinterpret messages that do not fit their preconceived views. Many may ignore politics altogether in the media, not watching news and current affairs programmes on television, and turning straight to the sports or fashion pages in newspapers. Yet it seems unlikely that the constant reiteration of a particular message does not have some effect, even if, and perhaps especially if, the main impact is subliminal. There is some evidence, for example, that newspapers can influence voting and perhaps on occasion swing elections. At another level radicals of all kinds argue that the mass media are biased towards establishment values, masculine attitudes, **capitalism** and consumerism, and it is this that legitimizes and reinforces the status quo. (For more on the mass media see Part V, pages 231–6.)

Materialism

Materialism in philosophy emphasizes 'matter' over 'mind'. In political theory it implies that only the material or physical world is relevant for the explanation of political and social phenomena. It implies a rejection of abstract moral, religious or spiritual values for a concentration on material interests and material welfare. Materialism can thus be contrasted with the idealism of **Plato**, **Kant** and **Hegel**, for whom knowledge related to

concepts

intangible ideals or ideas. **Marx** famously claimed to have found Hegel standing on his head and turned him the right way up. Thus Marx adapted Hegel's dialectic, applied by Hegel to the development of ideas, to the conflict between economic **class** interests over time, which became known as dialectical materialism or historical materialism. For Marx, all ideas, religious, moral or economic, were expressions of material interests. 'It is not the consciousness of men that determines their being, but on the contrary, their social being that determines their consciousness.'

Meritocracy

Meritocracy suggests another term of ancient Greek origin, but it was coined by Michael Young (in *The Rise of the Meritocracy* [1958]) to describe the rule of those with merit. 'Merit' might be held to involve a combination of aptitude and effort. This could be interpreted as rule of the deserving, the natural consequence of **equality** of opportunity and social mobility (although Young was actually rather critical of meritocracy). Indeed, recruitment and promotion based on merit, rather than bribery or social connections, may be regarded as a key principle of modern **bureaucracy**, as described by Max **Weber**. Yet talents are unequally distributed, so a meritocracy is by definition an **elite**, and not socially **representative** of the mass of the people. There is the added implication that they know better what the masses really want and need than the masses themselves. Thus meritocracy has questionable implications for democracy.

Militarism and military dictatorship

Militarism involves extolling military virtues, military discipline and military power. Ancient Sparta is often cited as an example of a militaristic state, along with some more recent or contemporary political societies. High spending on the armed forces, and a readiness to use them, might be taken as an illustration of militarism. The military may be extremely influential even in a **democracy**, because the armed forces are themselves big business, and the manufacture and sale of arms may be important to the national economy. Critics refer to the power of the military-industrial complex.

Where the armed forces are sufficiently well-equipped and numerous, their leaders may be tempted to seize political **power** and install a military **dictatorship**, as often happened in the past,

and is still not uncommon in the modern world (Finer, 1962). Generals may seize power in a time of (perceived) chaos, promising order and prosperity, and ultimately the restoration of civilian **democratic** rule, although they are often reluctant to relinquish power. A military dictatorship may be terminated by a counter-coup among the armed forces, to be followed by a new dictatorship under different personnel. It may ultimately collapse as a consequence of economic failure or (ironically) military failure. Thus the military junta in Argentina was brought down by its military defeat in the Falkland Islands (or Malvinas) in 1982.

Model

In politics and the social sciences generally the term **model** is used to describe a scaled-down simplified version of reality. Such models may be only verbally described, although they are often portrayed in diagrammatic form, involving highly simplified and abstract portrayals of significant relationships between institutions or variables. Particularly in economics, models are sometimes developed into workable computer simulations, into which key statistics can be fed to produce predicted outcomes. (The British Treasury has developed and used such models.) In politics, models are generally more simple and illustrative. Some models involve rival hypotheses about the working of the political system as a whole (such as **elitism** and **pluralism**), or part of it.

Monarchy

Monarchy is another term deriving from the ancient Greek, meaning literally rule by one. In practice the Greeks distinguished between monarchy (a traditional or legitimate single ruler) and tyranny (dictatorial rule by a usurper).

Monarchy was the dominant form of government in Europe from the Middle Ages through to the nineteenth century. In the Middle Ages the effective power of monarchy was often limited by the power of nobility and/or the church. While most kings owed their position to heredity, there were some survivals of (very limited) forms of elective monarchy (for example, in Germany). However, subsequently, monarchy became identified with rule by a single person owing his or her position to hereditary descent from previous rulers. In the seventeenth and eighteenth centuries some of these hereditary rulers appeared to have unlimited or absolute **power** (see **absolutism**). In the nineteenth and twentieth centuries monarchy was overthrown in some countries and limited in others. Most surviving kings and queens are **constitutional** monarchs. They reign but no longer rule. Some argue that monarchy retains some advantages for the role of formal head of state, others that the hereditary principle is inconsistent with **democracy**.

Multiculturalism

The term **multiculturalism** can be used in a largely descriptive way, simply suggesting that many societies and nations involve peoples with different cultures, languages and faiths living together. Multiculturalism in this descriptive sense is increasingly a feature of the modern world. From the 1970s onwards the term has also been used in a more prescriptive or normative sense, suggesting that the diversity involved in multiculturalism has positive benefits, and that governments should protect and support cultural diversity, rather than encourage the assimilation or integration of **ethnic minorities**. Multiculturalism in this normative sense recognizes and respects distinctive minority cultures. Indeed it is commonly argued that a variety of dress, food, customs and beliefs can enrich the whole community, creating an interesting and vibrant diversity. One consequence of multiculturalism has been the increasing acceptance of hyphenated identities that suggest a dual allegiance, such as Irish-American or British-Muslim or Black-British. Multiculturalism accommodates such multiple identities, and fits easily within the more complex interlocking political allegiances.

Yet there are also some issues over multiculturalism. Some fear that multiculturalism is dangerously eroding formerly common **national** values and identities. Others are less resistant to the ideal of multiculturalism, but point out that in practice those from different cultures commonly have minimal contact with each other, living separate lives in largely segregated communities, and that these are breeding grounds for damaging inter-communal conflict. Beyond that there are some concerns that multiculturalism, in so far as it legitimizes the continued use of minority languages and other distinctive cultural practices, may reduce the economic opportunities of those from minority backgrounds. Faster integration might enable them to compete more successfully, on equal terms.

Others again fear that multicultural values can be used to ignore or trump what they consider to be universal human **rights**. Thus under the influence of multiculturalism, a blind eye may be turned to practices unacceptable in a liberal democracy, such as forced marriages, the persecution of homosexuals, and limitations on freedom of speech. It sometimes appears difficult to reconcile respect for distinctive community identities and cultures with widely accepted individual rights, although critics (such as Bhikhu Parekh, 2000) suggest that some 'universal' human rights involve a strong western cultural bias, and undervalue alternative traditions (see Part V for more on multiculturalism).

Nation, nation-state and nationalism

A **nation** may consist of a **community** of people, bound together by some characteristic they all share and regard as important, such as a common language, religion, ethnicity or culture. Yet ultimately there are no objective criteria. A nation exists where a people feel they constitute a nation. Thus nations exist in the minds of their members. They are 'imagined communities' (Anderson, 1991).

The term 'nation' is sometimes used almost interchangeably with the term **state**, but while a nation is a community of people a state is a political and **governmental** unit. The term **nation-state** is used for a state whose subjects or citizens comprise those who belong to a single nation, however that is defined. Many older states were (and some today still are) multi-national, the consequence of past conquests, marriage alliances, and conventions governing the hereditary succession of rulers.

Nationalism is the political doctrine or **ideology** that nations should form states and states should consist of nations. A distinction is sometimes drawn between separation nationalism and unification nationalism. Separation nationalism involves a national minority within a multinational state seeking independence or national self-determination. Historical examples include Greece, Finland, and more recently Slovakia. Current examples of nationalist movements seeking independence include Quebec (from Canada) and the Basque separatists (from Spain). Unification nationalism involves peoples from separate states with a common sense of nationhood seeking to combine to form a new political union. Examples

concepts

include Italian and German unification in the nineteenth century, and more recently the unification of east and west Germany following the fall of the Berlin Wall.

There is disagreement over the emergence of national consciousness and nationalism. Some argue that a sense of national consciousness or national identity emerged in some communities many centuries ago (e.g. Greenfeld, 1992). Others suggest that a sense of nationhood is more recent, the product of industrialization, a **mass media** and mass education, and often shaped by states or ruling **elites** in their own interest. Gellner (1983: 55) observes, 'It is nationalism that engenders nations, and not the other way around.'

Although nationalism in theory is a principle with general application, in practice it is often expressed in a very specific and exclusive form. Some political thinkers (e.g. **Mazzini**) hoped that the general application of the principle of national self-determination would lead to a new international era of peace and cooperation between nation-states. Yet most nationalists seem less interested in national self-determination as a general principle than in the rights and grievances of their own particular nation. For such nationalists, 'the interests and values of their nation take priority over all over interests and values' (Breuilly, 1993: 2). Sometimes this has taken the form of an aggressive nationalism, under which the success of the nation in competition or conflict with other nations vindicates its own superiority.

The US President Woodrow Wilson tried to apply the principle of self-determination in the peace settlement at the end of the First World War. In practice the new nation-states established then commonly contained substantial minorities with different national identities and an enduring sense of grievance.

Nationalization and privatization

Nationalization involves the **state** (rather than private) ownership and control of key economic enterprises. The 'common ownership of the means of production' was a key **socialist** objective from the nineteenth century, as a means to secure a more **equal** society and a more efficient planned economy. Some socialists hoped this would involve effective 'workers' control' or producer cooperatives, although these hopes were substantially disappointed. In the twentieth century some **liberals** and **conservatives** in western Europe accepted **pragmatic** arguments for taking specific industries into state hands, particularly in wartime and the aftermath of war. Thus industries regarded as of strategic importance (for defence or other national purposes) and declining industries requiring state support for their concentration and rationalization were nationalized. In France some firms that had collaborated with the Germans, including the car manufacturers Renault, were taken over. A state-run industrial sector became part of the post-war consensus. Even socialist governments did not pursue wholesale nationalization, while other parties, such as European **Christian Democrats** and the British Conservative Party largely accepted the notion of a mixed economy.

The record of nationalized industries is contentious, although many were losing money before they were nationalized (Marxist critics suggest this explains why nationalization was not more strongly resisted). In general, they were not popular. **Neoliberal** critics argued they were inherently inefficient as they were effectively state monopolies, not subject to the discipline of the **free market**, and subject to endless political interference in key management and investment decisions.

The erosion of the post-war consensus and the rising influence of the free market ideas of neoliberals and the **New Right** led to the **privatization** (or denationalization) of many formerly state-run undertakings. Across Europe and elsewhere in the western world privatization was pursued by governments of the **right**, centre and even the **left**. Privatization brought in capital receipts for governments and the prospect of reducing the continuing burden on state finances of largely loss-making undertakings. Increased competition, it was argued, could only benefit consumers. In practice some state monopolies became privately owned and run monopolies, requiring the maintenance of some state regulation to protect consumer interests, and in some cases considerable ongoing state support, while other nationalized industries were forcibly broken up, causing problems for coordination. Governments soon discovered that denationalization did not depoliticize key issues around some industries.

Nature, natural law and natural rights

In political philosophy **nature**, what is natural or inborn, is contrasted with *convention*, meaning custom or practice. While nature is universal, custom and practice vary between and within societies. Some political theorists, including **Aquinas**, **Grotius** and **Locke**, argued that behind the varied positive laws of particular states there lay a universal **natural law**, with the implication that natural law provided a standard against which the laws of **states** could be measured. There was a further implication that where natural law and positive law clashed, it was natural law that was the higher law that should prevail. It was also commonly argued that there were universal and inalienable natural **rights** (see also **rights** and **law**).

In practice there were rather different understandings of nature, or what was natural. For some it was to be identified with an assumed original state of nature before the establishment of human society, **government** and civilization. For others nature was what was perceived to be common to all persons and societies. For religious thinkers, nature was simply what God intended for humankind, and thus natural law was, in effect, divine law.

Critics, such as Jeremy **Bentham**, ridiculed the whole notion of natural law and natural rights. Law and rights, he argued, had to be enforceable to be effective, and there was no means of enforcing natural law and natural rights. In practice, the concepts of natural law and natural rights were used to question and sometimes undermine positive law and legal rights.

Neoliberalism

Neoliberalism is a term commonly applied to distinguish modern economic **liberalism** from the progressive or social liberalism that had become dominant in parts of the western world in the course of the last century. The ideas were not new – they were derived from the **free market** economics of classical liberalism. Such free market ideas had become unfashionable in the decades immediately after the Second World War. Economic crises in the 1970s provoked a rethink, which involved a new interest in the free market or neoliberal ideas of **Hayek**, **Friedman**, and the rational or public choice school of **Buchanan**, **Tullock** and **Niskanen**. Some politicians and thinkers combined this economic liberalism with some features of traditional **conservatism** (see **New Right**).

New institutionalism

See **institutionalism and new institutionalism**.

New Right

The **New Right** is a term used to distinguish ideas and policies adopted from the 1970s onwards by politicians, parties and movements on the **right** of the political spectrum from many of the ideas and policies pursued by traditional right or **conservative** parties. The novel ingredient was the **free market** liberalism or **neoliberalism** of **Hayek**, **Friedman** and the **rational choice** school, rather than economic ideas of the old right (more wedded to **nationalism** and economic protectionism). However, the New Right involved a blend of neoliberal economics with elements of traditional conservatism. Leading converts included Keith Joseph and Margaret Thatcher in the British Conservative Party (which had previously embraced **consensus**, the mixed economy, the **welfare state** and planning), and the Republican administration in the USA of Ronald Reagan. New right ideas also increasingly challenged the formerly dominant ideas of **Christian democracy** and **social democracy** in much of western Europe.

Non-governmental organizations (NGOs)

A **non-governmental organization** (or **NGO**) is a term used principally in the study of **international relations** to describe international voluntary organizations that are part of neither **government** nor the commercial sector. They include organizations such as the International Committee of the Red Cross, Médécins Sans Frontières, Oxfam, Amnesty International and Human Rights Watch. The number of registered NGOs had risen to 37,000 by the year 2000 (Brown, 2005: 209). Some NGOs work closely with inter-governmental organizations (IGOs), such the United Nations. They have had considerable success in pressuring national **governments**, trans-national corporations (TNCs) and IGOs, particularly on human **rights** and **environmental** issues. The increasing importance of NGOs has been one element in the criticism of **realist** and neorealist state-centric theories of international relations.

Normative

The term **normative** is used to describe the *prescription* of rules (or norms). Much traditional political theory is normative, involving the prescription of preferred forms of **government**, political principles, obligations and **rights**. Modern political science, by contrast, aspires to be posi-

concepts

tive or objective, avoiding prescription in favour of accurate description and analysis. However, the distinction is far from water-tight. Some traditional political thinkers (such as **Aristotle** and **Machiavelli**) combined both prescription and an attempt at scientific analysis. Some modern political scientists (for example **Downs**, **Dahl**, **Putnam**) often seem to straddle the divide between positive analysis and normative recommendations.

Obligation

An **obligation** in general terms is any duty or act involving some form of moral compulsion. Thus a father may be considered to have an obligation to look after his children, an employer an obligation of care for his workers, a borrower an obligation to repay his debt. A distinction may however be drawn between a legal obligation, backed by clear enforceable sanctions against non-compliance, and a moral obligation, depending on individual conscience and social pressure.

Political obligation is commonly more narrowly defined in terms of the question, why and how far is a citizen obliged to obey the **state** (or the **government** of the day). This was a far from academic question in a world of political instability, involving frequent conflicts between rival claimants to political authority, **revolution** and civil war. Social contract theorists such as **Hobbes** and **Locke** derived the obligation to accept the **authority** of a government and obey its **laws** from a prior historical or hypothetical promise. Thus government rested on the consent of the governed. For some contract theorists the obligation to obedience was conditional only, depending on how far the sovereign kept to the terms of agreement. Accordingly Locke (but not Hobbes) conceded a limited right of rebellion. Yet regardless of whether such a contract or promise had ever been made, clearly most existing subjects had never formally promised obedience, as contract theorists generally acknowledged. Thus they argued (essentially following the arguments in **Plato's** *Crito*) that continuing to live in a state amounted to a tacit promise to recognize its authority.

The philosopher David **Hume** mocked not only the notion of an original contract, but the derivation of political obligation from a promise. His argument was simply that we should obey the state because society could not otherwise subsist, a **utilitarian** argument. Yet the notion that a government can forfeit the obligation of subjects to obey

it has endured. Indeed, **international law** and the proceedings of war crimes tribunals do not accept the familiar defence of those accused of war crimes that they were simply 'obeying orders', implying an obligation to disobey established political authority in certain circumstances.

Oligarchy

Oligarchy is a term derived from classical Greek, which means literally 'rule by the few'. Oligarchy may be contrasted with **monarchy** (the rule of a single person) and **democracy** (rule of the people, or of the many rather than the few). **Aristotle** distinguished between **aristocracy** (literally 'rule of the best', or on Aristotle's analysis rule of the few in the common interest) and oligarchy (rule of the few in their own interest). The rule of the few rather than the many was once regarded as normal and even desirable, but with the widespread acceptance of the norms of **representative democracy** it has become a pejorative term. Writing in the late nineteenth and early twentieth centuries against the democratic tide, the classical elitists (**Pareto**, **Mosca** and **Michels**) argued that oligarchy was in practice inevitable, even in states that claimed to be democratic, and Pareto certainly believed oligarchy was also preferable. More recently, radical **elite** theorists and **Marxists** have questioned neither the possibility nor desirability of democracy, but have pointed to the continuing concentration of **power** in the hands of the few in modern states that are supposedly democratic.

Pacifism

Pacifism involves the rejection of violence and war even in the face of aggression. Thus pacifists have refused to join armies and have resisted compulsory conscription, often facing prison or worse where a right to conscientious objection was not recognized. While some pacifists were prepared to join the fire service or medical service in times of war, others were opposed to any duties that might indirectly assist the war effort.

Some **anarchists** have also been pacifists. Political leaders who have renounced all violence and preferred to use peaceful resistance or **civil disobedience** include **Gandhi** and Martin Luther **King**

Patriarchy

Patriarchy means literally rule of the father. The patriarchal principle supported the inheritance of titles and property through the male line, and was considered to have implications for political authority. Thus the rule of the father of the family for **Aristotle** prefigured and justified the rule of kings over states. Filmer (1588–1653) derived the divine right of kings from the original gift of authority by God to Adam.

Today the term 'patriarchy' is used by **feminists** to mean male domination over women generally. While they argue, like Aristotle, that male **power** in society and government is analogous to and stems from the power of fathers within the family, unlike Aristotle they reject the whole principle and practice of patriarchy. For radical feminists patriarchy is all-pervasive, underpinning male domination and female subordination throughout society, even if there are formal legal commitments to gender **equality**.

Plebiscite

See under **referendum and plebiscite**.

Pluralism and neo-pluralism

Pluralism implies a broad range or plurality of organizations, interests and values, rather than a monolithic or **totalitarian** society and state where differences are not tolerated. Pluralists argue that **power** and influence are widely diffused rather than concentrated in the hands of the few or a single **elite**. While these assumptions are highly compatible with **democracy**, pluralists emphasize the importance of opportunities for ordinary citizens to influence the political process informally, particularly through involvement in **pressure group** activity, in addition to their inevitably more limited contribution to formal representative institutions.

Pluralists maintain this pressure group activity aids and improves the democratic process rather than subverting it (as some early critics had argued). In an open democratic society there are ample opportunities for anyone who wants to defend an interest or promote a cause to organize with others to influence decision makers and the wider public. This will commonly encourage those who take a different view to establish opposed groups, leading to a balance of interests (sometimes described as countervailing power). The information and arguments put forward by conflicting interests and causes put more relevant knowledge in the public domain, improve the quality of debate and aid decision making. Plural-

ists see this competition for influence between countless groups as the essence of democracy. They see governments as responding to the sum of group pressures, acting as neutral arbiters between conflicting interests in society.

Pluralism is closely linked with mainstream American political science. It grew out of the group theory of A. F. **Bentley**, developed and extended by David Truman, Nelson Polsby and especially Robert **Dahl**. Radical **elite theorists** and western **Marxists** are among their critics. Briefly, critics of pluralism argue that there are massive inequalities in resources and influence between some groups and others, and that the **state** is not neutral, but encourages some interests while effectively excluding others. Some of the argument has focused on case studies of specific political communities, both in the USA and elsewhere (see Part V).

Modern **neopluralists**, including Charles **Lindblom**, J. K **Galbraith**, and Robert **Dahl** himself in his later writing, accept that the state is not a neutral referee but an active participant in the game. While continuing to maintain that power and influence is fairly widely dispersed, they acknowledged that some interests, particularly business interests, have considerable practical influence while others may be virtually excluded from the political process. Some have viewed **corporatism** as a constrained variant of pluralism, in which free and open competition for influence between countless groups is replaced by a policy process involving a few peak or umbrella groups and government in a relationship of mutual dependence.

Police and police state

The **police** enforce the criminal law, and effective policing is important in any political community, particularly for those who are most vulnerable, including the very young, the old and minority groups, although a professional police force, separate from the armed forces, is a relatively modern development. Effective policing requires extensive powers and resources (including weaponry) to deal with lawbreakers, some of whom are among the most dangerous and ruthless elements in society, and in some circumstances police powers may be exceeded or abused. Unnecessary force may be used, correct procedures ignored and in extreme instances evidence fabricated or bribes taken. This raises the issue *Quis custodiet custo-*

concepts

des? (Who guards the guards?). While it is widely recognized that the police should be free from the detailed supervision of politicians, questions arise about police **accountability** and control, which different countries have sought to address in different ways. There are also questions surrounding the recruitment and composition of police forces. Where the police are drawn from a relatively narrow segment of society they may not enjoy the confidence and support of some sections of the community, who may view them as the enemy rather than their protectors.

Some countries are described as **police states**. Here the function of the police is to control rather than protect the public. Police powers are not checked, and they have wide discretion to act as they see fit, detaining whom they please and executing summary justice on them. Commonly such abuse of police power is associated with **dictatorships** and one-party states. Here the police are used to suppress opposition in a blatantly partisan way, and there is no pretence of even-handedness. (Examples include the role of the Gestapo in Nazi Germany and the KGB in the Soviet Union.)

Political parties

Political parties are often rather unsatisfactorily defined as political organizations that contest **elections** or seek to control **government**. However, parties in one-party dictatorships are not involved in effective competition for control of government, while many small parties that contest elections in democracies have no realistic expectation of **power**. Yet parties have clearly played a crucial role in modern politics and government, particularly in representative **democracies**.

Once party was widely condemned. Thus a founding father of the US Constitution, Thomas **Jefferson**, regarded party and faction as a damaging source of disunity in state and society. Yet it was in the USA that modern political parties developed. Party politics is still often deplored. However, political parties feature in virtually every modern democratic system, even where the prevailing political climate seemed initially hostile to them. That suggests that political parties are integral to representative democracy, and perform important functions.

❭ Political choice – it is largely through parties that voters are given an effective choice at elections between competing teams of political leaders, with distinctive policies and ideas. Although voters can choose independent candidates, overwhelmingly they prefer candidates with party labels. Thus in practice **representation** is through parties.

❭ Political recruitment – it is through parties that individuals are recruited and trained for political office (as ministers, elected representatives and so on).

❭ Reconciling and aggregating interests – while **pressure groups** 'articulate' or promote their own special interests, parties 'aggregate' or bring together a range of interests, and help transform a mass of sometimes conflicting demands into a coherent programme that can be placed before voters at elections. Larger parties almost inevitably involve coalitions of interests, with some internal tensions.

❭ Political participation – joining parties provides another opportunity for ordinary citizens to participate in the political process. Party members can help to select candidates for elections in their area, can increasingly contribute to the choice of party leaders and other party positions, and may seek to influence party policy.

❭ Political identity – parties have provided many people with a sense of their own political identity, as they willingly gave support and loyalty to a party over a lifetime (although note that identification with parties has weakened considerably more recently).

❭ Political communication – parties provide a two-way channel of communication between political leaders and their supporters. Party leaders will seek to convince their supporters of the merits of contentious policies. Party opinion may sometimes be an important constraint on the party leadership.

❭ **Accountability** and control – as government is effectively party government, it is principally through parties that government, at various levels, is held accountable for its performance, particularly at election times.

Some of these functions – particularly political recruitment, and to an extent reconciling and aggregating interests, participation and communication, have also been performed by parties in one-party states, although these will crucially not involve effective democratic choice, and only limited accountability and control.

Leading political parties in the middle of the twentieth century were mass parties, with millions of paid-up members within complex multi-tiered organizations. Although parties remain important in modern democracies today, membership and active involvement has fallen markedly almost everywhere, to such an extent that at local level, party organization may often be moribund. Thus some argue that parties today have become little more than electoral machines in which remaining rank and file members have little influence (see Part V for more on parties and party systems).

Politics

Politics is very variously defined, with definitions both reflecting underlying ideological assumptions, and influencing the scope of the subject and how it is studied. (For an extended discussion of the meaning of politics, see Part I, Section 1.)

Populism

The term **populism** has been used to describe specific political movements in the USA and Tsarist Russia in the late nineteenth century, although it has been more generally applied to political programmes designed to appeal to ordinary people. This might appear to be the essence of **democracy**, although the term populism is commonly employed in a pejorative way, to mean pandering to popular prejudices on issues such as capital punishment or immigration. Thus it is often argued, against populist demands, that elected politicians should lead rather than follow public opinion, and should exercise their own judgement rather than follow blindly the views of their constituents or the wider public (see **Burke**). In representative **democracies** populist politicians may appeal direct to the people, ignoring parliament and mainstream parties. Such politicians may have what Max **Weber** described as charismatic **authority**. They may also argue that the people rather than parliament should decide on key issues through **plebiscites** or **referendums** (plebiscitory democracy).

Postindustrialism and postindustrial society

Postindustrialism (or **postindustrial society**) is a term commonly used to describe a society or economy that is dependent no longer largely upon mining and manufacturing, but on services,

knowledge, information and communication. While many countries in the developing world remain preindustrial, and others are rapidly industrializing, most western economies may now be described as postindustrial. Note however that some states and societies (such as India) now play a key role in services, knowledge, information and communication, without ever having been extensively industrialized. A postindustrial society may have extensive social and political implications, for population distribution, class structure, interests, power, ideas and values. Daniel **Bell** wrote an influential text, *The Coming of Post-Industrial Society* (1976), which explored the concept and its implications.

Postmaterialism

Postmaterialism is a concept used to describe an attitude or culture that is concerned no longer largely with increasing material wealth and prosperity, but with personal fulfilment and maintaining and improving the quality of life and the environment. Post-material attitudes are commonly associated with advanced western economies where basic material needs have been substantially met, and much of the population enjoys material prosperity. According to Ronald **Inglehart** (1990, 1997), such a postmaterial culture is particularly evident among the younger generation in advanced capitalist economies. (See also Part V under 'Public opinion, political culture and democracy', page 215.)

Postmodernism

Postmodernism is a term that has been widely applied to developments in art, architecture, aesthetics and literary criticism, as well as psychology, philosophy and political theory. As with other terms with the prefix 'post' (such as '**postindustrialism**', 'poststructuralism' and 'postfeminism') there is some ambiguity over the relationship with the original term. Postmodernism may imply both a following on from, and a rejection of, modernism and modernity. Yet with regard to politics, postmodernism generally involved a repudiation of the Enlightenment and its trust in human progress, reason and science. Postmodernists adopted a sceptical attitude to the claims to objectivity and truth made by both natural and social scientists, including political scientists. Postmodernism thus involves an extreme form of relativism, or, as some critics would argue, nihilism.

Both postmodernism and the closely-related term post-structuralism became influential from the late 1960s onwards in French intellectual circles. Key thinkers associated with postmodernism include Lacan, **Foucault**, **Lyotard**, **Derrida** and **Baudrillard**, although both Foucault and Derrida subsequently dissociated themselves from the term. Some of them also vigorously disagreed with each other's ideas. While none of them were primarily political thinkers, they nevertheless had an important influence on the study of politics, in both Europe and the USA.

Lyotard famously characterized postmodernism as involving 'an incredulity towards meta-narratives'. What he meant by 'meta-narratives' was any theory, **ideology**, science or religion claiming to provide a general explanation of the world. He argued that such total doctrines had 'lost their credibility' in the post-Second World War era. No single theory could be given privileged status above others. Derrida is associated with the key postmodernist methodology of deconstruction, which re-emphasized the relativist message. Any text, such as a novel, poem, a historical account or a political document (such as a **constitution**) had multiple interpretations, among which none should be regarded as authoritative, not even that of the author. Such texts should be 'deconstructed' by readers to reveal other hidden meanings and often contradictory interpretations. Foucault's early work on the history of madness raised questions about the relationship between normality and abnormality, reason and unreason, while his later work explored the connection between the use of language and **power**. Baudrillard suggested that in the era of modern mass communication, media images had replaced reality, to the extent that it was impossible to determine what was real and what was unreal.

In some respects, such scepticism might be regarded as healthy (and indeed scepticism towards traditional authority was a feature of the Enlightenment and the **liberal** tradition that postmodernism rejected). Thus postmodernism particularly appealed to those who felt marginalized by mainstream western ideas, such as some radical **feminists**, and those belonging to all kinds of minorities. However, the thrust of postmodernism was subversive of all theories, including radical alternative perspectives, and all kinds of knowledge.

Power

Power is a key concept, arguably the central concept, in politics. It may be defined as the capacity to achieve desired goals, but this does not tell us much about the real essence of political power, which is difficult to pin down and even more difficult to measure. Sometimes power is equated simply with physical force. Thus the Chinese **Communist** leader **Mao Zedong** declared, 'Political power grows out of the barrel of a gun.' Yet much political power does not take such overtly coercive forms. The notion of business power, or the power of the church or of the press, or simply the power of ideas, implies that power can involve more subtle forms of control or influence, rather than physical compulsion.

While some power can be exercised unlawfully, or illegitimately (for example the power wielded by a robber, a rapist or a warlord), other power may be accepted and regarded as legitimate by those over whom it is exercised. **Authority** is the term commonly used for legitimate power. Lawful or legitimate power may be exercised by a recognized **government**, particularly today one that has been **democratically** elected, although it does not follow that all the power exercised by such a government will be regarded as legitimate. Moreover, even if power is willingly accepted and acknowledged, without any appearance of coercion, this may be the consequence of a more subtle exercise of power, which effectively tells people what to think (for example, through control of education or the **media**, and the whole process of political socialization).

As political power cannot be defined precisely and measured, in practice various surrogate measures are commonly used — formal responsibilities, numbers (of members, supporters, voters etc.), economic resources, military capacity (particularly in **international relations**, but sometimes within states), reputation (measured by 'experts' or in opinion polls). Any or all of these may contribute towards power, but none of them can be positively identified with power. Formal responsibilities can not always be exercised, while sometimes they are simply overridden. Public opinion may be a significant constraint on government, but it is also often ignored. The rich may often appear powerful, but income and wealth does not always seem to be able to secure desired outcomes. Nor does superior military capacity always prevail. Moreover some indicators clearly point in different directions. Thus the formal responsibilities or 'powers' of a president, chancellor or prime minister may remain the same throughout his or her period of office, yet the individual's effective power may be significantly affected by fluctuations in reputation over time.

Controversy over the distribution of political power persists. The American **pluralist** Robert **Dahl** defined power in terms of A getting B to do something he would not otherwise do. Dahl sought to measure this by studying decision making, exploring the influence of various interests on political decisions (such as education policy), and concluded that political power was fairly widely diffused in the **communities** he studied. Yet it is impossible to prove that the activities and influence of a particular group caused a specific outcome. Moreover, critics have objected that this focus on overt decision making ignores the capacity of dominant interests or **elites** to shape and influence the opinion of others, so that some issues do not come onto the political agenda at all (Lukes, 1974). Alternative approaches to the focus on decision making, for example tracing the links between members of elite groups in a political community to suggest the existence of a single ruling elite or establishment, may be suggestive, but hardly more conclusive. Thus political scientists continue to disagree over the extent to which political power is diffused or concentrated in any society or community.

Pragmatism

Pragmatism in politics involves hostility to theory and **ideology**, and a preference for practical experience. 'What matters is what works.' This approach has been most commonly associated with **conservative** thinkers (such as **Burke** and **Oakeshott**) and politicians, although it has also been linked with some politicians on the centre-left. Critics equate pragmatism with lack of principle, and following public opinion rather than leading it. For advocates it is about judging issues 'on their merits' rather than in accordance with preconceived ideas. It is however impossible to escape all theoretical assumptions. As the economist **Keynes** ([1936] 1964, chapter 24) declared, 'Practical men, who believe themselves exempt from any intellectual influences, are usually the slaves of some defunct economist.'

Pressure groups

In the study of politics a **pressure group** may be defined as any organized group that seeks to influence **government** and public policy at any level. They are organized, so they are not just a section of the public with an interest in common. They commonly have elected or appointed officers and paid-up members, and sometimes a formal constitution. They are thus to be distinguished from broader and looser social movements. They seek influence rather than direct control of power. They are usually seen as voluntary organizations, part of **civil society**, and outside government and the **state**.

Unlike **political parties**, pressure groups do not seek formal positions of political power, and they do not normally contest **elections** (although some have done, generally to advertise their case rather than with any realistic expectation of winning). While pressure groups 'articulate' interests, parties 'aggregate' interests. This means that pressure groups campaign for a specific interest or cause, whereas political parties that hope to attract a broad spectrum of public support must have a wide range of policies appealing to many different interests, which in turn requires accommodation and compromise.

The literature on groups is bedevilled by the absence of a generally agreed terminology. 'Pressure groups', 'organized groups', 'interest groups' and simply 'groups' are among the many terms commonly used to describe essentially the same phenomenon. 'Groups' and 'organized groups' seem too broad and insufficiently related to politics. 'Interest groups' has the disadvantage of cutting across a common distinction made between types of group – 'interest' and 'cause' groups. 'Pressure groups' has the merit of emphasizing the role of groups in the political process, bringing pressure to bear on government, although it perhaps exaggerates the importance of such pressure compared with the other roles of many groups that do not exist primarily for political purposes.

Analysis of pressure groups widely distinguishes between groups those *defending* the (self-) *interest* of a particular *section* of the community, and groups *promoting* a *cause*. (The italics emphasize words variously used to describe these groups, another instance of a lack of an agreed terminology.) This distinction between interest

concepts

and cause groups is generally useful, although there are some problems of classification at the margins. Another common distinction focuses on the relationship with government. Some are insider groups, with regular access to government, while others are outsider groups, excluded from consultation by government (Grant, 2000).

Beyond these issues of definition and classification there is an extensive debate over the role of pressure groups in the political system generally, and more specifically their contribution to **democracy**. (Some of these issues are addressed briefly under other key concepts, such as **elitism**, **pluralism** and **power**, and in more detail elsewhere in this volume, under 'elitism and pluralism' in Part II, Section 1 (pages 81–3), and under 'pressure groups' in Part V, pages 226–31.)

Privatization

See **Nationalization and privatization.**

Property

Entitlement to **property** and its distribution has been a central issue in political theory. Some thinkers have envisaged an original state of nature in which there was no private property, and where the fruits of the earth were enjoyed in common. In *A Discourse on Inequality*, **Rousseau** imagines that 'The first man who, having enclosed a piece of land, thought of saying "This is mine" and found people simple enough to believe him, was the true founder of civil society' (1984: 109). Rousseau appears to regret it, arguing that the human race would have been spared endless miseries and horrors if the claim had been resisted, but goes on to suggest that the acceptance of the institution of private property was perhaps inevitable.

Conservatives have seen few problems with private property, particularly land, once the most obvious source of status, wealth and income. While **liberals** have sometimes expressed strong reservations over the distribution of landed property in particular, they have generally strongly asserted the right to enjoyment of private property. Some **socialists** and **anarchists** have opposed all private property, arguing instead that goods should be held in common. The French socialist anarchist **Proudhon** famously declared that property was theft. While **Marx** and **Engels** sometimes disparaged property in general, it was specifically **bourgeois** property, the private ownership of the means of production, that they targeted. Both

soviet **communism** and, at one time but to a lesser extent, western **social democracy** sought to replace private ownership of industry with public ownership.

Although the majority of the population once had negligible private property, both in the west and in some of the rapidly expanding economies elsewhere, property ownership has become far more widely diffused. It is no longer unusual for ordinary working people to own their own homes, a range of luxury consumer goods, and stocks and shares and other forms of wealth. This suggests to conservatives that a 'property-owning democracy' is now a reality. Critics on the **left** of the political spectrum however argue that the distribution of income and wealth is as unequal as ever, and some argue that it is becoming more unequal. Redistribution to secure more **equality** and social **justice** is however strongly resisted on the **right** – particularly taxes on wealth and inheritance, and progressive income tax.

As well as arguments over the distribution of property, there are also increasingly arguments over its use. While at one time it was suggested that a man or woman was entitled to do what he wished with his or her own property, regardless of the social or environmental consequences, this has long not been the case. Today there are increasing legal restrictions on the uses to which property can be put.

Public choice theory

See **Rational choice theory and public choice theory.**

Public good

A **public good** is a good that has to be supplied to everyone if it is supplied to anyone, and from which no one can be excluded. Examples of such public goods include clean air, national defence, public parks and lighthouses. The market cannot be relied upon to supply such public goods, as charging is ineffective because it is difficult or impossible to prevent 'free riders' from benefiting from the good or service without payment. Such public goods may be supplied by public authorities, although they may also be provided by public subscription or private philanthropy.

Public interest

The **public interest** may be defined as the common interest, or the interest of the majority or the 'common good'. **Governments**, individual politicians and public officials may claim to serve the public interest. Sometimes a particular decision or policy is claimed to be 'in the public interest', while an alternative is 'not in the public interest'. Yet it is difficult to identify the public interest definitively. Very few decisions or policies can be said to benefit everyone.

Rational choice and public choice theorists are particularly sceptical over the claims made by politicians and public officials that they serve the public interest. These theorists do not recognize such apparently altruistic motives, but assume that all individuals, whether working in the public sector or the private sector, pursue their own rational self-interest. They claim that ministers or officials claiming to serve the public interest are really pursuing their own interests, for example seeking to advance their own careers.

Quango

Quango is an acronym (widely used in the USA and the UK) for **qu**asi-**a**utonomous **n**on-**g**overnmental **o**rganization. Exactly what organizations should be counted as quangos is contentious. Some quangos have important **executive** functions, some are quasi-**judicial**, some regulatory, while some are purely advisory. Examples of British organizations that have been described as quangos include regional development agencies (executive), the Employment Tribunal (quasi-judicial), the Audit Commission (regulatory) and the White Fish Authority (advisory).

Quangos are best thought of as appointed (rather than elected) agencies not directly controlled by elected politicians. In Britain the official description is 'non-departmental public bodies', indicating that they are not part of the **government** departments, nor staffed by civil servants. Other terms used to described these institutions include 'ad hoc bodies' (suggesting they are not part of the permanent machinery of government) and 'para-state organizations'. However, the acronym 'quango' has become the most familiar, even if the 'non-governmental' part of the description is rather misleading, as quangos are generally funded out of taxation, and ultimately (regardless of their 'quasi-autonomous' status) are part of government.

The growth of quangos has been widely criticized, from the centre and **left** on the grounds that these organizations are not democratically elected and are only weakly **accountable** to parliament and public, and on the **right** as part of a disguised and undesirable growth of government and public spending. A key issue is patronage: how are people appointed to quangos, and on what criteria? Pejorative terms to describe the phenomenon include 'the quango state', 'quangocracy', 'the appointed state' and 'the new magistracy'.

Yet it is generally conceded that some public functions (such as funding the arts, and much state regulation) need to be administered independently of the government of the day to promote public confidence in their neutrality. Also many advisory quangos usefully and cheaply tap expertise not necessarily available within the permanent government bureaucracy.

Race and racism

Race is a concept that has no scientific validity. In the nineteenth century it was widely believed (including by some scientists) that humankind could be classified into distinctive races (crudely identified by skin colour: white, yellow, brown, red and black) with measurable physical and mental differences. In Nazi Germany 'scientific racism' became a state-sponsored orthodoxy used to justify the treatment of 'non-Aryans' as inferior species, and ultimately, the extermination of the Jews in the Holocaust. Today, 'scientific racism' is totally discredited, although the term 'race' is still widely and loosely used, sometimes to distinguish cultural rather than biological differences. **Ethnicity** has become the approved term to describe such cultural differences, although official sources sometimes still use the term 'race', as in 'race relations'. Yet descriptions based on skin colour ('Blacks') or broad geographical background ('Asians') are in common usage, found in official documents, and to a degree are accepted by minority communities themselves, even though they involve gross over-simplification, and ignore substantial differences within these crude categories.

Racism, involving discriminating against those perceived to be of different racial origin, is still a feature of many modern societies, despite legislation outlawing discrimination and prejudice. Some writers have associated racism with economic deprivation and **class** relations under **capitalism**. Thus most 'Blacks and Asians' in countries where 'whites' are in the majority are employed in low-status manual work and live in racially segregated deprived urban areas. Here they compete for jobs, houses and services with white working-class people inhabiting the same deprived urban environment. Both white working-class racism and the aggressive response of some young Black and Asian males to white racism can be seen as a symptom of economic decline and deprivation. Yet economic deprivation hardly explains one of the most persistent forms of racism displayed by all classes over the centuries, anti-Semitism.

Some argue that racist attitudes are deeply embedded in popular culture, as a consequence of the historical experience of slavery and racial segregation in some countries (such as the USA) or colonial domination and exploitation in others (by for example the United Kingdom, France and Spain). American writers describe this culturally embedded racism as institutional racism, whereas in Britain the term is commonly applied more narrowly to persistent racist attitudes embedded in particular institutions, such as the police and the armed services.

Racism is routinely denounced by mainstream politicians, although some have not been above employing coded language to appeal to those concerned about ethnic tensions and immigration. Indeed, much of the expressed concern over 'immigration' and 'bogus asylum seekers' thinly conceals racist attitudes. Far-**right** politicians continue to use the language of race to exploit popular concerns over tensions between ethnic groups and over immigration. The 'war on terror' has exacerbated anti-Muslim feeling, and although this is strictly a religious rather than a 'race' issue, it has had some impact on Asians who are not Muslim. There have been periodic concerns over rising support for racist parties in a number of countries, including Austria, former East Germany, France and the United Kingdom.

While some would see integration and a colour-blind approach as the long term answer to racism, others assert the value of distinctive ethnic identities and the benefits of diversity, and argue for a positive acceptance of **multiculturalism**. Yet some fear that the perpetuation of difference may hinder mutual understanding and toleration, and reinforce prejudice, eroding any sense of a common national identity and allegiance. Others respond that multiple identities and allegiances are a feature of the modern world.

Rational choice theory is derived from classical economic theory, and assumes that individuals pursue their rational self-interest. Thus the starting point of analysis is the individual, not groups of people, nor society as a whole. Each individual is deemed capable of recognizing his or her own self-interest and pursuing it rationally. This assumption can be applied to voting, implying that individual voters will choose candidates and parties most likely to look after what they perceive as their own interest (lower taxes if they pay high taxes or improved public services if they are a beneficiary of such services).

Public choice theorists (such as **Buchanan**, **Tullock** and **Niskanen**) apply the assumptions of the pursuit of rational self-interest to the state, the public sector and public policy. They assume politicians, ministers and public officials are motivated to pursue their own rational self interest, in the same way as consumers and producers in the **free market**. However, in the absence of profits, those operating in the public sector will seek to advance their own careers, pay and conditions, by expanding their own departments and agencies ('bureau maximization' instead of profit maximization). Thus politicians and public officials in the public sector will favour increases in the size of **government**, public spending and taxation, without fearing the disciplines of the free market (ultimately business failure and bankruptcy). Voters and special interest groups who benefit from public services and subsidies, but who do not have to bear the full cost as taxpayers, may support such public spending and taxation. Public choice theory provides a plausible explanation of rising public spending and taxation in the post-war decades. It has become influential both in government circles and in the study of politics generally, but particularly in the USA.

Critics of rational choice theory and public choice theory may argue that individuals can act altruistically, preferring to pursue another's interest rather than their own. They may deny the assumption of rationality, suggesting that humans often follow their instincts or passions. They may reject the individualist assumptions, suggesting that individuals may be socially conditioned to act in the interests of others. Finally, it is

concepts

possible to accept the assumptions but reject the conclusions derived from the assumptions. Thus it is possible to argue that the pursuit of rational self-interest does not necessarily entail 'bureau maximization' (Dunleavy, 1991).

Rationalism

Rationalism assumes humans are, or should be, guided by reason, rather than instinct or emotion. It is a key assumption of the Enlightenment and **liberalism**. Liberals go on to assume that humans pursue their own rational self-interest, and that they are the best judge of their own interests. It has been commonly argued that reason is what distinguishes human beings from other sentient creatures, although it is far from generally agreed that all humans are capable of rational thought and conduct. Thus **Plato** argued that only a tiny minority of humans are ruled by reason, and the rest are governed by spirit or base appetites. Only those who were themselves ruled by reason should be entrusted with ruling others. **Conservative** thinkers such as **Burke** and **Oakeshott** have not only doubted the extent to which people are guided by reason, rather than instinct, tradition, or prejudice, but have explicitly criticized reason and rationalism. Thus for Oakeshott rationalism in politics is to be avoided. **Fascism** elevated spirit and emotion above reason. **Postmodernism** has questioned the Enlightenment trust in reason, knowledge and progress.

Some modern political science seems to suggest that human behaviour is not very rational (for example, some of the analysis of voting behaviour, and some theories of political communication). However, Herbert **Simon** advocated and defended a rational model of policy making against the rival incrementalist model of Charles **Lindblom**. Moreover, **rational choice theory** assumes the pursuit of rational self-interest in the public as well as the private sector. Some other approaches, particularly variants of **Marxism**, assume that the ideas and behaviour of individual humans are extensively socially conditioned, and thus they may be unable to recognize and pursue their own rational self-interest.

Realism and *realpolitik*

Realism, in politics, is commonly contrasted with **idealism**. Realism means seeing the world as it is rather than as one would like it be. **Thucydides**, the ancient Greek historian, **Machiavelli** and **Hobbes** have sometimes been cited as exemplifying the realist approach.

The term realism has been applied particularly to an influential interpretation of **international relations**. The study of international relations was initially given impetus by idealist assumptions over the potential to end war through collective security and to develop appropriate international institutions. The failure of these hopes between the two world wars led to the dominance of the realist interpretation of international relations associated with the work of E H **Carr** and Hans **Morgenthau**, and later the neo-realist work of Kenneth **Waltz**. (These realist assumptions have remained strongly in evidence among American neo-conservatives.) Realists and neo-realists have seen international relations as remaining essentially anarchic, and have stressed the continuing central role of states pursuing their own national interest through a readiness to use the military and economic resources at their disposal. This realist and neo-realist school has tended to be sceptical over the efficacy of international institutions and international law in dealing with threats to world peace. However, the growing importance of non-state actors (especially **non-governmental organizations** and trans-national corporations) in a globalizing world, coupled with the transformed international landscape following the collapse of Soviet communism, has led to a variety of challenges to the hitherto dominant neo-realist interpretation of international relations.

Realpolitik is a German word that expresses a hard-headed realist approach to domestic and international politics, involving a readiness to use all resources available, including military force, to attain one's ends. It has been associated particularly with the diplomacy of the nineteenth-century Prussian and German Chancellor, Bismarck, in his pursuit of German unification.

Referendum (or plebiscite)

A **referendum** or **plebiscite** allows voters themselves to decide directly on particular issues, rather than leaving them to the decisions of elected representatives. It has been used particularly to decide **constitutional** questions, but on a wide range of other issues in some countries. The term plebiscite is sometimes used interchangeably with referendum. However, sometimes it is employed more narrowly to describe a popular vote by

concepts

inhabitants of a particular territory on their political future (such as their independence or their transfer from one state to another). In some US states (such as California) under a device called the 'initiative', a proportion of citizens can force an issue (for example tax cuts or the legalization of cannabis) onto the ballot paper, for a decision by voters.

The referendum and other similar devices inject an element of direct **democracy** (or plebiscitory democracy) into a system of **representative** or parliamentary democracy, and appear to give more power to the people. They allow people to vote on specific issues that affect them, rather than leaving the decision to representatives who may ignore the opinion of those who elected them. It is also argued that the public debate around referendum questions submitted to the electorate helps to educate the public on the issues involved.

However referendums can involve a number of difficulties. First, who decides on the issues to be determined by referendum and who frames the questions? **Dictators** and charismatic leaders have sometimes made use of referendums to legitimize a preferred course of action. A question may be cleverly worded so as to encourage a desired answer. Equal time and equal resources may not be given to advocates of both sides, so the public debate may not be balanced and fair. A particular problem is that many issues cannot be easily framed to provide a straight choice between 'yes' or 'no'. There may be unanticipated problems in implementing the electorate's choice, particularly on tax and public spending cuts.

At another level it is argued that there is a conflict between the idea of direct and representative democracy, and between popular and parliamentary sovereignty. It is not easy to combine two methods of decision making based on different principles. Who decides what is to be determined by the direct decision of the people and what is to be determined by the people's elected representatives? One compromise solution that apparently preserves the principle of parliamentary **sovereignty**, and is used in the United Kingdom, is to consider referendums advisory only. Yet in practice it would be politically very difficult to disregard a clear majority decision on a reasonable turnout in a referendum, and UK governments have in practice regarded referendum results as binding.

Representation

Representation is a key but contentious concept in modern politics. Broadly, it involves a means by which an individual or small group is formally entrusted with promoting and defending the views and interests of many people (who may directly choose or **elect** the representative(s)). It has become the crucial element of the modern conception of **democracy**. Instead of direct rule by the people themselves, government is subject to the control of elected representatives of the people. Some would urge that these elected representatives should faithfully 'represent' the views of those they were elected to serve, even where they strongly disagree with those views. However, others (following Edmund **Burke**) have argued that representatives are not delegates, and they should use their own judgement of the public interest rather than reflect the views of their electors. This has become orthodoxy, although it might be noted that **socialists** and trade unionists have been more inclined to regard representatives as delegates. (See **democracy** and **referendum** for arguments about representative and direct democracy and the problems of combining elements of both.)

Another issue is how far any representative institution should be broadly socially representative, as well as formally elected. In practice many representative bodies at national, regional and local level are not socially representative. In most representative democracies women are under-represented, and **ethnic minorities** are often under-represented also. Some occupational backgrounds are over-represented (commonly, law and education) while others are under-represented. Elected representatives generally come from a restricted educational and social background, and are mostly middle-aged or elderly.

It is argued that an elected body can hardly be expected to be a microcosm of the electorate unless the electors' freedom to choose is considerably restricted. Others would argue that it is more important that representatives have the political skills necessary to serve their electors effectively, and these skills are inevitably unequally distributed in the population. There is considerable force in these arguments. Even so, if most representatives do not share and thus have no direct knowledge of the life and experience of those they represent, there may be an important

concepts

element missing from their debates and decisions. They may also appear increasingly remote from those they serve. In practice, many political parties have recognized that there is a problem, and have taken steps to make their candidates for election more socially representative, seeking to increase the number of women, ethnic minorities and those with alternative lifestyles. In some countries the electoral system has also been reformed with the aim or producing more socially diverse representatives.

Republic and republicanism

The familiar meaning of **republic** today is any state that is not a **monarchy**: in other words, most states in the modern world. A **republican** is someone opposed to, or seeking to abolish, monarchy. The term republic does however have other associations. It derives from the Latin *Res Publica* ('the public concern' or 'public affairs'). The original Roman Republic was established after the expulsion of the last of Rome's kings in 509 BC, and lasted until the formal establishment of the Roman empire under Caesar Augustus in 31 BC. This Roman Republic involved a mixed but substantially aristocratic or patrician system of government, headed by two elected consuls and the Senate (an assembly of patricians or noblemen), but with tribunes of the plebs looking after the interests of the common people. Writers like **Cicero** identified the Roman Republic with liberty and public service, and this became a model to be idealized and copied in subsequent ages. Republics flourished intermittently among the cities of Renaissance Italy, in the Dutch Republic of the late sixteenth and seventeenth centuries, and in England briefly in the middle of the seventeenth century. The republican ideal was later taken up with enthusiasm in the American and French revolutions, and by their subsequent imitators. In political thought this republican tradition is represented by thinkers such as **Machiavelli** in Renaissance Florence, Harrington in the seventeenth century and **Paine** in the eighteenth century in England, and **Madison** (particularly) among the founding fathers of the United States of America. For Madison a republic involved a **representative** but essentially mixed system of government rather than a pure democracy. Subsequently both in America and particularly in France, 'republic' became synonymous with **democracy.**

(Note that the latinized translation of the title of **Plato's** best known work *The Republic* is misleading. This has nothing to do with the republican tradition described above.)

Revolution

In politics the term **revolution** is commonly used to describe a substantial popular uprising that secures not just a change in the government but a change in the whole system of government, or 'regime change'. (Note however the term is sometimes employed more loosely to describe, by analogy, any major change, sometimes over a considerable period of time, as with 'the industrial revolution' and 'the behavioural revolution'.) A revolution may be distinguished from a 'coup', which involves a takeover of government at a more limited **elite** level. Key political revolutions that became models to imitate and/or examples to avoid were the French Revolution of 1789 onwards and the Russian Bolshevik Revolution of 1917. The American War of Independence is often also described as the American Revolution. Although the English Civil War is sometimes described as a revolution, this label is more commonly given to the replacement of King James II by William of Orange in 1688, the so-called 'Glorious Revolution', although this was more of a coup than a revolution. Revolutions involving significant regime change have been a recurring feature of the last two centuries around the world.

The causes of political stability and change have been explored by political thinkers from **Plato** and **Aristotle** onwards. This has become a major theme in the modern study of comparative politics. Theda **Skocpol** (1979) made her name with a comparative analysis of the French, Russian and Chinese revolutions. More recently, scholars have focused on the anti-**communist** revolutions of 1989 onwards in the former Soviet Union and eastern Europe. Ralf Dahrendorf wrote *Reflections on the Revolution in Europe* (1990) in conscious homage to the essay of Edmund **Burke** on the French Revolution 200 years previously.

Right

See **Left and right.**

Rights

Rights involve an entitlement to something – a right to life, a right to education, a right to expression, a right to work. They may be enshrined in specific **laws**, as for example a right to equal pay for men and women is in many countries. In some countries they may be listed in a charter of citizens' rights, the rights enjoyed by virtue of being a citizen of a particular **state**.

Yet it is often argued that these legal rights and citizen rights reflect some prior natural rights or universal human rights. Thus the American Declaration of Independence argues that 'all men are created equal and are endowed by their Creator with certain unalienable rights and that among these are life, liberty and the pursuit of happiness' (although these broad and undefined rights seem difficult to operationalize). Rather more specific are the rights listed in the *Declaration of the Rights of Man and Citizen* made by the French revolutionaries in 1789, and more detailed still are the United Nations Universal Declaration of Human Rights (1948) and the European Convention on Human Rights.

If rights were indeed 'self-evident', or universally acknowledged, there would be no need to proclaim them. Many of the rights that have been proclaimed as natural or inalienable human rights (for example freedom of expression, or gender equality) have been far from universally recognized over time. They are proclaimed to persuade people that they should be recognized.

Not everyone finds the notion of rights helpful. Jeremy **Bentham** mocked the whole notion of natural rights as 'nonsense on stilts'. The only right he recognized was a legal right, and he argued that natural rights had been invented 'to cut up law and legal rights'. **Marx** criticized not so much the principle but the particular rights enumerated in the *Declaration of the Rights of Man*, particularly the emphasis on rights to property and security. These were, he considered, the rights of egoistic man, 'an individual withdrawn into himself, his private interest and his private desires and separated from the community' (1975: 230–1).

Some suggest that what are proclaimed as universal human rights are only the rights recognized by dominant liberal western culture, and that the right of other cultures to be different should be respected. A problem here is that the 'rights of **communities**' (for example of religious or ethnic communities) may be employed to trump the rights of individuals and minorities. Thus respect for a particular cultural tradition might involve acceptance of discrimination against women or gays. This is one aspect of the continuing debate over **multiculturalism**.

Yet while some would deny the universality of human rights, others seek to extend rights further. The animal rights movement proclaims the rights of creatures incapable of expressing them themselves. The notion of animal rights implicitly conflicts with some traditionally recognized human rights, but there are some influential moral philosophers today (such as Peter **Singer**) who are prepared to make a case for the acceptance of animal rights.

Separation of powers

The notion of **separation of powers** requires that the main functions of the state – **executive**, **legislative** and **judicial** – should be clearly distinct and wielded by separate institutions. **Hobbes** and others forcefully declared that **sovereignty,** supreme power within the state, could not be divided. Other thinkers, following **Montesquieu**, have argued that the main powers or functions of the state could and should be maintained in separate hands in order to preserve the liberty of citizens and protect them from tyranny. Montesquieu considered that British government involved such a separation of powers, with the king and his ministers constituting the executive, parliament the legislature and an independent judiciary. Other observers (such as **Bagehot** [1867]1963) subsequently concluded that the executive and legislative functions in British government were interdependent and essentially fused, while even the judiciary were not truly independent.

Thus it was the American **Constitution** that first embodied the principle of the separation of powers. This declared that legislative powers were invested in Congress, executive powers in the President, and judicial powers in the Supreme Court and other inferior courts. Besides this apparently clear separation of the main power or functions of the state, the US Constitution also involved a separation between different levels of **government**, **federal** and **state**. In practice, the separation of powers in the US system of government did not and could not involve a complete separation of powers, as they were necessarily interdependent, but rather involved a system of 'checks and balances' designed to prevent the accumulation and centralization of power. These checks and balances are still widely approved in the USA, although over time there has been some criticism that the power of the presidency has increased at the expense of congress, and the federal government at the expense of states' rights. By contrast there are periodic concerns over 'gridlock', resulting from conflict within the system, commonly between president and congress frustrating the process of government.

The principle of the separation of powers, embodied in the US Constitution, has been widely imitated by other states, although the association of functions with specific institutions, and the constitutional machinery for dealing with disputes between them, vary considerably.

Social capital

The term **social capital** is used by the American political scientist Robert **Putnam** and his followers to mean the extent of social interaction and community engagement in any society. Thus active involvement in a bridge club, parent teacher association, trade union, church, political party or gun club would all count as part of social capital. Putnam has documented a marked decline in social capital in the USA, with, he argues, adverse implications for a healthy functioning **democratic** system. It is not yet clear how far other societies have experienced a comparable decline in social capital. However, critics suggest that Putnam underestimates the positive potential of new methods of communication via the internet which do not require physical association.

Socialism and social democracy

Socialism has been variously defined. Socialists in the nineteenth century emphasized **equality**, general social welfare rather than individual self-interest, cooperation rather than competition, planning rather than **free market** forces, common ownership rather than private **property**, or more specifically, collective ownership of the means of production. Thus socialism was seen as an alternative to **capitalism**. Arguably, socialists disagreed more over strategy than over values, some advocating a **revolutionary** route to socialism, others placing their faith in a more gradual evolutionary socialism, to be achieved through the ballot box and **representative** institutions, although this disagreement partly reflected differing political circumstances in particular states. Thus while both German and Russian socialists had been inspired by **Marx's** brand of revolutionary socialism, the two movements developed very differently. The German socialists openly organized a mass **political party**, won substantial electoral support and parliamentary **representation**, while their (much less numerous) Russian counterparts were constrained to operate clandestinely and mainly in exile. While the German party came to terms with a semi-parliamentary system and the norms of representative **democracy**, and over time, influenced by revisionism, modified their goals, the Russian party remained committed to revolution.

Both these parties were called **social democrat**, and before the First World War the terms socialism and social democracy were commonly used interchangeably. All socialists (including Marx) considered themselves democrats. Yet an already developing split among socialists was deepened by the successful Bolshevik Revolution in Russia, between those committed to parliamentary socialism and gradual reform rather than revolution, increasingly referred to as social democrats, and those socialists who remained committed to the revolutionary route. This split was institutionalized into rival international socialist organizations: the (social democratic) Second International and the (soviet dominated) Third International.

Social democracy has become a widely used term to describe a moderate, reformist (or revisionist) parliamentary form of socialism, rather than revolutionary or explicitly **Marxist** socialism or **communism**. Between the two World Wars there was generally bitter mutual antipathy between communists and social democrats in Europe, interspersed with limited periods of cooperation in 'popular front' coalitions. After the Second World War the split between the socialism practised in the Soviet Union and eastern Europe and that championed in the west was emphasized by the 'iron curtain' between them. In western Europe the values of social democracy were apparently so widely endorsed (even by other parties) that commentators talked of a 'social democratic consensus' in the post-war years. This consensus involved the acceptance of a mixed economy with a substantial **state** sector, increased **welfare** provision and progressive taxation, all of which were expected to lead, over time, to a more equal society. This social democratic consensus was challenged by a revival of **neoliberal** free market ideas in the west in the 1970s and 1980s, while the alternative 'really existing socialism' of the eastern bloc rapidly imploded after 1989. Moreover, the pressures of global capitalism made it increasingly difficult to pursue either socialism or social democracy in a single country. One commentator, Ralf Dahrendorf (1990: 38), declared, after the revolutions of 1989, that socialism in all its variants (including social democracy) was dead.

Yet the survival of socialism or social democracy depends on how these terms are defined. Parties describing themselves as socialist or social democratic have since been returned to power for significant periods in Sweden, France, Germany, Britain and elsewhere. Most of these have not only come to terms with capitalism and the free market, they have actively pursued the **privatization** of formerly state-owned enterprises. Political leaders argue they are maintaining traditional socialist or social democratic values, but reinterpreting them to meet altered circumstances.

Certainly it is difficult to identify social democracy any more with **collectivism** and **nationalization**. Fairness and **equality** are still enthusiastically endorsed by social democrats, although even in theory this means the pursuit of greater equality rather than absolute equality, and in practice it seems questionable whether even this limited goal has been achieved to any appreciable degree. Left-wing critics argue that party leaders and activists have become more middle class (embourgeoisement), no longer serve the workers they claim to represent and have ceased to be socialist in any meaningful sense. Yet there is little evidence of significant support for more traditional socialist policies from either a diminishing industrial working class or the broader electorate.

Social movement and new social movement

The term **social movement** is commonly used to describe a relatively loosely organized and informal combination of individuals and groups supporting a broad interest or cause. While a **pressure group** commonly has a formal organization, a clear leadership structure and a paid-up membership, a social movement may lack any organized structure, identifiable leaders and members, being composed instead of a fluctuating body of supporters and sympathizers, many of whom may not belong to any organized group. An example of an older social movement is the labour movement. Many of those who are considered part of the labour movement may be members of trade unions, other sympathetic organizations and sometimes **political parties**, but the labour movement is commonly considered to include all the labouring classes and those who sympathize with them.

The term **new social movement** has been used to describe a number of political movements that became prominent from the 1960s onwards, including the women's movement, the peace movement, the green movement, and more recently the anti-capitalist movement. While all of these included some formally structured pressure groups, there were many supporters and sympathisers who were not attached to any of these. Indeed, a loose informal movement was partly preferred for ideological reasons. Thus some **feminists** associate formal organizations, involving rules and hierarchies, with a male preference for order, **authority** and status, and seek less directed, more spontaneous and cooperative methods of working. Similarly, some peace campaigners and green activists positively reject leadership roles. The supporters of such new social movements commonly favour alternative forms of political activity, often including direct action rather than traditional pressure group methods. For movements operating on the fringes of legality (such as parts of the anti-capitalist movement and the animal rights movement), a lack of formal organization may have some practical advantages, making it more difficult for the authorities to determine the responsibility of individuals for particular actions.

These new social movements are associated with the **left** of the political spectrum. However, it should be noted that there has been a rise of **right**-wing protest movements in many countries, such as movements objecting to immigration, or objecting to restrictions on traditional countryside pursuits (such as shooting and hunting).

Sovereignty and independent sovereign state

Sovereignty means supreme power. Within a state it refers to the ultimate source of legal authority. While some thinkers (such as **Hobbes**) insist that sovereignty in a **state** cannot be divided, others (such as **Locke** and **Montesquieu**) argue that it can and should be. Thus many modern states follow the USA in separating the **executive**, **legislative** and **judicial** functions of the state, and some also have imitated the USA in dividing sovereignty between a **federal** and state level. Britain's political system, by contrast, is supposed to involve the principle of parliamentary sovereignty within

concepts

a unitary state: and the power of the Westminster Parliament is in theory unlimited. This parliamentary sovereignty is inconsistent with the ideal of the **separation of powers** (embodied in the US and many other constitutions). Some critics have attacked the principle of parliamentary sovereignty, while others have argued that recent developments in British government (EU membership, **devolution**, the increased use of **referendums**, and the Human Rights Act) have substantially eroded parliamentary sovereignty.

When used of the external relations of states, sovereignty refers to a state's ability to function as an independent entity free from external control or interference – as an independent sovereign state. The traditional interpretation of **international relations** as practised from the Treaty of Westphalia (1648) onwards has revolved around the interrelationship of such independent sovereign states. Today some supposedly sovereign states are perceived as the puppets of other states, and/or fail to maintain a monopoly of the legitimate use of physical force within their own borders. Moreover in an era of **globalization**, international relations are complicated by the growing importance of international institutions, **non-governmental organizations** (NGOs) and transnational corporations (TNCs), which appears to constrain the freedom of action of sovereign states. Within the study of international relations, **idealists** welcome these trends involving the increasing acknowledgement of both international obligations and international law by states. **Realists**, however, insist that the extent of change is exaggerated and that independent sovereign states, with their own economic and military resources, remain the crucial pieces in the game of international diplomacy.

State

The **state** may be briefly defined as a compulsory political association that has supreme **power** (**sovereignty**) over a particular territory. According to Max **Weber** 'the state is a human community that (successfully) claims the monopoly of the legitimate use of physical force within a given territory'. The concepts of force or power, sovereignty and **legitimacy** are closely bound up with most accounts of the state. The state may be defined narrowly, to include just the formal institutions of central **government**, or rather more broadly to cover local authorities and any other organizations funded by taxation.

'The state' in everyday language is sometimes used simply to mean 'the government', but while governments come and go, the state continues (although states can be destroyed by conquest, **revolution** or breakdown). States in practice have taken a wide variety of size and type, from small city states to extensive empires, from traditional autocracies to modern representative democracies, from unitary states to federal states (see **federalism**).

The functions or responsibilities of states vary in both theory and practice. Minimum (or 'nightwatchman') states largely confine their activities to defence and the maintenance of internal law and order. Others seek to exercise extensive powers over the outward behaviour and expressed beliefs of subject or citizens. **Welfare states** have assumed wide responsibilities for the provision of social services.

Attitudes to the state vary widely, reflecting very different ideological assumptions. **Anarchists** argue that states are inevitably oppressive, restricting freedom. People would be better off relying on peaceful voluntary cooperation in stateless societies. At the other extreme **fascism** was associated with a totalitarian theory of the state, under which the state was all-embracing, and excluded from no sphere of activity. **Conservatives** have generally emphasized the need for a strong state to protect people from external threats and internal crime and disorder. **Free market liberals** have tended to see the state as a necessary evil, but have sought to limit the power and scope of the state, excluding it from much economic and social activity, sharply distinguishing between the sphere of the state and **civil society**, or the state and the market. **Social democrats** have generally seen the state more positively, and have sought, through the electoral process, to capture and use the institutions of the state to achieve social reform. This is compatible with the **pluralist** assumption that the state is neutral between the various interests and pressures within a political **community**, as opposed to the **elitist** perspective that assumes that the state is controlled by, and serves the interests of a ruling elite or elites. **Marxists** contend specifically that the state in a **capitalist** society is bound to serve the interest of capital (although some Marxists allow that the state has 'relative autonomy' in pursuing that aim).

These different perspectives on the state not

only reflect very different assumptions about **human nature** and human potential, but also suggest very different answers to the questions posed by political theorists: why and how far should we obey the state? For some (such as **Bodin** and **Hobbes**) this **obligation** is unconditional. For others, such an obligation depends on the state's **legitimacy**. For democrats, legitimacy depends on the willing **consent** of the governed. For **nationalists**, the state to be legitimate has to be a **nation-state**, comprising all those who feel they belong to the nation (however defined). Revolutionary Marxists seek the overthrow of the capitalist state. Anarchists reject all states.

International relations as a discipline has long involved the study of the interaction of independent sovereign states. Until recently no other actors seemed to matter. Within the last century or so the growth of international organizations and **international law** has sometimes appeared to constrain states. The increased role of transnational corporations (TNCs) in an increasingly global economy and the growing influence of **non-governmental organizations** (**NGOs**) have arguably limited still further states' freedom of action. Indeed, some argue that **globalization** heralds the end of the nation-state (Ohmae, 1996). For others, the implications of globalization have been exaggerated and real power in international relations still lies with independent sovereign states. Yet in the modern world some states are clearly far more powerful and relatively more immune from international pressures than others. Some states struggle vainly to maintain order within their own territories. The problems of these 'failed states' sometimes appear contagious, to the extent that international bodies, or more commonly alliances of interested stronger states, are persuaded that outside intervention is necessary.

Structure and agency

The relative importance of **structure** and **agency** in politics has become a key theoretical debate. It is closely related to the old issue of free will and determinism. How far can individuals shape their own future? How far is their future shaped for them by the economic and social context in which they live? Structure may be defined as the context or environment in which individuals or groups operate. Agency refers to the ability of individuals or groups to affect their environment, and the ability of political actors to shape political outcomes.

Some theorists suggest that the capacity of any individuals or groups to change history is either highly constrained or almost non-existent owing to economic, social and ideological factors over which they have no control. This suggests there is no point in examining too closely the ideas and behaviour of politicians, such as presidents, prime ministers or chancellors. Instead we should seek to understand the whole economic, social and political system, and examine the deep underlying structures that shape political change. Others implicitly or explicitly maintain that individual or group action can make a decisive difference. Both **pluralists** and **rational choice** theorists assume that individuals on their own or in combination shape political outcomes. Structuralist is the name given to those political theorists who emphasize the importance of structure and context over human agency.

Terrorism

Terrorism is a term that has long been applied, and one with which the world has unhappily become reacquainted, but it is nevertheless difficult to define uncontentiously. It has become a cliché that one person's terrorist is another person's freedom fighter. Thus the German occupiers of France and the Vichy French government regarded those French who actively resisted the occupation as terrorists. Following the liberation of France these 'terrorists' were regarded as heroes and liberators. Much the same was true of nationalist leaders rebelling against colonial governments and racist regimes. Nelson Mandela was widely regarded as a terrorist, not only by the apartheid government in South Africa, which successfully prosecuted him for treason and sentenced him to life imprisonment, but also by many in the west who later venerated him.

Terrorism is generally envisaged to involve random and indiscriminate attacks on people, including not only rulers, government officials and the armed forces, but ordinary civilians. The shock effect of such attacks achieves considerable publicity, of a kind not easily secured by more peaceful means, although the suffering of innocent victims can arouse revulsion and damage the cause. While terrorism is usually associated with opponents of the **state** and dominant classes, the term 'state terrorism' suggests that governments also can use terror deliberately to create a climate of fear and crush opposition. Thus Robespierre in revolutionary France and Stalin in the Soviet Union employed terrorism as deliberate policy.

There has been much recent discussion of global terrorism, acts of terror perpetrated across the world's continents, much of it attributed to the al Qaida network of Islamic fundamentalists. Terrorist atrocities in New York, East Africa, Bali, Saudi Arabia, Istanbul, Madrid and London have been plausibly connected to al Qaida, although it appears much of the initiative and planning was more local. The continued threat of global terrorism has had massive implications for domestic policy on security and civil liberties, and even more far-reaching consequences for western foreign policy. Some argue that the western 'war on terrorism' has stimulated an increase in terrorism rather than checking it.

Third way

Broadly speaking, the **third way** is a term that has been sometimes employed to describe a different option, making unnecessary a choice between two unpalatable alternatives. Thus Mussolini presented **fascism** as a 'third way' between soviet **communism** and **free market capitalism**. Others have used the 'third way' in the sense of a 'middle way' or centrist philosophy between **left** and **right**. The then Conservative rebel, Harold Macmillan, used the term 'middle way' in the 1930s to describe his own brand of progressive **conservatism**. In the 1990s the term 'third way' was linked with, among others, Blair's 'New Labour' in Britain, Bill Clinton's Democrat administration in the USA and the Social Democrat-led government of Gerhard Schröder in Germany. Schroder used the term 'new middle'. Blair argued, 'The solutions of neither the old Left nor the new Right will do. We need a radical centre in modern politics.' The British sociologist Anthony **Giddens** (1998) described the third way as updated **social democracy**, while some critics saw it as a cloak for the acceptance of **neoliberal** free market ideas by social democratic parties. Others considered there was more rhetoric than substance in the term. It has been less used since some of the leading politicians associated with it have left office.

Toleration

Toleration involves not interfering with the ideas and practices of others, even if they are strongly disliked or disapproved of. The principle of toleration is commonly expressed in relation to religious observance, and more broadly in favour of freedom of speech, a principle is expressed in words commonly (but incorrectly) attributed to **Voltaire**: 'I disapprove of what you say, but I will defend to the death your right to say it.'

Although the principle of religious toleration is now widely accepted at least in the west, it was certainly not the case in the past. Religious unorthodoxy or heresy was regarded as a threat to the established religion and frequently the **state** as well. It was seen as endangering the mortal souls of the people. Thus religious minorities invariably suffered persecution, and sometimes expulsion or extermination. Catholics in Protestant states, and Protestants in Catholic states were seen as potential traitors or **terrorists**. The carnage involved in the wars of religion in the sixteenth and seventeenth centuries in Europe did something to change attitudes. **Spinoza**, **Locke** and later **Voltaire** championed religious toleration – although even for Locke toleration did not extend to Roman Catholics or atheists. In the nineteenth century John Stuart **Mill** ([1859]1972) advanced the classic case for full freedom of speech. For Mill this did not just involve freedom from legal penalties or government restrictions, but freedom of the individual from the stifling control of public opinion, the 'tyranny of the majority'.

Religious toleration no longer appeared an issue in much of the modern world until recently, when a number of *causes célèbres* raised once more the scope and limits of religious toleration. In Britain the *fatwa* declared by Ayatollah Khomeini in Iran against Salman Rushdie, author of *The Satanic Verses,* forced him into hiding under police protection for years. The death threat was real. Criticism of the Muslim faith by the director Theo van Gogh led to his murder by an Islamic fundamentalist. Yet Christians have also shown intolerance of perceived criticism of their religion. Demonstrations by Christians resulted in the closure of performances of a musical deemed insulting to Christianity. Some argue that freedom of speech should not involve the licence to insult the deeply held beliefs of others. Respect for minorities in a **multicultural** society, it is argued, requires some restraint on what have been described as 'communal libels'. Yet religious toleration is an argument against the persecution of believers because of their beliefs, not for their protection from any criticism of their religion that they may deem offensive.

Totalitarianism

Totalitarianism was a label initially applied to Italian **fascism** and German Nazism to describe a new kind of **dictatorship** involving a monolithic and all-embracing **state** controlling every aspect of political and social life. 'Everything for the state, nothing outside the state, nothing against the state' as the Italian fascist leader Mussolini put it. Thus the totalitarian state dissolves the liberal distinction between the state and **civil society**. The term 'totalitarianism' was later employed in the west to describe also the **communist** one-party dictatorships in Russia, eastern Europe and China, implying that the similarities between communism and fascism were more marked than the differences. Critics argue that this application of the term was a product of cold war propaganda and ignored the substantial differences between communism and fascism. Key theorists of totalitarianism include Hannah **Arendt**, Karl **Popper** and Friedrich and Brzezinski (1963).

Tradition

Tradition is the term used to describe the handing down of ideas, values and practices from one generation to another. **Conservatives** attach value to tradition, which they see as embodying the accumulated wisdom of the past (see **Burke** and **Oakeshott** among key thinkers). Whole **communities** may venerate traditional practices, and derive comfort from them. However, the Enlightenment viewed tradition with suspicion, as embodying outdated ideas and customs that could no longer be rationally upheld. **Utilitarians** (such as **Bentham**) applied the test of utility to all traditional institutions and practices, and found many of them wanting. **Liberals**, **socialists** and reformers, and revolutionaries generally have similarly embraced **rationalism** and criticized traditionalism for endorsing the status quo and existing unjustified privilege and **power**. **Fascism** in practice often involved a curious marriage of modern technology with many traditional values, which was perhaps part of its appeal to traditional communities facing rapid economic change.

Utilitarianism

Utilitarianism is a moral and political theory that suggests that **laws**, institutions and policies should be judged by their utility (or usefulness), the test of which is how far they promote the hap-piness of the greatest number. Jeremy **Bentham** was the leading proponent of classical utilitarianism, although he acknowledged a debt to previous writers, including the Scottish philosopher David **Hume**, the French writer Helvetius and the Italian criminologist Beccaria. Bentham assumed that all humans pursue pleasure and avoid pain, and that, quantity of pleasure being equal, no pleasure should be ranked more worthy than another. The greatest happiness of the greatest number could be assessed by a 'felicific calculus' balancing the total quantity of pleasure against the quantity of pain resulting from any act. Bentham was converted by his friend James Mill to **representative democracy**. This, he thought, was the only system that could ensure that governments would pursue the happiness of the greatest number rather than the greatest happiness of themselves. Although he thought that the greatest happiness of the greatest number would be secured most readily through the **free market**, increasingly he came to favour government intervention to correct problems arising from free market forces.

John Stuart **Mill** championed Benthamite utilitarianism but departed from Bentham in one significant respect, arguing that 'some *kinds* of pleasures are more desirable and more valuable than others' ([1861]: 8). The notion of 'higher pleasures' introduces a complicating factor in Bentham's 'felicific calculus'. However, both Bentham and Mill applied utilitarianism in a radical way, and their ideas were influential with British socialists, such as Beatrice and Sidney **Webb**.

Utopia (and utopianism)

Utopia was the name Sir Thomas More [1516] gave to his account of an ideal community on an imaginary island. It has since been applied to any fictional account of an ideal political community, from **Plato's** *Republic* through to the modern socialist and anarchist utopias devised by thinkers such as Fourier and **Kropotkin**. Some, such as the British socialist Robert **Owen**, tried to establish such model communities in practice, at New Lanark in Scotland and New Harmony in the USA More generally, the term 'utopian' and 'utopianism' has been employed to mean any idealistic proposal or scheme deemed unrealistic by others. It was in this spirit that **Marx** and **Engels** described Saint-Simon, Fourier and Owen as 'utopian socialists' in *The Communist Manifesto* ([1848]). While they had a socialist vision of a future socialist society, their socialism lacked a scientific analysis of social change, and consequently a realistic strategy for achieving socialism. Marx's own notion of the 'withering away of the state' has been deemed utopian by some critics.

Welfare state

A **welfare state** is concerned not just with the minimum classical **liberal** functions of the state – defence against external threats, the maintenance of internal order, and the protection of **property** – but with the provision of public welfare services, particularly education, health and social security 'from the cradle to the grave'. Many western **states** developed such welfare services from the late nineteenth century onwards, although the pattern of provision, and the means for financing it, differed somewhat from state to state. The proportion of public spending and national income devoted to such welfare services grew rapidly after the Second World War, creating economic and political difficulties. In some respects it could be argued that the welfare state was the victim of its own success, as health and welfare benefits increased life expectancy, and increased demand for retirement pensions and health and social service for the elderly. This has sometimes led to cutbacks in some of these services, and increased reliance on family and **community** care. The pressures of **globalization** have also been sometimes blamed for cuts in welfare provision.

thinkers

introduction to part IV:
key thinkers

This section concentrates on *thinkers*, political philosophers or political scientists who have made a significant contribution to political ideas and the analysis of politics. It excludes almost all those who are best known for practising politics, although the distinction is not always clear cut. The *thought* of some (such as Gandhi and Stalin) is remembered substantially because of what they *did*.

Any list of key thinkers is likely to be contentious for both its inclusions and exclusions. A standard criticism is that they largely consist of 'dead white males'. This is certainly true here. They are mostly dead, and predominantly white and male. Yet they are substantially representative of the writers cited and studied on politics courses around the western world, and reflect the bias in human society over the whole period in which politics has been studied systematically. While additional modern political thinkers and political scientists might have been included, that would have made the list far longer, and perhaps even more contentious. Reputations rise and fall, and it is far from clear which of those writing today will still be studied by generations to come. Thus this list is very sparing in including those who are still living. (However, many more recent writers are cited in Part V, which reviews key areas of research in politics today.)

finding your way around Part IV

While some of the more important thinkers are given extended entries, the ideas of others are discussed more briefly, and in some cases there is little more than the briefest of biographical details, with key publications. If you want to learn more about them you will need to look at other sources (see guidance on further reading in Part VII, Section 2). The same cross-referencing system is employed as in Part III and elsewhere in the book. Thus there is **bold brown text** for other key thinkers mentioned that have their own separate entries in this part, Part IV, and **bold text** for key terms concepts, explored in Part III. There are also, where appropriate, cross-references (in brackets) to other parts of the book.

Adorno

Theodor W. Adorno (1903–1969) was a leading social philosopher who was part of the Frankfurt school, and was associated with critical theory. Born in Frankfurt with a father of Jewish descent, the rise to power of Hitler led him to quit Germany for first England and then the United States, returning to a professorship at Frankfurt after the war. He is still most well-known for *The Authoritarian Personality* (1950), a study of **fascist** psychology based on research he directed. He also wrote on the negative influence on contemporary society of the **mass media** and mass culture, which he considered rendered people docile and passive.

Almond

Gabriel Almond (1911–2002) was an outstanding American political scientist through a long career extending from the 1930s right up to his death. He played a key role in the **behavioural revolution** that moved the study of politics away from **constitutions** and governmental institutions towards such areas as **political culture** and socialization. He also was influential in shifting the study of comparative politics (see pages 88–9) away from a narrow focus on a few western systems of government to include the non-western world. His most celebrated work *The Civic Culture* (with Sidney Verba, 1963) involved a cross-national survey of political cultures in five states. Almond and Verba suggested that what they called a civic culture was most compatible with political stability and **democracy**.

Althusser

Louis Pierre Althusser (1918–1990) was an influential French **Marxist** philosopher and member of the French **Communist Party**. Suffering from mental instability, he strangled his wife in 1980. Diagnosed as having diminished responsibility, he was committed to a psychiatric hospital, and after his release, lived quietly in retirement until his death. In his key work *For Marx* ([1965] 1969), Althusser criticized rival interpretations of **Marx's** thought, particularly those involving crude economic determinism and others that drew particularly on Marx's 'humanist' early writings. He argued that there was an 'epistemological break' between Marx's early and later writings. Only the theory of historical **materialism** tentatively outlined in *The German Ideology* (1845) but more fully developed by the mature Marx in *Capital* had real explanatory power and was truly scientific. Althusser is regarded as the leading exponent of structural Marxism. He argued it was necessary to go beyond an **empirical** approach focusing on isolated aspects of observable human behaviour to understand the 'deep structure' underlying the complex relations of social and economic processes in totality. Some of the implications of Althusser's interpretation of Marx were explored further by Nicos **Poulantzas**.

Aquinas

St Thomas Aquinas (1225–1274) is still widely regarded as the supreme Catholic theologian and philosopher, and much of the political thinking of the modern Roman Catholic church is based on 'Thomist' principles. ('Thomism', derived from Thomas, is the name commonly used to describe the thought of Aquinas.) He was born in southern Italy, and joined the Dominican order in 1244. He studied at Naples, Paris and Cologne before returning to teach in Paris and then various centres of learning in Italy. In the twelfth and thirteenth centuries the main works of **Aristotle** had been rediscovered in western Europe, in part via Muslim Spain. Key texts were translated from Greek to Latin, while the interpretation of Aristotle was strongly influenced by Arab scholars such as Avicenna and **Averroes**. The church was initially uncertain how to regard this new teaching, linked with infidel sources, and there were attempts to ban it. Aquinas instead sought to reconcile the rediscovered philosophy of Aristotle with Christian theology, or reason and faith. *Summa Theologiae* is regarded as his key work. While he agreed with Aristotle that man was by nature a social and political animal, he considered the earthly state could never be a perfect community, and that man required God's grace and the Christian virtues to lead a good life. Thus he argued, 'Grace does not do away with nature but perfects it.' Yet the principles of law and government could be derived from **natural law**, common to all men (see Aquinas, 1948).

Arendt

Hannah Arendt (1906–1975) was a political thinker known mainly for her exploration of **totalitarianism**. A German Jew, she fled Nazi Germany and eventually settled in the USA. Her key book *The Origins of Totalitarianism* (1951) argued that both Nazi Germany and Stalinist Russia involved an essentially new totalitarian system of **government**, in which all institutions and interests were subordinated to the **state** through ideological indoctrination and **terror.** Some critics objected to the equating of Stalinism with Nazism. In a later book *Eichmann in Jerusalem* (1963), arising from the capture, trial and execution of the Nazi Adolf Eichmann for his role in the Holocaust, Arendt used the striking phrase 'the banality of evil' to describe Eichmann's attitude and behaviour. Some Jewish critics thought Arendt diminished Eichmann's personal responsibility for his crimes.

Aristotle

Aristotle (384–322 BC) was a Greek philosopher and political thinker. He was born at Stagira in Thrace, and studied under **Plato** in Athens from 367, leaving the city after Plato's death in 347. In 343 he became tutor to the young Alexander, son of Philip of Macedon, although curiously perhaps, he did not seem to have recognized the longer-term implications of the empire founded by his former pupil for the future of small Greek self-governing political communities, like Athens. Subsequently he returned to Athens, where he opened his own school, the Lyceum. Fears for his own safety following the death of Alexander (known as the Great), and an upsurge of anti-Macedonian feeling, led him to flee Athens in 323, to die in Euboea the following year.

'It's all in Aristotle' has long been a familiar saying among modern writers on politics. He is widely considered one of the greatest political thinkers of all time (although some, including Thomas **Hobbes** in the seventeenth century and Karl **Popper** in the twentieth have been less impressed). Although Plato's pupil, Aristotle came to disagree with much of Plato's philosophy, particularly his theory of knowledge. His approach to the study of politics was also markedly different. Although like Plato he had clear ethical assumptions, he was less interested in abstract political ideals, and more concerned with political practice.

Thus he was a pioneer in the study of comparative politics (see page 88). He and his pupils are known to have surveyed 158 constitutions, of which the only account surviving is of Athens. Aristotle's *Politics* draws extensively on his knowledge of the Greek city states of his own day.

In his *Politics* Aristotle classified political systems using two criteria. The first was simply the number of those directly involved in government (one, few or many). The second criterion involved a rather more subjective judgement as to whether rulers served their own interest or the general interest. This led to a typology with six types of government. Under this classification the rule of one in the general interest (**monarchy**) was the best form of government, while the rule on one in his own interest (tyranny) was the worst.

In comparing political systems he was rather less critical of **democracy** than Plato, but considered that a mixed system of **government** was the most practicable. He argued that man was naturally a social and political animal. Anyone outside the *polis* (roughly translated as city state) was either a beast or a god. However, he assumed that slavery was natural. Unlike Plato, he held conventional views on gender relations and the family, and defended private **property**.

Aristotle wrote extensively on a range of subjects, but key works as far as the study of politics is concerned are the *Politics* and the *Nichomachean Ethics*. Aristotle's writings were translated into Arabic in the Middle Ages and had a significant influence on Islamic thought. Through **Aquinas** in particular Aristotle became a major influence on later medieval Christian philosophy and political thought.

Table 4.1 Aristotle's classification of systems of government

	Ruling in interest of all	Ruling in own interest
Rule of one	Monarchy	Tyranny
Rule of the few	Aristocracy	Oligarchy
Rule of the many	'Good' democracy (polity)	'Bad' democracy (mob rule)

Arrow

Kenneth Arrow (1921–) is an American economist whose work on social theory has had an influence on the study of politics and particularly democracy. Arrow's book *Social Choice and Individual Values* (1951) demonstrated that it was impossible for any method of **election** to produce a fair and accurate reflection of the aggregate choice of voters (Arrow's 'impossibility theorem'). William Riker later showed the importance of Arrow's work for political scientists, especially for **democratic** theory, although Riker considered Arrow's work more damaging for populist interpretations of democracy than for liberal representative democracy.

Augustine

St Augustine (354–430) was one of the first thinkers to explore the relations between religion and the **state**, a key theme of medieval political thought, which now appears of increasing significance in the modern world. He was born in north Africa, still then part of a Roman empire which under the emperor Constantine had become officially Christian, but faced increasing threats from without and within. Some indeed considered that the Christian religion was one of those threats, as the whole-hearted exclusive commitment and loyalty required by some church leaders had damaging implications for both the empire and political **authority** generally. Although his mother was a Christian, Augustine himself was not particularly committed to the faith in his early years. He went through a fairly dissolute period as a student in Rome. In his *Confessions* he records praying, 'Give me chastity and continency – but not yet!' After further studies in Milan, where he fell under the influence of St Ambrose, he experienced a dramatic conversion to a Christian religious vocation. He returned to Africa in 388, and served as bishop of Hippo from 395 until his death in 430, when the city was under siege from the Vandals.

In his key work *The City of God* Augustine contrasted the earthly city or pagan state with the kingdom of Christ, and examined the implications of Christian faith for politics and **government**. While he agreed with pre-Christian writers such as **Plato** and **Cicero** that the state and **civil society** were both natural and necessary, he denied that fallen man could aspire to the good life or the good society. True **justice** could not be achieved on earth. Yet while the ultimate commitment of the Christian was to the Christian community on earth and the kingdom of heaven thereafter, Christians should obey earthly rulers and behave as good citizens.

Averroes

Averroes (Ibn Rushd) (1126–1198) was born in Cordoba, then a leading intellectual centre of Muslim Spain. The Islamic world had taken up with enthusiasm Greek philosophy, translating works into Arabic. Averroes was the last and greatest of the Arab philosophers, providing commentaries on **Plato** and translations of and commentaries on **Aristotle's** *Ethics*. The latter was subsequently translated into Latin, and had a significant influence on **Aquinas** and late medieval political thought in the west.

Bagehot

Walter Bagehot (1826–1877) was a leading British political commentator of his day, remembered for *The English Constitution* ([1867]1963), which famously distinguished between the 'dignified' and 'efficient' parts of the largely unwritten British **constitution** (a distinction that can be readily applied to other constitutions). Bagehot rejected received opinion on the **separation of powers**, and saw the cabinet as the efficient secret of British government, binding the **executive** to the **legislature**. Some later observers in the second half of the twentieth century (such as John Mackintosh and Richard Crossman) concluded that prime ministerial government had subsequently replaced Cabinet government, which had become another dignified rather than efficient part of the constitution. Whether they were right or not is less important than the general point that **power** in government is not necessarily located where constitutional texts suggest, and moreover can change over time.

Bakunin

Michael Bakunin (1814–1876) was a Russian revolutionary **anarchist** who spent periods of his life in prison. Unlike some anarchists who were pacifist, Bakunin advocated violent struggle and acts of **terrorism**. He and **Marx** competed for control of the First International, from which he was expelled in 1872. Bakunin warned of the likely outcome of Marx's notion of the dictatorship of the proletariat.

Barry

Brian Barry (1936–) is a British moral and political philosopher who has taught in universities in the United Kingdom and the USA His work straddles the divide between traditional political philosophy and modern analytical political science, notably in an influential early work *Sociologists, Economists and Democracy* (1970), which involved a critical analysis of the work of **Downs**, **Olson**, **Almond**, **Easton**, and **Lipset** among others. He is best known for his work on social **justice**, on which he was a champion and interpreter of the work of John **Rawls**, who he claimed had relaunched political philosophy. Barry's own work on justice includes consideration of international and inter-generational justice. Key works include *Theories of Justice* (1989), *Justice as Impartiality* (1995) and *Why Social Justice Matters* (2005). He has also written *Culture and Equality: An egalitarian critique of multi-culturalism* (2001a).

Baudrillard

Jean Baudrillard (1929–2007) was a leading French thinker, associated with **postmodernism.** Although he began as a **Marxist** he was later to reject Marxism, becoming increasingly preoccupied with the impact of modern mass communication. He described the condition of the present age as one of 'hyper-reality', with signs, images or symbols ('simulacra') obscuring or replacing reality. Some of his pronouncements were both paradoxical and provocative. Thus he claimed in 1991 that the first Gulf War 'did not take place' and suggested that the 9/11 attacks on the Twin Towers had nothing much to do with religion or a clash of civilizations (see **Huntington**) but were a reaction against **globalization**. His work has attracted considerable controversy. One otherwise respectful obituary began, 'Jean Baudrillard's death did not take place' (*Guardian*, 8 March 2007).

Bell

Daniel Bell (1919–) is an American political sociologist. He is still perhaps best known for *The End of Ideology* (1960). This argued that political differences in the post-war western world were increasingly over technical means rather than ideological ends. The contending ideologies, Stalinist **communism** and **fascism**, that had divided the world earlier in the twentieth century were destroyed or discredited. The very term **ide-**ology and all political 'isms' appeared suspect. **Downs** had already argued that two-party systems were likely to promote competition over the political middle ground, and Bell's 'end of ideology' thesis matched perceptions of a growing political **consensus** (or agreement) in the USA, Britain and the west generally. Critics objected that the presumed 'end of ideology' actually involved the dominance (or **hegemony**) of a particular **liberal capitalist** ideology in the west. Moreover, the growth of political dissent in the 1960s and 1970s (for instance the peace movement, radical **feminism**, the **neoliberal** revival, **green thinking**) soon suggested the obituary for ideology was premature (although Francis **Fukuyama** was to suggest a similar thesis following the end of the cold war).

Bell's influential later work *The Coming of Post-Industrial Society* (1973) argued that the society created by the industrial revolution based on manufacturing industry was being replaced by a **postindustrial** society involving a shift from manufacturing to a service economy, in which information and communication would be key resources. He later coined the term 'information society' to describe the post-industrial economy. Others used the term 'knowledge economy'. Bell has been credited for predicting important developments, then in their infancy, that had considerable implications for politics.

Bentham

Jeremy Bentham (1748–1832) was a British legal and social reformer and political theorist who founded **utilitarianism**. A scathing critic of the doctrine of **natural rights**, which he called 'nonsense on stilts', he championed instead the principle of utility. He asked of any social institution or **law** the question, 'What use is it?' Any such institution or law, however venerable and sanctified by **tradition** and long usage, that failed the utility test, should be abolished or radically reformed. Utility was measured by the pain and pleasure produced for individuals, counted as equals. The principle on which society should be managed (and the aim of **government**) should be to achieve 'the greatest happiness of the greatest number'. One of his passions was penal reform, and Bentham designed, on paper, a massive model prison, the Panopticon, in which prisoners would be comprehensively supervised in all their activities. Although proposals to build the prison were approved by Parliament, implementation of the scheme was obstructed.

Bentham added parliamentary reform to his other causes after James Mill, the father of John Stuart **Mill**, converted him to the principle of **representative democracy**, as the means to ensure that government would in practice be forced to consider the interests of the majority. Although he was also associated with classical economists who advocated the principle of laissez-faire and a minimal **state**, Bentham became convinced of the need for increased state intervention in a variety of fields, and for a reformed state **bureaucracy** that would be fit for purpose. Thus Bentham's **liberalism** did not take the form of pure classical **free market** liberalism but pointed forward to the interventionist New Liberalism of the late nineteenth and twentieth centuries. In the second half of the twentieth century, **neoliberals** like **Hayek** were severely critical of Bentham's 'constructivist rationalism' which they felt was responsible for the growth of the state bureaucracy and **welfare** provision they deplored. The later career of Bentham's secretary, Edwin Chadwick, personified the tensions in mid-nineteenth century liberalism. Chadwick was the architect of the New Poor Law (1834), which embodied market principles on the one hand, but led to the creation of a new state bureaucracy on the other, and Chadwick himself went on to become the leader figure of the interventionist Public Health movement. Bentham himself died in 1832, the year of the great Reform Bill. In accordance with his wishes his body was preserved, dressed in his own clothes, and kept in a glass case in University College, London.

Bentley

Arthur Bentley (1870–1957) was a pioneering American political scientist in the first part of the twentieth century. He may be considered one of the founders of modern **pluralist** theory. As a precursor of the **behavioural** approach, he was sceptical towards formal political institutions, and drew attention to the crucial importance of pressure groups in his key work *The Process of Government* (1908).

Berlin

Isaiah Berlin (1909–1997) was an influential British **liberal** thinker. He was born in Riga, Latvia, from which his family fled to Russia in 1915 and then England in 1920. He secured a double first at Oxford University in Greats (Greek and Latin language and literature) and in Philosophy, Politics and Economics. After graduating, he continued to teach and work at Oxford until his retirement in 1971. His writings were wide-ranging, but he is particularly remembered for an essay, 'Two concepts of liberty' (1958), republished in Berlin's own *Four Essays on Liberty* (1969) and in various anthologies of modern political thought. In this essay he distinguished between 'negative' **liberty**, essentially the freedom of the individual from external interference and from oppression of various kinds, and 'positive' liberty, the freedom of individuals to develop and realize their true potential. While the latter might appear to some (including New Liberal thinkers such as **Green**) to involve a fuller, richer freedom, Berlin considered the notion of positive liberty to have damaging and possibly even **totalitarian** implications. It could be used (and had been used) to justify interference with the freedom of individuals to further their 'real' higher self-interest as opposed to their own immediate wishes and desires. Thus their 'real will' (what they would want if they were sufficiently enlightened), could be used to over-ride their actual preferences Even more dangerously, their 'real will' might be identified with the wider will of the community of which they were a part. Berlin acknowledged that sometimes people may be coerced for their own good, but argued that it is a 'monstrous impersonation' to argue that they really want what they are coerced to do.

Bernstein

Edward Bernstein (1850–1932) was a leading German revisionist **socialist**. He sought to update **Marx** in the light of subsequent history and the failure of some of Marx's predictions (such as the disappearance of intermediate classes and the impoverishment of the industrial working class). He argued that a modified **capitalism** could be transformed gradually into socialism. He was denounced by other **Marxists** (such as Karl **Kautsky**, **Lenin** and Rosa **Luxemburg**), and his influence declined in his own lifetime, although most western socialist parties subsequently followed the route he recommended.

Beveridge

William Beveridge (1879–1963) was an influential British liberal social reformer and economist. He worked with Beatrice and Sidney **Webb** on their report on the Poor Law (1909) and advised Lloyd George on pensions and national insurance, contributing to the ideas of the New Liberals before the First World War. He was director of the London School of Economics (LSE) from 1919–37. In the Second World War he worked for the government, delivering the landmark report on *Social Insurance and Allied Services* (1942), known as the Beveridge report, that provided the basis for the post-war **welfare state**. His work and that of **Keynes** helped to establish the post-war **consensus**, often described as the 'Keynes–Beveridge consensus'. Although his ideas contributed significantly to the post-war Labour government, he remained a **liberal**, and after receiving a peerage in 1946 he later led the Liberal Party in the House of Lords.

Bodin

Jean Bodin (1530–1596) was a French political theorist who argued that only unconditional obedience to a single absolute **sovereign power** could provide internal security and order within a **state**. His key work was *Six livres de la republique* (1576) often referred to simply as the *Republic*.

Buchanan

James M. Buchanan (1919–) is an American economist largely responsible, with Gordon **Tullock**, for the establishment of the **public choice** school (also known as **rational choice**, or the Virginia school – both Buchanan and Tullock taught at university there). Public choice theory has had a massive impact on the study of politics, particularly in the USA but also more generally. Buchanan and Tullock argued that the rational choice assumptions made by economists for the behaviour of producers and consumers in the market should also be applied to the behaviour of those in the public sector. This had critical implications for the role of government and the state generally. Their key work was *The Calculus of Consent* (1962).

Bull

Hedley Bull (1932–1985) was the leading figure in the 'English' school of **international relations**, although he originated from Australia. In his key work *The Anarchical Society* (1977) he argued that **nation-states** remained the main actors in an international society characterized by **anarchy**, in the absence of any effective international authority. Yet anarchy did not necessarily advocate the pursuit of state interests at all costs,

leading to international disorder and war, as states recognized some **obligations** to each other and from prudence and fear states seek to preserve a balance of power.

Burke

Edmund Burke (1729–1797) is now regarded as a founder of modern **conservatism**. Yet this is a rather surprising verdict on a Whig politician and writer who for most of his life was a scathing critic of King George III and British government policy towards America and India. He parted company from the Whig leader Charles James Fox and much of his party over the French **Revolution**, which they initially welcomed, but he condemned from the outset. His essay *Reflections on the Revolution in France* (1790), which was vigorously attacked by radical critics like Tom **Paine**, has become a key text for conservatives everywhere, but particularly in the English-speaking world.

The problem with the French Revolution for Burke was that it involved an attempt to build a new system of **government** and a new society on first principles without reference to the past. Burke thought that the French Revolution differed markedly from Britain's own revolution a century earlier, the so-called 'Glorious Revolution' of 1688 that all Whigs celebrated, as this drew on the past. Burke explicitly compared the state with a living organism, like a plant, that may be pruned or grafted but not torn up by the roots. Instead, reform should be more limited and cautious, and should grow out of the past, and be based on precedent and **tradition**.

While the eighteenth century has been called the 'age of Enlightenment' or 'age of reason', Burke challenged prevailing rationalist assumptions. He argued that most people are not ruled by reason, but guided by emotions and feelings. Individuals would be better advised to rely on the wisdom inherent in tradition and custom rather than attempt to pursue their own rational self-interest. Provocatively, Burke championed what he called 'prejudice' against 'naked reason'.

Burke, like all conservatives, defended private **property**, and justified its unequal distribution. He argued that 'the characteristic essence of property, formed out of the combined principles of its acquisition and conservation, is to be unequal'. Great concentrations of property 'form a natural rampart about the lesser properties in all their gradations'. Thus any threat against the property of the very rich threatens property rights in general. Burke also strongly upheld rights of inheritance.

Burke's old associates accused him of betraying his past principles. Yet while he had been a critic of particular government policies and of abuses of power he had never been a radical, nor committed to notions of popular **sovereignty**. Burke as Member of Parliament sternly declined to be instructed by the electors of Bristol in 1774. 'Your representative owes you, not his industry only, but his judgement; and he betrays instead of serving you, if he sacrifices it to your opinion' (1975: 157). This has become the classic justification for the independence of elected **representatives**, as against the populist principle that, as delegates, they should faithfully reflect the interests and views of their electors.

Carr

E. H. (Edward Hallett) Carr (1892–1982) is perhaps best known as a British **Marxist** historian, particularly for his massive *History of Soviet Russia*. However, he made his name as an **international relations** theorist, particularly for his *The Twenty Years' Crisis* (1939). This book trenchantly advanced Carr's own realist position against the then dominant liberal internationalism that he described as **utopianism**. He argued there was no harmony of interests in international relations. **States** cloaked the pursuit of their own interests in the language of morality. The failure of liberal internationalism to check aggression and preserve peace and stability in the period between the two world wars (the 'twenty years' crisis' of Carr's title) undermined faith in **liberal idealist** theories of international relations. It led to the dominance of **realist** and neo-realist theories in the study of international relations in the post-war decades.

Comte

August Comte (1798–1857) was a wide-ranging French philosopher who coined the term 'sociology' to describe the 'new science' of society. He was the champion of positivism, of positive rather than normative social science, arguing that it was important to understand actual human behaviour, how things were as they were, rather than asking metaphysical questions about why they existed. As such he was the forerunner of the twentieth-century **behavioural revolution** in the social sciences, including politics. He foresaw a society organized on scientific and technocratic

lines in which decisions would be taken by qualified experts in the interests of the community as a whole, but not by the people themselves. He was thus hostile to **democracy**. To help overcome divisive conflict in modern society Comte advocated what was to be in effect a new religion, the religion of humanity, to replace Christianity. Although his scheme for a new religion provoked considerable ridicule, Comte's influence on the subsequent development of the social sciences and the practice of **government** was considerable, particularly in his native France.

Cicero

Marcus Tullius Cicero (106–43 BC) was a Roman lawyer, statesman and political theorist. He made his name in the law courts, studied oratory in Greece, and served as consul, the highest position in the Roman republic, in 63 BC. Subsequently, he fell from favour and spent more of his time writing on law and politics. A keen advocate of the **republican** constitution as well as Roman **law**, he was killed in the period of political turmoil following the assassination of Julius Caesar, and thus did not live to see the emergence of the Roman empire which marked the end of the republic.

He popularized key ideas from Greek philosophy, particularly the notion of **natural law**, derived principally from the Stoics. He described the Roman state as *res populi* or *res publica* (the affair of the people). It existed to serve its people and political **authority** was ultimately derived from the people. Yet although he argued that all men are **equal** in essential respects, he did not favour **democracy** but championed the mixed **constitution**, which he saw embodied in the Roman republic. Key works are his *Republic* and *Laws*.

Crosland

Anthony Crosland (1918–1977) was the leading **social democrat** (or revisionist) thinker in the British Labour Party in the decades after the Second World War. His key work *The Future of Socialism* (1956) argued that **nationalization** of industry was irrelevant in an era when effective control of business was increasingly divorced from its ownership. He believed **Keynes** had shown that a **capitalist** economy could be effectively managed without resort to nationalization. Crosland defined **socialism** in terms of increasing **equality**, and this was being achieved, he thought, through increased **welfare** provision on the one hand and progressive taxation on the other, thus redistributing the fruits of economic growth, without necessarily making anyone worse off in absolute terms. He subsequently held various Cabinet posts in the Labour governments of Wilson and Callaghan. In government, his expectation of continuing substantial economic growth proved over-optimistic, but he remained committed to public spending and his interpretation of socialism.

Dahl

Robert Dahl (1915–) is widely considered an outstanding modern American political scientist and political theorist. He is particularly associated with the study of **power**, which he interpreted in terms of the simple formula that A has power over B if he can get B to do something he would not otherwise do. (Others have criticized this as involving too narrow a view of power, focusing on observable decisions.) Dahl is a key figure in the **community** power debate between **pluralists**, who are argue that power is dispersed, and **elitists** who claim it is heavily concentrated in the hands of the few, a governing elite or elites. *Who Governs?* (1961), his study of decision making in New Haven, Connecticut, concluded that there was no single elite guiding decision making in the town, but rather that power was relatively widely dispersed through the effective influence of many **pressure groups** on the decision-making process in various policy arenas. His theory of **democracy** (he prefers the term 'polyarchy') rests heavily on the ability of ordinary people to influence governmental decision making though such participation in pressure group activity. His writings on democracy include *A Preface to Democratic Theory* (1956), *Polyarchy: Participation and opposition* (1971) and *Democracy and its Critics* (1989).

De Beauvoir

Simone de Beauvoir (1908–1986) was an influential French **feminist** thinker. Her key work, *The Second Sex* [1949], anticipated most of the analysis of the 'second-wave' of feminism by American, Australian and British feminists some 20 years later. Drawing on history, biology, psychology, sociology, literature, and the existentialist philosophy of her long-term partner Jean-Paul **Sartre**, she sought to explain why women constituted a 'second' or inferior sex in society, with less freedom to shape their own destiny. She argued that contemporary images of femininity were learned rather than natural, and advocated full **equality** for women and a balanced relationship between the sexes, in which both men and women enjoyed **freedom**.

Derrida

Jacques Derrida (1930–2004) was perhaps the most widely respected of the French **postmodernist** thinkers (although he dissociated himself from the label), holding prestigious posts in a number of French and American universities and receiving prizes and honorary doctorates around the western world. He is particularly associated with the term 'deconstruction', involving deep analysis of a text to uncover multiple interpretations, with the implication that none of these interpretations should be privileged over the others. Critics have accused Derrida of obscurity, relativism and nihilism. Supporters have claimed his ideas have political relevance. While he was not notably active in politics he supported progressive causes.

Deutsch

Karl Deutsch (1912–1992) was born in Prague, where he studied at the German University and Charles University, before emigrating to the United States in 1938, where he subsequently taught at Yale and Harvard. He is regarded as one of the pioneers of modern political analysis, particularly the application of quantitative methods and cybernetics to social science, and contributed notably to the study of **nationalism** and political communication. A key work is *The Nerves of Government* (1963).

Downs

Anthony Downs (1930–), made his name as an American political scientist with the publication of *An Economic Theory of Democracy* (1957). This applied the theory and methods of economics to the analysis of the competition between **political parties** for votes and support. A key assumption in economics is that individuals both as consumers and producers pursue their own **rational** self-interest. This compares with approaches to the study of politics derived from sociology or psychology that suggest that much political behaviour, (for example, voting behaviour) is not particularly rational. Downs assumed that parties, like entrepreneurs in the market place, sought to maximize their support by increasing their share of the political market by finding out what

thinkers

the majority consumers or voters wanted, and promising to supply it. Ideas and policies found to be unpopular are jettisoned. In a two-party system (like that in the USA and until recently the United Kingdom), the competing parties seek to maximize their vote by competing for the political centre ground. This book was a key inspiration for the growth of **rational choice** (or **public choice**) theory, which now dominates the US political science and has a strong influence on the study of politics in the United Kingdom and elsewhere. Downs himself contributed significantly to public choice theory with his later book *Inside Bureaucracy* (1967). This applied the assumption of the pursuit of rational self-interest to those working inside **bureaucratic** organizations, particularly in the private sector. William **Niskanen** has developed further the application of public choice theory to the behaviour of bureaucrats.

Duverger

Maurice Duverger (1917–) is perhaps the outstanding French political scientist of the second half of the twentieth century. His work was founded on extensive empirical research. He is perhaps best known for his study of **political parties** published in 1951. His typology of parties is still extensively applied, particularly the distinction between elite and mass parties, although the latter have recently suffered a substantial decline both in formal membership and activism almost everywhere. What came to be called 'Duverger's law' suggested a strong correlation between the 'first past the post' electoral system and a two-party system (for example in the United Kingdom, although here this correlation seems weaker today than from 1945–70). Duverger's approach to the subject of politics (first published as *Sociologie Politique* in France in 1966 and translated into English as *The Study of Politics* in 1972) has also been influential. He likens politics to the two faces of Janus, one involving conflict and **power,** the other unification and integration. Politics is about both conflict and compromise, the resolution of conflict. Duverger is an academic who has more recently played an active political role, as a Member of the European Parliament from 1989–94, sitting with the European Socialist Party.

Dworkin, Andrea

Andrea Dworkin (1946–2005) was an extremely controversial American radical **feminist**. She was active in **left**-wing causes before her experience of an abusive marriage in the Netherlands turned her also into a radical feminist, inspired by the writings of Kate **Millett** and others. She became a leading figure in campaigns against violence against women, which she linked with pornography, arguing that it involved the domination, humiliation and dehumanization of women (*Pornography: Men possessing women*, 1979). With Catharine **MacKinnon** she campaigned to use civil rights legislation to combat pornography. However, her controversial and provocative style led even some feminists to conclude that her influence was counterproductive for the women's movement. Some criticized what they saw as her repressive attitude to sexuality.

Dworkin, Ronald

Ronald Dworkin (1931–) is an American legal and political theorist who has taught at Yale, Oxford and London universities. As a legal theorist he disagreed with the English legal theorist H. L. A. Hart whose legal **positivism** involved a separation of **law** and morality. As a political theorist he has made a significant contribution to the modern debate on **equality**, **liberty** and **rights**. A key work is *Taking Rights Seriously* (1977).

Easton

David Easton (1917–) is a Canadian political scientist, known principally for applying systems theory (derived from cybernetics) to politics (Easton, 1965). The political system is seen as responding to inputs or influences (demands and supports) from its environment, converting these into policy outputs (or decisions), which in turn affect the environment, and leading to new inputs. The systems approach was particularly fashionable in the 1950s and 1960s, and fitted **pluralist** assumptions. Critics argued that the systems approach only offered another description of the political system using different terminology. The systems approach also appears to ignore or downgrade the **state** and its institutions and personnel, implying these involve little more than a mechanism to convert inputs into outputs, without any autonomous **power** of its own.

Engels

Friedrich Engels (1820–1895) is known largely as the junior partner in his celebrated intellectual collaboration with **Marx**. Born in Westphalia, the eldest son of a wealthy textile manufacturer, he was drawn into radical young Hegelian and **communist** circles as a student in Berlin. Nevertheless he went on in 1842 to work in the family business in Manchester, combining his own employment in the services of **capitalism** with research that exposed the consequences of capitalism in *The Condition of the Working Class in England* (1845). His close collaboration with Marx dates from their meeting in Paris in 1844. They worked together on *The Holy Family*, the unfinished *German Ideology*, and most notably, *The Communist Manifesto* (1848). After the failure of the 1848 revolutions Engels rejoined the family firm in Manchester, where he also enjoyed riding to hounds with the Cheshire hunt. Yet he remained a committed communist **revolutionary**, whose own comfortable circumstances allowed him to subsidize the impoverished Marx, while he worked on *Das Kapital*. After Marx's death in 1883, Engels edited the second and third volumes of *Kapital*, and continued to popularize his partner's ideas. How far he protected Marx's legacy is contentious. Thus his interpretation of dialectical materialism (for instance in *Anti-Duhring*) was perhaps less subtle than Marx's own. Engels also lived to witness the rise in the electoral fortunes of the German SPD, the **social democrats**, and came to envisage the possibility of **socialism** through the ballot box. Undoubtedly, however, Engels considerably assisted the growth of **Marxism**, widening its appeal, not least to women. *The Origin of the Family, Private Property and the State* explored gender relations and the subordination of women, an issue relatively neglected by Marx.

Foucault

Michel Foucault (1926–1984) was an influential French philosopher, and regarded as a leading influence on structuralism and **postmodernism**, although Foucault himself rejected categorization. In *Madness and Civilization* (1965) and *Discipline and Punish* (1977) he argued that our changing perceptions and techniques for dealing with both lunatics and criminals involved, not progress and a more scientific and humane approach to the treatment of deviants, but institutionalization and social control that was dehumanizing. A particular target was Jeremy **Bentham** and his proposed model prison, the 'Panopticon'. Foucault saw the asylum and the prison as metaphors for modern institutions generally and the social control of

whole peoples. In *The Archaeology of Knowledge* (1972) and other works on language he connected the 'discourses' or 'discursive formations' used to legitimize modern 'scientific' approaches with **power**. Narrative and discourse reflected power. This connection of power with language is particularly suggestive for students of politics.

Friedan

Betty Friedan (1921–2006) remains the most well-known modern American **feminist** writer. Her best-selling book *The Feminist Mystique* (1965) argued that women had been manipulated into believing that their fulfilment lay in marriage and passive domesticity by women's magazines and the advertising industry. She spoke for millions of American women who felt imprisoned in the home and family, and precipitated the formation of a mass movement in 1966, the National Organization of Women (NOW), of which she became the first president. This did succeed in achieving some legal changes, and more important changes in attitude, not only in the USA, but elsewhere in the west. Radical critics however pointed out that women had manifestly failed to secure equality with men, suggesting that Friedan's **liberal** feminist analysis and strategy did not go far enough. Friedan responded to her critics by placing more emphasis on child care provision and maternity leave in her later book *The Second Stage* (1982), although she also argued that the shock tactics of the radicals had sometimes been counterproductive and had alienated some women.

Fukuyama

Francis Fukuyama (1952–) sprang to fame for an article entitled 'The end of history?' originally published in 1989, the year of the fall of the Berlin Wall, and reproduced in expanded book form as *The End of History and the Last Man* (1992). Essentially it argued that history, in the sense of a conflict between rival **ideologies**, and rival economic and political systems, was at an end. The cold war between **communism** and **capitalism** was over and **liberal** capitalism had won. Inevitably, Fukuyama's thesis provoked comparisons with the earlier *End of Ideology* (1960) of Daniel **Bell**. As with Bell's book, Fukuyama's bold thesis was rapidly overtaken by events. Other forms of ideological and cultural conflict soon replaced the now redundant competition between a liberal capitalist west and Marxist-Leninist east, and history seemed far from over. Fukuyama has since produced further controversial books on social trust (1996) and the biotechnology revolution (2002), incidentally acknowledging in the latter that history is not at an end. Although he was until recently regarded as a neo-conservative, initially strongly advocating armed intervention in Iraq, he has since distanced himself from neoconservatism, criticizing the conduct of the Iraq war and American foreign policy generally. He now favours US support for international institutions, with military force only employed as a last resort.

Galbraith

John Kenneth Galbraith (1908–2006) was a celebrated Canadian economist and political thinker who advised several US presidents from F D Roosevelt to Kennedy, and was professor of economics at Harvard. Some of his many books became best sellers, particularly *The Affluent Society* (1958) and *The New Industrial State* (1967). He was a pluralist who coined the phrase 'countervailing power' to describe US political economy in *American Capitalism* (1952). In his later work he advocated increased spending on education and social **welfare**, and criticized the neglect of the public sector and the growth of **inequality** and poverty in the USA, helping to inspire the 'war on poverty' of Presidents Kennedy and Johnson. His influence on **government** waned subsequently and as a progressive **liberal** who favoured government spending and redistribution he incurred the hostility of **neoliberals** like Milton Friedman.

Gandhi

Mohandas Karamchand (more commonly known as Mahatma) Gandhi (1869–1948) led the ultimately successful campaign for Indian independence, but was perhaps more remarkable for his beliefs and methods than for his political achievements. Born and brought up in Porbandar, Kathiawar, in India, with the support of his family he went to London to study law, where he also became active in the vegetarian movement. He returned to India and a lucrative legal practice in Bombay, which he gave up in 1893 to live in poverty and practise law in South Africa on behalf of the Indian community, who routinely experienced racial discrimination and injustice. Thoroughly radicalized, in 1914 he returned to India, where he soon became the acknowledged leader of the Home Rule movement. Totally committed to non-

violence, he led campaigns of **civil disobedience** involving passive resistance to forward the cause of independence. It may be questionable how far his pacifism would have been successful against a more ruthless enemy, but it achieved a moral **authority** that for a time united Indians across barriers of caste, language and religion. The British government negotiated with Gandhi to secure the independence of India after the Second World War. However, religious divisions between Hindus and Muslims prevented the emergence of a single **state** for the whole Indian sub-continent. Gandhi was appalled by the sectarian violence in the period leading up to independence, and tried to check it. He was assassinated by a Hindu fanatic in 1948.

Giddens

Anthony Giddens (1938–) is a British sociologist whose prolific output has had a significant impact on the study of politics. His theory of structuration, an approach to the problem of **structure and agency**, has been particularly influential. He insisted that neither social structure nor individual human agency had primacy but both were 'flip sides' of the same coin. We should recognize the duality of structure. Human agents make social structures but are in turn constrained by them. Key works included *Central Problems in Social Theory* (1979) and *The Constitution of Society* (1984). More recently Giddens has focused on the concepts of modernity (incidentally dismissing the notion of **postmodernity**) and **globalization**, and has contributed to the debate on the development of political ideas, particularly the **Third Way**, in *Beyond Left and Right* (1994), *The Third Way* (1998), *The Third Way and Its Critics* (2000) and *The Global Third Way Debate* (2001). He received a life peerage in 2004.

Godwin

William Godwin (1756–1836) was an English **anarchist** who was against all forms of **government**, but was also a **pacifist** opposed to violent **revolution**. His most celebrated work *An Enquiry Concerning Political Justice* (1793), involved an extremely optimistic view of **human nature**. Humans were **rational**, naturally benevolent towards each other and cooperative. **State government** should be replaced by self-government, and people should live together in small self-governing local **communities**. Issues would be resolved by rational debate. Reason, he thought, would lead people to a voluntary system of **communism**. Godwin was briefly married to the feminist writer Mary **Wollstonecraft**. Their daughter, also called Mary, married the radical poet Shelley, who later expressed some of Godwin's political ideas in verse.

Gramsci

Antonio Gramsci (1891–1937) was perhaps the most influential twentieth-century western **Marxist**. Born in Sardinia, he won a scholarship to the University of Turin, and was active as a young man in the Italian socialist party before the First World War. He enthusiastically welcomed the Russian Revolution of 1917 and in post-war Italy supported the factory council movement. He helped form the new Italian Communist Party (PCI) in 1921 and went to Moscow as the party's delegate to the Third International in 1922. Returning to Italy in 1924, he was elected to parliament, two years after Mussolini had become prime minister following the **fascist** 'march on Rome' In 1926 he was arrested and imprisoned for the rest of his life. It was while he was in captivity that he wrote *The Prison Notebooks* [1929–35]. Gramsci sought to explain the survival of **capitalism** in the western industrialized world and the failure of the working **class** to develop a revolutionary consciousness. His answer was linked to his key concept, **hegemony**. Although the ruling class could ultimately resort to coercion, most of the time they could rely on the consent of the ruled because of their effective dominance (or hegemony) over ideas and thought generally, resulting from their control of the economy, state, culture and education. The **state**, Gramsci argued, involved force plus **consent**. The role of a **revolutionary** party was to develop working-class self-consciousness to create an alternative counter **ideology** to challenge and ultimately overcome the dominant **bourgeois** ideology. Gramsci urged a strategy of working with other progressive forces in society to this end, arguably supporting the kind of approach the PCI was later to take in Italy after the end of the war and the fascist dictatorship. However, the relationship between Gramsci's ideas and the subsequent euro-communism of the Italian Communist Party is contentious.

Green

Thomas Hill Green (1836–1882) was an Oxford philosopher who was a key influence, along with

Leonard **Hobhouse** and John Hobson (1858–1940), on the development of British **liberalism** towards the New Liberalism of the late nineteenth and early twentieth centuries. Green's key work, *Lectures on the Principles of Political Obligation* [1881], was published after his early death. Influenced by ancient Greek philosophy and German idealism (particularly **Kant**), Green criticized aspects of earlier schools of liberalism, including both classical laissez-faire liberalism and Benthamite **utilitarianism**. He rejected what he saw as an artificial antithesis between the individual and society. A political **community** was a partnership for the common good. Each individual had **obligations** as well as **freedoms**. True freedom involves not simply the satisfaction of appetites, but self-development, in common with others. This justified **state** intervention, particularly in education and health, both for the common good and to allow individuals to make the best of themselves. This positive liberty (freedom *to*) might be contrasted with the negative liberty (freedom *from*) associated with classical **free market** liberalism. (Isaiah **Berlin** later famously explored the implications of these two concepts of liberty.)

Greer

Germaine Greer (1939–) is a particularly controversial **feminist** writer and broadcaster, who was born and brought up in Australia but has since lived and worked mainly in England. Her best-selling book *The Female Eunuch* (1970) brought feminist ideas to a much wider audience. While critical of the role of the western nuclear family in the subordination of women, Greer, in her later work *Sex and Destiny* (1984), argued in favour of the extended family, familiar in Asian, African and Mediterranean cultures. She remains the most well-known feminist in Britain, but her undoubted 'star quality' and her enjoyment of controversy have not always endeared herself to other feminists and the women's movement generally.

Grotius

Hugo Grotius (1583–1645) was a Dutch lawyer who is widely considered to have laid the foundations of modern **international law**. Like many classical and medieval thinkers before him he considered **natural law** as the foundation of the **law** of **states**, but argued that it also should govern relations between states in his key work *De Jure Belli ac Pacis* (Concerning the Law of War and

Peace, 1625). He asserted, as a central principle of international law, that states and their **governments** should uphold treaties freely entered into. Only a defensive war, he argued, could be a just war. His ideas are still widely cited in modern theories of **international relations**, particularly by the English school.

Habermas

Jurgen Habermas (1929–) is a wide-ranging German social and political theorist, who is generally considered the leading thinker of the second generation of the Frankfurt School of critical theory. Unlike many fashionable modern thinkers Habermas defends the Enlightenment, which he sees as a still unfinished project to create a modern free and rational society. This has brought him into conflict with **postmodernists** such as **Derrida** and **Lyotard** who have reacted against the Enlightenment and its trust in human reason, science and progress. In *The Structural Transformation of the Public Sphere* (1962), Habermas deplores the decline of what he saw as a once vigorous public sphere of political debate with the growth of a commercialised mass media. In *Knowledge and Human Interests* (1971) he argues that people are effectively manipulated in modern capitalist society where everything is treated as a commodity. In his *Legitimation Crisis* (1975) Habermas claims the modern capitalist state is facing a combination of crises. State intervention to deal with or avoid economic crisis risks creating crises of rationality, **legitimacy** and motivation. However his key work is *The Theory of Communicative Action* (volume 1, 1984, volume 2, 1986), where he displays his confidence in the potential for rational communication based on mutual trust and **consensus**. In his more recent work he has apparently modified his earlier hostility to **capitalism**, which he now sees as compatible with a **democratic** society.

Hayek

Friedrich August von Hayek (1899–1992) was the outstanding **neoliberal** thinker of the twentieth century. Born and educated in Austria, where he worked as an economist, he moved to the London School of Economics (LSE) in 1931, becoming a British citizen in 1938. He left the LSE for the University of Chicago in 1950, and moved from there to the University of Freiburg in Germany in 1962, until his retirement in 1968. He was awarded the Nobel Prize for economics in 1974, was made

a Companion of Honour in Britain in 1984, and received the US Presidential Medal of Freedom in 1991. His ideas have been influential throughout the western world, but have perhaps had most impact in his native Austria, his adopted country, Britain, the USA, and finally Germany, where he died in 1992.

Hayek's *Road to Serfdom* (1944) involved an attack on all forms of state economic planning, not just the **collectivist** planning advocated by **communists**, left-wing **socialists** and **fascists**, but the modest state intervention practised by **social democrats**, many **conservatives** and 'social' or 'new' **liberals**. Hayek argued that state economic planning was not only less efficient than resource allocation through the **free market**, it also involved, inevitably, an oppressive interference with individual **liberty**, or in his words a 'road to serfdom'. Hayek opposed any attempt by government to promote social (or distributive) **justice**. He argued that it would lead to constant and extensive control of individuals, which was inconsistent with a free society, in pursuit of an unobtainable ideal. The legitimate role of government, according to Hayek, was to provide a framework of law and order within which the free market could flourish, and this he outlined in his later major work *The Constitution of Liberty* (1960). Here he did however allow that governments might provide a minimal safety net for particularly needy individuals.

Hayek's uncompromising free market convictions naturally brought him into conflict not only with socialists but with Keynesians, who believed in government management of the macroeconomy, and all those governments and politicians across the political spectrum who favoured the development of a **welfare state** in the post-war period. For much of this time Hayek's classical liberalism (or neoliberalism) was at odds with prevailing economic and political orthodoxy. However, the problems encountered by governments attempting to manage the economy on Keynesian lines brought Hayek's free market ideas back into fashion. In Britain, the Conservative leader Margaret Thatcher (prime minister 1979–90), was a self-proclaimed admirer, and there was further support for his ideas from President Reagan's Republican administration (1980–88).

Hayek himself always denied that he was a conservative. Conservatism had not in the past been wedded to free markets. Perhaps Hayek also bore in mind the interventionist record of past

Conservative governments in Britain, as well as the continuing emphasis of continental European conservatives and **Christian democrats** on planning and social welfare. Instead, Hayek called himself a classical liberal or old Whig. In the USA he is generally described as a 'libertarian'. Whatever label is used, Hayek's influence not just on political thought but on the practice of government has been considerable.

Hegel

George Wilhelm Friedrich Hegel (1770–1831) was a German philosopher and political thinker. Born in Stuttgart, he later taught at the universities of Jena, Heidelberg and Berlin. His key political work is *The Philosophy of Right* [1821], but his writings on logic also had important implications for political theory. Thus he argued that classical formal logic is static and intellectually limited. Instead, he suggested that human knowledge commonly progresses through a dynamic process of argument, that he called *dialectic*, involving the statement of a *thesis*, its opposite or *antithesis,* and a *synthesis* incorporating elements of the original thesis and its antithesis. This becomes a new thesis, initiating a new antithesis and synthesis, and so on.

In *The Philosophy of Right* Hegel applies his dialectical analysis to three levels of human social interaction, the family, **civil society** and the **state**. Within the family people may pursue 'particular altruism', putting the interests of other family members before their own, but the family is a natural rather than a rational form of association and inherently unstable. Civil society involves 'universal egoism', the general pursuit of individual self-interest in the wider **community**, although people honour their contractual obligations in the market place. The state, however, is an ethical community which involves a synthesis of the values of the family and civil society, and is characterized by universal altruism, the whole community acting for the common good rather than individual self-interest. Thus for Hegel it is only within the modern state that human beings can realize their true rational **freedom** in company with their fellows. For Hegel humans are naturally social animals and can only fulfil themselves through society and political community. Thus he holds an organic theory of society and the state.

Hegel has been variously interpreted. Although he has been accused of being a political reactionary, celebrating the Prussian state that he served, he supported the constitutional and legal reforms undertaken in Prussia, and so advocated limited rather than absolute monarchy. The 'young Hegelians' (including especially **Marx**) applied his ideas in a radical or even **revolutionary** way. While Hegel applied his dialectical method to the development of ideas, and human progress towards greater self-knowledge and freedom, Marx later applied it to material circumstances, particularly **class** interests (hence *dialectical materialism*). In the later nineteenth century Hegel's thought particularly influenced the English idealists, including T H **Green**, and Bosanquet, notably in their emphasis on positive rather than negative liberty and their general commitment to state action to enlarge freedom. Subsequently, some western thinkers (such as **Popper**) detected dangerous **authoritarian** and even **totalitarian** tendencies in Hegel's thought. His ideas have been more sympathetically re-examined by others.

Hirschman

Albert O. Hirschman (1915–) is an American economist who has been described as inhabiting a grey zone between economic and political theory. He was born in Berlin, and educated in Paris, London and Trieste. He helped many European intellectuals escape from the Nazis, and emigrated to the USA himself in 1941. After the war he held economics posts at Yale, Columbia and Harvard, where he worked on the political economy of development. To students of politics he is best known for his influential book *Exit, Voice and Loyalty* (1970), the title of which lists the three main responses open to dissatisfied consumers, employees or citizens. They can leave (exit), they can oppose (voice) or keep quiet (loyalty). As Stoker (2006: 74) has pointed out, exit is the classic economic mechanism. In a **free market**, if consumers are dissatisfied, the answer is easy; they can go elsewhere. They do not have make a fuss. Voice is the classic political mechanism, exercised for example through such means of political participation as voting, joining **pressure groups**, protesting or taking direct action. Voice requires more effort and carries more costs for the individual than exit. Moreover it may not be successful. (This is one reason why Stoker concludes that political decision making involves 'designed-in disappointment'.)

Hobbes

Thomas Hobbes (1588–1679) is perhaps the most celebrated English political philosopher. He was born in the year of the Spanish Armada. Hobbes claimed that his mother, seeking to flee the threatened invasion, gave birth to twins, himself and fear. Later, fear was to form a significant element in his political thought. Educated at Oxford, he was unimpressed by the philosophy of **Aristotle**. His political ideas were shaped by the conflict between King Charles I and Parliament that led to the English Civil War, the execution of Charles and the 'Commonwealth' of Oliver Cromwell. Already by 1640 he had become an advocate of absolute **monarchy,** and fled to France with the summoning of the Long Parliament. His thoughts on government were set out in *De Cive* (1642). From 1646 he briefly became tutor to the young exiled Prince Charles. In 1651 he published his great work *Leviathan*.

As in his early works, in *Leviathan* Hobbes advocated virtually total obedience to an absolute **government** as the only alternative to **anarchy**. He argued that humans were competitive, selfish and acquisitive. Their life without a supreme government to keep them in order would be 'solitary, poor, nasty, brutish and short', and would involve a war of every man against every man. To avoid this nightmare, men rationally agreed to surrender their right to govern themselves to a common **sovereign** in a contract or promise. Some political thinkers used the notion of a social contract to suggest a two-way bargain between sovereign and subjects, arguing that if the sovereign failed to maintain his side of the bargain, his subjects were no longer bound to obey him. For Hobbes the surrender of power by subjects was unconditional and permanent. If sovereignty was limited or divided, anarchy would result.

Yet his justification of **absolutism** did not involve the conventional royalist argument based on the divine right of kings, but was essentially **utilitarian**. The sovereign should be obeyed because of the peace and security the sovereign provided. For Hobbes the identity of the sovereign was less important. Indeed, he argued that the sovereign power could be either a single person or an assembly, but not both. Hobbes' message could be interpreted to mean simply, 'Obey the powers that be.' If a former ruler had effectively lost sovereign **authority**, and could no longer provide the peace and security associated with sovereignty, the rational solution was for subjects to transfer their allegiance to the new sovereign. The argument was not spelled out in the *Leviathan*, but in 1652 Hobbes returned to England and made his peace with Oliver Cromwell. Subsequently, after the restoration, he was recognized by his former pupil, by then King Charles II and brought back to court for a time, until his alleged atheism scandalized the courtiers. He continued to work and write until his death in 1679.

Hobhouse

Leonard Trelawney Hobhouse (1864–1929) was a British **liberal** political philosopher who was an influential figure in the emergence of the New Liberalism that favoured increased state intervention in the early twentieth century. In *Liberalism* [1911] he was prepared to justify extensive interference with the **free market** to secure 'the right to work' and 'the right to a living wage'. Although Hobhouse was influenced by the **idealism** of T. H. **Green**, he became critical of the influence of **Hegel**, in particular on the New Liberalism. Hobhouse's book *The Metaphysical Theory of the State* [1918] vigorously attacked *The Philosophical Theory of the State* (1899) by Green's disciple Bernard Bosanquet.

Hooker

Richard Hooker (1554–1600) was an English theologian and philosopher who provided theoretical support for the Elizabethan church and state. In his key work *Of the Laws of Ecclesiastical Polity* (1592) he upheld the Church of England as an acceptable middle way between Roman Catholicism and Puritanism, and justified the royal supremacy over the church. Like some other thinkers of the early modern period he assumed that legitimate **government** originated from a contract, and thus ultimately rested on the **consent** of the governed. However, he did not draw radical conclusions from this assumption (as did some later contractarian theorists), but lauded, and preached loyalty to, the English **constitution**. He is thus regarded as part of the English **conservative** tradition of political thought.

Hume

David Hume (1711–1776), a hugely influential Scottish thinker, was celebrated in his own time as a historian (a five-volume *History of England*,

1754–62) and is today viewed chiefly as a major philosopher (*A Treatise of Human Nature*, 1739–40), but his contributions to political thought are also important, although not easy to summarize. As a philosopher he was both an **empiricist** and a sceptic. Reason is limited and 'the slave of the passions'. Our ideas are derived from the experience of our senses. An association or correlation of events cannot prove a cause and effect. This emphasis on the limitations of reason and human intelligence is compatible with a form of **conservatism**, and Hume's own political sympathies were Tory. A brief essay, *Of the Original Contract* [1748], typifies his common-sense approach to politics. In it he robustly demolishes the argument of those like **Hobbes** and **Locke** that our obligation to obey **government** depends on some (implicit or explicit) contract or promise. Instead, Hume argues that we obey government 'because society could not otherwise subsist'. This might be described as a **utilitarian** argument. Indeed, Hume was claimed as a forerunner by the utilitarian thinker Jeremy **Bentham**, although Hume did not share Bentham's **rationalist** and reformist convictions.

Huntington

Samuel P Huntington (1927–) is an American political scientist, and a professor at Harvard University. An influential but controversial book was *Political Order in Changing Societies* which appeared in the same year, 1968, that saw radical political protest by students in both the USA and western Europe. He subsequently turned his attention to the comparative study of the process of **democratization** that he saw as developing in the course of the twentieth century in three 'waves', with intervening reverse waves (*The Third Wave: Democratization in the Late Twentieth Century*, 1991). More controversial still was *The Clash of Civilizations,* published as an article in 1993, and later expanded for publication in book form as *The Clash of Civilizations and the Remaking of World Order* [1996]. This argued that cultural (and religious) divisions transcending **state** boundaries had replaced **ideological** conflict between sovereign states in the post cold war world. Huntington's thesis was widely seen as prophetic of the apparently growing threat to the west from radical Islam, as represented by the attack on the Twin Towers of 9/11. Some critics accused Huntington of legitimizing the subsequent 'war on terror' and the western invasion of Afghanistan

and Iraq, although he was not an enthusiast for extensive 'humanitarian intervention'. Others argued that his analysis was over-simplified, taking insufficient account of the extensive internal differences within civilizations and cultures.

Inglehart

Ronald Inglehart (1934–) is an American political scientist whose work has focused on changes in **political culture**, particularly in advanced western industrial states. He argued in a seminal article ('The silent revolution in Europe: intergenerational change in post-industrial societies', 1971) that increased affluence and security had led to changes in political attitudes among the younger generation towards **postmaterial** values that emphasized quality of life rather than economic achievement. This theme was further explored in later works, such as *Culture Shift in Advanced Industrial Society* [1990], and *Modernization and Post-Modernization: Cultural, economic and social change in 43 societies* [1997b]. More recently he has (with Pippa Norris) in *Sacred and Secular: Religion and politics worldwide* [2004] explored the contrast between the growth of secularization in the western industrial societies and the strong maintenance of traditional religious convictions elsewhere, particularly those living in poorer societies and failed **states**.

Jefferson

Thomas Jefferson (1743–1826), among his many other wide-ranging interests, furnished some of the key ideas behind the American Revolution. As an active politician and statesman he helped shape the United States of America in its early years. Born and brought up in Virginia, where his education introduced him to the ideas of the Scottish Enlightenment, he was elected as delegate from his state to the Continental Congress of 1776, and drafted the *Declaration of Independence*, with its celebrated preamble:

> We hold these truths to be self-evident, that all men are created equal, that they are endowed by their Creator with certain inalienable rights, that among these are life, liberty and the pursuit of happiness. That to secure these rights, governments are instituted among men, deriving their just powers from the consent of the governed.

thinkers

Jefferson's eloquently stated ideals have remained an inspiration, and not only to Americans. If Jefferson's passionate commitment to **equality**, **liberty** and universal human **rights** was incompatible with his own position as a slave owner, it was a contradiction widely shared in the new political state and society he helped to create in America.

Jefferson subsequently served as American Minister in Paris (1784–9) where he witnessed the beginning of the French **Revolution** and advised Lafayette on the *Declaration of the Rights of Man* (1789). Thus he provides a crucial link between the American and French revolutions. Back in America he served in Washington's government from 1789–93 and became the third president of the United States (1801–9). He played a key role in the early US **party** system, standing for the rural interests of the majority of American voters against the business interests of the federalist party.

Kant

Immanuel Kant (1724–1804) was an outstanding German philosopher, who was born in Konigsberg (then in East Prussia), where he later taught at the university and spent the rest of his life. He is widely considered to be the last great thinker of the Enlightenment. His key works include *Critique of Pure Reason* (1781), *Critique of Practical Reason* (1788) and *Critique of Judgement* (1790) (all in Kant, 1970). Although he was not primarily a political thinker, his writings on ethics in particular have made a significant influence on political thought. For Kant, morality springs from the exercise of human reason by **free** individuals. It does not rest on religion or other forms of **authority**. Kant's main moral principle (or 'categorical imperative') was, act only on the maxim through which you can at the same time will that it should become a universal law. In other words, we should act only as we would be happy for others to act in the same circumstances. Kant's best-known moral principle is that we should treat other people as ends, never as means. Thus we should do good for its own sake, not for any benefit it might bring.

Kant also anticipated elements of later liberal **international relations** theory in his essay *Perpetual Peace* (1795), where he argues that nations, for the sake of their own security, should seek a 'federation of peoples' to prevent war. This would not involve a global **state**, but would rest on an 'equilibrium of forces' (or balance of **power**).

Peace would be aided by the mutual interest of nations in trade and commerce, which cannot coexist with war, so that wherever a threat of war emerged, nations would seek to avoid it by mediation. Kant also argued that **republics** were much less likely to go war, as the citizens who decided the issue would suffer the consequences. Modern international relations theory notes that in practice **democracies** rarely make war on other democracies (see Kant, 1970).

Kautsky

Karl Kautsky (1854–1938) was a leading German **socialist** thinker, responsible with **Bernstein** for the 1891 Erfurt Programme of the Social Democratic Party, which committed it to a Marxist programme. Subsequently he rejected Bernstein's revisionism, insisting on the inevitability of **class** conflict. Yet he was committed to the **democratic** route to power, and after he criticized the Bolshevik Revolution he was in turn attacked by **Lenin** as a renegade. After the war he played a leading role in the Second International.

Keohane

Robert Keohane (1941–) is a leading American writer on **international relations**. In a volume he co-edited with Joseph Nye, *Transnational Relations and World Politics* (1971), much greater importance was attached to the role and influence of non-state actors in international relations, in contrast to the **state**-centred approach of orthodox **realist** theory. In 1977 Keohane and Nye published *Power and Interdependence* (3rd edn 2000), their own theory of international relations, based on the notion of complex interdependence, involving both state and non-state actors.

Key

V. O. Key (1908–1963) was a leading American political scientist who played a significant role in the **behavioural revolution** in the study of politics. He was particularly associated with the statistical analysis of voting, and public opinion data. His publications include *Politics, Parties and Pressure Groups* (1942), and *Southern Politics in State and Nation* (1950).

Keynes

John Maynard Keynes (1883–1946) was a celebrated British economist whose work had major implications for politics. He worked in the

British Treasury during the First World War, and attended the post-war treaty negotiations, writing a celebrated critique of the outcome, *The Economic Consequences of the Peace* (1919). In the 1920s he advised the Liberal Party on economic policy. In 1936 he published the *General Theory of Employment, Interest and Money*, which became the 'bible' of what came to be known as Keynesianism, and provided the theoretical underpinning for **government** management of the economy in the post-war decades.

Briefly, Keynes advocated leaving the micro economy to market forces, but recommended government management of aggregate demand in the macro economy through fiscal and monetary policy to stimulate or depress demand (depending on circumstances) to maintain steady economic growth, and full employment without inflation. His ideas became official orthodoxy during the Second World War (which saw Keynes back at the Treasury). They were later endorsed with enthusiasm by both progressive **conservatives** and **Christian Democrats**, anxious to avoid the economic difficulties of the inter-war years (particularly high unemployment) as well as by **social democrats** searching for some form of state planning and managed **capitalism**.

With social **welfare** reforms (in Britain associated with William **Beveridge**), Keynesian economic policy provided the basis for the post-war political **consensus**. Keynes died soon after the war ended, so did not live to see the use (or sometimes misuse) of his ideas in the post-war period. While Keynes saw his theory as an equilibrium theory, designed to tackle both inflation and depression, governments predominantly sought to maintain full employment by boosting demand, mainly through increasing government spending. This contributed to inflationary pressures, culminating in an inflationary crisis in the 1970s that partially discredited Keynesian ideas and led to the increased influence of **neoliberal** thinkers, such as **Hayek**, Friedman, and the **public choice** school.

King

Martin Luther King (1929–1968) was a Baptist minister who became leader of the civil **rights** movement in the United States. He sought to end various practices that discriminated against American Blacks, successfully campaigning in the southern states against segregation on the buses and in schools, and to ensure that the right to vote was conceded and exercised. Inspired by the example of **Gandhi**, he was committed to 'active non-violence', although his moderation did not please some Black leaders (such as Stokely Carmichael) who advocated less pacifist and more assertive tactics. However, many found King's oratory inspiring. In 1963 he led a march of 200,000 to Washington, where he delivered his celebrated speech with the reiterated phrase, 'I have a dream.' In 1964 he was awarded the Nobel Prize. In 1968 he was assassinated. His life and work helped transform race relations in the United States.

Kropotkin

Prince Peter Kropotkin (1842–1921) born a Russian nobleman, and educated in a military academy, was converted to **anarchism** in 1872 and became involved in the Russian populist movement. Imprisoned for his **revolutionary** activities he escaped in 1876 and spent most of the rest of his life in exile. He returned to Russia after the revolution in 1917 but soon became disillusioned with the new Bolshevik regime. His funeral provoked a mass anarchist demonstration in 1921. His key work was *Mutual Aid* (1902). Here he argued for cooperation rather than competition and conflict. He claimed that cooperation and mutual aid were in accordance with nature generally and human nature, strongly disagreeing with the views of **Hobbes** on the subject. While personally opposed to violence, he considered a popular uprising a precondition of an anarchist society. The repressive **state** would be replaced by a loose federation of small self-governing local **communities**.

Kymlicka

Will Kymlicka (1933–) is a Canadian political philosopher who has particularly explored the issue of group rights of minority cultures, such as the Quebecois (French Canadians) and Inuit Indians in Canada, the aborigines in Australia and the Maori in New Zealand. Key works that tackle some of the philosophical issues involved include *Liberalism, Community and Culture* (1989) and *Multicultural Citizenship* (1995). In *Contemporary Political Philosophy* (1990) he examines major schools in modern philosophy, and critically analyses the work of some leading modern thinkers, including John **Rawls**, Robert **Nozick** and Ronald **Dworkin**

Lasswell

Harold Lasswell (1902–1978) was a pioneering

American political scientist, who emphasized that politics was about **power**. His book *Politics: Who gets what, when how?* (1935) is regarded as a classic text. He also contributed notably to the study of **political communication**, and wrote provocatively on the subject of propaganda.

Lazarsfeld

Paul Lazarsfeld (1901–1976) was a leading American sociologist. Born in Vienna, he received a doctorate in mathematics, and soon applied his quantitative skills to the study of sociology. He moved to the USA in 1933, where he worked at Newark, Princeton and Columbia, undertaking mass market surveys, and his approach to the collection and statistical analysis of data had a major impact on social science methodology. He was the lead author of the first substantial survey of voting behaviour, *The People's Choice* (Lazarsfeld, Berelson and Gaudet, 1944).

Lenin

Vladimir Ilich Ulyanov (1870–1924), who later took the name Lenin, was born in Russia to a middle-class family. After his elder brother was hanged for his part in a plot to assassinate Tsar Alexander III in 1887, Lenin himself became a committed **revolutionary**. He joined a small group of **Marxist** intellectuals in St Petersburg, where he was arrested and imprisoned in 1895. He was then exiled to Siberia in 1897, before moving to Switzerland where he joined other Marxist emigrés in 1900. There he edited and contributed to the Marxist paper *Iskra*, and published *What is to be Done?* (1902). In 1903 Lenin divided the Russian Marxist party, the Social Democrats. His supporters, briefly the majority, were dubbed Bolsheviks, and his opponents Mensheviks (after the Russian terms for majority and minority groups).

In 1914 Lenin realized that war could lead to the downfall of the Russian Tsarist state, and seized the opportunity provided by the February Revolution of 1917 to return to Russia and eventually seize power for the Bolsheviks in October. He proclaimed 'all power to the soviets' (workers' councils) and dissolved the elected Russian parliament, consolidating the Bolshevik hold on power by abolishing other parties, making peace with Germany and winning the subsequent civil war between the 'red' and 'white' forces in Russia. In 1921 he exchanged his early 'war **communism**', which had damaged the Russian economy, for a

more moderate New Economic Policy. His death in 1924 provoked a power struggle among the leading Bolsheviks which eventually resulted in the **dictatorship** of Stalin, and the elimination of Lenin's leading associates.

Lenin, as a successful Marxist revolutionary, effectively created **Marxism-Leninism**, the dominant interpretation of Marxism in the twentieth century. Although he was widely seen as a rigidly orthodox Marxist, he adapted and reinterpreted Marx's thought to meet conditions in Tsarist Russia, where **capitalism** was relatively undeveloped and both the **bourgeoisie** and industrial proletariat relatively weak. This meant winning support from the peasants. Yet Russian Marxists could not hope to build a mass party as the German **social democrats** had done, as in Tsarist Russia political opposition was necessarily underground and clandestine.

In *What Is To Be Done?* Lenin argued for a small party of dedicated revolutionaries to act as the intellectual 'vanguard' of the working class. He advocated what came to be called 'democratic centralism', involving ruthless party discipline once policy had been decided upon. Marx's notion of a temporary dictatorship of the proletariat evolved under Lenin to mean a more lasting dictatorship of the Communist Party, acting on behalf of the working class. After the Bolshevik Revolution Lenin created a one-party state, but argued that what he called soviet **democracy** or proletarian democracy was far more democratic than bourgeois democracy, which in practice excluded the working class from active involvement. Lenin's interpretation of democracy was to become the orthodoxy not only in the Soviet Union but also in the so-called 'people's democracies' of eastern Europe and elsewhere.

Lenin's most important contribution to Marxist theory was perhaps *Imperialism, the Highest Stage of Capitalism* (1916). Here he argued that the apparent failure of Marx's prediction of the increasing exploitation and 'immiseration' of the working class in the most advanced capitalist countries was due to the acquisition and exploitation of colonial empires, which enabled leading capitalist states to postpone the impoverishment of their own working classes. His analysis not only provided a plausible explanation of the apparent decline of working-class militancy in the west, but also increased the appeal of Marxism-Leninism to anti-colonial movements.

thinkers

Lijphart

Arend Lijphart (1936–) is a political scientist who was born in the Netherlands, but has worked mainly in the USA, and holds dual American and Dutch citizenship. The contrast between 'consensus' democracies (such as his native Netherlands) and majoritarian democracies (such as the USA) has informed much of his work. His first major book involved a study of Dutch politics, *The Politics of Accommodation* (1967), where he developed the concept of consociation. He later applied it to other societies divided on ethnic, religious or linguistic lines.

Lindblom

Charles E Lindblom (1917–) is a leading American political scientist. He remains best known for his advocacy of incremental decision making, which he provocatively described as 'The science of muddling through' (1959), rather than the rational decision-making model put forward by Herbert Simon. For Lindblom incrementalism (or policy making by a series of small incremental steps) is a better description of how policy is generally made in practice. However he also argued that it is a better prescriptive model of how it should made, as it is less risky and generally reflects a degree of consensus among affected interests (arising from what Lindblom described as 'partisan mutual adjustment'). Lindblom was also influenced by the pluralism of his colleague Robert Dahl at Yale University, although in his book *Politics and Markets* (1977) he noted the privileged position of business, and the limits on effective competition both in the market place and politics. Because of these departures from classical pluralism he is sometimes described as a 'neopluralist'.

Lipset

Seymour Martin Lipset (1922–2006) was an American political sociologist. He is still best known for *Political Man: The social bases of politics* [1960]. However, his interests roamed widely over the whole field of politics, including the relationship between economic development and democracy, right-wing extremism in America, and the reasons for American exceptionalism (the failure of socialism to make political headway).

Locke

John Locke (1632–1704) was an extremely influential English political thinker. He was personal physician and adviser to the Earl of Shaftesbury, who served briefly as a minister under the restored monarchy of King Charles II, but subsequently led the parliamentary opposition to the court. Locke left England for Holland following Shaftesbury's fall and death in 1683. He only returned after the 'Glorious Revolution' of 1688, in which the Catholic James II (brother and successor to Charles II) was replaced by the protestant Dutch prince, William of Orange, and his wife Mary (protestant daughter of James). Although Locke's two *Treatises on Civil Government* [1690] seem to have been largely written before 1688, they provided a theoretical justification for the revolution of that year.

Locke, like Hobbes, envisaged an original state of nature in which there was no government, followed by a contract to establish a society and government. Yet Locke's state of nature was less fearful than that of Hobbes, It is 'a state of liberty, yet it is not a state of licence'. Men enjoyed natural rights in the state of nature, including, crucially, a right to property, which individuals acquired initially through mixing their own labour with natural resources, although government was necessary to increase the security of property. Locke's contract involved a conditional rather than total surrender of power to the sovereign. Government depended on the consent of the governed. The authority of government was limited rather than absolute, and the powers of government should be separate rather than concentrated. If the sovereign infringed the rights of his subjects, they were entitled to resist.

All these ideas, natural and inalienable human rights, government by consent, limited government, the separation of powers, and a right of resistance to, and ultimately rebellion against, an arbitrary or tyrannical government, became key concepts in liberal thought. They seemed to underpin the British system of government as it evolved after 1688. Less questionably they helped inspire the American Revolution and underpinned the constitution of the USA, as well as subsequent political developments both in Europe and the wider world.

Whether Locke would have approved these developments is questionable. Although for Locke government depended ultimately on the consent of the governed, he was certainly no democrat. While all men were free and equal in the state of nature, the right to property was entirely consis-

thinkers

tent with considerable **inequality** in possessions and **power**. Indeed, Locke's political theory has been held to justify not only the effective **oligarchy** of rich landowners in eighteenth-century Britain, but also of emerging **capitalism** both in Britain and the western world. Thus C.B. Macpherson described the ideas of both Hobbes and Locke as *The Political Theory of Possessive Individualism* (1962). There were also limits to Locke's liberalism. Even his eloquent defence of religious **toleration** (in his *A Letter Concerning Toleration* [1689]) did not extend to Catholics or atheists. Yet, irrespective of his limitations, John Locke remains a crucial figure in the liberal tradition.

Lovelock

James Lovelock (1919–) is a British scientist and environmentalist. He is best known for the Gaia hypothesis. Gaia was the name of a Greek goddess of the earth. Lovelock adopted the name to personify the notion of the earth and the earth's atmosphere as a living organism, in danger from **environmental** pollution, and specifically global warming. Unlike other environmentalists he has become a keen advocate of nuclear power, as the only feasible way of halting global warming. A recent book expounding his ideas is *The Revenge of Gaia* (2007).

Luxemburg

Rosa Luxemburg (1871–1919) was a Polish revolutionary **socialist**, committed to the international working class and influential in German and Russian socialist circles. She vigorously attacked **Bernstein's** revisionism but also criticized **Lenin's** views on **party** organization. She favoured mass strikes and demonstrations as a means to **revolution**. She was imprisoned for her anti-war views in the First World War, and brutally murdered by counter-revolutionary solders in the abortive German revolution at the end of the war. She subsequently became an iconic figure in western **Marxist** circles, rivalling **Trotsky** as a source of inspiration.

Lyotard

Jean-François Lyotard (1924–1998) was a leading French **postmodernist** philosopher. His book *The Postmodern Condition* (1979, English translation, 1984), has become a key text for understanding postmodernism. Lyotard argued that the modern industrial age was over, and with it the Enlightenment faith in human reason, science and progress. The modern age had brought some benefits, but also destructive wars and other man-made disasters, bringing disillusion with the Enlightenment project. Modernism had thus been superseded by **postmodernism**, characterized by an 'incredulity towards meta-narratives', a famous phrase of Lyotard's. By 'meta-narratives (or grand narratives) he meant any theory, religion, philosophy or **ideology** purporting to explain the world or its history. Postmodernism instead emphasized difference and diversity. This opposition to 'grand narratives' appealed to some radical alternative perspectives, such as radical **feminism**, critical of mainstream (or 'malestream') interpretations of the world. Yet critics have pointed out that the postmodernist rejection of *all* meta-narratives included radical alternatives such as feminism (and, some argue, even postmodernism itself).

Machiavelli

Niccolò Machiavelli (1469–1537) lived in Florence through a turbulent period of its history as an independent state. After the expulsion of the Medici rulers of the city, he served the Republic of Florence as a diplomat until the Medicis were returned to power. He wrote his most well-known work, *The Prince*, as a kind of unsolicited job application to the restored Medici rulers, an application which proved unsuccessful, perhaps unsurprisingly in view of his **republican** sympathies, evident in his previous employment and in his later books, the *Discourses* and *The History of Florence*.

Machiavelli's thought has been very variously interpreted. For many his cynical political **realism** was profoundly shocking and immoral. Thus in *The Prince* he advised rulers to break their word when the occasion demanded. 'Since men are a sorry lot and will not keep their promises to you, you need not keep your promises to them. A prince never lacks legitimate reasons to break his promises.' Yet while it was not necessary for a prince to have all the virtues, 'it is very necessary for him to appear to have them'. In a similar vein he advises that it is better for a ruler to be feared than loved, as men are 'ungrateful, fickle, simulators and deceivers, avoiders of danger, and greedy for gain' and not to be relied upon. 'Thus fear will more effectively compel their obedience than love.' To his outraged critics, Machiavelli was 'old Nick', the devil, shamelessly advocating immoral conduct. To others, Machiavelli might rather be considered the first modern political scientist, describing and analysing politics as it is, rather than as it ought to be. For others again, Machiavelli's real political convictions are not to be found in *The Prince* but in his other writings, where his republican ideals are manifest. Thus Machiavelli belongs in the great republican tradition of thought. Yet although the *Discourses* suggest where his real political sympathies lay, it has been argued that both books display a similar pessimistic view of **human nature**, and a similar political realism.

MacIntyre

Alasdair MacIntyre (1929–) is an influential Scottish-born moral and political philosopher who has taught at a wider range of universities in Britain and the USA. His key work is *After Virtue* (1981). He is regarded as an important modern **communitarian** theorist, although he is difficult to classify as he draws on ideas from a wide range of thinkers, including **Aristotle**, **Aquinas**, and **Marx**.

MacKinnon

Catharine MacKinnon (1946–) is an extremely influential American **feminist** lawyer and theorist. As a lawyer she played a key role in using anti-sex discrimination legislation to help women sue against sexual harassment at work. Her book *Sexual Harassment of Working Women* (1979) became the standard authority on the subject. Her work in this field has changed the law, opinion and practice. She represented the actress who had appeared in the pornographic film *Deep Throat* under the name Linda Lovelace, but later accused her husband of abusing her and forcing her to make the film. With Andrea **Dworkin**, MacKinnon campaigned to use civil rights legislation against pornography. She has contributed notably to feminist theory with her books *Towards a Feminist Theory of the State* (1989) and *Sex Equality* (2007). She insists that feminist theory is derived from the specific experiences of women, hitherto ignored. She argues that knowledge is **power**. Power means that your view of how things are is generally accepted. Powerlessness means your view of how things are is marginalized or ignored. Feminism is about giving a voice to women's own experience of how things are.

Madison

James Madison (1751–1836) was a major American thinker and statesman, the 'Father of the Constitution'. A critic of the Articles of Confederation, the first **constitution** of the United States of America which had newly won independence from Britain, he led the struggle to revise them in the Constitutional Convention of 1787, helping to devise what was in effect a new system of government. He then (along with Alexander Hamilton and John Jay) co-authored *The Federalist Papers* (1787–8), a series of essays that defended the new constitution against its critics. Subsequently he helped promote and defend the Bill of Rights (1791), comprising the first ten amendments to the American Constitution. From 1801–9 he served as Secretary of State under Thomas **Jefferson**, and succeeded Jefferson as America's fourth president (1809–17).

While Madison thought that political **authority** was ultimately derived from the people, he feared strong popular influence on **government**. He distinguished between a **republic**, by which he meant a representative system of government, and a pure **democracy**, which he argued was 'incompatible with personal security or the rights of property'. In a **representative** system, he argued, 'the public voice, pronounced by the representatives of the people, will be more consonant to the public good than if pronounced by the people themselves' (*Federalist Paper* no. 10). The American Constitution, defended by Madison, did place some limits on direct popular control of government, although not all the checks and balances built into the constitution operated as intended (thus the president was effectively directly elected by the people rather than freely chosen by members of the electoral college). However, the main elements of the **federal** system of government, as advocated and defended by Madison, remain in place, and the federal principle has since been adopted in many other countries.

Maistre

Joseph de Maistre (1753–1821) was born in Chambéry, then part of Savoy, belonging to the King of Sardinia. He was a French-speaking Savoyard of French descent who initially welcomed the French **Revolution**. However, after the French invasion of Savoy he denounced it and became a leading spokesman for Catholic authoritarian counter-revolution from his exile initially in Switzerland and later in Russia, where he served as the ambassador for the King of Savoy until 1817. Like Burke he is regarded as an important **conservative** thinker, but while Burke was prepared to accept moderate pragmatic reform, de Maistre was an uncompromising advocate of papal and royal **authority**, and reactionary conservatism.

Malthus

Thomas Malthus (1766–1834) was an English clergyman and economist, whose main claim to fame was his *Essay on the Principle of Population* (1798), in which he argued there was a natural tendency for population to rise faster than the means of subsistence – thus undermining hopes of raising living standards. It was this work that substantially contributed to the reputation of economics as the 'gloomy science'. Economic growth and increased prosperity in the west subsequently suggested that Malthus had been too pessimistic. More recently **green** thinkers have rediscovered the message of Malthus that there are limits to growth, and the dangers of a continued rise in population.

Mao

Mao Zedong (or Tse-tung) (1893–1976) was born to a farming family in Hunan, but discovered **Marxism** in Beijing and was among the founders of the Chinese **Communist** Party in 1921, influenced by the recent success of the Bolsheviks in Russia. Just as **Lenin** had adapted **Marx** to Russian circumstances, Mao similarly reinterpreted Marxism for a predominantly agricultural society, emphasizing the **revolutionary** potential of the peasantry. The communists initially supported the Kuomintang, founded by the nationalist leader Sun Yatsen in 1924 to combat the chaos of rival warlords into which China had slipped after the abdication of the last emperor in 1912, but Sun Yatsen's successor Chiang Kai-shek turned ruthlessly against them. Mao led a break-out of the remains of Communist forces and a 'Long March' to the relative safety of north-west China. Following this feat Mao was the unchallenged leader of the Chinese Communists. Subsequently the Communists worked with the Kuomintang in guerrilla campaigns against the Japanese occupation, but after the defeat of Japan, the Red Army fought against Chiang Kai-shek's nationalist forces in a civil war from which the Communists under Mao emerged victorious in 1949. Their victory owed little to Soviet communism or Stalin, who had earlier advised working with the Kuomintang, and Mao in power developed his own distinctive and more populist version of Communism, that led ultimately to a Sino–Soviet split that was never entirely healed.

Yet although Maoism appeared to be a more **populist**, less **authoritarian**, version of Marxism, it was arguably as damaging to China as Stalinism had been to Russia. Mao periodically sought to revitalize his party through encouraging the active participation of ordinary members against the party **elite**. Yet his Great Leap Forward, an attempt at rapid industrialization through grass roots enterprise, proved an economic disaster, while his cultural revolution, in which young Red Guards denounced party officials, academics and professionals (including sometimes their own parents) for **bourgeois** behaviour and revisionism, was deeply divisive and damaging. It was in the latter period that *The Thoughts of Chairman Mao* (known more familiarly as *The Little Red Book*) received a world-wide circulation. After his death his successors continued to pay lip-service to Mao and Maoism, but have not protected his legacy. While they maintained the political control of the Communist Party and ruthlessly suppressed demands for political freedoms, they introduced extensive economic reforms, encouraging private enterprise and **free market** forces. In a period of rapid industrialization and rising living standards, it appears that it is the peasantry who were championed by Mao who have been largely left behind.

Marcuse

Herbert Marcuse (1898–1979) was a German thinker and member of the Frankfurt School who escaped Nazi Germany to live and work in the USA. His writings, particularly *One Dimensional Man* (1964) became particularly influential among **left**-wing student circles in the 1960s, and he was briefly regarded as an iconic figure in the abortive 1968 **revolutions** in France and elsewhere. Like other members of the Frankfurt School he sought to combine a broadly **Marxist** approach, minus its economic determinism, with insights from other strands of thought, particularly Freudian psychology, but unlike them he retained his revolutionary enthusiasm until the end of his life.

Marsiglio

Marsiglio (or in Latin Marsilus) (c.1275–c.1342) was born in Padua, and subsequently taught at Paris. His key work *Defensor Pacis* (Defender of Peace) was written in 1324. This has to be seen

thinkers

in the context of the long conflict between church and state in the Middle Ages, between the spiritual power of the church and papacy, and the temporal power of emperors and kings. Contrary to the arguments of those who argued that temporal rulers should be subject to the supreme power of the pope, the supreme head of the church, Marsiglio maintained that the two spheres were quite separate. The pope and the church should not interfere with the **government** of **states**. Popes had no powers to dethrone emperors, as had been claimed. Marsiglio also challenged the ecclesiatical hierarchy, arguing that the pope was subject to the community of the faithful, represented by a General Council of the church. Unsurprisingly, the teaching of Marsiglio was widely condemned by the Catholic Church. His ideas to some degree anticipate the more secular politics of the post-reformation period.

Marx

Karl Marx (1818–1883) was born in Trier in the German Rhineland to a Jewish family who had converted to Protestantism. Neither faith meant much to Marx, who later declared that religion was the opiate of the people. He studied at the University of Berlin, and there became one of the circle of 'young Hegelians', who interpreted **Hegel's** thought in a radical direction. He then devoted himself to radical journalism until his paper the *Rheinische Zeitung* was suppressed by the government. He married his childhood sweetheart Jenny von Westphalen in 1843, and moved to Paris where he associated with French **socialists** and other German exiles, including notably Friedrich **Engels**, with whom he formed a lifelong intellectual partnership. In 1848, a year of **revolutions** in Europe, Marx and Engels wrote *The Communist Manifesto,* still the most succinct and accessible introduction to Marx's ideas. Following the failure of the revolution they settled in England, the Marx family in London, Engels in Manchester where he managed a branch of his family's textile business and subsidized the impoverished Marx, who apart from occasional journalism devoted himself to studying in the British Museum, and writing *Capital*. From 1864 until 1872 he and Engels were actively involved in working-class politics in the International Working Men's Association, in which Marx clashed with followers of the anarchist **Bakunin**, leading to the collapse of what was subsequently known as the First International.

Marx's thought involved an adaptation and synthesis of German philosophy, French revolutionary **socialism** and British political economy. From **Hegel** Marx derived the philosophy of history and specifically the dialectic, the notion of progression through thesis, antithesis and synthesis. Yet while Hegel used the dialectic to describe the development of ideas, Marx applied it to the material world, to productive forces, interests and classes, hence 'dialectal materialism'. Hegel's political views have been various interpreted as **liberal**, **conservative** or reactionary. Marx was a revolutionary. He observed that 'Philosophers have only interpreted the world in various ways, the point is to change it.' However, he differed from leading contemporary socialists like Fourier or **Owen** in being comparatively uninterested in designing model socialist societies. Instead he devoted his energies to analysing **capitalism** and its internal contradictions, which would eventually (he thought) lead to revolution and socialism.

To do this he studied the British classical economists, Adam **Smith** and particularly David Ricardo). He argued that while **capitalism** was promoting the growth of income and wealth on an unprecedented scale, it was increasingly polarizing society between two key **classes** with conflicting interests. These classes were the **bourgeoisie** (or capitalists) who owned the means of production, and the industrial working class (or proletariat) who owned only their own labour. These industrial workers were increasingly alienated from the labour process and the goods they produced. Competition between capitalists would intensify the exploitation of the workers, and their immiseration (increased poverty) would lead to revolution and the establishment of socialism, requiring a brief **dictatorship** of the proletariat to prevent counter-revolution and bring about ultimately a **communist** society. This would be organized on the principle 'from each according to his abilities, to each according to his needs'. Class conflict would be at an end. The **state**, which Marx saw substantially as the instrument of the dominant economic class, would ultimately 'wither away'.

After his death Marx's influence rapidly grew among socialists the world over, inspiring revolutions in Russia, China and elsewhere, and a collectivist economic system that appeared to be a practical alternative to western capitalism. **Marxism** thus became the state-sponsored

thinkers

orthodoxy over a large part of the globe. Marx himself might not have approved. In the various avowedly Marxist regimes established long after Marx's death, the temporary 'dictatorship of the proletariat' proved both lasting and highly centralized. The state, far from 'withering away', became omnipresent. From 1989 onwards, most of these regimes have been overthrown or transformed. In many countries where Marx was formerly revered he has since been repudiated.

Yet irrespective of the fate of the regimes associated with his name, Marx remains an important figure in the history of political thought, and in the practice of political science. Many key concepts integral to the modern study of politics derive from Marx. He demonstrated the importance of economic interests and economic conflicts in the real distribution of **power** and influence in political systems. He may in the process have exaggerated the role of economics, coming close to economic determinism, and underestimating the importance of political and social divisions that are not primarily economic – those based on **nation**, **ethnicity**, religion or **gender** for example. His analysis of capitalism was penetrating and (on the development of monopoly capitalism and **globalization**) prophetic, even if his central prediction of its eventual inevitable collapse seems further off than ever.

Mazzini

Giuseppe Mazzini (1805–1872) was an Italian **nationalist** writer and political activist. He founded Young Italy in 1831, to work for a united Italian **republic**, and Young Europe in 1834, to encourage nationalism elsewhere in Europe. He argued that a Europe of **nation-states**, with peoples free from foreign domination, would live in peace with each other. He headed the short-lived Roman Republic established after the 1848 **revolutions**. Although he lived to see a united Italy, he was disillusioned by the manner in which it was achieved (diplomacy and war rather than a popular uprising) and by the form the new Italy took (a **monarchy** rather than a **democratic** republic).

Michels

Robert Michels (1875–1936) was a German sociologist who was initially a **Marxist**, but after teaching in Italian universities became, like **Pareto** and **Mosca**, a key exponent of **elitism**. Elite theorists argued that despite the apparent growing

acceptance of **democracy**, **power** in society was inevitably concentrated in the hands of minorities – small elite groups. Michels argued this was true not only of society as a whole but of all organizations within society, 'Who says organization, say **oligarchy**' (or rule of the few). This was what he described as 'the iron law of oligarchy.'

In his best known book *Political Parties* [1911] he tried to show that this was true even of **political parties**, such as **social democratic** parties, that had a mass membership and were explicitly committed to democratic principles and procedures, and where the **leadership** was elected. He argued that any large organization required permanent leadership and specialized officers, who take key decisions, and that ordinary members lack the time and skill to exert effective **accountability** and control. Rank and file members are relatively disorganized, and want and respect strong leadership. Internal party democracy is in practice impossible. Michels concluded, 'The socialists might conquer, but not **socialism**, which would perish in the moment of its adherents' triumph.' The analysis of Michels is persuasive even, and perhaps especially, for those who find his conclusions distasteful. For many ordinary members of socialist parties it is unhappily confirmed by the periodic 'betrayal' of socialist objectives by the party leadership. Leaders may respond that they must bear in mind not only the views of party activists but actual and potential voters, who may not share the views of members. Pleasing activists may spell electoral disaster. Inevitably also the leadership is constrained by the economic pressures of a **capitalist** economy, and the prevailing norms of a traditional parliamentary system.

Miliband

Ralph Miliband (1924–1994) was a leading British **Marxist** historian and political thinker. Born in Brussels in a Jewish family as Adolphe Miliband, he escaped with his father to England in 1940 following the German invasion of Belgium. In England he changed his first name to Ralph, and studied politics at the London School of Economics (LSE) under the socialist Harold Laski. He later lectured at the LSE until 1972 when he became professor of politics at Leeds University. His book *Parliamentary Socialism* [1963] argued that the British Labour Party had consistently over time given priority to parliamentary institutions, procedures and values over **socialism**, and, by implication, that the parliamentary route to socialism was inherently flawed. He and his friend, the historian John Saville, employed the term 'labourism' rather than socialism to describe the ideas of the Labour Party.

In *The State in Capitalist Society* (1969) Miliband argued that power in Britain was effectively concentrated in the hands of interconnected **elites**. This provoked a celebrated debate with Nicos **Poulantzas** in the *New Left Review* (1969, 1970). At the end of his life, following the collapse of the USSR, Miliband reaffirmed his own socialist convictions in *Socialism for a Sceptical Age* (1994). Ironically, his sons David and Edward, who helped to see this last book through to publication, were both to become Labour MPs and subsequently ministers in the UK's New Labour government.

Mill

John Stuart Mill (1806–1873), an English philosopher, is regarded as a the quintessential **liberal**. His father James Mill is credited with converting his friend, the **utilitarian** philosopher Jeremy **Bentham** to representative **democracy**. Another close associate was the economist David Ricardo. These three were the dominant early influences on John Stuart Mill's own thought. Indeed, it appears he was educated to champion their cause. He was taught Greek from the age of three, Latin from eight, and began the study of logic and political economy at ten. On top of this rigorous cramming, he was also expected to instruct his younger siblings, and work as his father's secretary and research assistant. In 1826 he suffered a mental crisis, widely interpreted as a reaction against his somewhat unnatural upbringing. He read romantic poetry, and came to question the limitations of the Benthamite utilitarian philosophy in which he had been brought up. He began to study a wider range of ideas, including those of Coleridge, Carlyle, Saint-Simon, **Comte** and **Tocqueville**.

In 1843 Mill published *A System of Logic* and in 1848 the first edition of *Principles of Political Economy*. These two substantial works made his reputation, although his fame today rests more on his later essays. In 1851 he married (after the death of her husband in 1849) Harriet Taylor, whom he had first met in 1830. Her influence on his writing survived her death in 1858. Key works included *On Liberty* [1859], *Representative Government* and *Utilitarianism* (in Mill, 1972, and many other modern editions), both published in 1861. *The Subjection of Women*, completed the same year, was not to be published until 1869, when its radical stance on women's liberation created a scandal. In the interim Mill served as an MP for Westminster from 1865 until 1868, in which brief period he unsuccessfully advocated women's suffrage and proportional **representation**. His step-daughter, Helen Taylor, set up a Women's Suffrage Society, with Mill's enthusiastic support. She subsequently prepared Mill's *Autobiography* for publication after his death in 1873.

Of all Mill's works, the essay *On Liberty* is perhaps best known and most widely quoted. It is a passionate plea for full **freedom** of thought and expression. He argued that the only grounds for interfering with the liberty of any individual were to prevent harm to others. This individual freedom should include 'liberty of expressing and publishing opinions', full 'liberty of tastes and pursuits' and freedom to unite with others 'for any purpose not involving harm to others'. Mill argued vehemently the benefits to society of these freedoms, and the advantages to be derived from the encouragement of individuality. He was worried that social pressures would produce too much conformity of opinion and conduct, fearing what **Tocqueville** had called the 'tyranny of the majority'.

For this reason Mill, though a consistent advocate of representative **democracy**, was concerned by 'its natural tendency … towards collective mediocrity'. In *Considerations on Representative Government*, he argued that those who were illiterate or in receipt of poor relief should be excluded from the franchise, and suggested extra votes for those with superior education. However, he also demanded votes for women on the same terms as men. He urged active citizen participation, anticipating that this would promote the political education of the electorate.

In *Utilitarianism,* Mill defended a significantly modified version of Jeremy Bentham's creed. Bentham had assumed that all men pursue pleasure and avoid pain, but had been indifferent to men's choice of pleasures. To Mill some pleasures were higher than others. 'It is better to be a human being dissatisfied than a pig satisfied; better to be Socrates dissatisfied than a fool satisfied.' In rejecting Bentham's simple hedonism, however, Mill created additional problems in measuring happiness.

thinkers

Mill's last major work to be published in his lifetime, *The Subjection of Women* (1869), was actually completed much earlier in 1861, the year of the start of the American Civil War, on which Mill sided decisively with the north on the slavery issue. Mill provocatively compared the position of women in Britain with that of slaves in the American southern states. Critics at the time were outraged particularly by Mill's 'indelicate' references to the physical and sexual abuse of women. While most male commentators since have not given this work as much serious consideration as his other writings, modern radical **feminists**, by contrast, have generally focused on the limitations of his 'liberal feminism'.

Millett

Kate Millett (1934–), a leading American radical **feminist**, adapted the term **'patriarchy'** (literally 'rule of the father') to mean substantially the universal power that men have over women. In her ground-breaking book *Sexual Politics* (1970) she drew on examples from modern literature to demonstrate the routine physical and more specifically sexual **power**, and abuse of power, of men over women that transcends **class** and **culture**. In focusing on domestic and sexual relations between men and women she purposely enlarged the scope of politics beyond the explicitly public arena to the private sphere of home and bedroom, illustrating the radical feminist slogan, 'the personal is political'.

Mills

C. (Charles) Wright Mills (1916–1962) was an American sociologist, who taught at Columbia University from 1946 until his death. He is remembered particularly by political scientists for his key work *The Power Elite* (1956), which became a crucial text in the debate between **elitists** and **pluralists** over the nature and reality of contemporary political **power**. In this book he explored the emergence in the USA of a military elite with close links with the industrial elite (hence a 'military-industrial complex') and also with the political elite. Although C. Wright Mills himself was never wholly convinced by the ideas of **Marx**, he strongly influenced some contemporary western **Marxists**, particularly the British socialist Ralph **Miliband**, who dedicated *The State in Capitalist Society* (1969) to his memory.

Montesquieu

Charles, Baron de Montesquieu (1689–1755) was a French political thinker who satirized French society and institutions in his *Lettres Persanes* (1721). He studied **Hobbes**, whose pessimistic view of **human nature** he criticized, and the political writings of John **Locke**. His key work *The Spirit of the Laws* [1748] included a flattering analysis of the English **constitution**. He thought this involved a **separation** of **executive**, **legislative** and **judicial powers**, in contrast with the concentration of authority in the hands of **absolutist monarchs** common at the time elsewhere in Europe. Ultimately, it was to become clear that there was no clear separation of powers in Britain, but it was an understandable interpretation of the evolving British system of government in the early eighteenth century.

Morgenthau

Hans J. Morgenthau (1904–1980) was the most influential writer on **international relations** in the 1940s and 1950s. His **'realism'** can be seen in part as a reaction against the **'idealism'** in international relations in the inter-war period, which optimistically assumed that international cooperation and collective security could avoid the carnage of another world war. Morgenthau himself escaped from Hitler's Germany and found refuge in the USA, where he was a professor in the University of Chicago. His key work *Politics Among Nations* [1948] argues that, despite the growth of international institutions and cross-national interests, **states** remain by far the most significant actors in international relations. States pursue their own national interests defined in terms of power.

Morris

William Morris (1834–1896) was an English **socialist** thinker who founded the arts and crafts movement and subsequently, in 1884 the Socialist League. His rejection of modern industrial production and enthusiasm for hand-crafted work by individuals and small cooperatives appeared **utopian** and even reactionary to critics, but his romantic and idiosyncratic interpretation of socialism was influential in the English-speaking world.

Mosca

Gaetano Mosca (1858–1941) was an Italian sociologist and political thinker, one of the classical **elitists** who argued that minority rule was inevitable, even in a **democracy**. His key work was *The Ruling Class* [1896]. Yet unlike fellow elite theorists Pareto and Michels he later became more sympathetic towards **representative government**, becoming an elected deputy in 1908 and serving briefly in the government, before becoming a senator in 1919. The introduction of a universal franchise had not led to the excesses that he, as a **conservative**, had feared, and seemed compatible with the limited government that he favoured. Thus he did not support Mussolini, and in 1924 spoke in the Senate to 'almost lament' the downfall of the parliamentary government that he admitted he had always sharply criticized. It was a muted dissent, but he declined to embrace **fascism** for the remainder of his life.

Naess

Arne Naess (1912–) is a Norwegian philosopher whose academic interests included **Spinoza**, **Gandhi** and Buddhism. However his most widely-known work was done after he retired from his university chair at Oslo in 1970. It was then that he developed his deep **green** or deep ecology ideas, expressed in key articles in 1973 and 1985, and in his later book *Ecology, Community and Lifestyle* (1989). He personally engaged in direct action to further his deep green agenda, chaining himself with other protestors to rocks to oppose plans to bid a dam in a Norwegian fiord in 1970, a demonstration that was ultimately successful.

Nietzsche

Friedrich Wilhelm Nietzsche (1844–1900) was and remains a very controversial German philosopher, partly because some of his ideas were later used (or misused) by the Nazis. Nietzsche was mad for the last 11 years of his life, looked after by his mother and sister. His sister later became an enthusiastic Nazi and interpreted her brother's thought to anticipate elements of Nazi ideology, particularly *The Will to Power* [1901], put together from discarded scattered notes of Nietzsche after his death. While Nietzsche was opposed to the **racism** and **nationalism** that later became key features of Nazism, his notion of a 'superman' above conventional morality in his best-known work *Thus Spake Zarathustra* [1883–4] has been seen as the template for charismatic leaders like Hitler and Mussolini. In his other writings, such as *Beyond Good and Evil* [1886] Nietzsche famously

proclaimed not only the death of God, but the end of any prospects of establishing universal objective truth. Thus Nietzsche can be seen as a precursor of **postmodernist** thinking.

Niskanen

William Niskanen (1933–) is an American economist whose work on **bureaucracy** has had particular implications for the study of public sector organizations and officials. In his key work *Bureaucracy and Representative Government* (1971) he argued that, in the absence of market competition and considerations of profit, public sector bureaucrats, in the interest of increasing their own status, income and job satisfaction, would pursue bureau maximization (increasing the size of their organization's work, employment and expenditure) rather than profit maximization. His analysis provided a rationale for the steady growth of public sector employment and expenditure, and was seized on by the **New Right** in the USA and United Kingdom. The British political scientist Patrick Dunleavy has used **rational choice** assumptions to argue that public sector bureaucrats pursue bureau *shaping* rather than bureau *maximizing* (for example, because senior bureaucrats may benefit from contracting out some activities).

Nozick

Robert Nozick (1938–2002) was an American political philosopher, best known for his book *Anarchy, State and Utopia* (1974). Nozick himself was more of an old-fashioned laissez-faire **liberal** than an **anarchist**. He resembles anarchists in his extreme mistrust of government, particularly **government** intervention in the interests of redistribution and **social justice**. While the French anarchist **Proudhon** had famously declared **property** to be theft, and anarchists have generally favoured the abolition of private property, Nozick asserted the inviolability of property **rights**. Like John **Locke** he connected the individual's right to **liberty** with the right to property, which he derived, also like Locke, from labour. But however property was initially secured, individuals had an absolute inalienable right to acquire, own and transfer property. Nozick opposed any attempts by the **state** to take property from the rich to give to the poor in the interests of social (or distributive) justice, a concept Nozick did not recognize. Thus he objected to redistributive taxation, which he

thinkers

regarded as the extraction of enforced labour from those required to pay such taxes. His book can be seen as a reply to John **Rawls'** *Theory of Justice*, published three years earlier, and a continuation of an argument between two strands of liberalism (economic and social liberalism, or classical and 'new' liberalism). It was also an argument within the philosophy department of the University of Harvard, where both men taught.

Oakeshott

Michael Joseph Oakeshott (1901–1990) was an influential English **conservative** thinker who was professor of political science at the London School of Economics from 1951–1968. *Rationalism in Politics and other essays* (1962) is the best introduction to his thought. The title essay involves a wide-ranging attack on what he calls '**rationalism** in politics'. His targets include the French and American **revolutions**, **liberalism**, **socialism** and, effectively, all modern political doctrines or **ideologies**, including some apparently close to his own ideas, such as the **neoliberalism** of **Hayek**. Thus Oakeshott observes tersely of Hayek's *Road to Serfdom*, 'A plan to resist all planning may be better than its opposite, but it belongs to the same style of politics.' Significantly, while Hayek rejected the conservative label, describing himself as a liberal, Oakeshott identified with conservatism, but for him it was not a doctrine but an attitude of mind. 'To be conservative is to prefer the familiar to the unknown, to prefer the tried to the untried, fact to mystery, the actual to the possible, the limited to the unbounded.' His preference for limited gradual reform is reminiscent of Edmund **Burke**. Thus, according to Oakeshott, the conservative accepts that innovation may sometimes be necessary, but 'he will find small and slow changes more tolerable than large and sudden: and he will value highly every appearance of continuity'.

Olson

Mancur Olson (1932–1998) was an American economist and social scientist whose work had a significant impact on the study of politics. His reputation still rests largely on his first book *The Logic of Collective Action* (1965). This uses economic analysis to explain why small special-interest groups often seem to have a bigger impact on public policy than larger interests, such as taxpayers and consumers. **Pluralists** had argued that the cumulative impact of countless competing groups would serve the interests of the majority in an essentially democratic process. Countervailing power would prevent any small interest group unrepresentative of wider opinion from obtaining too much influence. Olson showed why this is not necessarily true. Individual taxpayers and consumers have little motivation for expending their energies on organizing and lobbying to protect their interests, because the costs in time and energy outweigh the potentially small benefits, and they can 'free ride' on the lobbying of others. By contrast, members of small trade associations and producer groups are strongly motivated to organize and push policies with potentially large benefits for themselves, for example involving protection or public subsidies. The costs are spread among the generality of taxpayers and consumers who will have little incentives to organize against them. Subsequently, Olson applied his economic analysis to explain political change, particularly in *The Rise and Decline of Nations* (1982) and his last book *Power and Prosperity* (2000).

Ostrogorski

Mosei Ostrogorski (1854–1919) was a pioneering Russian political scientist. His celebrated work *Democracy and the Organization of Political Parties* ([1902] two volumes, the first on Britain, the second on the United States) argued that **political parties** were increasingly dominated by their unrepresentative mass membership, with damaging implications for **representative democracy**. Robert **Michels**, by contrast, later argued that power in mass parties was in practice wielded by the parliamentary **leadership** and the party **bureaucracy**. Subsequent research on parties has tended to confirm the analysis of Michels rather than Ostrogorski.

Owen

Robert Owen (1771–1858) contributed to a distinctive British version of **socialism** in various ways in his writing and political activities. He first established his reputation by demonstrating that it was possible to make money as an enlightened employer at the model factory and community he established at New Lanark in Scotland, although his more socialist community, New Harmony, which he later tried to establish in America, proved less successful. In *A New View of Society* [1813] he argued that man's character was shaped by his social environment. He later became closely involved in early British trade unionism, and the cooperative movement. His socialism emphasized peaceful, gradual reform and working-class self-help. **Marx** and **Engels** in the *Communist Manifesto* regarded Owen as a **utopian socialist**, with a socialist vision of the future, but no practical strategy to achieve it.

Paine

Thomas Paine (1737–1809) was a radical thinker who was closely involved in the politics of three countries, his native Britain, America and France. In 1774 Benjamin Franklin helped him to emigrate to Pennsylvania, where he wrote radical journalism. After war broke out between the American colonies and Britain Paine wrote *Common Sense* [1776] which urged a declaration of independence. He served as a soldier in the rebel cause, and his writings continued to influence the debate on American politics. In 1781 he was sent on a mission to France, and returned to England in 1787. There he published *The Rights of Man* [1791–2] which supported the French **Revolution** against the criticism of Edmund **Burke** in *Reflections on the Revolution in France* [1790]. Accused of treason, and burned in effigy by a patriotic mob, he escaped to France in 1792, became a French citizen and was elected to the revolutionary Convention, arousing the anger of the Jacobins by opposing the execution of Louis XVI. Imprisoned, and fortunate not to lose his head in the Terror, he wrote *The Age of Reason* [1794, 1796], which attacked organized religion and alienated many of his old friends in America, so that when he returned there in 1802, he was ignored and died uncelebrated in 1809. William Cobbett, the former Tory and once fierce critic of Paine, who became a convert to radicalism, sailed to America in 1819 to bring back the bones of his old enemy home. These bones were lost at sea but Paine's writings continued to win support for his brand of radical **liberalism**, **republicanism** and **democracy.**

Pareto

Vilfredo Pareto (1848–1923) was an important Italian economist as well as a political sociologist. In this latter capacity he was an **elite** theorist. He argued that all societies are divided into a minority or elite which rules, and a majority that is ruled. Rule is exercised by a combination of cunning and persuasion on the one hand and physical force on the other, through types of leaders Pareto describes as 'foxes' and 'lions' respectively. Elites may be periodically overthrown; for history is 'a graveyard of elites', but they will be replaced not by **democracy** and rule of the masses but by a new elite, in accordance with his notion of the circulation of elites. He was scornful over the prospects for real democracy. The introduction of universal suffrage made no difference, as Pareto held that it was always an **oligarchy** that governs. He was equally contemptuous of **Marxism**. Real **socialism**, like real democracy, was impossible for someone who believed that the rule of some kind of elite in its own interest was inevitable. Italian **fascists** admired and honoured Pareto, but he did live long enough after Mussolini took power in Italy, in 1922, to discover the reality of fascism in action.

Parsons

Talcott Parsons (1902–1979) was an important American sociologist, whose theory of structural-functionalism and understanding of the social system strongly influenced the study of politics in the 1950s and 1960s, particularly the systems approach of David Easton. A 'system' is a complex whole of which the parts are interdependent. 'Functions' fulfil societal needs, and operate within broader social structures and social norms to contribute to the smooth operation of the social system, a whole. The social system is in equilibrium when its different parts are operating together smoothly. Any disturbance to equilibrium normally triggers adjustments elsewhere in the system and a return to equilibrium. The systems approach thus emphasizes stability and consensus and downplays radical change and conflict. This was a problem for radical sociologists and also for political scientists. It was argued there was an inbuilt **conservatism** in the model; existing features of the social and political system were assumed to be functional or necessary for system maintenance. Critics suggested that the theory involved description rather than critical analysis. Consequently, Parsons' approach rather fell from favour from the 1970s. However, the development of modern political science in the middle of the twentieth century cannot be understood without reference to Parsons and structural-functionalism. Key works include *The Structure of Social Action* [1937], *The Social System* [1951], *Economy and Society* [1956] and *Structure and Process in Modern Societies* [1960].

thinkers

Pateman

Carole Pateman is a British political theorist and feminist who studied at Oxford and went on to teach at universities in Australia and the USA. She is perhaps best known still for her first book, *Participation and Democratic Theory* (1970), in which she argued for an extension of effective participation, including participation in the workplace, to complement **representative democracy**. Participatory democracy, she argued, would promote a sense of political efficacy, reduce alienation and apathy, encourage a concern with the wider public interest and assist the political education of citizens. Later books have included *The Problem of Political Obligation* (1979) and *The Sexual Contract* (1988), the latter focusing particularly on the marriage contract and the institution of marriage, and their continuing implications for the subordination of women.

Pericles

Pericles (c. 495–429 BC) was the leading Athenian general and statesman of his age. In 431 BC he led Athens into the long Peloponnesian war with Sparta, chronicled by the historian Thucydides, who put into the mouth of Pericles a great funeral oration over the first who died in battle in that war. How far this great speech reported by Thucydides, many years after the event, reflects the real ideas of Pericles is uncertain. However, it eloquently celebrated Athenian **democracy** and the values of **freedom**, **toleration**, and active **citizenship** linked with it, while ignoring its flaws, most notably the acceptance of slavery. The speech remains a source of inspiration for those who favour participatory democracy.

Plato

Although Plato (427–347 BC) lived and wrote nearly two and a half millennia ago, he is still widely regarded as one of the greatest philosophers and political theorists who has ever lived. His extensive surviving writings are still studied and argued over in universities across the world. Born in an aristocratic family in Athens after the death of **Pericles** and the great period of its democracy, he grew up during the long war with Sparta, culminating in Athens' defeat, and the brief tyranny of the Thirty. The subsequent restoration of democracy led to the trial and execution of his great teacher, **Socrates**, in 399, an event that seems to have profoundly influenced his own political outlook. Later he founded and directed the Academy (c. 385), where one of his pupils was **Aristotle,** who was to criticize some of Plato's ideas.

Plato's surviving writings take the form of dialogues in which his teacher **Socrates** plays the leading role. Those generally considered early works may represent the arguments of Socrates himself, while in middle and later dialogues (such as *Republic, Statesman, Laws*) 'Socrates' is reckoned to be the mouthpiece of Plato's own views. Some of the presumed earlier and shorter dialogues are perhaps the best introduction to Plato's work. These include the *Apology, Crito, Gorgias* and *Protagoras*. They also involve genuine debates, illustrating what is reckoned to be the Socratic method of question and answer to arrive at a greater understanding of specific ethical and political questions. In the early dialogues these questions included how far one should obey the **state** (even to the extent of acquiescing in one's own unjust death sentence) or how far political skills can be taught.

The Republic, the most celebrated and widely read of all Plato's writings, is a much more complex work covering aspects of philosophy, ethics, psychology, education, economics, aesthetics and even medicine, as well as politics. It begins as a genuine dialogue in which Plato and his companions discuss the meaning of **justice**. One speaker, Thrasymachus, defines justice as the interest of the stronger party. Everyone seeks their own selfish advantage and pleasure. They are only deterred by the fear of punishment. The successful tyrant who is powerful enough to satisfy his own desires is the happiest of men. The rest of *The Republic* (which involves less genuine debate, and more of a monologue by 'Socrates' with supportive interjections by his pupils) can be seen as Plato's refutation of this cynical position. He outlines an ideal state, in which the 'guardians' or rulers (who can be male or female) emerge from a long and rigorous educational regime, culminating in the study of philosophy, because only philosophers have real knowledge rather than mere beliefs or opinions. Philosophers, Plato argues, should be rulers, and rulers should be philosophers, because only the true philosopher knows justice and the other virtues, and can be trusted to pursue the interests of the whole community rather than his or her own selfish interests. Indeed, the true philosopher would prefer a life of intellectual

thinkers

contemplation, and must be persuaded to accept the burden of government in the wider public interest. If the idea of the philosopher king appears bizarre today, the notion that only those who do not want the job should be entrusted with political power is attractive.

While some of Plato's prescriptions may appear alien in the modern world, much of his political analysis remains acutely relevant. Thus his account of political change in *The Republic* remains penetrating. Particularly memorable is his portrait of the apparently successful tyrant, who is 'really the most abject slave, a parasite of the vilest scoundrels. Never able to satisfy his desires, he is always in need ... . His condition is like that of the country he governs, haunted throughout life by terrors and convulsed with anguish.' The tyrant's lot is thus far from enviable. The description might be aptly applied to many modern **dictators.**

If Plato roundly condemns tyranny, his approach to politics in *The Republic* and in other works such as the *Laws* is also profoundly hostile to **democracy**. Partly this perhaps reflects his own experience of Athenian democracy in decline and in particular the trial and execution of his teacher Socrates (referred to in the questionably authentic *Seventh Letter*). Yet essentially it derives logically from Plato's theory of knowledge, which is to be sharply distinguished from the mere beliefs or opinions of the multitude. Only the select few can attain real knowledge, after a long and rigorous system of education (outlined in the *Republic*). It follows (from this premise) that **government** is a matter for the expert, not for the ordinary man. It involves doing what is right rather than what pleases the public, compared by Plato to a great beast. Some modern commentators (such as **Popper**) have attacked Plato for his hostility to the values and practices of democracy. Others argue that it is unhistorical to seek to apply Plato's interpretation of the very different society and political systems of Greece in the fourth century BC to those of the modern world. However, it is clear that Plato was profoundly unsympathetic to the democratic values of **freedom**, participation and **toleration** emphasized in the speech which **Thucydides** puts into the mouth of **Pericles.**

Popper

Sir Karl Popper (1902–1994) born an Austrian Jew, escaped from Vienna in 1937 shortly before Austria was absorbed into Hitler's Third Reich, and taught in New Zealand, and then from 1945–69 at the London School of Economics. Popper was best known in the period immediately after the Second World War for his two-volume work *The Open Society and Its Enemies* (1945). Popper's 'open society' was the free, **liberal**, **democratic** western tradition. Its 'enemies' included some of the great names of political thought, including **Plato**, **Hegel** and **Marx**. Popper advocated piecemeal social reform rather than sweeping **utopian** reform. In *The Poverty of Historicism* (1957) he criticized those who claimed to have discovered laws of historical development.

Popper is perhaps most remembered today for his earlier work on scientific method. *The Logic of Scientific Discovery* (1934, English translation 1959) argues that nothing can be definitely proved by induction, generalizing from repeated observations. Instead, scientific method proceeds on the basis of 'conjectures and refutations' seeking to falsify (or refute) provisional hypotheses (or 'conjectures'). An hypothesis expressed in such broad or imprecise terms that it cannot be tested and (potentially) falsified is unscientific. It follows that all scientific knowledge (including the social sciences) is provisional rather than certain. This notion of 'falsifiability' as the basis of scientific method remains influential.

Poulantzas

Nicos Poulantzas (1936–1979) was a Greek-born **Marxist** thinker who spent most of his working life in Paris, where he held various university posts. He was strongly influenced by the writings of **Gramsci** and various French Marxist thinkers, particularly the structural Marxism of Louis **Althusser**. He committed suicide in Paris in 1979.

Poulantzas was involved in a celebrated dispute with **Miliband** in the pages of *New Left Review* (1969, 1970). Miliband had sought to demonstrate the close connections between the state **elite** and business. To Poulantzas this was irrelevant. He argued that the **state** is bound by its structural role within a **capitalist** society to further the interests of capitalism, regardless of whether the state's personnel come from the capitalist **class** or have social links with capitalism. Yet he also maintained that the state enjoys relative autonomy, and does not necessarily act at the behest of capitalists or specific capitalist interests. Rather the state seeks to manage class forces so as to unite sometimes conflicting

thinkers

interests within capital, and subtly divide and control other classes. His theory is elaborated in *Political Power and Social Classes* (1968) and *Classes in Contemporary Capitalism* (1975). However he also explored contemporary political developments, such as the collapse of military **dictatorships** in his native Greece, Spain and Portugal. His last book *State, Power and Socialism* (1978) recognized the importance of **new social movements** and explored the problems of transition to **democratic socialism.**

Proudhon

Pierre-Joseph Proudhon (1809–1865) was a **revolutionary** French **socialist** and **anarchist**. In an early publication he famously asked the question 'What is property?' supplying his own answer 'Property is theft!' Following the failure of the 1848 revolution in which he played a conspicuous but unconstructive role, he devoted most of the rest of his life to political theory, rejecting **government** and advocating mutualism.

Putnam

Robert D Putnam (1941–) is an American political scientist mainly known today for his work on civic engagement and **social capital**. He first came to prominence for his comparative study of the attitudes of political representatives and activists in Britain and Italy, *The Beliefs of Politicians* (1973). He followed this with broader comparative surveys of political **elites** (1976) and **bureaucrats** and politicians (1981). In a comparative study of regional governments in Italy, *Making democracy work: Civic traditions in modern Italy* (1993), Putnam first identified the importance of what he called 'social capital' (the extent of face-to-face social interaction and **community** engagement) for a healthy functioning **democratic system**. This echoed a key theme of a celebrated earlier study, *The Civic Culture* (1963), by **Almond** and Verba (which specifically involved a study of Italian political culture, as one of five national political cultures).

Putnam went on to suggest that social capital was declining in modern America in a seminal article published in 1995, and followed this up with extensive research into levels of social and communal interaction in the USA, documented in *Bowling Alone: The collapse and revival of American community* (2000). 'Bowling alone' was a metaphor for the solitary private leisure pursuits of Americans which were apparently growing at the expense of more social, interactive pursuits. Putnam argued that the decline of even such apparently apolitical activities as social dining and bridge clubs had damaging implications for civic engagement and democracy.

His work on social capital has provoked an extensive debate. Some have questioned whether the apparent decline in social capital in the USA is replicated in other western societies, pointing to increased participation in some forms of **pressure group** activity. Others have criticized some of Putnam's assumptions. Thus some 'solitary' activities that do not involve face-to-face interaction, such as communication via the internet, may not be damaging for democracy but may even assist more direct participation in politics.

Rawls

John Rawls (1921–2002) has been credited with reviving political philosophy almost single-handed after it was declared dead in the 1950s, with his *A Theory of Justice* (1971). Here he is concerned with the issue of distributive or social **justice** (basically how resources and goods should be shared out fairly between people), a preoccupation of political philosophers since the earliest times. He criticized the **utilitarian** conception of justice, as 'the greatest happiness of the greatest number' might involve sacrificing the interests of individuals or minorities to the greater good.

Rawls postulates a purely hypothetical 'Original Position' (with some similarity to the 'state of nature' in the work of **Hobbes** and **Locke**), in which people are placed behind a 'veil of ignorance'. They know nothing of the society to which they are to belong and their position within it, nor do they know what talents and abilities they have themselves. It is however assumed that they know certain 'primary goods' – **rights, liberties**, opportunities, income and wealth, respect – will be useful to them, and that they will want as much of these as possible. What moral principles would be agreed by people who are ignorant as to whether they will be advantageously or disadvantageously placed? Rawls suggests two principles (or effectively three, as his second principle is subdivided). Firstly, each person should have an equal right to the most extensive liberty, as long as this does not infringe the liberty of others (sometimes called the 'liberty principle'.

thinkers

Secondly, social and economic inequalities should be arranged so as to be of the greatest benefit to the least advantaged (referred to as the 'difference principle') and attached to positions and offices open to all under fair **equality** of opportunity (the 'equal opportunity principle').

What Rawls called 'the difference principle' is the most important and contentious. He assumes people in a hypothetical state of ignorance about their own prospects would opt for a society and system of justice in which even the worst off would have sufficient resources to enjoy a reasonable life. Rawls' concept of 'justice as fairness' was seized on by progressive **liberals** and **social democrats** as justifying some **state** intervention to secure a measure of redistribution so as to assist the least well-off, through the tax and **welfare** system. Critics such as Robert **Nozick** argue that the difference principle in practice will interfere with the liberty principle, which Nozick claims should be paramount.

In his later work *Political Liberalism* (1993), Rawls substantially maintained the principles outlined in *A Theory of Justice* (with minor modifications). He further argued that these principles could be agreed by rational persons with very different world views. They did not depend on a political consensus. In *The Law of Peoples* (1999) Rawls considered the application of the principle of 'justice as fairness' to **international relations**. He argued that, in the interests of international stability, liberal societies should tolerate 'decent hierarchical' societies that discriminated against minorities. He also denied that the 'difference principle' could be used to justify massive redistribution of global resources between states. Here Rawls disappointed some of his liberal allies and supporters. He is still, however, considered a massive figure in modern political philosophy.

Rokkan

Stein Rokkan (1921–1979) was a Norwegian political scientist, and a professor in comparative politics at Bergen University. He worked with Seymour **Lipset** with whom he co-edited the influential text *Party Systems and Voter Alignments* (1967). He also studied and wrote about state and nation building in Europe. Key works included another co-edited book *Building States and Nations* (with Shmuel Eisenstadt, 1973) and *Economy, Territory and Identity* (1983), co-authored with Derek Urwin.

Rousseau

Controversial in his own lifetime, Jean-Jacques Rousseau (1712–1778) remains a contentious figure. Although he never advocated **revolution**, his writings inspired some of those who, after his death, were to lead the French Revolution. The first modern thinker to champion **democracy,** he raised doubts over its feasibility, while scornfully rejecting the **representative** democracy that was to become its characteristic modern form. Some critics have even argued that his ideas anticipate aspects of twentieth-century **totalitarianism**, although others insist that he belongs in the great **republican** tradition.

Although Rousseau wrote in French and spent most of his working life in France, he was not French by birth or upbringing. He was born and brought up in the French-speaking Swiss city state of Geneva, and this shaped his political sympathies. In a note at the beginning of his key work *The Social Contract* (1762) he writes of Geneva, 'I was born into a free state and am a member of a sovereign body.' His political theory reflects experience of his native city and knowledge he had acquired of the political thought and practice of the small city **states** of ancient Greece and the early Roman Republic, rather than the powerful and geographically extensive states and empires of his own day.

Rousseau opens *The Social Contract* with the famous declaration, 'Man is born free but everywhere he is in chains.' Before the establishment of **government** and civilization man enjoyed natural **liberty**. In Rousseau's earlier work *A Discourse on Inequality* (1755) there is an element of nostalgia for the loss innocence and freedom of primitive man in his natural state. He is a 'noble savage', free to make his own choices, driven by the instinct of self-preservation but capable of pity and sympathy for his fellow creatures. Yet while Rousseau's imagined state of nature was not, like that of **Hobbes**, a nightmare world of brutality and fear, it limited human capacities. These could only be realized in a civil **community**. Thus man is prepared to join with others in a social contract, and surrender his natural liberty in exchange for civil liberty. 'To be subject to appetite,' Rousseau argues, 'is to be a slave, while to obey the laws laid down by society is to be free.' His assumption here is that those who obey the laws have had a part in making them. Rousseau's social contract is not, like that of **Hobbes**, an unconditional surrender of **power** to a sovereign, nor even, like **Locke's**, a conditional surrender that can be revoked if the sovereign fails to maintain his terms of the contract. Rousseau argues that **sovereignty** can never be alienated. In other words supreme power remains with the people. Only in such a political society could man still retain (or regain) freedom.

Popular sovereignty was a revolutionary doctrine. It committed Rousseau to a form of **democracy**. Yet he remained sceptical whether democracy was really practical. He explicitly rejected **representation** as a means of realizing democracy. The general will of the people, he argued, can not be represented. The English, he thought, were mistaken in believing they were free. 'They are free only when electing members of parliament, and then revert to slavery.' Thus Rousseau favoured direct rather than representative democracy. Such a system could only work, he thought, in a small state where everyone could be gathered together and knew each other, and where there was considerable **equality** of wealth. These were conditions that ruled out most of the states of Rousseau's own day. Thus he pessimistically noted 'Were there such a thing as a nation of Gods, it would be a democracy. So perfect a form of government is not suited to mere men.'

Rousseau assumed not only active citizen participation in making the **laws** that all must obey, but virtual unanimity. Laws must reflect not the will of the majority but the 'general will', the will of all, considering not their own particular interest, but the general interest. Yet Rousseau acknowledges this may be difficult. 'Left to themselves, the People always desire the good,' but 'they do not always know where that good lies. The general will is always right, but the judgement guiding it is not always well informed.' Thus, Rousseau concludes, a **legislator** is necessary. Rousseau had in mind the example of great lawgivers in ancient Greece – he cites Lycurgus of Sparta. Yet, to some critics, Rousseau's notion of a general will interpreted by a charismatic individual sinisterly foreshadows the popular **dictatorships** and **totalitarian** pseudo-democracies of the twentieth century.

Said

Edward Said (1935–2003) was a controversial Palestinian intellectual whose ideas have some continuing relevance for students of politics.

He was born in Jerusalem to wealthy Christian Palestinian parents during the period of the British Palestinian mandate, and was educated in what he described as 'elite colonial schools' in Jerusalem and Cairo. He completed his education in the USA at Princeton and Harvard, eventually becoming professor of English and comparative literature at Columbia University. His key work *Orientalism* (1978) had implications far beyond the study of literature. In it he argued that both western academic studies of eastern culture as well as western popular conceptions of 'the orient' were inevitably conditioned and warped by western power and colonial dominance over the east. (The argument owed something to the work of Michel **Foucault** who had argued that prevailing interpretations of reality necessarily reflected **power** relations.) Western conceptions of the orient in turn influenced political attitudes and judgements. *Orientalism* was hailed as a masterpiece by some, and sharply criticized by others. Said remained to his death a distinctive champion of the Palestinian cause, and Palestinian refugees. Although he initially supported the two-state solution to the Palestinian question, he later advocated a single state in which Jews and Arabs would have equal rights.

Sandel

Michael Sandel (1953–) is a modern political philosopher who made his name with his criticism of John **Rawls'** *A Theory of Justice* in his own book *Liberalism and the Limits of Justice* (1982). Along with his own tutor Charles **Taylor**, Alasdair **MacIntyre** and Michael **Walzer**, Sandel is regarded as one of the leading **communitarian** thinkers, emphasizing the reciprocal ties between persons and the **community** of which they are a part, in opposition to **liberal individualism**.

Sartori

Giovanni Sartori (1924–) is an Italian political scientist who has held chairs in his native Italy and in the USA. He has worked extensively in the field of comparative politics. Key works include *Parties and Party Systems* (1976) and *The Theory of Democracy Revisited* (1987).

Sartre

Jean-Paul Sartre (1905–1980) was the most celebrated **left**-wing French intellectual in the decades following the Second World War. His existentialist philosophy was expressed in his novels and plays as well as his key philosophical work *Being and Nothingness* (1943), which emphasized the need for individuals to assert their own **freedom**, unconstrained by conventions and expectations. However, while critical of its determinist strand, he was increasingly drawn to **Marxism**, which he sought to reconcile with existentialism. A committed political activist, he subsequently gave largely uncritical support to the French **Communist** Party and the Soviet Union. His influence on the young was already declining before his death, replaced by a younger generation of Marxist intellectuals and **postmodernist** thinkers. The work of his longtime partner, Simone **de Beauvoir**, has perhaps lasted better.

Schumacher

E. F. (Fritz) Schumacher (1911–1977) was a German-born economist who had been initially interned in Britain in the Second World War, to be rescued by **Keynes**. He was to write Keynes's obituary for *The Times,* although he was already beginning to question aspects of Keynesian economics. Much later, his book *Small is Beautiful* (1976) challenged the then fashionable presumption in favour of large scale enterprises and economies of scale. It made a significant contribution to **green thinking**, which favours **decentralization** and more local production of goods and services.

Schumpeter

Joseph Schumpeter (1883–1950) was born and educated in Vienna, and was briefly finance minister in the new Austrian Republic in 1919, but subsequently emigrated to the USA where he became a professor of economics at Harvard. In his most celebrated work *Capitalism, Socialism and Democracy* (1943) he argued that modern **representative democracy** did not (and should not) involve government by the people in the sense of their active participation in political decision making. The real initiative came not from the people themselves but from political **leaders** and their parties, rival **elites** periodically competing for public support. The majority were simple not capable of rational choice on political issues, and could only be expected to choose, like consumers in the market place, between rival teams and programmes at periodic elections. Thus 'the democratic method is that institutional arrangement for arriving at political decisions in which individuals acquire the power to decide by a competitive struggle for the people's vote'. Schumpeter's modified theory of democracy, with its restricted and passive role for ordinary people, is sometimes termed 'democratic elitism'.

Simon

Herbert Simon (1916–2001) was an American thinker with expertise in a number of fields. His work on decision making, the subject of his first book *Administrative Behaviour* (1947), is of particular relevance to politics and public administration. Here he put forward an ideal model of **rational** decision making, according to which the administrator should not start with aims and objectives because these might close down possible options. Instead he should start with the situation, consider all the options, all the consequences arising from each option, and select the option with the greatest net benefits. This, Simon recognized, was an ideal that could rarely be attained in practice, because of lack of perfect information, lack of time and perhaps lack of skills. Administrators thus normally have to operate with 'bounded rationality'. In practice they may not be able to optimize (find the one best solution) but 'satisfice' (continuing to search until a tolerably satisfactory solution is found). Simon's work on decision making influenced much subsequent theory and practice. Charles **Lindblom** designed his own rival model of policy making, **incrementalism**, in direct response.

Singer

Peter Singer (1946–) is a controversial Australian moral philosopher, who is best known for *Animal Liberation* (1975), a book that has had a major influence on the animal rights movement. He argues that all creatures capable of suffering are entitled to equal consideration. Treating animals differently from humans he describes as a form of discrimination, 'speciesism' (analogous to **racism** or sexism). Using animals for food causes unnecessary suffering, thus Singer advocates vegetarianism and a vegan diet. His general moral philosophy is **utilitarian**, set out in his book *Practical Ethics* (1979). Some of his applications of his moral theory have aroused controversy, such as his justification of euthanasia, abortion and even infanticide in certain circumstance. In a celebrated essay 'Famine, affluence and morality' (1972) he argued that it is morally indefensible for people to

thinkers

enjoy luxury goods and an affluent lifestyle while others starve. Giving money to avoid famine is not 'charity'. 'We ought to give the money away, and it is wrong not to do so.'

Skocpol

Theda Skocpol (1947–) is a leading American political scientist at Harvard University. She published *States and Social Revolutions: A comparative analysis of France, Russia and China* in 1979, and continued her exploration of **revolution** in *Social Revolutions in the Modern World* (1994). She co-edited an influential study *Bringing the State Back In* (Evans et al., 1985). She has also written extensively on American **democracy**, **government** and public policy.

Smith

Adam Smith (1723–1790) is remembered today as the founding father of classical economics, but he was also an important moral philosopher, holding a chair in the subject at the University of Glasgow from 1752–64. Both his economics and his ethics had had important implications for politics. He was a close friend and associate of the philosopher and historian David **Hume**. Both men were Scots, with closer intellectual ties with France rather than England. They are key figures in what is described as the Scottish Enlightenment, which was an important element of the wider European Enlightenment of the eighteenth century.

In *The Theory of Moral Sentiments* [1759] Smith argued that mutual sympathy was the basis of human cooperation, but introduced the notion of the 'hidden hand' of market forces as a key to increasing prosperity. In *The Wealth of Nations* [1776] he developed further the role of individual self-interest in promoting general well-being through the hidden hand of the **free market**. It followed that attempts to interfere with or restrain the operation of free market forces, either by the **state** or by other interests, were generally detrimental to the 'wealth of nations'. Smith also demonstrated the impact of specialization and the division of labour on productivity and national prosperity.

Smith was both the prophet and champion of industrial **capitalism** and the free market. Yet he also recognized that the provision of some goods and services, for example defence, public works, and education, could not or should not be left to the market. Much of the continuing debate over the legitimate role of the state in economic activities originated with Adam Smith. Although he is most commonly cited by modern **neoliberals** to support their anti-state free market convictions, parts of his writing can also be used to justify the moderate state intervention advocated by modern **social liberals** and **social democrats**.

Socrates

Socrates (c. 469–399 BC) was a celebrated Athenian philosopher who lived through the great days of the city under **Pericles**, and the ensuing long war between Athens and Sparta. This war ended with the defeat of Athens in 404, and the brief replacement of the Athenian system of **democracy** by the tyranny of the Thirty. After democracy was restored, Socrates was put on trial for corrupting the young. He conducted his own defence provocatively, and was condemned to death by drinking hemlock. His death sentence has long been regarded as a serious stain on Athenian democracy. The attitude towards democracy of Socrates himself is unclear, although some of his associates were certainly its enemies and his pupil **Plato** was very hostile.

The teaching of Socrates himself was oral, so that we rely on his contemporaries and pupils, principally Plato, but also, among others, the historian Xenophon and the playwright Aristophanes, for our knowledge of his ideas and methods. Their testimony is somewhat contradictory. However, particularly in his so-called earlier dialogues, Plato may have provided a tolerably accurate portrait of Socrates himself and the 'Socratic method'. This involved rigorous cross-examination of the ideas expressed by others, exposing weaknesses and inconsistencies in their thinking. In Plato's *Apology*, Socrates, in the course of his defence at his trial, describes how the oracle at Delphi had declared there was no one wiser than himself. Aware that he had no claim to wisdom, Socrates cross-examined many men considered wise in an attempt to disprove the oracle's verdict. He concluded from his enquiries that the reputation of these men for wisdom was unjustified, and that they, like himself, knew nothing of importance. However, he was conscious of his own ignorance, and they were not, and to that extent he was wiser than they were.

Sorel

Georges Sorel (1847–1922) was a French thinker

associated with syndicalism and anarcho-syndicalism, involving **revolutionary** industrial action and direct workers' control, rather than seeking power through **electoral** and parliamentary means. Sorel emphasized the importance of myths in sustaining revolutionary consciousness and workers' solidarity, particularly the myth of the general strike, as a means to bring **capitalism** down. His ideas were influential in radical trade union circles before and after the First World War.

Spencer

Herbert Spencer (1820–1903) was a British philosopher whose strong laissez-faire **free market liberalism** was reinforced by Darwin's theory of evolution, and the notion of the survival of the fittest. He was strongly opposed to the interventionist New Liberalism that became influential towards the end of his life. His extensive writings include *Social Statics* [1850] and *The Man versus the State* [1884]. While his reputation has declined in Britain he is still rated highly by some American **neoliberals**.

Spinoza

Baruch (Benedict) Spinoza (1632–1697) was a Dutch Jewish philosopher who vigorously defended **free** speech and religious **toleration**. His political thought was influenced by **Hobbes**, but unlike Hobbes he believed in limited **government**, and favoured **democracy**. Key works include the *Tractatus Theologico-Philosophicus* [1670] and his posthumously published *Ethics* (see McShea, 1968).

Stalin

Joseph Stalin (1879–1953) was born Josef Vissarionovich Dzhugashvili but adopted the name Stalin (meaning 'man of steel') when he became an active Bolshevik **revolutionary**. He was not a leading figure in the 1917 Russian Revolution, but became a member of the ruling politburo and, in 1922, General Secretary of the Communist Party. He used this administrative post to strengthen his own power base in the party, and after Lenin's death in 1924, over time, skilfully outmanoeuvred his opponents, such as **Trotsky**, to become Lenin's successor, establishing a ruthless dictatorship. His contribution to **Marxist-Leninist** theory was relatively thin, including his writings on the nationalities issue and his support for the idea of '**socialism** in one country', in response to Trotsky's doctrine of 'permanent revolution'. It

was the practice of his **government** that added the term 'Stalinism' to political vocabulary. This included the extermination of millions of peasants who resisted the forced collectivization of agriculture, and the show trials and executions of those perceived as traitors to the regime, who included nearly all Lenin's leading Bolshevik colleagues who survived long enough to become victims of Stalin. The excesses of his rule were denounced, after his death, by his eventual successor as Soviet leader, Nikita Khrushchev.

Tawney

Richard Henry Tawney (1880–1962) was a British economic historian and Christian **socialist**. While many socialists around the world have been indifferent or hostile to religion, Christian socialism has been a significant strand in the British labour movement. Some Christian socialists were Roman Catholics (such as John Wheatley) but rather more were Protestant nonconformists, particularly Methodists (such as Philip Snowden). R. H. Tawney combined socialism with Anglicanism. Key works were *The Acquisitive Society* [1921], *Religion and the Rise of Capitalism* [1926] and *Equality* [1931].

Taylor

Charles Taylor (1931–) is a Canadian political philosopher, who held professorial chairs at Oxford, where he taught Michael **Sandel**, among others, and McGill University, Montreal. He tried four times unsuccessfully to secure election to the Canadian House of Commons as a candidate of the New Democratic Party. His key work is generally thought to be *Sources of the Self: The making of modern identity* (1990). He argues that the self can only be understood in terms of the **community** of which it is a part, and not as an isolated individual, as suggested by **liberals**.

Thoreau

Henry David Thoreau (1817–1862) was an American radical individualist thinker. In *Walden* [1854] he described how he pursued self-sufficiency living in a cabin at Walden Pond. He asserted, 'That **government** is best which governs not all.' He justified resistance to **authority** and **civil disobedience** on grounds of conscience, particularly on the issue of slavery. Prison, he argued, was 'the only house in a slave-state in which a free man can reside with honour'.

thinkers

Tocqueville

Alexis de Tocqueville (1805–1859) was born into a French Catholic aristocratic family which fully supported the restored Bourbon **monarchy** of Louis XVIII and Charles X. This French aristocrat is today chiefly known for his celebrated and generally sympathetic two-volume study *Democracy in America*. (The first volume was published in 1835, the second in 1840.) The still relatively new system of **democracy** in America was then regarded with considerable curiosity tinged with apprehension in Europe. Tocqueville went to America in 1831 with a commission from the new French government to research the American penal system, but his real interest was in wider American society and its political system. The result of his extensive travel and research has been described as 'the greatest book ever written on America'. It is still regularly cited by American politicians.

While he was well aware of some of the theoretical issues surrounding the development of the American **constitution**, Tocqueville was more interested in the practice of American democracy. He was particularly impressed by the active participation of American citizens in the **government** of their own localities. 'The strength of free nations resides in the township.' He repeatedly emphasized the importance of **decentralization** in the American political system. However, he was concerned over what he called 'the tyranny of the majority' in democratic society, a key phrase that has entered the language. Tocqueville also wrote eloquently on the condition of American Blacks, roundly condemning slavery but observing pointedly that **racial** prejudice appeared stronger in those states that had abolished slavery than in those where slavery still existed. While he was assured that freed slaves had the legal right to vote in America, he noted that they were effectively prevented from exercising these **rights**.

Trotsky

Leon Trotsky (1879–1940) was a leading Russian **Marxist revolutionary** politician and thinker, whose ideas ultimately became more influential on the **socialist left** in the west than in the **communist** bloc. He was born Leon Bronstein, but assumed the name Trotsky after he became a Marxist revolutionary. An early associate of **Lenin**, Trotsky famously predicted that the **democratic** centralism advocated in Lenin's *What Is To Be Done?* would mean 'the party organization substitutes itself for the party, the central committee substitutes itself for the organization, and, finally, a '**dictator**' substitutes himself for the central committee.' Yet Trotsky was not definitely aligned with either the Bolsheviks or the Mensheviks after the party split in 1903. He played a leading role in the abortive 1905 revolution, and in 1917 joined Lenin. After the Bolshevik Revolution he negotiated the Treaty of Brest Litovsk with Germany, and then led the Red Army to victory over the Whites in the Russian Civil War. He then appeared to be Lenin's leading lieutenant and potential successor, but in the struggle for power after Lenin's death Trotsky was distrusted by the old Bolsheviks, and was eventually outmanoeuvred by the party secretary, **Stalin**, who controlled the **bureaucracy**.

While Stalin advocated 'socialism in one country', Trotsky assumed that the communism could not triumph in Russia without revolution elsewhere, and continued to champion 'permanent revolution'. He was exiled in 1929, fiercely denounced the show trials and executions of the 1930s in which Stalin eliminated almost all the surviving old Bolsheviks, and was finally killed in Mexico by a Stalinist agent in 1940. Trotskyism as an alternative to Stalinism continued to attract a following among western **Marxists** throughout the period of the cold war. Trotsky was always the most readable of the Russian Marxists, and his own account of the Russian Revolution and its subsequent betrayal won admirers, as did a monumental biography by Isaac Deutscher. In the communist world, while some victims of Stalin were subsequently rehabilitated, Trotsky was not, and he remains a marginalized figure following the implosion of communism in Russia and eastern Europe.

Tullock

Gordon Tullock (1922–) is an American economist. Together with James Buchanan he wrote *The Calculus of Consent* (1962), a classic work of the **public choice** school that became massively influential in American political science. Other works include *The Politics of Bureaucracy* (1965), and *On Voting: A public choice approach* (1998).

Voltaire

François-Marie Arouet Voltaire (1694–1778) was a celebrated thinker of the French Enlightenment.

thinkers

Voltaire was a noted critic of the nobility and clergy, but not of the monarchy, favouring a benevolent despotism. He was a supporter of religious **toleration** and **freedom** of thought, although he did not say the words commonly attributed to him, 'I disapprove of what you say, but I will defend to the death your right to say it' (actually uttered by S. G. Tallentyre). He is most remembered today for his satire *Candide* (1759).

Waltz

Kenneth N Waltz (1924–) is the leading modern **realist** or neorealist American **international relations** theorist. In his key work *Theory of International Politics* (1979) he argued that the international system remains one of **anarchy** in which **states** have to look after their own interests in the absence of effective higher **authority** to which they might defer. In looking after their own security, states have to consider the threats posed by other states. To reduce such threats, state foreign policy seeks to build alliances to secure a balance of **power** and thus create and maintain stability in the international political system. The balance of power between the USA and its allies on the one hand, and the USSR and its allies on the other, appeared to be an example of such an (apparently stable) international system at the time of writing. Some **liberal-pluralist** critics argued that Waltz's account was unduly state-centred, involved oversimplified assumptions about the making of state foreign policy and the pursuit of national interest, and downplayed the importance of international institutions and **non-governmental organizations** (**NGOs**). Other critics considered that Waltz underplayed the impact of a **globalized capitalist** economy on international relations. The unanticipated end of the cold war provided further problems for the neorealists. Yet realist and neo-realist assumptions about international relations have remained influential, not least in the foreign policy of the USA.

Walzer

Michael Walzer (1935–) is a modern American moral and political philosopher, associated with **communitarianism** (along with Alasdair **MacIntyre**, Michael **Sandel** and Charles **Taylor**) and with his criticism of John **Rawls** and his theory of **justice**, for example in *Spheres of Justice* (1983). Walzer has also revived the notion of the just war in *Just and Unjust Wars* (2000), upholding the general principle of non-intervention in the internal affairs of independent **sovereign states**, although allowing a case for humanitarian intervention in very rare circumstances.

Webb

Sidney Webb (1859–1947) and his wife Beatrice Webb (1858–1943) formed such a close-knit intellectual partnership that they are best treated together. The young Beatrice Potter combined formidable intellectual tastes with beauty, and had a youthful crush on the radical Liberal and subsequent Liberal Unionist politician Joe Chamberlain, before she married the clever but less charismatic Sidney Webb in 1892. They became leading figures in the Fabian Society, a small but influential **socialist** group, named after the Roman general who had defeated Hannibal by patient delaying tactics (declining to fight him in open battle), and committed to gradual reform through the ballot box rather than **revolution**. The Webbs were active in founding the London School of Economics in 1895, indicative of their own enthusiasm for reform based on social science research. They believed that their practical common-sense socialist ideas would, over time, permeate society. Initially they were prepared to work through any politician (including the young Winston Churchill) who would listen to them, but they became increasingly committed to the Labour Party. Sidney Webb helped draft the original Clause IV of the party's constitution (1918), with its celebrated commitment to common ownership of the means of production, distribution and exchange. He later served as Labour minister in MacDonald's governments in 1924 and 1929–31. Subsequently the Webbs visited Stalin's Russia, whose socialist system they endorsed with naïve enthusiasm, ironically, as Stalin's interpretation of socialism was far removed from the gradual parliamentary socialism with which they were identified.

Weber

Max Weber (1864–1920) is now regarded as one of the most important social and political thinkers of the twentieth century, and a founding father of sociology. He was born in Erfurt, the son of a prominent German politician. The family moved to Berlin in 1869. He studied law, history, economics and philosophy, and later taught economics at Berlin and politics at Heidelberg, but gave up teaching after he quarrelled with his father and his health broke down. In 1904 his celebrated essay *The Protestant Ethic and the Spirit of Capitalism* was published. At the end of the First World War he was involved in peace negotiations at Versailles, and was a member of the commission that drafted the Weimar **constitution**. He returned to teaching at Vienna and then Munich, where he died of pneumonia in 1920. Much of the writing for which he is now most well known was published after his death.

In contrast with **Marx**, who believed that economic interests ultimately determined political and social change, Weber thought that historical development was the consequence of a more complex interplay of social, cultural and religious forces. Thus he famously argued that the rise of **capitalism** in the west was assisted by the emergence of Protestantism, and more specifically Calvinism. Calvinism aided capitalist accumulation, as this was interpreted as a sign of divine favour. Puritanism also encouraged ploughing back income and wealth into new enterprise rather than wasting it in conspicuous consumption.

To cope with studying the complexity of society and social change, Weber made use of what he described as 'ideal types', involving abstract exaggerations of features of real life. Thus ideal types are simplified explanatory tools or models providing insights into complex social reality. '**Capitalism**', '**authority**', '**bureaucracy**', '**class**' and 'status' are among the key concepts that Weber analysed in this way.

Weber's analyses of **power**, **authority**, **legitimacy**, the **state** and **bureaucracy** are particularly important for students of politics. Power he saw as the ability to gain one's ends despite the resistance of others. Ultimately power relies on the threat of physical force. Weber famously defined the state as a human **community** that (successfully) claims the monopoly of the legitimate use of physical force within a given territory. Yet a key word here is 'legitimate'. Weber recognized that power is often widely accepted as legitimate, and used the term 'authority' to describe legitimate power. He argued that legitimate power or authority could be derived from three main sources. It may be traditional, arising from age-old custom and practice, such as the authority of a hereditary ruler. It may stem from the personal qualities or charisma of a particular **leader**. Weber believed the characteristic modern form of authority was legal-rational, based on clear written rules and

procedures. Here obedience is essentially to the position rather than the person who occupies the position, as long as that person has been appointed or **elected** according to recognized rules and procedures. Both **representative democracy** and bureaucracy involved legal-rational authority.

Weber saw **bureaucracy** as the predominant form of organization in the modern world in both the public and private sectors. His ideal type of bureaucracy involved a number of features, including a hierarchical structure, with a clear chain of command, adherence to impersonal written rules, recruitment and promotion by merit and recognized professional qualifications, and the separation of work from private life. Yet while Weber thought bureaucracy was a **rational** and efficient form of organization, he had some concerns that it might effectively supplant democracy.

Wendt

Alexander Wendt (1958–) is a German-born scholar who completed his education in the USA, where he is now a leading **constructivist** theorist of **international relations**. He published two key articles 'The agent/structure problem in international relations theory' (1987) and 'Anarchy is what states make of it: the social construction of power politics' (1992), both of which questioned the **realist** and neo-realist assumption that international relations were shaped by enduring material objective factors. He argued instead that key concepts (such as **anarchy**) were not immutable but socially constructed (or interpreted) by key actors, such as **states**, and so were capable of evolving over time. His book *Social Theory of International Politics* (1999) outlined his own approach to the study of international relations; the title suggests it was conceived as a direct response to the key work of Kenneth **Waltz** (1979).

Wildavsky

Aaron Wildavksy (1930–1993) was an American political scientist who taught at the University of California, Berkeley, and published prolifically on a wide variety of topics. He is perhaps best known among political scientists for his work on policy analysis, including *Implementation* (with J. Pressman, 1973), *The Politics of the Budgetary Process* (Heclo and Wildavsky, 1974), and *The Art and Craft of Policy Analysis* (1980). His book (with Hugh Heclo) *The Private Government of Public Money* (1974) is widely regarded as a classic study of

thinkers

British public administration. He has also written on the American Presidency, cultural theory and **environmentalism.** He co-authored *Risk and Culture* with the anthropologist Mary Douglas.

Wollstonecraft

Mary Wollstonecraft (1759–1797) was a pioneer English **feminist**, who sought to apply **liberal** values to the position of women. She associated with radical nonconformists and enthusiastically supported the French **Revolution**. Her book *A Vindication of the Rights of Man* (1790) followed the publication of the revolutionary 'Declaration of the Rights of Man and Citizen' of 1789 and was written in direct response to the *Reflections on the Revolution in France* of Edmund **Burke** [1790]. Her key work *A Vindication of the Rights of Women* (1792) followed two years later. In it she argued that women were as **rational** as men, and as rational creature should be entitled to the same **rights** as men. **Rousseau** had argued in *Emile* that women were different in nature from men, and 'woman is made to please and to be in subjection to man.' Wollstonecraft vehemently disagreed. If women's nature appeared different this was because of social conditioning. Women should not be dependent on men for their subsistence, and made, by this dependence, virtual slaves. She placed strong emphasis on women's education as the key to their emancipation.

After several unhappy relationships Mary Wollstonecraft in 1797 married the anarchist thinker William Godwin, who was later to write her biography. She died soon after the birth of their daughter Mary, who later married the poet Shelley and as Mary Shelley wrote the horror story *Frankenstein.*

research

introduction to part V:
key research and debates

This part of the book introduces students to some key theoretical debates and research in modern political science. The topics discussed are illustrative rather than comprehensive in scope, and intended to stimulate interest and raise questions rather than provide answers.

The first five topics (on political culture, voting, parties, pressure groups and political communication), focus substantially on the involvement of the masses in politics, and are particularly critical for the viability of representative democracy, now ostensibly the dominant political system in the modern world. The next two topics, on public administration and governance, focus more closely on the machinery of government and the state, on the policy-making process and policy outputs and outcomes.

There follows a discussion of the increased significance of identity politics and the linked debates around multiculturalism. These raise questions over allegiance and obligation that are important for the politics and government of states, but also transcend political borders and have major implications for global politics, peace and security. The international dimension is clearer still on the last three topics (democratization, globalization and international relations). The rapid expansion in the number of states embracing representative democracy is potentially the most important political development of recent decades, yet raises issues about the quality and stability of democratic systems, with implications for both domestic politics and relations between states. Similarly, the nature and extent of globalization and its influence on both state and global politics has become a major focus of research. Finally, a rich mixture of developments in world politics and new theoretical perspectives is transforming the study of international relations.

Part V draws on much that has gone before. Thus attention was drawn to the considerable diversity of approaches to the study of politics across countries and institutions in Part I, and this is evident in this part of the book. The topics discussed here also explore some of the practical implications of the theories and approaches discussed in Part II. They inevitably draw on many of the key concepts outlined in Part III, and the key thinkers mentioned in Part IV.

research

Public opinion, political culture and democracy

The **behavioural** revolution in political science involved a shift in focus away from normative political philosophy on the one hand and the formal institutions of **government** on the other, towards the systematic analysis of the political attitudes and behaviour of the masses. It was plausible that what ordinary people knew and thought about politics (their '**political culture**') substantially influenced their political behaviour, and their participation in the political process. This was of particular concern in **liberal democratic** political systems that placed a high premium on the political commitment and participation of their individual citizens.

> *It was plausible that what ordinary people knew and thought about politics substantially influenced their political behaviour, and their participation in the political process.*

The argument goes back a long way. **Tocqueville** connected the flourishing of democracy in America in the 1830s to the attitudes and values of its people, long before the term 'political culture' was coined, and more systematically measured. 'To have a hand in the government of society, and to talk about it, is the most important business, and, so to speak, the only pleasure an American knows' (Tocqueville, [1835]: 284). It is impossible to know how far Tocqueville's judgement would have been supported by more systematic statistical analysis of American opinion then. A century later, American political scientists such as V. O. **Key** (1961, 1966) were able to undertake mass surveys of public opinion and subject the findings to thorough statistical analysis. However, the results were still subject to conflicting interpretations. While Key continued to believe his own extensive surveys of American public opinion were quite compatible with the notions of rational participation in the political process, others discovered that the average American citizen was neither especially politically knowledgeable, nor discriminating. Such views had significant implications for explanations of voting behaviour, both in America and elsewhere (see below).

Political culture

While the USA was a rich seam for surveying public opinion, other American political scientists, fully committed to a comparative approach, sought to measure and analyse political knowledge and attitudes across countries. In a pioneering study **Almond** and Verba (1963) supervised in-depth opinion surveys in five countries, the USA, the United Kingdom, Mexico, West Germany and Italy, and discovered considerable differences in their national political cultures. West Germany they found had a 'subject' political culture, in which people neither expected nor wanted to have much influence on government. Italy had a more 'parochial' political culture, in which people identified with their own area rather than the country as a whole, with negative implications for participation in national politics. Survey evidence suggested the USA had a more 'participant' political culture, in which citizens both wanted and expected to have political influence, although the downside of this active citizenship was that Americans had less respect for the **law** and **authority** generally. Almond and Verba concluded that Britain (whose political culture was then characterized in terms of 'homogeneity, consensus and deference') came closest to what they regarded as an ideal 'civic' culture, which blended elements of a subject and participant culture. Thus the British combined respect for the

> *Almond and Verba supervised in-depth opinion surveys in five countries and discovered considerable differences in their national political cultures.*

research

law and legitimate authority with confidence in their ability to influence the political process.

Almond and Verba assumed that political culture had major implications for political behaviour, and more specifically, for a flourishing **democracy**. Thus we might conclude that some nations and some cultures are more suited to democracy than others. Yet of course changes in political practice and political behaviour may lead to changes in political attitudes. The apparently successful operation of democracy over a period may transform political attitudes. Recognizing that political cultures can evolve over time, Almond and Verba later sought to repeat their research, and found some significant changes (Almond and Verba, 1980). Germans now took political participation and civic responsibility more seriously, while national confidence had declined in both Britain and the USA. These changes might be seen as the consequence on the one hand of Germany's economic miracle and continued political stability, and on the other of severe economic and political problems in the UK and USA.

Although Almond and Verba's research and analysis was impressive in breadth and depth, not everyone was convinced by their conclusions. One criticism was that in seeking to characterize national political cultures, they had downplayed or ignored evidence of significant subcultures, based for example on region, **ethnicity**, **class** or gender. Thus some observers in the post-war period perceived a marked contrast between **elite** and mass culture, and identified a distinctive working-class political subculture in western countries like Britain, Italy and Germany (Norris, 1971). In the USA there are distinctive subcultures associated with the south, and with particular ethnic minorities (such as blacks and Hispanics). Feminists have often claimed that women's political attitudes and behaviour are significantly different from men's. The whole concept of a national political culture thus may obscure substantial political divisions within a nation, derived from people's very different experiences of life and work.

Political consensus?

Yet others would still perceive a shared national political **consensus** that transcends such divisions. Such a consensus may simply reflect real political homogeneity, the absence of deep social and economic divisions. Alternatively it may reflect a willing compromise and sharing of power between different interests and subcultures, in what **Lijphart** (1977) has termed a consociational democracy. However, not everyone would accept that such a political consensus either exists in practice or should exist. For **Marxists** the consensus was a phoney or imposed consensus which did not reflect the real interests of the poor. People were effectively conditioned what to think by their upbringing, their education, the **media** and the whole economic and social system they experience, so that they could not conceive of any realistic alternative. The Italian Marxist Antonio **Gramsci** used the term '**hegemony**' to describe the dominance of **bourgeois** ideas under **capitalism**. Steven Lukes (1974) has suggested that that the most subtle and effective use of **power** is the power to shape, in effect, how people think. It is a point made in a rather different way by **Foucault** and leading **postmodernist** thinkers, who argue that knowledge, and the language used to express knowledge, reflects power, an argument taken up by some **feminists**.

> For Marxists the consensus was a phoney or imposed consensus that did not reflect the real interests of the poor.

Post-material culture?

For all kinds of reasons the study of **political culture** and even the term itself rather fell from academic favour. Yet some political scientists continued to examine the impact of people's attitudes and values on their political behaviour. Thus Ronald **Inglehart** (1977) has found evidence for a change to '**postmaterial**' values in advanced western states. The hypothesis suggests that a new political generation who take for granted levels of material prosperity and security are inclined to value postmaterial goals, including quality of life and self-fulfilment. This may be exemplified by the emergence of new social movements (such as the women's movement, the peace movement, the green movement) and new forms of political participation (the politics of protest rather than more formal electoral and parliamentary procedures). Some of this might be regarded as healthy for democracy, although not perhaps traditional representative democracy.

Yet it has also been noted that the evidence for such 'post-material' values is more sparse in eastern Europe and other parts of the globe where living standards are rather lower, and there is an understandable continuing attachment to 'material' values. Indeed, much of the early enthusiasm of former communist societies in eastern Europe for democracy and the European Union was perhaps bound up with the hope and even expectation of the enjoyment of western living standards. One cynical observation was 'democracy comes on four wheels', implying that these former **communist** peoples desired the same cars and other consumer goods widely enjoyed by advanced western democracies. Certainly there seems to be less enthusiasm for **green ideas**, green pressure groups and green parties in some of the newer European democracies. Yet if material prosperity is important for democratic stability, much rides on the prospects for rapid economic growth among relatively disadvantaged countries.

Social capital

Despite the recent rapid spread of regimes formally endorsing democracy around the world, the long-term future of this system of government is hardly assured, even in apparently mature stable democracies. More than any other political system, democracy depends on the willing political support and participation of ordinary people. In long-established democracies the general decline in voter turnout, the sharp fall in membership and active involvement in **political parties**, and survey data indicating growing distrust with elected politicians and the whole political process all suggest a growing crisis of confidence in democracy. Some argue that there is a marked decline in engagement with the public sphere, a retreat into the private world of work, leisure and family that bodes ill for the health of democracy.

Some argue that there is a marked decline in engagement with the public sphere, a retreat into the private world of work, leisure and family that bodes ill for the health of democracy.

The work of Robert **Putnam** on **social capital** is often cited in this connection. Putnam has had a long interest in the influence of political attitudes on the functioning of democracy. An early book *The Beliefs of Politicians* (1973) concentrated on the views of political elites, comparing the attitudes of politicians and party activists in Britain and Italy. His later work has focused on wider social attitudes and behaviour. Thus in his comparative study of regional governments in Italy, *Making Democracy Work: Civic traditions in modern Italy* (1993), he first identified the importance of what he called social capital (essentially the extent of social networks and community engagement) for a healthy functioning democratic system. He went on to argue that social capital was declining in modern America in a seminal article published in 1995. He proceeded to document this thesis with extensive research into levels of social and communal interaction in the USA, published in *Bowling Alone: The collapse and revival of American community* (2000). 'Bowling alone' was a metaphor for the solitary leisure activities of Americans, apparently increasing at the expense of more social, interactive pursuits. Putnam argued that the decrease of even such apparently apolitical activities as social dining and bridge clubs involved a decline in social capital, with damaging implications for civic engagement and democracy.

Putnam's work is substantially in the tradition of research into political culture established by Almond and Verba. Over time he has directed his interest to three of the five countries studied by them (the United Kingdom, Italy and the USA), although the focus of his work is distinctive. His social capital thesis has been influential and has provoked an extensive debate. Some have questioned whether the apparent decline in social capital found in the USA is replicated in other western societies, pointing to increased participation in some forms of **pressure groups** and social movements (e.g. Hall, 1999). However, another line of criticism is directed at Putnam's assumptions. Thus it is arguable that some 'solitary' activities that do not involve physical social interaction, such as communication via the internet, may not be damaging for democracy but may even assist more direct participation in politics (e.g. Margetts, 2002: 201). Others again are critical of the whole concept of social capital and its underlying implications. Thus Theda **Skocpol** (1996: 20–25) complained that Putnam's approach assumed that 'spontaneous social association is primary and government and politics are derivative'.

Elections and voting

Research into elections and voting was a key aspect of the **behavioural revolution** (see Part II, Section 2). Voting was in many ways an ideal subject for this new approach to the study of politics. It involved studying the political behaviour of the masses rather than **governments** or **elites**. It was well suited to the essentially inductive methodology of behaviouralism, which consisted of deriving generalizations or hypotheses from a mass of data. It offered almost unlimited potential for the application of quantitative techniques to correlate election data with a mass of other statistical information. Finally, early research matched closely the then dominant perspective of political sociology.

Sociological approaches to voting

Thus pioneering studies of **elections** emphasized the importance of social characteristics, such as **class**, religion and **ethnicity**, in influencing and, it appeared, almost determining political allegiance. The authors of *The People's Choice*, the first large-scale study of voting behaviour in the USA (**Lazarsfeld** et al, 1944: 27) bluntly concluded that 'a person thinks, politically, as he is socially. Social characteristics determine political preference.' British election studies from 1945 onwards seemed to confirm the importance of social factors, particularly occupational class, in explaining party choice. In a much-quoted verdict, Peter Pulzer in 1967 declared, 'class is the basis of British politics; all else is embellishment and detail.' Research into voting on the European continent also showed significant correlations with a range of social factors, and not just occupational class. Religion, language, and urban/rural cleavages were among the factors that seemed to explain party preferences in specific European democracies (Lane and Ersson, 1999).

British election studies from 1945 onwards seemed to confirm the importance of social factors, particularly occupational class, in explaining party choice.

A rather more sophisticated model of electoral choice was introduced by a number of researchers at the University of Michigan (*The American Voter*, Campbell et al, 1960). This argued that the specific social characteristics of an individual voter exposed him or her to important influences (such as family, friends, neighbours, colleagues at work) that shaped his or her party allegiance or 'identity'. This party identity, once formed by the process of political socialization, tended to be stable over time. The Michigan model, as it was called, was initially used to analyse American elections, but was soon exported elsewhere. Butler and Stokes (*Political Change in Britain*, 1969) applied a similar approach to British elections. Their model suggested that parents' social class and party were particularly significant in influencing party identity. They also argued that the political circumstances prevailing when young adults were first eligible to vote helped to shape enduring political attitudes. The evidence implied that new voters determined whether they were Republican or Democrat, Labour or Conservative, Christian Democrat or Social Democrat, and tended to maintain that allegiance over time, with only a small minority of 'floating voters' prepared to switch their support from election to election. Surveys also suggested such floating voters were, in the main, more politically ignorant and apathetic than those who strongly identified with one party.

Some found the conclusions from all this research into voting rather disturbing. If most voting was habitual and depended on the accidents of birth and upbringing, it did not seem particularly rational. How could governments be properly accountable to voters who, it appeared, were not carefully weighing their record against the promises of the opposition, but merely recording their tribal loyalties to a particular party? The evidence seemed to confirm the views of those, like Joseph **Schumpeter**, who had argued that most voters were politically ignorant.

Economic models of voting

Those who found the analysis of voter behaviour from sociological surveys disturbing could consider an alternative approach inspired by economics. *An Economic Theory of Democracy* (Anthony **Downs**, 1957) started from the assumption that voters did behave rationally. Using simple economic models Downs demonstrated that in a two-party system both major parties would compete to occupy the political central ground to maximize their vote (the analysis does not hold for a multi-party system). This seemed to provide theoretical support for the strategies generally (but not invariably) followed by US and UK parties. **Rational choice** theorists subsequently assumed that all political actors, including voters, acted in their own economic self-interest (an assumption that has implications for many other forms of political behaviour besides voting).

If these notions of voters pursuing their rational self-interest had remained just deductions from the kind of assumptions about human behaviour that classical and neoclassical economists had long routinely made, they would not have challenged the received wisdom from the patient and thorough research of political sociologists. Yet economic models of voting did receive some support from new empirical research. Thus in Britain, Ivor Crewe found increased evidence of significant issue-based voting in British General Elections between 1974 and 1992. The party that had a lead in opinion polls on key salient issues was most likely to win. By 1992 Crewe was arguing that economic

research

prosperity was the crucial issue influencing party choice, overriding other issues on which the (then) opposition Labour party held the lead (see Denver, 2003: 100–1). Research by David Sanders (reported in Denver, 2003: 114–18) suggested a close correlation between economic indicators (relating to both the real economy and expectations) and party fortunes. Thus the (economic) 'well-being' factor seemed a key to election success. This matched closely the received political wisdom among Bill Clinton's Democrats in the USA in the 1990s, who coined the aphorism, 'It's the economy, stupid!' It also corresponds with an older cynical explanation of the behaviour of French voters in two ballot elections – that they vote with their heart in the first round and their wallet in the second (when the result really matters).

> The (economic) 'well-being' factor seemed a key to election success.

Another British political scientist, Patrick Dunleavy (1979, 1980) found that 'consumption cleavages' or divisions in the electorate over the consumption of services (such as housing, transport, health and education) had implications for party choice. Those substantially dependent (from necessity or choice) on the public provision of these services were significantly more likely to support the Labour Party than those who made less use of state services, regardless of their own role in the production process (as blue or white-collar workers). This reflects what could be seen as another interpretation of economic self-interest. Those who benefit from these services will want more public spending on them, and will accept the corollary of higher taxation. Those who make little use of them will oppose high taxes to pay for them.

Electoral volatility

It sometimes appears that just as a broad consensus is becoming established among political scientists, events conspire to undermine it. No sooner had the importance of economic well-being become widely (but never universally) accepted as the predominant factor influencing voting, when along came 9/11, the 'war on **terror**' and the acutely controversial invasion and occupation of Iraq. The support of the Spanish **conservative** government of Anzar for the Iraq war, closely followed by the Madrid **terror** bombings, led to the government's defeat. The war also seems to have substantially eroded support for Blair's Labour Government in 2005 and for the US Republicans in 2006. Of course it can be argued that war was a substantial drain on the economy of the USA and the United Kingdom, and diverted resources from domestic spending programmes. Yet it does seem that foreign policy can, on occasions, swing elections.

> The evidence indicates a marked decline in party identification from the 1970s to the present day.

However, one generalization about modern voting does seem to be validated by comparative research as well as trends within single countries, and that is a pattern of declining party loyalty almost across the board. The evidence indicates a marked decline in party identification from the 1970s to the present day. Fewer voters identify themselves as Republican or Democrat, Labour or Conservative, Communist, Social Democrat, Christian Democrat or Liberal. This can be substantially explained in terms of what is described as 'partisan dealignment', a weakening of the links between political parties and social groups. Class voting seems to have markedly declined everywhere, while religious, regional or ethnic identities have generally declined as factors influencing party loyalty and electoral choice. Voters have become more volatile, more prepared to switch their party support from one election to another (Denver, 2003: 66–94).

One indication of this greater electoral volatility can be seen in the readiness of voters to switch parties between different stages of the electoral process (as in the French two-ballot system), or between different levels of election (such as federal, state and local), or when faced with different **electoral systems**. What has surprised commentators is the way in which voters have responded in often quite sophisticated ways to the potentialities of specific electoral systems, such as the additional member system used in Germany, Scotland and Wales, or the single transferable vote in Ireland (now used in both north and south). There has been an associated increase in tactical voting, that is voters opting to cast a vote for their second or third-choice party in certain circumstances. Those who were once sceptical over the impact of significant tactical voting have now conceded its growing significance. One example involves electors in first past the post systems (as in the United Kingdom) switching from their preferred party to one most likely to defeat a hated opponent that otherwise might win. Another illustration involves Germans who support major parties but vote tactically instead for minor parties who are potential coalition partners, to help them surmount the 5 per cent threshold to secure representation in the German Bundestag.

Declining turnout

Much of this greater electoral volatility seems healthy, indicating, some may argue, a more discriminating and sophisticated electorate using the franchise to achieve a preferred outcome, and to penalize or reward parties for their performance in government or opposition. This seems to match more closely the optimistic assumptions of the early theorists of modern **representative democracy**. Yet another general trend in recent elections almost everywhere is rather more disturbing – the widespread marked decline in turnout levels.

Relatively low turnout levels, sometimes below 50 per cent even for presidential elections, have long been a feature of the USA. Yet in the immediate post-war era in western Europe turnout levels were generally high, with often 80–90 per cent of those eligible to vote choosing to do so. Indeed, rational choice theorists found these high turnout levels rather baffling, as their own analysis suggested voting was not rational for individuals, as the cost (in terms of effort) was unlikely to be balanced by any reward directly resulting from their own participation in the process. The notion that voters might feel morally obliged to vote as a civic duty was not easily compatible with rational choice assumptions. Perhaps more voters have concluded that voting is indeed irrational, or perhaps they have abstained for other reasons, yet whatever the explanation it has damaging implications for the legitimacy of representative democracy.

> Relatively low turnout levels, sometimes below 50 per cent even for presidential elections, have long been a feature of the USA.

Commenting on the drop in turnout in British general elections between 1997 and 2001, from 71 per cent to 59 per cent, Whiteley et al (in Norris, 2001: 222) observe, 'If this is not a crisis of democratic politics in Britain, then it is hard to know what would be.' Declines of turnout of 10 per cent or more over the post-war period have also been noted in Austria, France, Japan, New Zealand, Switzerland and the USA, with lesser but still significant drops in turnout in many other countries (Hague and Harrop, 2007: 127). Levels of turnout also vary markedly between types of election. Local elections and increasingly elections for other bodies, such as the European Parliament, attract far lower

research

levels of participation than national elections involving a potential change of government and policy. These trends have led to concerns over increased political apathy. (However, the first round of the French presidential election of 2007 produced a surprisingly high 85 per cent turnout.)

Here it might be noted that even the study of elections and voting, commonly associated with the purist scientific detachment of the behaviouralist revolution, has more normative aspects. Thus practical ways of raising turnout levels have been discussed, along with the case for more extensive use of the ballot box, for example employing more **referendums**. While the first aim is certainly normative but relatively uncontroversial, the second is more contestable. Moreover, the two aims may be in conflict, as one suggested explanation for lower turnout levels is increased voter fatigue, arguably the product of increased numbers of elections and referendums.

The cumulative body of research into elections and voting over the last half century or more is vast and in many ways impressive. We know far more about voting as a result. Lessons have been learned and applied not only by political scientists, but by practising politicians, and to a degree by voters. Yet research, however extensive and thorough, can never be conclusive. The rules under which elections are conducted change. The electorate changes over time. Politicians and parties change. Techniques of political communication change. Above all, political circumstances change. Thus trends that are identified may always be halted or reversed. However much we think we already know about elections and voting, there will always be new trends, new correlations and new tentative hypotheses to explore. Voting will remain a fertile field for new research as long as elections and the ballot box feature in modern political systems.

Political parties and party systems

Parties and party systems have been an important focus of political analysis and research because they have long seemed crucial to the process of politics and government in modern **democratic** states especially, as the celebrated Italian political scientist Giovanni **Sartori** demonstrated in his key study *Parties and Party Systems* (1976).

Types of parties

Organized political parties of some kind or other now feature in every continent and in most countries, including virtually all representative democracies, as well as quite a few **states** whose democratic credentials appear more questionable. Some classification is important to provide a framework for analysis of what has become a very crowded field, although it is not easy for find a clear basis for a typology. Parties differ considerably in their size, longevity and general importance. Many parties that feature in **elections** are tiny and ephemeral, yet some others have played an important role in the politics of their country for a century or more.

> *Organized political parties of some kind or other now feature in every continent and in most countries.*

Clearly parties can also differ radically in their aims, principles and policies. They are frequently categorized according to their apparent location on the **left–right** political spectrum (see key concepts, page 139). Thus parties are characterized as left, centre, or right, with gradations within each category ('extreme left', 'centre-left' 'far right' and so on). Such a typology relates principally to ideas, although it also reflects associated interests, particularly **class** interests. **Socialist**

research

parties claim to represent the interests of the working class. Centre and right parties that champion 'free enterprise' commonly draw their main support from, and represent the interests of, the middle classes. Yet in many countries, particularly on the European continent, there have long been other social cleavages (religious, urban/rural, linguistic and ethnic) that cut across economic class divisions and may considerably complicate both ideological conflict and the party system (Lane and Ersson, 1999).

One simple distinction, still commonly cited in textbooks, is that between **ideological** and **pragmatic** parties. In practice, parties of the left were rather more likely to endorse formally political values and aims, sometimes in their **constitution** (as with the British Labour Party's commitment to common ownership in clause IV of its constitution). Although some parties of the right, influenced by **neoliberal** ideas, proclaimed their **free market** principles with as much ideological fervour as the socialist opponents, the traditional **conservative** line was to abhor ideology. Thus they boasted instead of their flexible, pragmatic and 'common sense' approach to the problems of government. Yet such parties often showed considerable ideological consistency in practice, while left-wing parties commonly displayed some flexibility in interpreting their core principles. This is hardly surprising. A party that shows no consistency loses credibility, while one that has no capacity to adapt to altered circumstances dooms itself to irrelevance. Thus the distinction between ideological and pragmatic parties was always relative rather than fundamental.

The French political scientist, Maurice **Duverger** ([1954] 1970) provided a typology of parties according to their organizational features. Yet at least two of his categories are now of more historical than contemporary importance. One, the 'cell party' based on Lenin's organization of the Russian Bolsheviks around the principles of an elite 'vanguard' party and 'democratic centralism' and later imitated by other communist parties, is today of sharply diminished significance. Similarly, the militia party, organized as a fighting force on military lines, was linked with **fascist** and quasi-fascist parties particularly in the inter-war period, and appears less relevant today (although it might still be an appropriate description for some parties in the Middle East). Examples of another of Duverger's categories, the 'caucus' (or 'cadre') party formed by loose groupings of politicians in national parliaments and assemblies, could still be found in the post-war period (for example, the French Radical party), but these increasingly found it difficult to compete effectively with his remaining type, the 'branch' or 'mass' party.

Mass parties

Mass parties were commonly formed initially outside parliament and retained a strong extra-parliamentary organization. Such parties had a formal democratic constitution, a clearly identified **leadership** accountable to millions of paid-up members recruited in a comprehensive system of local branches, and supported by a national (and often also regional organization) employing full-time salaried professional staff. This model, developed by left-wing parties such as the German Social Democrats, was increasingly imitated by parties of the right and centre. Thus Duverger's 'branch' or 'mass' party was already established as the norm in the post-war period.

In such mass parties there was always some apparent potential for tension or conflict between the parliamentary leadership and their 'grass roots' membership. In an early study of parties in Britain and the USA the Russian **Ostrogorski** (1902) raised fears that radical and unrepresentative extra-parliamentary elements might effectively dictate to the more moderate parliamentary leadership. Beer (1982) quotes Lowell to suggest that Ostrogorski's fears were exaggerated in British parties then, and cites Robert McKenzie (1963) to reaffirm that they were still exaggerated in the 1950s and 1960s. **Michels** in his key work *Political Parties* ([1911] 1962) provides a plausible explanation why this should be so, even in left-wing parties with an ostensible commitment to intra-party democracy. Party **elites** are organized, cohesive, full-time and relatively expert, as well as enjoying the supported of a professional central **bureaucracy**, while the mass membership is relatively disorganized and lacks professional support. Thus the central party machine continues to dominate, leaving grass roots members and other critics (e.g. **Miliband**, 1972) to complain of the 'watering down' of party principles and 'betrayal' by their leaders.

Yet Ostrogorski drew attention to an enduring problem still faced by parties today. Effectively they have to satisfy two overlapping but distinctive markets, the mass of voters and party members. This mattered less when many party voters were also party members, or at least identified strongly with their party, as was arguably the case when truly mass parties flourished, in the middle of the twentieth century. The problem has been intensified by developments in recent decades. Almost everywhere, party membership has declined sharply, and the active membership even more so. Effectively, most modern political parties retain the organizational trappings of the mass party without the mass membership that is its main feature and justification. Today, commonly only a tiny minority of voters are active paid-up members of political parties. These party activists may be untypical of ordinary voters not only in their continued involvement with parties, but also in their age and social background, and, more significantly, in their ideas and policy preferences. May's 'special law of curvilinear disparity' suggests that party members are more extreme or radical than party leaders and voters (May, 1973). However, this plausible hypothesis does not always seem to be borne out by empirical research.

The decline in party membership is bad news for parties that depend substantially on their members, to some extent for money, but to a much greater extent for unpaid work in maintaining a grass roots organization and, in particular, fighting **elections**. Parties that do not listen to their dwindling active supporters risk alienating this important resource.

Grass roots members often retain (or have more recently acquired) some significant powers, including the selection of party candidates locally, and commonly a role in electing the party leader, and some (generally limited) scope for influencing party policy. In extreme cases these powers can saddle parties with an unelectable leader and programme, where party activists are markedly out of line with voters. Moreover, party leaders seeking to broaden and modernize the party's image by, for example, adopting new policies and selecting more women and **ethnic minority** candidates, can be effectively frustrated by elderly unrepresentative local party activists with traditional ideas. Even more serious was the threat of 'entryism', the deliberate penetration of a party's membership by an organized extreme faction that does not share the party's aims, or even necessarily its commitment to parliamentary democracy. Thus in the UK the Trotskyist Militant Tendency was able to take control of several constituency Labour Parties in the early 1980s (Seyd, 1987: 50–4).

Catch-all parties

Some analysts suggest that some of the more electorally successful modern parties seek to avoid this problem by radically transforming themselves, marginalizing their members, and pursuing a pragmatic and consensual approach designed to appeal to as many voters as possible. Such parties are described as 'catch-all' parties, a term introduced by Kirchheimer (1966) and early applied to the German Christian Democratic Union (CDU) and subsequently also to its main rival, the Social Democratic Party (SPD) after its repudiation of **Marxism**. Panebianco (1988) used the term 'electoral-professional parties' to describe much the same approach.

> *The 'catch-all' or 'electoral-professional' party unashamedly seeks power rather than the representation of any social group.*

The 'catch-all' or 'electoral-professional' party unashamedly seeks power rather than the representation of any social group (such as the working class or the Catholic Church). Instead it seeks support wherever it can be obtained, using modern marketing techniques. Rather than depending substantially on the subscriptions, donations and fund-raising of members, the catch-all party seeks funding from a variety of sources, including large organizations and wealthy individuals. Such catch-all parties may be dominated by charismatic leaders who reach out directly to voters through the **mass media** rather than through the party organization. To this extent, party members may seem to matter less. Critics argue that the party leadership may deliberately change procedures to bypass grass-roots party activists or reduce their influence. Thus, for example, postal elections are adopted for party positions, and the internet used for communicating directly with members, instead of the traditional reliance on attendance at party meetings, dominated (it is argued) by a hard core of activists less susceptible to the blandishments of the leadership or the media.

Cartel parties?

Some observers have taken this analysis further, proposing a new type of 'cartel parties' (Katz and Mair, 1995). The notion of a cartel is drawn from monopoly capitalism, where a small number of businesses that dominate an industry or sector of the economy collude to limit competition between each other, and to exclude potential new rivals. Thus established leading 'cartel' parties seek to maintain their dominant position in the political market place, by for example determining rules for the state funding of parties, and for the use of state-owned or regulated media, commonly based on the proportion of votes or seats gained in past elections. This renders them less dependent on their diminishing grass roots membership, but also makes it difficult for new parties to mount an effective challenge as they have less access to state funding and the media. Thus the party system becomes fossilized, with a cosy limited competition between a small number of established parties. However, the evolution of party systems in some countries suggests that established parties are not invariably successful in preserving their cartel. Thus older established parties have sometimes suffered meltdown, while the emergence of new parties has not been prevented (see below).

Party systems

The extent of party competition has varied considerably both between countries and often within countries over time. Sometimes there appears to be no effective competition. One-party systems can result from deliberate limits on party competition, simply banning other parties as in many former communist states or in right-wing dictatorships. Alternatively, even where other parties are free to fight elections, one party may remain overwhelmingly dominant. This was sometimes the case in former colonies, where one party or movement was closely associated with the successful drive for independence (as was the Congress Party in the first decades of India's independence).

research

In a pure two-party system, two major parties dominate elections and representation in assemblies, and, between them, monopolize control of government. The long duopoly of the Republicans and Democrats in US politics is the clearest example of a two-party system. However for periods in its history the United Kingdom has had a two-party system by most if not all criteria, and some other states in the English-speaking world have also for a time had substantially two-party systems. Yet two-party systems are now relatively rare.

Multi-party systems may feature three, four or more major competing parties, and commonly involve coalition government. A distinction is sometimes drawn between stable multi-party systems, and unstable multi-party systems. In the former it seems relatively easy to form a stable coalition government, perhaps because ideological differences are not wide or deep (as in the case in the Netherlands and Sweden). In the latter, perhaps because of the existence of substantial extremist or anti-system parties, it is difficult to form any kind of government with prospects of an enduring majority. Examples include the Fourth French Republic (1946–58) and until recently, Italy.

Why do some countries have two-party systems and others multi-party systems? Maurice **Duverger** plausibly connected two-party systems to the first-past-the-post electoral system (sometimes termed 'Duverger's law'). Certainly the most conspicuous examples of a two-party system (the USA and until recently the United Kingdom) have both long used the first-past-the-post method of election (more accurately described as the single-member simple plurality system). Third and minor parties, particularly those whose support is geographically widely dispersed (such as the Liberals, Liberal Democrats and Greens in the United Kingdom) are seriously under-represented in such a system. By contrast, more proportional systems allow smaller parties like the German Free Democrats or Greens to survive and thrive (see Box 5.1).

Yet as numerous critics have observed, there are many exceptions to Duverger's law. There is no simple correlation between electoral systems and party systems (Lijphart, 1994). Multi-party systems often appear to reflect multiple and cross-cutting social or ideological cleavages. **Lipset** and **Rokkan** (1967) argued that the party systems of the 1960s were frozen, reflecting the social cleavages of the 1920s. Duverger himself acknowledged that the French Fourth Republic's multi-party system reflected three such cross-cutting divisions (planning versus the free market, religion versus anti-clericalism, and support for, and opposition to, the Soviet Union).

research

BOX
5.1

the contrasting electoral and governmental fortunes of the German Free Democrats and the British Liberal Democrats

Both the British Liberal Democrats and the German FDP (Free Democrats) are liberal parties. Their MEPs sit with the European Liberal and Democratic and Reform Party in the European Parliament. In national elections the Liberal Democrats have secured a much larger share of the vote (around a fifth of the vote in recent General Elections) than the German FDP (5–8 per cent of the vote). Yet the Liberal Democrats have never secured a share of seats in the House of Commons comparable to their share of votes. By contrast, the FDP have not only normally secured a proportion of seats in the German Bundestag close to their share of the vote, but have frequently featured in coalition government with both the Christian Democrats and the Social Democrats. Neither the Liberal Democrats nor their Liberal predecessors have been a part of UK Cabinet government since 1945.

Party systems and political stability

Those who live in what are sometimes called 'majoritarian' systems, where essentially two major parties compete to win power and form a single-party majority government, may assume that this is a key factor in promoting governmental longevity and political stability. By contrast, a multi-party system commonly producing coalition government can appear a recipe for instability. Indeed it may sometimes appear difficult to form any kind of government with prospects of an enduring majority. Examples include the Fourth French Republic (1946–58) and until recently, Italy, where governments lasted sometimes only weeks or months before they fell, precipitating frequent political crises. Yet elsewhere, over much of Europe (particularly Germany, the Netherlands and Denmark), a multi-party system and coalition government have appeared consistent with considerable political stability.

Arendt **Lijphart** has championed proportional electoral systems, multi-party systems and coalition government as key aspects of what he has described as consociational democracy, which he has argued is particularly suitable for societies that are deeply divided along lines of culture, language, religion, ethnicity or ideology. Proportional representation, multi-party systems and power-sharing in government protect the interests of minorities more effectively than majoritarian systems, which may effectively and permanently exclude some minority interests from the political system, and promote alienation and disaffection. A consociational democracy, by contrast, promotes compromise and consensus, because no single section of society can hope to control power on its own and all must work with others. Particular sections of society (especially where these are largely associated with geographical areas) may also be given considerable autonomy through a federal system or devolution of power. Lijphart has argued that such consociational or consensual democracies score higher on a range of indicators, favouring welfare provision, foreign aid and environmental conservation (Lijphart, 1999).

The future of parties and party systems

We have seen that **Lipset** and **Rokkan** considered that the party system of the 1960s remained relatively frozen. This appeared largely true then of most of the western world (although France was one significant exception). Much later, the notion of the cartel party (Katz and Mair, 1995) provided a persuasive explanation for the relative stability of party systems. Yet recently, the weakening of party identities and loyalties and increasing electoral volatility have introduced much more unpredictability into party systems even in mature democracies. Party politics has become both more confusing and perhaps more interesting. Parties with long strong traditions can suddenly face melt-down, as the Canadian Conservatives and the Italian Christian Democrats (in 1994) have found. New major parties, like Berlusconi's Forza Italia, have come from nowhere into government.

Political circumstances have sometimes precipitated major shifts. Thus the fall of the Berlin Wall, and the ensuing collapse of **communism** in the former Soviet Union and eastern Europe, had massive implications for the countries directly affected. In the new successor democratic or quasi-democratic regimes in eastern Europe and the former Soviet Union, a range of new parties have flourished briefly in a shifting constellation of political forces. Yet the fall of communism in the east also had major implications for western communist parties. Most of the former Italian Communist Party (which had long pursued its own version of Eurocommunism) successfully reinvented itself as the Democratic Party of the Left, to become the major political force inside the Olive Tree Alliance that has since enjoyed periods in government. The less flexible French Communists have continued to decline.

Inglehart's (1971, 1977, 1990) theory of **postmaterialism** suggests that changing values in advanced western democracies have created new issues and political forces. Such post-materialist ideas have often involved a different style of politics, with new **social movements** making use of direct action to bypass representative institutions and established parties. Yet post-materialist ideas have also had some impact on the party scene, most notably with the increased presence of green parties, although only in Germany has a Green Party made substantial political headway, culminating in a share in government from 1998 until 2006. Yet other new parties, such as populist far-right **racist** parties, in such countries as France, Italy, Austria and former East Germany, seem to reflect more the resentments of the poor and marginalized than any post-material values.

Some of the new parties have been described as 'anti-parties', as they involve a rejection of traditional party politics. The rise of such anti-parties and the decreasing numbers of people identifying with traditional parties, and the sharper decline in those prepared to join and participate in them, suggests a crisis for political parties. They no longer seem to offer a major channel for ordinary citizens to participate in politics. They often seem out of touch with the core interests in society they claim to represent. They are more closely identified with **government** and the **state** than the people. In these circumstances some commentators have begun to talk of a party-less democracy. Whether this is feasible is questionable. Organized political parties have been a feature of virtually all representative democracies. More direct democracy might reduce the need for parties as intermediaries between state and people, but this would involve far more active citizen participation. As parties have lost some legitimacy as a consequence of reduced participation by ordinary citizens, it appears rather optimistic to expect that an increase in effective citizen participation may allow modern democracies to do without parties.

> *Some of the new parties have been described as 'anti-parties', as they involve a rejection of traditional party politics.*

Pressure groups and social movements

The importance of organized groups and **social movements** in the political process has already been acknowledged in several earlier parts of this book. Issues surrounding the definition and classification of **pressure groups** and broader (and less organized) social movements, as well as some theoretical concerns have already been briefly explored under relevant key concepts in Part III (and see Grant, 2000). There is further reference to the role of organized groups in Part II, particularly under the headings 'elitism and pluralism' 'the behavioural revolution' and 'rational choice'. Here some of the research issues and theoretical debates around pressure groups and new social movements are examined further.

Attitudes towards pressure group activities have varied over time and space. Once, if their significance was recognized at all, they were widely seen as sinister 'hidden persuaders' potentially subverting the democratic process. Indeed French political culture still remains rather suspicious of the legitimacy of group influence on government, perhaps influenced by **Rousseau's** criticism of sectional interests articulating their own 'partial will' at the expense of the general will of the French people. Many modern American political scientists, by contrast, have seen pressure group activity as the very essence of a modern pluralist participative **democracy**. Yet this orthodoxy has been challenged from the **left** by radical **elitists** and from the **right** by **neoliberals** and **rational choice** theorists.

Development of the study of pressure groups

It was Arthur **Bentley** (1908) who first insisted on the vital importance of organized groups in the political process, maintaining, 'All phenomena of government are phenomena of groups pressing one another.' However, in the USA the study of pressure groups really took off with the **behavioural revolution**. David Truman reaffirmed the key role of groups in *The Governmental Process* (1951). Robert **Dahl** (1956, 1961) and Nelson Polsby (1963) went on emphasize their importance for democracy. In the United Kingdom a spate of books on pressure groups from the late 1950s onwards, including those by Samuel Finer (1958), John Stewart (1958) and Allen Potter (1961), indicated that there also the significance of organized groups for politics was finally appreciated.

Detailed research has sometimes involved an in-depth case study of the political influence of a particular group (e.g. Eckstein, 1960 on the British Medical Association). Alternatively it has focused instead on the relative influence of a variety of groups on a specific key decision or important policy field (Crenson, 1971 on air pollution in US steel towns). Other researchers studied the methods and apparent influence over a period of years of a number of several similar kinds of groups (such as, for example, **environmental** groups). Another favoured approach was to examine group influences in a specific local political **community**, such as a town, or city. A series of studies of this kind helped fuel the community power debate (see Box 5.2), which provided further ammunition on both sides of the long-running argument between **elitists** and **pluralists**.

BOX 5.2 the community power debate

Much of the argument between elitists and pluralists has focused not on the distribution of power at the level of the **nation-state** but on detailed case studies of the political influence of various local interests in specific urban communities, both in the USA and elsewhere. Thus Floyd Hunter's path-breaking *Community Power Structure* (1953) apparently demonstrated that the political process in one US city (Atlanta, Georgia) was dominated by business interests, while ordinary people were marginalized and blacks totally excluded. By contrast, Robert **Dahl's** celebrated study of New Haven, Connecticut, *Who Governs?* (1961) seemed to establish that there was no single elite dominating the decision-making process and that political influence was widely diffused, in accordance with pluralist assumptions. The work of French Marxists (e.g. Castells, 1977) suggested that urban power reflected the interests of national and local capital, with only limited autonomy for the local state apparatus. In Britain a series of case studies of urban politics threw up a range of evidence on the influence of particular interests on council policy (e.g. Hampton, 1970; Dearlove, 1973; Newton, 1976; Saunders, 1980) Broadly speaking, the empirical research arising from this community power debate has tended to confirm the initial assumptions of theorists on each side. Pluralists discover influence is fairly widely dispersed, while elitists find it is concentrated. Moreover, even if the research findings are accepted for particular communities, it is by no means clear any broader generalizations about the influence of interests or the distribution of power can be derived from them. Thus some have concluded that such case studies can only be illustrative: they do not prove anything.)

research

Pressure groups and participation

Pressure groups are considered important, particularly in relation to democracy, because of the extensive opportunities they apparently provide for citizen participation in the political process. **Elections**, by comparison, afford only very infrequent, limited and blunt means for citizens to influence policies that affect them. **Political parties** offer some scope for further participation, but many observers have concluded that ordinary members, even if they are active, can have only a very limited input into party policy, and ultimately public policy. According to the Canadian political scientist Robert McKenzie, 'There can be no doubt that pressure groups, taken together, are a far more important channel of communication than parties for the transmission of political ideas from the mass of the citizenry to their rulers' (1958).

> *Pressure groups are considered important because of the extensive opportunities they apparently provide for citizen participation.*

This judgement seems even more valid today. Parties were still mass parties when McKenzie wrote. Since then, parties almost everywhere have lost members, often heavily (see preceding section). In the United Kingdom fewer than 2 per cent of citizens belong to political parties, while some leading groups such as the National Trust or the Royal Society for the Protection of Birds (RSPB) number millions of members (Maloney, 2006). Increasingly it appears that those citizens who wish to engage in politics are far more likely to do so through single-issue groups than though parties. Such groups offer almost limitless opportunities for ordinary people to seek to influence policy on specific issues that affect or concern them on a continuous basis. Unlike parties, which are almost bound to compromise and temporize in seeking to construct an electoral coalition, pressure groups can campaign single-mindedly and passionately for the particular interest or cause that is the reason for their existence.

Some of the participation is, in practice, rather limited. Many large pressure groups, such as Friends of the Earth and Greenpeace are what are sometimes described as 'chequebook groups'. 'Signing a cheque or completing a direct-debit form is the beginning and end of the involvement for the majority of supporters' (Maloney, 2006: 109). The evidence suggests that most of the supporters neither expect nor want a more active role. The money they provide helps to finance specific campaigns by professionals. Thus much of the effective competition between groups is not between their (sometimes substantial) paper membership but between their respective leaders, spokespersons and a small number of paid professional staff. Most group leaders and spokespersons are either elected by a tiny minority of members, or not elected at all and virtually self-appointed. It is not even always clear that groups really represent the interests of members or those they claim to serve. One survey has shown that most charitable groups ostensibly serving the interests of disabled people actually represent the interest of those caring for the disabled rather than the disabled themselves, who often have other priorities (Drake, 2002). Some groups, rather more ambitiously, claim to speak for the 'silent majority', but while the majority remains silent this is a claim that it is rather difficult to validate.

The role of pressure groups remains at the heart of the argument between pluralists and elitists (see Part II, Section 2). Thus if pluralists emphasize the extensive opportunities for popular participation, offered by countless competing groups, elitists counter with evidence that these opportunities are used far more by the higher socio-economic classes.

'Those who potentially have the most to gain from the system (disadvantaged groups) participate the least' (Maloney, 2006: 116). As Schattschneider (1960: 35) observed much earlier, 'The flaw in the pluralist heaven is that the heavenly chorus sings with a strong upper class accent.' As a result of this in-built bias, 'Some issues are organized into politics and some are organized out of it' (Schattschneider, 1960: 71).

Pressure groups and the policy process

Moreover, while pluralists focus on the large number of groups involved in the policy process, elitists respond that these groups are not competing on anything like equal terms. Groups vary in resources, in finance, leadership, organization, skills, and most crucially, access to decision makers. Although by implication they are outside government, some groups can have a very close relationship with government, as the now common distinction between 'insider' and 'outsider' groups acknowledges (Grant, 2000). Some groups are pushing at an open door, while others are effectively locked out. Government is not passively responding to the sum of group pressure, as systems theory sometimes implied, nor is government some kind of impartial referee of group demands. Rather, government is an active participant, with its own interests to advance and defend. It needs information, advice, expertise, and sometimes active cooperation from a variety of groups, and thus routinely consults them. Yet other groups that either have less to offer, or are known opponents, will not be on the inside track.

Too close involvement with government can carry risk for groups, who may, for example, sometimes feel obliged to make compromises to preserve their own privileged insider status. In the process they may become incorporated and emasculated, alienating some of their own members and supporters. Ultimately this can provoke splits and the formation of new groups. Yet generally access to government brings some clear advantages to groups in term of information about government proposals, and opportunities to promote their own interests and influence policy. Indeed, it sometimes happens that government departments or other public agencies come to serve the interests of their own client groups or those they are supposed to regulate, rather than the wider public. Examples of such 'agency capture' have often been observed in the USA.

Many theoretical approaches assume a relationship of mutual dependence between government and groups. Charles **Lindblom's** incremental model of policy making envisaged groups as an integral part of the policy process. Governments routinely consult affected groups and interested parties, and make a series of minor (or incremental) adjustments in policy as the consultation proceeds through what Lindblom describes as 'partisan mutual adjustment'. Richardson and Jordan (Richardson and Jordan (1979); Jordan and Richardson (1987)) argued that in particular areas of policy (such as education, health and transport) there are 'policy communities' consisting of relevant government department and agencies, and associated group interests (such as relevant trade unions and professional associations, and consumer groups). **Liberal corporatist** theories suggested there was a more systematic relationship between government and key interests representing labour and **capital**. Instead of the **pluralist** model of unlimited numbers of groups freely competing to influence government, corporatism implied a limited number of peak or umbrella groups in close collaboration with government (Schmitter, 1979). The work of Rhodes (1997) on governance assumed that business and voluntary groups were closely involved with public sector bodies in partnerships and policy networks.

research

Criticism of group influence

Much of the earlier criticism of the mutual dependence of government and leading groups came from the left, from Marxists (e.g. Ralph **Miliband**) and radical elite theorists (e.g. C. Wright **Mills**), who objected to what they saw as the excessive influence of business or the 'military-industrial complex'. (Indeed, neo-pluralists such as **Galbraith**, **Lindblom** and **Dahl** himself have acknowledged the key role of business interests.) Other radical critics have contended that not just the economically deprived but women, **ethnic minorities** and those with unconventional life styles or sexual preferences were effectively excluded. However, from the mid-1970s onwards some of the strongest attacks came from **neoliberals** (e.g. **Hayek**, Friedman) and rational choice theorists (e.g. **Buchanan**, **Tullock** and **Niskanen**). They argued that a close and symbiotic relationship between government agencies and their client groups, particularly those in receipt of **welfare** services, was effectively driving the growth of government, public spending and taxation.

Indeed the American economist Mancur **Olson** (1965) demonstrated that there was a 'free rider' problem with group influence. A group may devote substantial effort and resources in pushing policies that materially benefit its members. However, as the cost is spread broadly and thinly over the generality of taxpayers and consumers, these have little incentive to spend the time and energy required to organize in opposition to the group's proposals. Yet this argument seems to apply more obviously to producer groups keen to secure subsidies or restrict competition than to client groups in pursuit of higher welfare payments and improved public services. Most of the empirical evidence suggests that these interests are among the least likely to be effectively organized, and even if they are, they will probably be among those 'outsider groups' that do not enjoy a cosy relationship with government. Such outsider groups may simply lack access as they do not know how the system works, although this may also be because their aims and interests are fundamentally at variance with the government. In such circumstances, neither the groups nor the government may see much point in consultation.

Social movements

Social movements may be outside the customary processes of consultation for some similar reasons. The term 'social movement' is used to describe a loose coalition that may include some more organized groups as well as unattached individuals, who nevertheless may identify strongly with the movement. Examples of such social movements include the women's movement, the peace movement, the green movement, the anti-capitalist movement, and specifically in the USA the Christian coalition. They lack formal structure, designated officers and lists of members, and are too broad and amorphous for any of the customary processes of consultation, although there may be other additional reasons why conventional forms of political involvement are avoided (Byrne, 1997).

A looser informal movement may be preferred for ideological reasons. Thus some feminists associate formal constitutions, rules and hierarchical structures with a male preference for order, **authority** and status, and seek less directed, more spontaneous and cooperative methods of working. Similarly, some peace campaigners and green activists reject leadership roles, seeking radical alternative ways of organizing politics and society. Thus they may deliberately avoid traditional pressure group methods of seeking influence, through direct contact with government bureaucracy, or through lobbying parliament, elected politicians and parties. They may prefer direct action, and semi-spontaneous protests and demonstrations. These may be strictly non-violent, although some working within new social movements may be prepared to break the law deliberately. For some movements, such as the animal rights movement, that contain activists prepared to use violence against property, and sometimes against people, a loose organization without identifiable leaders and members makes it more difficult for the forces of law and order to pin responsibility for activities on individuals. Modern methods of communication, including mobile phones and the internet, have substantially helped the planning of protests and other political activities, despite the absence of formal organizational structures and leadership roles.

Most protest movements indulging in direct action and challenging the legitimacy of government and the whole political system have been associated with the **left** of the political spectrum. However, in recent years some protest movements on behalf of causes or interests more often associated linked with the **right** have emerged. The Christian Coalition in the United States has clear links with the Republican Party, whose policies it has sought to influence on a number of specific issues (such as the family, marriage, abortion and sexual orientation). Similarly, the Countryside Alliance in the United Kingdom, while seeking to exploit a number of rural grievances, is really focused on the hunting issue, and while it claims all party-support has a substantial overlap with membership of the Conservative Party, to whose candidates it has lent organizational support in recent elections. Motorists and hauliers opposed to high fuel taxation or speed cameras constitute another right-wing social movement. As for some left-wing movements, some activists have been prepared to confront authority and break the law.

While the importance of groups and social movements in the political process is now almost everywhere conceded, their role in public participation, their influence on public policy, their relationship to the distribution of power, and their general contribution to democracy remain rather more contested.

Political communication

Communication has always been important for politics. Ancient empires could not have been governed and maintained without effective means of communication. Without reliable sources of information efficient administration is impossible, and information needs to be collected and communicated. Nor are the 'black arts' of propaganda and 'spin' essentially new. Governments of all kinds have sought to promote a favourable image of themselves, and an unfavourable image of their opponents, both at home and abroad. However both the channels of communication and the techniques for using them have been transformed extensively and dramatically over the last century, and particularly in the last few decades, than any other aspect of politics. The study of political communication has thus become ever more important for political scientists.

> *Governments of all kinds have sought to promote a favourable image of themselves, and an unfavourable image of their opponents.*

The mass media

The modern **mass media** have progressively transformed political communication. They have facilitated the transfer of messages to a mass audience both for commercial enterprises and for the state and the public sector. More recently they have assisted a growing two-way flow of communication that enables the masses to talk back. In rapid succession, print media, including particularly mass-circulation newspapers, film, radio, television and the internet have brought changes in the scope of political communication and the techniques required for successfully exploiting new facilities. A 1960s media guru, Marshall McLuhan, coined the snappy formula 'the medium is the message'. What he meant by this was that each medium of communication has its own distinctive characteristics, which help shape and even determine the message that comes across. The implications for politics have been massive.

There are, broadly, three main views of the role and power of the media. The **pluralist** model suggests that the media present a wide diversity of views, aiding public debate and the democratic process, enabling people to make up their own minds on important political issues. The media has an important 'watchdog' role on behalf of the people, over government and powerful interests in society, and thus promotes effective public accountability. The 'dominant values' model suggests that the media reflect the values of political elites (**Miliband**, 1973: 196–214; Hermann and Chomsky, 1988), or as **Marx** put it, 'The ruling ideas in every age are the ideas of the ruling class.' Ownership and control of the media are heavily concentrated, reflecting the concentration of wealth, income and power in society. Accordingly, the media only represent a relatively narrow range of views, and minority perspectives are given little space or airtime, while those who appear to deviate from prevailing norms – single mothers, striking workers, asylum seekers – are scapegoated. Finally, the market model suggests that the media are largely driven by market or commercial considerations. Owners, editors and producers seek to maximize returns by increasing circulation or audience share. Thus the media deliver what the public wants. From this perspective the widely perceived 'dumbing down' of political coverage by the media reflects the public's lack of interest in politics.

How far are the media biased and what form does the bias take? The definition and measurement of bias is problematic (McQuail, 1992). The evidence is suggestive but inconclusive. In so far as the media are necessarily involved in the selection and prioritization of news, they are inevitably biased, although the direction of that bias is more contestable. Thus in most mature western **democracies** many national newspapers openly support a range of parties and political viewpoints. However, a partisan press is partially offset by radio and television, sometimes legally obliged to provide more 'balanced' coverage, and more recently by the internet, apparently supporting pluralist assumptions.

The increased commercialization of the media, accompanied by the general decline in public service broadcasting, lends some support to the market model that suggests that the media are simply responding to public tastes and preferences. Thus their only real bias is towards making money. Yet there are many examples of wealthy individuals acquiring and using media outlets unashamedly to exercise political influence rather than make money, and of press owners appointing and sometimes removing editors, and sometimes intervening more directly to ensure their papers reflect their own political views (Street, 2001: 124–44). Critics point to increased cross-media concentration, with business conglomerates involving press, television, radio and internet interests, and to the power of individual media tycoons such as Rupert Murdoch and Silvio Berlusconi.

It is usually parties and politicians of the **left** who complain most bitterly of press bias, although it was a British Conservative politician, Baldwin, who most memorably attacked the power of newspaper owners, who had, he claimed, 'power without responsibility, the prerogative of the harlot throughout the ages'.

Media influence

How far, however, does media bias affect political behaviour? It was once widely assumed that the modern mass media gave governments extensive power to mould and shape political opinion and behaviour if they chose to use it. Indeed regimes that have been described as 'totalitarian' employed their control of the press, film and radio to 'indoctrinate' their subjects through deliberate political propaganda. The scope for successfully moulding political opinion and behaviour now appears somewhat reduced by the globalization of communication, suggesting that it is now far more difficult for ruling elites in any state to immunize its peoples from the contamination of different political cultures, as in the past. The failure to exclude foreign currents of thought and culture were arguably factors in the collapse of former **communist** regimes, and of apartheid South Africa.

An influential theory, backed up by some research, suggested that in western democracies the media served to reinforce rather than change political views. According to this interpretation, people do not passively accept political communication imparted by the media, but 'filter out' messages that do not match their own preconceived ideas. They do this through a process of selective exposure, selective perception and selective retention. Thus many people tend to read newspapers and watch programmes that support their own political viewpoint, and ignore alternative perspectives. When they do encounter conflicting political positions they reinterpret them to match their own preconceptions. Moreover, they remember selectively, only recalling evidence and arguments that fit in with their own ideas and forgetting those that do not (Blumler and McQuail, 1968).

> *Many people tend to read newspapers and watch programmes that support their own political viewpoint, and ignore alternative perspectives.*

Yet as critics have noted, much of the research supporting this filter and reinforcement model was conducted some time ago, and largely focused on television, and more specifically on UK party election broadcasts, where the political bias is transparent and often unsubtle (Denver, 2003). However many of the messages conveyed by the mass media are not so immediately obvious, and work at a subliminal level. Where words are employed, catchy slogans or brief soundbites (which, American research suggests, are becoming shorter) are preferred to reasoned argument and long speeches. They work, like most advertising, by dint of repetition. Some of the messages conveyed by the press are not contained in reasoned articles, but in headlines, photographs and cartoons, images that even the most apolitical readers may absorb subliminally, before turning to features on celebrities or sport.

Television in particular is a visual medium, and here it is visual images rather than words that carry the most potent messages. A celebrated example is the 1960 US presidential election where the underdog Jack Kennedy turned the election after a debate simultaneously broadcast on television and radio. While those who only heard the debate concluded that both candidates had performed equally well, or that Kennedy's opponent Nixon had shaded it, those who watched on television judged Kennedy the clear winner. It was the pictures that had done it (White, 1962: 279–95). Today, many media advisers to politicians particularly favour the wordless photo opportunity, on the assumption that political leader surrounded by beaming nurses or school pupils conveys concern for

research

health or education far more immediately and subtly than do detailed policy commitments or statistics. Photo opportunities also offer fewer hostages to fortune.

In most countries, however, there are constraints on the coverage of the electronic media, frequently requiring balance in the coverage of parties and politicians, particularly during election campaigns, although this does not prevent accusations of bias by parties. Constraints on television coverage of politics and election campaigns vary. Some countries, most notably the USA, allow the purchase of television advertising spots by election candidates, parties and pressure groups, while other countries do not. Thus groups such as the National Rifle Association (NRA) can spend millions of dollars for commercials attacking and discrediting politicians who advocate gun control. Many countries, but not the USA, give free time to parties to put their message across. Many, but not the United Kingdom, have copied the US televised debates between presidential candidates for their own leading politicians at elections (Hague and Harrop, 2001). The effect of all this coverage is difficult to assess. However, surveys into the political impact of television on voting and party allegiance have generally concluded that it is minimal, apparently confirming the prevailing sense of television's political neutrality.

Many media advisers favour the wordless photo opportunity, on the assumption that a political leader surrounded by beaming nurses or school pupils conveys concern for health or education far more immediately and subtly than detailed policy commitments or statistics.

It might be thought that the increasing importance of television would deprive the press of their former political influence. It is true that newspaper reading has declined, substantially in some countries (Hague and Harrop, 2001; McNair, 2003). Yet the press remains influential, particularly in shaping the political agenda. Because television is more constrained by obligations of political balance, it is often inhibited from coverage that might be interpreted as damaging to particular politicians or parties. The press has no such inhibitions, and thus often determines what is newsworthy, leaving television to follow the press agenda. More contentious is the role of the press in influencing the outcome of elections. Unlike television, newspapers are often shamelessly partisan, and this open bias extends not just to editorials and expert comment and analysis, but to their whole coverage of the news. Some observers suggest that this press bias has a very limited impact, as most people choose papers that match their own political leanings, and thus their bias only reinforces, instead of changing, party support. Yet there is some evidence of significant press influence on the outcome of some elections. Citing research on the UK 1992 Conservative victory in the General Election, the top-selling tabloid paper boasted that it was 'The *Sun* wot won it'. Opposition Labour leaders may have believed it, judging from the efforts they subsequently made to persuade the media magnate Rupert Murdoch, who owned the *Sun*, to change sides and support Labour in subsequent elections. Yet at least Murdoch is not himself a practising politician, unlike Silvio Berlusconi, a multimedia tycoon who leads a political party and has served as Italy's prime minister, whose own papers and television channels have been accused of flagrant political bias.

Other researchers have been more interested in the power of the media to shape the interpretation of news stories and political attitudes over a period. Some have perceived a persistent establishment and management bias in most of the mass media, including television, citing in particular the coverage of industrial policy and foreign policy. Others have blamed the media for a declining trust in politicians, parties and the political process

research

generally, suggesting that political satire and the inquisitorial interrogation of politicians has created a mood of cynicism that is damaging for democracy (Lloyd, 2004).

Government communication and 'spin'

Yet others blame government and politicians themselves for increased public mistrust, particularly for the use of 'spin', originally an American term for putting a favourable gloss or interpretation on events, and now widely familiar. Whether it is called 'spin' or something else, it is not new, but as old as politics itself. What is relatively recent is the publicity that some advisers on communication, or 'spin doctors', have drawn on themselves. The most effective 'spin' is unobtrusive, so that people do not realize that a particular political story has been spun. The high public profile of people like Alastair Campbell, Prime Minister Blair's outspoken press secretary and later director of communications, meant that they became the story, and damaged the government they were trying to promote, as Campbell himself came to realize.

However, governments need to communicate effectively (Phillis Report, 2004). Frequently new laws, new taxes, new benefits and services need to be advertised, or they will fail in their purpose. There are also important public health and safety campaigns that require promotion, on for example the risks of AIDS, smoking, alcohol abuse, drugs and fireworks. Government advertising is big and expensive business. Yet there are important ethical issues surrounding such advertising. A government initiative may require promotion if it is to be successful, but this may implicitly involve the promotion of the government itself and the party that controls the government. Thus government advertising requires careful scrutiny and control. It is also the case that parties, both in government and in opposition, need money to put their own case across if there is to be an effective democratic debate between them. Either the money has to come from sometimes questionable private sources, with the suggestion that political favours are being bought, or it has to come from the state. In many countries there is already state funding of parties.

New media

So far little has been said of the momentous but contested implications for politics of the internet. Use of the internet has grown massively and rapidly world-wide. In advanced western states most people already have access to the internet and are making increasing use of it. The importance of this new media has also been appreciated quickly by governments and politicians. Government departments and agencies, political parties and many individual politicians have their own websites to facilitate direct communication with the public, cutting out the 'middlemen' (and they are still largely 'men') who control older established channels of communication. How far these increasingly sophisticated websites impact on the general public is questionable. It may be that relatively few internet consumers are looking for information on politics. There is little evidence as yet of an appreciable influence of the internet on voting, for example. Polling opinion on the internet has become common, and there is potential for the casting of votes on the internet, but it would need careful safeguards.

> *Use of the internet has grown massively and rapidly world-wide. The importance of this new media has also been appreciated quickly by governments and politicians.*

Some argue that the internet offers exciting opportunities for **democracy**. The established mass media involve largely a top-down model of political communication, from **elites** to the masses. While newspapers have sometimes claimed to be the voice of the people; they are more accurately the voice of their proprietors, editors and professional journalists. Readers may contribute letters, but these are organized, selected and edited by the professionals. The same is true of television and radio. Despite the popularity of phone-in programmes, overall output is controlled by managers and journalists. The internet, by contrast, is a form of communication that is open to anyone who has access to it. Anyone can put their own thoughts on the internet, unselected, unedited and largely uncensored. They can also do it anonymously, if they wish. Many millions (71 million in 2007) have taken the opportunity to publish their own weblogs (or 'blogs') on the internet. Thus the internet is truly democratic, making a reality of 'free speech'.

Others object that this freedom involves licence to bully, insult and slander, and use racist, sexist and homophobic language, without risk, under cover of anonymity. There is no effective quality control on the web. Much of the material placed on the internet is interesting, and some is brilliant. However, blatant falsehoods can be purveyed as easily as truth. The web offers opportunities for pornographers, fraudsters, conspiracy theorists, political extremists of all kinds, and indeed terrorists. How far these abuses can be controlled without damaging the exciting potential of the internet to enlarge a genuine democratic freedom of debate remains to be seen (Sunstein, 2001; Hague and Harrop, 2007: 127).

Overall, it is difficult to exaggerate the impact of all the mass media on the way the world and politics are perceived. Our own direct experience is inevitably so limited and partial that we depend on the media for much of what we think we know about politics. **Postmodernist** thinkers like **Baudrillard** have argued that the mass media are now so all-pervasive that media images are the new reality. It is such images of the Gulf War, or the east Asian tsunami, or the attack on the Twin Towers, that many millions around the world have seen in newspapers, on television and the internet. It is through the prism of the media that we learn to interpret such events, which are only 'news' because of media coverage. When the 'story' is rendered stale by repetition and is displaced by other stories, the event is no longer in the public eye, and experienced as 'real', even though its effects, in terms of human suffering, may continue and even intensify long after it have ceased to be news.

Public administration and public sector management

A major sub-discipline of politics has long been the study of public administration. This focuses on the institutions and processes of **government** and the **state** rather than the wider political process, although there are some of the usual difficulties in defining public administration more precisely and distinguishing it clearly from private administration (Dunsire, 1973). It was once widely assumed that public administration was governed by different principles from the private sector, motivated by a concern for the coordination of services in the wider public interest rather than competition and the pursuit of private profit. (This assumption was later challenged, with implications for the autonomy of the subject.) Within the study of government, there was a particular interest in the state **bureaucracy**, the public officials responsible for advising on and implementing policy, their background, recruitment and training and their relationship with elected politicians (Crozier, 1964; Albrow, 1970).

The study of public administration has commonly involved a mutual dependence between academics and reflective administrators. Many of its pioneers were not ivory-towered academics, but hands-on practitioners, drafted in by government to improve the organization and decision making of government, or sometimes academics who went on to become politicians and test their own assumptions. (A celebrated example of the latter was Woodrow Wilson, a former university politics teacher who became US President.) The approach to the study of public administration has often been unashamedly normative, seeking to improve the organization and processes of government (Nelson, in Goodin and Klingemann, 1996: 558–66).

However, the approach to the subject in different countries has also been influenced by distinctive national **political cultures**, particularly attitudes to the state and the public sector. Thus in France the state has long been perceived positively, as the embodiment of the French Republic, 'one and indivisible'. There, state officials still constitute an extremely prestigious **elite**, specifically trained for this purpose. Top French civil servants are graduates of the elite and highly selective postgraduate *Ecole Nationale d'Administration* (ENA), sometimes nicknamed '*enarques*' (Cole, 1998: 104–8). Yet some of the outstanding French politicians of the Fifth French Republic, including Presidents Giscard d'Estaing and Chirac, were also graduates, for in France there is no rigid distinction between a political and a civil service career (as there is, for example, in Britain). There is also considerable movement between the private and public sectors, reflecting a strong interdependence between the state and business.

In Britain, as in France, top civil servants were selected from among the best brains in the country, but with little in the way of specialist training (Fulton Report, 1968). Reforms designed to address this problem had only limited impact. Thus a new Civil Service College, introduced in response to Fulton, never acquired a status remotely comparable to that of the French ENA. (Both the name and objectives of the institution have since been changed.) In contrast with the fluid interrelationship between politics and administration in France, British civil servants were expected to refrain from overt political activity and serve governments of different parties impartially. Indeed the study of public administration in Britain has sometimes resembled government with the politics taken out. Nevertheless, the higher civil service appeared extremely influential, with some critics even suggesting that they were the real rulers of Britain.

> There are commonly demands for more political and administrative decentralization, transferring decision making downwards to local communities and front-line workers.

In the USA attitudes to government and public service have generally been less positive. The **executive**, and often the **federal** government in particular, have been seen as a potential threat to individual **freedom** and initiative, while the public bureaucracy was unfavourably compared with the competition and enterprise of the private sector. Public officials are less prestigious than in France or Britain, and they are also more vulnerable to political change, as an alteration in party control at any level of government commonly results in extensive changes at the official level also (reflecting what is described as the 'spoils system'). Past concerns over the venality and corruption of public officials drove a reform agenda, particularly in city government. It is perhaps no accident that **public choice** theory, which assumes that public officials are motivated by their own rational self-interest, took off in the United States. There, reform of the public sector has commonly involved making it more like the private sector.

There is only scope here to discuss briefly some of the key themes within the study of public administration. One is the structure and organization of government, and the various ways in which its work can be divided up into departments and agencies. Closely linked with this is the division of responsibilities between different levels of government. There are commonly demands for more political and administrative **decentralization**, transferring decision making downwards to local **communities** and front-line workers. Yet this can lead to increased problems in the coordination of policy and services, and almost inevitably involves disparities in service levels between areas. However, the analysis and reform of the organization of departments and of the territorial administration of government has been a recurring concern of academics as well as administrators.

Bureaucracy

Another theme relates to the recruitment and training of the public bureaucracy. **Weber's** model of bureaucracy provides a useful starting point (see page 113), although features of his model are far from universal in state bureaucracies around the world. In many countries recruitment and promotion are still by patronage rather than qualifications and expertise, decisions are not reached by applying impersonal rules, but more arbitrarily, and bribery is endemic. Even in advanced western states the impartiality and incorruptibility of state officials cannot be guaranteed, although there is a general presumption in favour of the impartiality and integrity of public servants. Criticism is more commonly expressed over their expertise and competence. This sometimes reflects the dominance of a particular area of expertise, such as law (notably in Germany and Japan), although this is now rivalled by economics in some countries. The United Kingdom has traditionally recruited top university graduates (especially Oxbridge) regardless of the relevance of subjects studied.

However, recruiting the best brains available for public service tends in practice to mean they come from a fairly restricted educational and social background, and are thus not socially representative. A long-standing criticism of the 'Oxbridge' dominance of the British higher civil service has been more recently matched by criticism of the '*enarques*' in France. The alienation of **ethnic minority** communities from the state in both countries has been exacerbated by their relative exclusion from the highest levels of state service, despite efforts to reduce the unconscious institutional **racism** that has sometimes effectively discriminated against minorities. This is one area where the USA has perhaps been more successful, with a record of positive discrimination in favour of disadvantaged groups. But in so far as this may involve recruiting those with inferior qualifications, this is perceived as unfair (and illegal in the United Kingdom), and may result in lower standards of service.

Studies of the power and influence of state bureaucracies necessarily involve some of the usual problems of definition and measurement. The cynical assumption that democracy in practice involves bureaucracy, the rule of officials, is lent some support by manifest evidence that officials are far more numerous, more permanent, more expert and experienced than the politicians to whom they are supposedly accountable. Yet detailed studies suggest a more complex reality, variable over time and space. We have already seen that in France there is often movement between bureaucratic and political roles, and leading officials and politicians come from similar backgrounds. While in Britain there is a more rigid distinction between political and civil service careers, leading members of each have more in common than divides them. Although the post-war growth in the size of the public sector across the western world has been partly attributed to its own power and influence, by the same token the subsequent failure of that same public bureaucracy to resist cuts in its own personnel and budgets implies its relative impotence. (Note, however, the arguments of Dunleavy, 1991, on this issue.)

Government and the market

In and around the 1970s there was much criticism of 'big government', and not just from **neoliberals** and public choice theorists (see Part II, Section 2, pages 90–2). It was widely asserted that problems of inflation, policy failure and budgetary crisis that emerged in many advanced western states around that time were a consequence of the growth of government and of government spending and taxation. Pressures of **globalization** seemed to require a freer labour market and less expensive social protection and provision. At the same time demographic change (particularly an ageing population) rendered existing state pension and **welfare** schemes increasingly expensive and, it appeared, unsustainable. Thus the growth of the state was halted and partially reversed in a number of western countries. A general presumption in favour of state provision was replaced by a presumption in favour of the **free market**. Remedies included slimming down the state, **privatizing** some former state-controlled activities and exposing others to more competition both from the private and voluntary sectors and within the public sector, particularly through the development of internal markets. Increased emphasis was placed on decentralization of services and on consumer choice (Self, 1993; Walsh, 1995; Greenwood et al, 2001; Hughes, 2003).

These developments threatened the notion of public administration as a distinctive subject. A fashionable new title for the subject area was 'public sector management', implying that it was simply a sub-branch of the general study of management, whose core principles applied to both the private and public sector. This was underlined by the widespread introduction of private-sector principles, techniques, and often personnel into the management of the public sector in many western countries under the general heading of the 'New Public Management' (NPM). Much of this involved increasing the autonomy of managers and reducing effective political **accountability** and control. The political context within which public administration had traditionally operated was marginalized. Yet it was never possible to take politics out of the administration of public services that had massive implications for citizens both as consumers and taxpayers.

> The new institutionalism has particularly emphasized the importance of organizational cultures on the behaviour of members of organizations.

The new **institutionalism** (see pages 94–6) has substantially revived the study of institutions, including state institutions, but with a broader and more political focus than traditional public administration. The new institutionalism has particularly emphasized the importance of organizational cultures on the behaviour of members of organizations. Thus public sector bureaucrats may be socialized into accepting norms of public service, and are not necessarily solely motivated by naked rational self-interest. They may internalize a public service ethic. However, collective institutional cultures that affect individual behaviour may vary between different parts of the public sector and across different occupations within it. The values and rules of conduct associated with professional ethics influence professionals working within the public service.

Public policy and governance

Rationalism and incrementalism

Public administration has been particularly associated with the organization of **government** and institutions, although it has also been concerned with the process of government. In the USA, there has long been a particular focus on the theory and practice of policy making, initially to encourage a more **rational** or scientific approach to the process of government. The rational model of decision making associated with Herbert **Simon** (1947), assumed the decision maker should, ideally, start from the situation, trace through all possible courses of action and their consequences, and choose the one with greatest net benefits or least cost. Yet Simon recognized that much decision making does not and indeed cannot follow this ideal approach. Decision makers are commonly limited by lack of time, information and skills, so that they cannot find the optimum solution, and in practice are only able to search for a solution that appears tolerably satisfactory. Thus in his more realistic model they 'satisfice' rather than 'optimize' (terms incidentally now familiar in the study of microeconomics). It may be noted that Simon's approach is unashamedly prescriptive or normative. This is how administrators *should* behave. He was not primarily concerned with how administrators behave in practice, although he was prepared to temper his recommendations with a degree of realism.

Charles **Lindblom** (1959) is substantially responsible for the rival approach to policy making, **incrementalism**. He argued that decisions were not commonly made by a single detached administrator, impartially assessing options, but commonly emerged over time, with contributions from many individuals and groups. Indeed Lindblom built pluralist assumptions into his model. Various interests may have a significant input into the policy process, and there may be considerable conflict and bargaining between groups, which Lindbom describes as 'partisan mutual adjustment', leading to a rather disjointed policy process. As a consequence, much policy is likely to involve not major radical shifts but small 'incremental changes' to past policy. Lindblom's model, which he provocatively described as 'the science of muddling through', appeared closer to the way much policy actually seemed to emerge.

> Lindblom's model, which he provocatively described as 'the science of muddling through', appeared closer to the way much policy actually seemed to emerge.

Indeed, incrementalism appeared to provide a very close fit to the way budgetary policy in particular was made, as confirmed by many leading researchers (Heclo and **Wildavsky**, 1974). In practice, despite attempts to introduce a more 'rational' public expenditure planning process, budgets normally involve small-scale changes to last year's budget after extensive bargaining between vested interests both inside and outside government. Thus incrementalism appeared a good descriptive model of the policy process. Yet for Lindblom incrementalism would lead to better decisions than Simon's rational model, partly because it was more likely to be acceptable as it assumed accommodation and compromise, and partly because small-scale shifts in policy were less likely to involve catastrophic mistakes. Thus incrementalism was a prescriptive as well as a descriptive model. Lindblom recommended 'muddling through' as likely to produce better results, to the delight of those public servants who had been 'muddling through' their whole working lives.

Not everyone shared their enthusiasm. Critics reluctantly agreed that Lindblom may have provided a tolerably accurate model of the way much policy was made in practice, but they thought it should be possible to do better. Some critics suggested there was an inbuilt **conservative** bias in incrementalism, as most policy will closely resemble past policy on which it is based. Yet if existing policy is failing badly, radical change may be necessary. Lindblom argued that quite radical changes in policy may take place over time as the cumulative outcome of a series of incremental shifts, although critics countered that without any sense of strategic direction a series of incremental shifts might simply involve going round in circles. To a degree Lindblom (1979, 1980) has taken this particular point on board, conceding the need for some forward planning and 'strategic analysis' in later versions of his model.

There have also been attempts to construct 'mixed' models of the policy process, incorporating elements of rationalism and incrementalism, such as the 'mixed scanning' of Amitai Etzioni (1967).

Governance

Interest in the process of policy making has fed into more recent debates over governance (see also Part I, Section 1). **Governance** became a fashionable term in the analysis of politics in the 1990s, particularly following the publication of Osborne and Gaebler's *Reinventing Government* (1992). 'Governance,' they proclaimed, 'is the process by which we collectively solve our problems and meet our society's needs. Government is the instrument we use.' The emphasis on governance as a process gave it a wider, more inclusive, sense than government. Governance involves 'us' as well as 'them'. It transcends the distinction between politics and government, and between state and civil society. It covers both the 'inputs' and 'outputs' of the systems model. It includes not only elected politicians but appointed officials and anyone else involved in the decision-making process, not just government departments, but all kinds of other public offices and agencies, including **quangos** (quasi autonomous non-government organizations). It covers not just the public sector, but the private and voluntary sectors, in so far as they help to 'collectively solve our problems and meet our society's needs.'

Moreover, in a celebrated Osborne and Gaebler metaphor, governance is about 'steering' rather than 'rowing', or 'enabling' rather than directly 'providing', goods and services. Thus government and other public agencies are in the business of leading or persuading rather than necessarily commanding and controlling. Similarly, there is no assumption of a hierarchical 'command and control' relationship between the institutions and individuals involved in particular policy areas, such as education or transport. Partnerships and networks may be a more common form of organization, requiring a cooperative and diplomatic relationship between equals rather than between superior and inferior. They may often cut across the normal functional and departmental divisions of government. What emerges from this process is more fragmentation and diversity rather than the homogeneity and uniformity once associated with policies and services in centralized sovereign states.

What all this means for the state and government is contentious. One implication is that government should do less, while society should do more. Hence the term employed by Peters (1997: 56–7), 'societal governance.' Rhodes (1997: 46–60) rather more provocatively talks of 'governing without government', and suggests that the state has been 'hollowed out' (1997: 17–19). Yet although 'governance' seems to involve a reduced role for the state, as traditionally conceived, it also paradoxically involves a broader interpretation of the public sphere. Thus governance includes not only **privatized** activities, no longer formally part of the state, but still extensively subject to state **legislation** and regulation (and sometimes state subsidy), but also the private and voluntary sectors in so far as they contribute to, and are affected by, public policy. Business companies and voluntary bodies involved with public agencies in partnerships and networks are very much part of the governance process.

research

BOX 5.3 from government to governance: the shifting focus

Old government	New governance
The state	The state and civil society
The public sector	Public, private and voluntary (or 'third') sectors
Institutions	Processes
Organizational structures	Policies, outputs, outcomes
Homogeneity, uniformity	Diversity, fragmentation
'Rowing', providing	'Steering', enabling
Commanding, controlling, directing	Leading, facilitating, collaborating, bargaining
Hierarchy and authority	Partnerships, networks, task forces, cross-cutting agencies

Source: adapted from Leach and Percy-Smith (2001, tables 1.1 and 1.2).

The new (or newish) world of governance is not without problems. For those in government, leading, enabling and cajoling rather than ordering and controlling require different and more difficult skills. The proliferation of partnerships and networks can have some obvious advantages. It may bring in more knowledge, skills and resources. Ideally, it may assist the dispersal and **decentralization** of power, providing wider opportunities for active participation by groups and interests outside government. It may also help to build a wider and more genuine **consensus** behind policy. Yet it may increase the complexity of the policy process, to the extent that it is no longer clear who is in charge, and who carries the can for failure. There is often a fundamental but not transparent inequality between what those involved in partnership and networks bring to the table in terms of resources and **power**. Some may be only token participants, while others dominate proceedings. There can be significant problems for effective **democratic** control. Too much influence may be conceded to specialist minority groups or business interests. Sometimes it may appear as if government has increasing responsibilities and decreasing power for the effective exercise of those responsibilities.

Multi-level governance

So far the emphasis has been on the horizontal relationships between public agencies and private and voluntary-sector bodies at the same level of government, yet there is an increasing complex relationship between different levels of governance, which is inevitably multi-layered. Governance operates at a number of levels, from the immediate neighbourhood or **community** to the **global**, including local, regional, state, **federal** (where applicable) transnational and international levels. Thus a French citizen is affected by decisions

> *Governance operates at a number of levels, from the immediate neighbourhood to the global.*

taken at the level of the commune, department, region, nation, European Union and international level (for example, the United Nations, G8, World Trade Organization, International Monetary Fund and so on). Yet France is still, in terms of constitutional theory at least, a unitary state, the Fifth French Republic 'one and indivisible'. The position is more complicated in federal states, like the USA and Germany, where **sovereignty** is formally divided between two levels. It is arguably still more complex in what might be described as 'quasi-federal' states such Spain and the United Kingdom, where substantial powers have been **devolved** to nations or autonomous regions, but without any formal transfer of sovereignty.

In both federal systems and those states where sovereignty is formally concentrated, it is difficult and frequently impossible to assign functions, policies and services exclusively to one level of government or governance. A few policies are still substantially determined at central or federal government level, such as foreign and defence policy. However even these policy areas may be significantly affected by international bodies (such as the United Nations) or transnational bodies (such as the European Union), and by treaty obligations (such as NATO, the North Atlantic Treaty Organization). They can also on occasion be influenced by subnational pressures. Other policies, such as trade, agriculture, education, transport, health and social policy, may be determined at a number of different levels, with considerable multi-way influence between levels. The extent of local autonomy or discretion may vary significantly between states, but where responsibility for specific policies or services have been substantially devolved there may as a result be considerable diversity in policy and service levels between different parts of the country within a single state. This will not always be welcomed. Indeed variations in services, and sometimes in charges, between different areas of the same state, can provoke outrage. Some argue strenuously that all state citizens in the same circumstances should be treated equally, and not be subject to what is sometimes described as a 'postcode lottery'.

The diversity involved in this complex world of 'multi-level governance' can be confusing. It makes it more difficult to determine where power really lies, who really 'calls the shots'. There are some sceptics who suggest the whole picture is wildly exaggerated. The reality, they suggest, is still of a world where key decisions are taken at the level of the sovereign **nation-state**. This is even the case in ostensibly international bodies, such as the United Nations, G8 or World Trade Organization, which are composed of member states, and where decisions commonly emerge from negotiations between state governments (see for example the **realist** and neorealist theories of international relations, Part II, Section 2, pages 103–7). Moreover in many states it is argued that power is not effectively decentralized or devolved. **Legislation** remains largely or exclusively a central function, while the bulk of taxation is determined at central level. While responsibility for services may be delegated to local or regional levels of government, it is the centre that determines the legal framework and the centre that largely still holds the purse strings, and 'he or she who pays the piper calls the tune'. Thus real power in central–local relations remains with the centre. Indeed some advocates of more local or regional autonomy in unitary states, or of state rights in federal systems, lament what they see as increased centralization of policy making in recent decades.

Identity politics

Social characteristics and identity

Much of the research by sociologists and political scientists has sought to correlate political attitudes and behaviour with various more or less objective social characteristics. For most of us it is not difficult to tick the relevant boxes. Some details concerning ourselves are routinely recorded in official documents: sex, age, home address, and for some purposes marital status, nationality and perhaps religion. A full census and some surveys will require further information, such as occupation (commonly sorted into a number of categories

research

or classes), and increasingly **ethnic** background (with a choice of categories such as Black African, Black Caribbean, Asian) which may be more problematic for some respondents.

Such ethnic monitoring is more contentious, but useful (for example, to provide hard evidence of the extent of discrimination and disadvantage experienced by **ethnic minorities**). Putting on one side some of the problems of definition, classification and measurement, political scientists can learn much from correlating these social characteristics with political attitudes and behaviour (as we have seen already in earlier discussions of political opinion, voting, and involvement with **political parties** and **pressure groups**).

Yet however dispassionately or otherwise government statisticians or social scientists may classify us, we are also defined by others and by ourselves, and this labelling also has considerable political implications. These identities may be largely historically determined or socially constructed rather than personally chosen, although some such identities we may tacitly accept, while others may be more actively endorsed, and still others may be directly challenged. Thus while 'sex' is an (almost inescapable) biological category, 'gender' is socially constructed, a category which carries with it a whole bundle of expectations about the respective roles of men and women. Many women and some men have sought to challenge these expectations and redefine male and female roles. However, partly as a consequence of continued discrimination, for some women their gender is the most important thing about them, and has major implications for their political attitudes and behaviour.

> While 'sex' is an (almost inescapable) biological category, 'gender' is socially constructed, a category which carries with it a whole bundle of expectations about the respective roles of men and women.

In an era of rapid social, economic and political transformation and potentially extensive personal mobility, the labels given to individuals and groups, and the identities that appear meaningful and help to make sense of people's lives, may also change. We may come to see ourselves differently and embrace new identities over a lifetime. A refugee who has escaped persecution may enthusiastically adopt a new nationality. Another migrant may want to rediscover his or her roots and reconnect with the past. Sometimes those who are called names by others may defiantly adopt them. Old beliefs may acquire new meanings. Identities may be essentially socially constructed but they are also enthusiastically endorsed by individuals and internalized. Identities exist in the mind.

Some people identify positively with the social groups into which they are divided by statisticians and social scientists, with their generation, with their home area, or their occupational **class**. However, 'identity politics' commonly transcends these divisions and relates to perceived national identity, ethnicity, religion and culture. These identities may have significant implications for political attitudes and behaviour, particular insofar as they transcend existing state borders.

Nations – imagined communities

National identities are of course far from new. The **nation** has long appeared the most significant political community in the modern world. The doctrine of 'national self-determination', proclaimed by the Italian **Mazzini** and later by US President Woodrow Wilson, assumed that nations should be able to determine their own future, and become independent self-governing states, or '**nation-states**'. Gellner (1983) succinctly defined nationalism as 'a political principle which holds that the political and national unit should be congruent'. In other words nations should form states, and states should consist of nations.

It is however worth recalling that most states in history have not been nation-states, but were carved out by conquest and sometimes by their rulers' marriage alliances, and commonly bequeathed by principles of hereditary succession, almost regardless of the **culture** and identity of their subjects. The concept of the nation has only become the basis for a state's legitimacy in modern times. Yet a nation has never been easy to define. It may be described as a **community** of people bound together by some characteristic that they share, such as a common language, religion, culture or ethnicity. Yet ultimately there are no clear objective criteria. Nations exist in the minds of their members. They are 'imagined communities' (Anderson, 1983).

There is considerable continuing disagreement about the origins of nationalism and the nation-state. Some authorities discern the development of national consciousness in the early modern period from the sixteenth century onwards (Greenfeld, 1992: 14). Others date the growth of nationalism from industrialization, modernization and changes in communication from the late eighteenth or early nineteenth century, (Hobsbawm, 1990; Gellner, 1992; Breuilly, 1993; Alter, 1994). Some see it as a political doctrine initially promoted by radical intellectual **elites** opposed to traditional rule (Kedourie, 1993), but then taken up by some governing elites and more conservative interests as an officially state-sponsored nationalism to reinforce the allegiance of other, potentially revolutionary, classes to the state. As Gellner (1983: 55) tartly observes, 'it is nationalism that engenders nations rather the other way around'. From this perspective, national identities were promoted and learned rather than innate. Yet they subsequently proved difficult to manipulate and control.

Moreover national identities can evolve and change over time in altered circumstances. Thus states that were the products of nationalism and the doctrine of national self-determination (such as Belgium, Italy, Czechoslovakia and Yugoslavia) have faced their own separatist nationalist movements that have destroyed or threatened the survival of the state. Older states like Britain and Spain, once widely considered 'nation-states', have experienced nationalist pressures that have already led to significant devolution of power and could lead eventually to the break-up of the existing state and the creation of new nation-states (Nairn, 1981, 2000).

Some nevertheless see national consciousness and the nation state as declining forces in the modern world, threatened by **globalization** and the emergence of new region states (such as the European Union) on the one hand (Ohmae, 1996) and by other essentially transnational loyalties and identities on the other (**Huntington**, 2002). Yet there is little sign in the modern world of the impending demise of nationalism. Indeed it has recently flourished particularly in former **communist** countries where a counter-ideology stressing universalism and international working-class solidarity have been inculcated for half a century or more. While nationalism appears logically redundant in a post-industrial globalized world, it continues to deny predictions.

However, 200 years of nationalism have generally failed to produce a world of homogeneous nation-states. The complex inter-settlement of peoples with different identities renders the creation of pure nation-states, with coherent and defendable borders

> Most states in history have not been nation-states. The concept of the nation has only become the basis for a state's legitimacy in modern times.

but without significant minorities, almost impossible. In addition, extensive migration over the last century, and particularly the last half century, has created sizeable ethnic minorities in many states that were once more ethnically and culturally homogeneous.

'Race' and ethnicity

Race and ethnicity are highly contested terms. While it was once thought there was scientific support for the division of humanity into distinctive 'races' with their own skin colour (white, black, brown, yellow, red), it is now accepted that that there is no biological justification for the concept of race. Yet if 'race' is in scientific terms meaningless, the term 'race' remains in common use, often in a pejorative sense, and also finds its way into official language, particularly with reference to 'race riots', 'racial discrimination' or 'race relations'. Clearly racism and racist attitudes persist.

Ethnicity is another problematic term that is not easily separated from overlapping concepts such as nation, culture and race. Ethnic divisions were once associated particularly with language and culture in Europe (Lane and Errson, 1999: 53–65). It was once widely anticipated that the political implications of such ethnic cleavages would decline with modernization, hastening the decline of minority languages and cultures (**Lipset** and **Rokkan**, 1967). In practice the opposite has happened. Traditional ethnic minorities have been politically mobilized, and in some cases have inspired separatist **nationalism** (see above). Languages that once appeared in terminal decline have been revived, and these linguistic and associated cultural identities have become of increased political significance.

Yet today the term 'ethnic minorities' is less likely to be applied to such traditional minority cultures. In western Europe it is chiefly used in practice to describe minority groups marked off from the majority population by their relatively recent arrival as immigrants or descendants of immigrants, and often also by their distinctive appearance in terms of skin colour and dress, and sometimes their religion. The ethnic minorities that arouse particular popular, media and official attention and concern in western countries are non-white and/or non-Christian. Thus the term 'ethnic minorities' has become an accepted substitute for the discredited notion of 'race'. However, it is sometimes also used for some white Christian minorities, such as Irish or Poles, or Eastern Europeans.

Elsewhere in the western world there are ethnic minorities who may be clearly marked off from the majority community by their physical appearance, but who are not relatively recent immigrants but indigenous. Such indigenous minorities include the Inuits of Canada, the native Americans (or 'red Indians') of the USA, the Maori of New Zealand and the aborigines of Australia. In these states it is indeed the white majority, descendants of European settlers, who are the immigrants. In the USA (and also in the Caribbean and parts of Latin America) there is also a substantial non-indigenous black population, most of whom are distantly descended from unwilling immigrants from the African continent. The USA also has substantial communities of more recent immigrants from parts of Europe and Latin America, and these retain elements of their distinctive cultures.

Ethnic cleavages in other parts of the world are different again. Over the African continent it is white-skinned people who constitute minorities of various sizes (mostly tiny, but still significant in South Africa). The once sizeable east African Asian community has largely been either forcibly expelled or effectively pushed out. State boundaries largely mirror colonial boundaries that substantially ignored tribal divisions, and these continue to bedevil internal relations in many African states. These divisions are further complicated by religious differences, particularly between Christians and Muslims in states such as Nigeria and the Sudan.

Over much of Latin America ethnic differences, while still significant, are substantially blurred by substantial inter-settlement and inter-marriage. Thus it is difficult to estimate with any precision the various ethnic groups of a country like Brazil, which is one of the most racially mixed countries of the world. Although it seems there is a correlation between poverty and colour, race relations has not featured on the Brazilian political agenda (see Al Montero in Kesselman et al, 2000). There is also considerable ethnic diversity in Asia, most notably in India, with a wide range of languages, castes and religions (see Atul Kohli in Kesselman et al, 2000) but also in countries like Iran, Malaysia and Indonesia.

Such ethnic identities may be of crucial significance for political attitudes and behaviour. Where minorities face discrimination and prejudice it is hardly surprising that they may appear politically apathetic or alienated, with damaging implications for civil order and national unity. Yet minorities that are too small or geographically dispersed to be considered a nation rarely constitute a threat to the survival of the state, unless they can make common cause with comparable groups in other states that share their ethnic background, language or particularly religion.

Religion

Although from the late Roman empire to the seventeenth century religious divisions were of crucial importance to both the government of political communities and inter-state relations, for most of the period from the eighteenth century onwards they appeared to be of declining political significance. While both the civil wars and interstate wars of the sixteenth and seventeenth centuries had a substantial religious component, the major wars of the eighteenth century were dynastic and colonial, while those of the nineteenth and twentieth centuries were national and ideological. The eighteenth-century Enlightenment assisted the development of more sceptical attitudes towards religious belief and the growth of secularism (see Part II, Section 1).

Yet in the last part of the twentieth century some detected a significant religious revival in many parts of the world (e.g. **Huntington** [1996]: 64–6, 95–101). According to Huntington the main traditional religions of the world have all experienced a resurgence, involving an 'unsecularization' of the world. Huntington ([1996]: 97) connects this religious resurgence with 'social, economic and cultural modernization'. As 'people more from the countryside to the city, and become separated from their roots ... they interact with large numbers of strangers' and 'they need new sources of identity, new forms of stable community'. Thus religion becomes more crucial to personal identity in a bewildering, shifting world. The argument is inherently plausible, although it is illustrated by quotations and examples rather than conclusively demonstrated. In some parts of the world the evidence for a religious resurgence is rather shaky. Lane and Ersson (1999: 44–53) quote statistics for church attendance across western Europe, and conclude that 'all religions have lost members'. Yet this does not necessarily contradict Huntington's general point, and the evidence he cites for a religious revival in for example the former Soviet Union and eastern Europe.

Huntington's main thesis is that cold war conflicts between two rival ideologies have

> In the last part of the twentieth century some have detected a significant religious revival in many parts of the world.

been effectively replaced by the resurrection of older clashes between rival civilizations. For Huntington ([1996]: 47), 'religion is a central defining characteristic of civilizations,' although language and other aspects of culture are also significant. He lists seven or eight major civilizations: Sinic (or Chinese), Japanese, Islamic, Hindu, Orthodox, Western, Latin American and perhaps African. Of Huntington's civilizations three are clearly identified by religion (Islamic, Hindu and Orthodox), although he also associates western civilization with western (that is non-Orthodox) Christianity, and this western Christianity is also an equally crucial element of Latin-American civilization. Yet his other civilizations are less clearly associated with a single dominant religion.

However, largely since Huntington's book appeared, his observations on the increase in fundamentalist religion in particular has been apparently dramatically confirmed by series of **terrorist** acts inspired by Islamic fundamentalism. 'The clash of civilizations' has been translated in media and popular images into a class between the west and militant Islam. This appears to have substance, in that for some Muslims their religious identity also determines their political loyalties, and these transcend state borders. Clearly they also perceive a global clash between the west and Islam.

Yet while subsequent events appeared to validate a narrow version of Huntington's thesis, his broader framework appears less convincing. The civilizations he identifies are contestable at the margins, as he partially admits himself in the case of African and Japanese civilization. The notion of an Orthodox civilization also seems somewhat strained. Is the division between western and orthodox Christianity really so much more significant than that between Catholicism and Protestantism? Moreover there is hardly a distinctive Latin American civilization.

He pays little attention to the major cleavages within civilizations, for example in the west, between Europe and the USA as well as between secularism and religion, and within Christianity. If the unity of the west is exaggerated, much the same applies to his other civilizations, the divisions between Sunni and Shia interpretations of Islam for example, and very different views of the relations between Islam and the state in, for example, Turkey, Egypt and Iran. Thus Salwa Ismail (in Leftwich, 2004) convincingly argues that 'there is no single Islamic conception of politics'.

We could also ask whether it is really Chinese and Hindu civilizations that are providing a challenge to the west. Rather it seems to be the Chinese and Indian states and economies that are providing an increasing threat to western economic and technological leadership. Hindu fundamentalism may have implications for Indian domestic politics, but not much yet for **international relations**. The clashes some see between Asian values and western values (see for example the views of Parekh, 2000, quoted on page 252) transcend Huntington's civilizations, four of which are substantially Asian.

Altogether it appears that religious identities may have increased significance for politics after a long period of generally declining religious influence, but it does not necessarily follow that the most important global political divisions are between distinctive civilizations of which 'religion is the central defining characteristic'.

Multiculturalism

At one level the term **multiculturalism** simply describes this cultural diversity, which has become an inescapable fact of life in many states and societies around the world. These states and societies contain peoples from different ethnic backgrounds who may speak different languages, belong to different religious faiths and follow different moral codes, dress and behave differently and eat different foods. While multicultural states and societies are sometimes associated particularly with the modern world, many historical states contained considerable diversity (for example, the Ottoman, Austro-Hungarian and Russian empires).

Yet if the existence of cultural diversity cannot be disputed, it is very variously regarded, and policies to cope with it are hotly contested. The term 'multiculturalism' has also been employed in a more normative sense, implying a welcoming of cultural diversity and recognition of the distinctive cultures of minorities. One contentious issue for public policy is how to balance national unity and cohesion with diversity. It is an issue that has been addressed by political scientists, studying the impact of cultural diversity across nations (e.g. Huntington, [1996]) and also by a number of political philosophers (**Kymlicka**, 1995; Parekh, 2000; **Barry**, 2001a, 2001b).

Much past practice involved the assimilation of minority cultures. For many individuals and whole communities this was what simple self-preservation and self-interest required. The conquered were commonly persuaded to adopt the language and religion of their conquerors. Those who declined to assimilate, like many Jews, found their prospects at best limited. Yet those Jews who did assimilate, including some who were baptized as Christians, and others who effectively discarded or marginalized their faith to become, as they imagined, fully integrated into their host communities, discovered they were still labelled as Jews, discriminated against, persecuted and even exterminated. With a terrible irony, it was the German Jews who seemed the most thoroughly integrated in Europe who faced the Holocaust. Many other immigrant communities who had been effectively driven out from where they had come by persecution or poverty were only too happy to assimilate, and to identify with their new countries, and in some cases they were welcomed by host communities, and in others accepted over time.

For some critics of multiculturalism, assimilation remains imperative. **Huntington** ([1996]: 305–6) sees multiculturalism as a serious threat. For him cultural diversity involves 'schizophrenic torn countries … not belonging to any civilization and lacking a cultural core'. He argues that 'History shows that no country so constituted can long endure.' He criticizes immigrant communities who reject assimilation 'and continue to adhere to and to propagate the values, customs and cultures of their home countries', instancing Muslims in Europe and (to a lesser extent) Hispanics in the USA. Huntington particularly deplores a 'small but influential number of intellectuals' who 'in the name of multiculturalism' have 'attacked the identification of the United States with Western civilization, denied the existence of a common American heritage, and promoted racial, ethnic, and other sub-national cultural identities and groupings'. He found the 'multicultural trend' manifest in a variety of legislation that followed the civil rights acts of the 1960s and the 'encouragement of diversity' in the 1990s by the Clinton administration. He warns that 'If assimilation fails … America will become a cleft country with all the potentials for internal strife and disunion that entails.'

> For some critics of multi-culturalism, assimilation remains imperative.

Huntington's own conclusions rest on wide-ranging historical and comparative analysis. Yet even his reading of American history is not altogether persuasive. He refers, reasonably, to the problem the American founding fathers had of coping with diversity, but implies that this involved the sacrifice of diversity to unity. In practice the invention of **federalism** enabled them to accommodate substantial diversity, and it was this institutional device

research

that subsequently helped other states to balance unity and diversity. Indeed, the USA might qualify as one of **Lijphart's** 'consociational democracies', providing political stability in divided societies (Lijphart, 1977), but for its first-past-the-post **electoral system** and its two-party system (although America's federal structure cloaks considerable internal differences within its two parties).

To outsiders, the USA has been fairly successful in reconciling unity and diversity, as demonstrated by the widely acknowledged hyphenated identities of Americans. There are Irish-Americans, Polish-Americans, Greek-Americans, Italian-Americans, Jewish-Americans and indeed Hispanic-Americans, all contributing to a rich cultural mix. Their continued loyalty to 'the values, customs and cultures of their home countries' does not seem to interfere with their common allegiance to the USA. The civil rights legislation of the 1960s and the Clinton administration's encouragement of diversity sprang in large part from specific past failures to accommodate important minorities which can hardly be themselves blamed for any failure to assimilate fully, Blacks and native Americans.

Native Americans were there first. It was the European colonists who were immigrants. The sizeable Black slave population at the time of America's Declaration of Independence were immigrants of a sort, but had not asked to be there. **Tocqueville**, who admired many features of early American democracy, was scathing in his observations on American treatment of these 'other races'. 'Oppression has deprived the descendants of the Africans of almost all the privileges due to human beings!' Even if a slave gains his freedom 'he often feels independence as a shackle heavier than slavery itself'. As for the indigenous population, Tocqueville comments on the speed of their displacement by Europeans, that there has never been 'so swift a destruction'. He quotes from the plaintive petition of the Cherokee to Congress in 1829, 'What crime have we committed which could deprive us of our country?' (Tocqueville, [1835]: 370–6, 396).

It is hardly surprising that minorities that have experienced prejudice, discrimination and oppression may have some problems identifying with 'their' nation, and may seek to recover some of their old cultural identity. Moreover, it is to the credit of some of the majority community that they recognize historical injustices in the treatment of minorities, and seek to protect what remains of their culture and their rights. Will **Kymlicka**, a Canadian political philosopher who has explored issues around multiculturalism, has focused particularly on the rights of 'minority nations' everywhere, but notably in his own Canada. He cites the native Inuit and the Quebecois, descendants of the French who had settled in Canada before the British. Kymlicka (1995) argues that such 'minority nations' deserve special group rights to self-government, through, for example, devolution or federation, and perhaps ultimately independence.

Kymlicka does not think that all ethnic minorities should be entitled to such rights, which spring from specific historical circumstances. Thus there is some obligation on voluntary immigrants into a state to assimilate. However he urges that immigrant communities should be allowed to maintain their distinctive cultures through recognition of what Kymlicka calls 'polyethnic' rights, including some exemption from general laws, on, for example, school dress codes or animal slaughtering. Some minorities might additionally need '**representation** rights' to compensate for their under-representation in political institutions and society generally.

While cultural diversity may pose problems for political unity and stability, it is not clear, even on purely pragmatic grounds, what is ultimately the most appropriate answer, assuming the rejection of extreme 'solutions' involving ethnic cleansing. Huntington may

research

be right in assuming that concessions to minorities may sometimes impair the unity and stability of the state, although they may also be the only terms on which the state may endure. There are difficult questions over the balance to be struck between diversity and unity in any political community. Only the future course of history will make it clear whether those states that have made concessions to minorities, sometimes involving significant devolution of power (as in Canada, Belgium, Spain and the United Kingdom) will survive or not. Even if such states break up it does not necessarily follow that concessions should not have been made. Political separation may sometimes be the best or least worse alternative for most of those directly involved.

> *There are difficult questions over the balance to be struck between diversity and unity in any political community.*

Moreover it should not be assumed that identities and allegiances are necessarily exclusive (as Huntington sometimes seems to imply). Persecution may intensify particular identities so that they become dominant or even exclusive, but that is hardly inevitable in pluralist democratic societies, where multiple identities and allegiances are surely to be expected (see Box 5.4).

BOX 5.4 self-identities of individuals from Black and Asian ethnic minorities in Britain

39 per cent saw themselves as 'fully British.'
A clear majority thought they were 'mainly' or 'fully' British.
22 per cent of Blacks thought they were 'not at all British'.

Some individual views

I am British and mixed race, with Indian and Irish parents. I can be proud of that. But forms asking me to identify my ethnic group never quite seem to offer the right box.

Sunder Katwala, general secretary, Fabian Society

I am a Muslim Kashmiri but also a Yorkshire lad who loves his fish and chips and his curry and chapati.

Lord Ahmed, Labour peer

For me being a British East African Asian is as important as being a thirty-something, single, gay Londoner.

Sham Sandhu, television controller

I define myself as black British, but most importantly as tri-cultural: Ghanaian, Grenadian and English.

Kwame Kwei-Armah, playwright and actor

Source: derived from the *Guardian*, 21 March 2005.

Group rights and universal human rights

One offshoot of the debate over multiculturalism has been an acrimonious argument over the notion of group **rights**. The notion of group rights has become particularly contentious, partly because of the potential for conflict with the rights of individuals, proclaimed as universal in many celebrated documents, such as the Declaration of the Rights of Man and

Citizen (1789) and the United Nations Universal Declaration of Human Rights (1948). The political philosopher Bhikhu Parekh (2000: 137) has argued that such documents embody western **liberal** ideas and ignore or downplay other (for example Asian) values of 'social harmony, respect for authority, orderly society, a united and extended family and a sense of filial piety'. Human beings are not the same everywhere, but 'culturally embedded, in the sense that they are born into, raised in and deeply shaped by their cultural communities'. The implication is that the beliefs and practices of these cultural communities should be respected, even where they may appear to conflict with universal rights.

The liberal British political philosopher Brian **Barry** (2001b) disagrees completely. He argues that Parekh's approach 'is liable to be harmful to women and children in minority communities and to those within them who deviate from prevailing norms'. Respecting the values embedded in a particular culture might entail accepting discrimination on grounds of gender or caste, and legitimizing prejudices on sexual orientation. Cultural norms can be employed to trump minimal universal norms, including women's rights, gay rights and even rights to freedom of speech and expression. Barry goes on to point out that the appeal to abstract universal rights has been a driving force behind the transformation of the legal status of women around the world. He similarly notes that the advance of the rights of American blacks depended on similar abstract principles. Respect for traditional cultural norms would have justified the continuation of discriminatory sexist and racist practices. This does not necessarily reject the notion of any group rights, as advanced by Will Kymlicka. Indeed, Barry implicitly endorses the rights of women, ethnic groups, gays and others, but he does not think that respect for minority cultures can justify any infringement of universal human rights.

Democratization

The rise of **democracy** has been the most remarkable political development of modern times. At the beginning of the twentieth century only a handful of states had **governments** that were directly **elected** or accountable to elected **representative** assemblies, and even these restricted the franchise to men. Most of the world's population had no say in their own government. Some lived under traditional autocracies or **dictators**, while many others were colonial subjects of European powers that might practice democracy at home but regarded it as inappropriate or premature for their empires abroad. Yet by the end of the twentieth century nearly two-thirds of the world's states and a majority of its peoples lived in states that appeared to meet the basic minimum criteria for democracy (Stoker, 2006: 27). Democracy had become the norm. Indeed, it is now widely regarded as the only legitimate form of government.

> *At the beginning of the twentieth century only a handful of states had governments that were directly elected or accountable to elected representative assemblies, and even these restricted the franchise to men.*

Democratization (or the transition to democracy) has become an important focus for research within the broad field of comparative politics (Whitehead, in Goodin and Klingemann, 1996: 353–71). Behind democratization studies there is generally an implicit but fairly clear normative presumption in favour of **liberal** democracy, as at least a better form of government than the alternatives, as Churchill once suggested (see Box 5.5). Some **international relations** scholars also argue that the spread of democracy assists world peace and stability, as the record shows that democratic states tend not to fight each other. (For a discussion of the relationship between democracy and peace see Burchill, in Burchill et al 2005: 58–62).

BOX 5.5   Winston Churchill on democracy

No-one pretends that democracy is perfect or all-wise. Indeed it has been said that democracy is the worst form of Government except all those other forms that have been tried from time to time.

Speech in House of Commons, *Hansard*, 11 November 1947, col. 206.

The rise of democracy: three waves

The rise of democracy was not smooth and continuous. **Huntington** (1991) has suggested that historically it advanced in three 'waves', with some 'reverse waves' in between, when a number of democracies were overthrown. In the first 'long wave' some 30 democracies were established over a century or so in the period leading up to the aftermath of the First World War. Yet it was soon clear that the war had not 'made the world safe for democracy'. The 20 years from the rise to power of fascism in Italy in 1922 'saw an accelerating, increasingly catastrophic, retreat of liberal political institutions' (Hobsbawm, 1994: 111). The outcome of the Second World War and post-war decolonization by former **imperial** powers led to another significant expansion of democracy. However, this second wave of democratization was also partially reversed from 1958 onwards as a number of relatively recently established democratic regimes in South America, Africa, Asia and even Greece in Europe succumbed to dictatorships of various kinds. Since 1974 there has been a substantial 'third wave' of democratization. Firstly, democracy was re-established in Greece, Spain and Portugal and in some states in Africa and Latin America. Then the break-up of the former Soviet empire and the discrediting of the rival concept of **communist** 'people's democracies' led to a substantial further increase in western-style liberal democratic systems.

Studying how and why democratic institutions spread in the past may provide important clues to the prospects for the consolidation and extension of democracy. In the earliest cases the development of democracy came from within societies. Subsequently there were models to emulate: the republican model of the USA and France or the constitutional **monarchies** of Britain and northern Europe. Yet if there was external influence there was no external pressure, at least until the end of the First World War. Then, in 1919 the US President Woodrow Wilson, British Prime Minister David Lloyd George and French premier Georges Clemenceau together 'determined what countries should exist … what their boundaries should be and who should rule them' (Huntington [1996]: 91). The principle of self-determination, championed by Wilson, implied democratic **nation-states**, and new European states were created on this basis. Yet the principle of self-determination was not applied to colonies of the victors, nor to the defeated nations. Unsurprisingly, perhaps, the new democratic Weimar Republic in Germany, associated with defeat and victors' justice, always had problems with legitimacy, and following the economic slump was swept away by Hitler and the Nazis, who went on invade and destroy

research

nearly all the surviving democracies and semi-democracies of continental Europe. Thus much of Huntington's first 'reverse wave' of democratization was the consequence of external pressure, although there were strong indigenous currents hostile to democracy in countries such as France as well as Italy and Germany.

The second wave of democratization was initially stimulated, in Europe, by external pressure, namely the defeat of the Axis powers. For much of continental Europe this was welcomed as a liberation. Liberal democratic institutions were restored rather than imposed in former German-occupied countries freed by western forces. However, in eastern Europe 'people's democracies', which were effectively one-party communist states, emerged in those areas occupied by the Soviet army. In Germany the western-occupied zones became the German Federal Republic, while in the east a new German Democratic Republic (GDR) was established as a client state of the Soviet Union. The prospects for democracy in the Federal Republic were hardly auspicious, but the victorious allies had learned some lessons from the First World War and treated the defeated Germany more generously, assisting its economic revival and its political and economic integration into what was to become the European Union. Assisted by the German economic miracle, the new democracy over time acquired increased legitimacy with its people (in marked contrast to the fortunes of the Weimar Republic earlier).

External influences were also evident in the democratic systems in many newly independent states established in many former western colonies. Yet in Africa in particular few of these post-colonial parliamentary regimes survived unscathed. Brian **Barry** (in Goodin and Klingemann, 1996: 545) observes that on key criteria 'almost every African state is a worse place to live now than it was at the time of decolonization'. Yet it is the colonial powers that bear substantial responsibility for this state of affairs. Although some claimed they were preparing colonies for independence and democracy, in practice this preparation was initially slow and perfunctory, and later rushed and ineffectual, as military, economic and political problems forced a rapid run-down of empire. It did not help that colonial borders almost nowhere coincided with ethnic and tribal divisions, so that the new states were hardly natural political **communities**. Among the consequences were bitter internal conflicts and civil wars, and the persecution and sometimes ethnic cleansing of minorities.

Huntington's third wave of democratization began in Greece and the Iberian peninsular. In Latin America the transition from dictatorship to democracy in Spain and Portugal aroused considerable interest, with obvious implications for other countries in the Spanish-speaking world, which had its own extensive experience of military dictatorships. Civil–military relations have been a continuing concern to those engaged in, or studying, the process of establishing or re-establishing democratic government (Whitehead, in Goodin and Klingemann, 1996,: 356–7). In Latin America an added complication was the preponderance of US power, commonly exercised to safeguard what were taken to be US interests rather than promote democracy. Thus dictators friendly to the USA were often preferred to elected governments that appeared to pose a threat (as in Chile). However, in those countries that have long experience of military dictatorship like Argentina and Chile, democracy seems at last to have been successfully restored.

In Asia there were some similar concerns. Military dictatorship has been a feature of many regimes there also. Moreover, the attitude of the west has been ambivalent in terms of the promotion of democracy, since it long preferred to prop up autocracies and dictatorship in Iran, South Korea, Indonesia and Iraq, and is still helping to maintain them in Saudi Arabia and Pakistan. For those countries where freely contested elections and parliamentary institutions have been introduced, there are continuing issues around the compatibility of western-style democracy with Asian values. Surprisingly, in view of initial dire predictions, it is Indian democracy, despite all its problems, that endures as the beacon of Asian democracy. Overall, however, the growth of democracy in Asia has been partial and erratic. Thus despite massive economic change in China there has been no progress towards democracy. Recent attempts to import western democratic systems into Afghanistan and Iraq following their invasion have proved particularly problematic.

The most substantial boost to western liberal democracy, superficially at least, was provided by the sudden collapse of the former Soviet empire. Most of the former Soviet satellite states in Eastern Europe have now been substantially locked into the democratic west by membership of the European Union, although there are some indications of declining enthusiasm for democracy, at least in terms of electoral turnout (Stoker, 2006: 41). The democratic future of the successor states of the Soviet Union, including Russia, seems less assured.

The triumph of liberal democracy?

There has to date been no substantial reversal of Huntington's 'third wave' of democratization, which started well before the collapse of the Soviet empire, but was massively assisted by it. It appeared that liberal democracy had finally and conclusively triumphed. Indeed there was some early optimism arising from survey evidence of 'high levels of support for basic democratic principles' in what were termed the 'new democracies' that the prospects for democracy were positive (Dalton, in Goodin and Klingemann, 1996: 340). Some of that optimism persists. Thus Ronald **Inglehart** has drawn comfort from a substantial survey of public opinion across over 80 countries that showed substantial agreement across the globe with the statement, 'Democracy may have its problems but its better than any other form of government' (1999–2002 www. worldvaluessurvey.org). Inglehart emphasizes that this general preference for democracy is endorsed by Muslim and Arab opinion.

> It appeared that liberal democracy had finally and conclusively triumphed.

However Stoker (2006: 28–9), who refers to these findings, comments that 'the response of citizens in many countries also suggests that they are able to distinguish between the *idea* of democracy and its, often less than perfect, *practice*' (Stoker's italics). Some of the 'new democracies' established towards the end of the twentieth century have not been consolidated. Indeed, in some so-called democracies there is 'little attention to individual rights' and 'democracy does not extend much beyond the election itself' (Hague and Harrop, 2007: 49). One key test of democratic consolidation is the peaceful turnover of governments in competitive elections (Huntington, 1991: 266, 306; Przeworski, 1991: 10). Some formally democratic regimes established after the break-up of the former Soviet Union, as well as some African states, clearly fail this test. Individual human rights (including freedom of expression) that are considered fundamental by liberals are also rejected by a number of Asian democracies as inconsistent with their values and culture.

Thus a new distinction between 'liberal' and 'illiberal' democracies has been coined (Hague and Harrop, 2007: 49–52). In illiberal democracies 'democracy does not extend far beyond the election itself'. Elections are mixed with authoritarian leadership. Rights are not respected, particularly those of political opponents. Thus illiberal democracy is

research

'democracy without turnover and competition without alternation' (Huntington, 1991: 306). While Huntington did not think this half-way house could last, some of these 'illiberal' or 'semi' democracies (for example in sub-Saharan Africa) have already survived for many years. Some observers have concluded that illiberal democracy is not 'a mere way-station on the road to further democracy' (Case, 1996, quoted in Hague and Harrop, 2007: 52). It may indeed be a 'stable compromise' – a sufficient minimum of democratic forms to satisfy international organizations and world opinion without providing an effective challenge for established elites. 'Illiberal democracy' may be here to stay.

Clearly there is no sharp distinction to be drawn between new and established, liberal and illiberal, democracy. There are significant shortcomings in many democratic regimes, including some of the longest established (Hague and Harrop, 2007: 51, box 3.5). Rather, there is a range of relevant criteria, on which some countries score relatively well and other relatively poorly, with a number somewhere in the middle, so that it is a matter of fine judgement on which side of the liberal/illiberal divide they should be placed. However, one source (Karatnycky, 2006, quoted in Hague and Harrop, 2007: 52) suggests that as many as 30 countries that hold competitive elections (including Indonesia, Nigeria, Turkey and many other 'new democracies' in Africa, Latin America and Asia) fail to qualify as fully fledged democracies.

What is democracy?

There are clearly continuing issues of definition and interpretation here around the notion of democracy itself. Western liberal democracy, dependent on the principle and practice of representation, is marked off from the older idea of direct democracy, as practised, albeit imperfectly, by ancient Athens. Yet western liberal democracy makes only minimal demands of its citizens. Some critics have long urged that there is scope for some more direct citizen participation in modern democracies beyond periodically registering a vote (**Pateman**, 1970). Indeed the new media have made this technically more feasible. Others plainly fear that attempts to increase participation in an era of declining engagement with politics could be counter-productive (Stoker, 2006: 151–62).

It is worth recalling that communist states claimed to be democratic. Lenin argued that Soviet or proletarian democracy was 'a million times more democratic than any bourgeois democracy'. He maintained that the formal equality of **bourgeois** democracy concealed massive inequality, and that the masses were effectively excluded from power (**Lenin**, 1918, in Rosen and Wolff, 1999: 103–4). Liberal critics would of course point to the absence of effective electoral choice and individual freedom in communist states. Nevertheless some on the left in the west were once prepared to argue that the 'people's democracies' of the communist world involved a valid alternative interpretation of democracy which prioritized economic equality over individual freedom (although others pointed to substantial inequality within communist states). Few would now justify the practice of the so-called 'people's democracies', but the debate over the compatibility of western democracy with massive economic inequality continues. While it was once assumed that democracy involving political equality would, over time, promote greater social and economic equality, this has not happened. Indeed, in some western democracies the gap between rich and poor appears to be widening. Some would continue to argue that this undermines the principle of political equality involved in 'one person, one vote, one value'.

research

Today the debate focuses more on other variants of democracy, such as 'Asian' democracy. Some variants of Asian democracy (for example Malaysia and Singapore) have representative institutions and regular, free elections, but place a higher premium on order and social cohesion rather than individual human rights. Thus it is argued that these states take a more 'organic' view of democracy which emphasizes the maintenance of social harmony, and the need to reflect the basic values of their people. (For more on the issues involved in the debate over Asian values and democracy, see the previous section on multiculturalism, and particularly the views of Parekh, 2000, and Barry, 2001a and 2001b.)

Yet when all allowances are made for problems in defining democracy, and in assessing levels of democracy in specific states, the extent and quality of democracy matter. They matter both for their peoples, and potentially for world peace, which is why so much attention has been focused on the process of transition to and consolidation of democracy. It is an unfinished story, which is why democratization is likely to remain a major focus of research in politics for many years to come.

Globalization

Globalization is a thoroughly contested concept. It has been variously defined, measured, dated and explained. Some have questioned the whole phenomenon (Hirst and Thompson, 1999), or used dismissive terms such as 'globaloney' to describe it. Against such sceptics, Scholte (2005) has persuasively argued that globalization is a reality, has largely occurred over the last half century, and has been characterized by the shrinking of social space and the spread of transplanetary and supraterritorial connections between peoples.

Global political economy

One of the most familiar aspects of globalization has been the establishment of a global political economy, sometimes characterized as 'hyper-capitalism'. Certainly it seems that globalization has intensified business concentration and created not only global markets, but cross-border mergers and acquisitions, leading to international oligopoly. To critics and opponents, much of this has appeared malign. Globalization has been blamed for cuts in **welfare** provision (Teeple, 1995; Mishra, 1999) and reductions in labour protection in many western states. It is argued that within the new globalized economy, generous welfare provision and restrictions on hours of work can no longer be afforded, because of the impact of international competition from low-regulation, low-wage and low-tax economies. Some of the anti-globalization protest movements have been stimulated by the erosion of accustomed levels of welfare and labour conditions, which has been blamed, not always fairly, on globalization.

> *Globalization has been blamed for the increase in inequality between the richer and poorer states world-wide.*

Globalization has also been blamed, perhaps more fairly, for the increase in inequality between the richer and poorer states world-wide. Free trade in many foods and raw materials has pushed down wage rates to near starvation levels in some countries, while the continuation of protection for western industry and agriculture for other products has restricted the scope of competition from which poorer states might otherwise benefit. Dominated by the commercial decisions of powerful multinational corporations whose turnover far exceeds their own gross national product, and burdened by debt to the wealthy nations and international organizations, poorer states appear helpless in the face of economic forces they cannot control. This massive global imbalance between rich and poor, or north and south, has fundamental implications for **international relations**. For their own security, richer states need to work to together to mitigate the worst effects of global poverty, and this is a priority for the relevant international agencies.

The global environment

Equally manifest are the global implications of the use of scarce resources and of **environmental** pollution. In the past, much of the concern expressed was over the rate of resource depletion, particularly fossil fuels, and some of the environmental and political consequences of the search for new secure sources of these fuels to satisfy the insatiable demand of advanced western states. The politics of oil has become a particular problem, with some obvious consequences for the foreign policy concerns of western states. More recently, most concern has been expressed over the consequences of global industrial activity and patterns of consumption upon the environment, and especially the now almost universally conceded threat of global warming. This, alongside other concerns such as holes in the ozone layer and acid rain, has effects that ignore state borders and are genuinely transplanetary. They too require cooperation between states, not just the west but other fast industrializing world powers such as China and India, as well as other actors on the international stage. Yet it is far from clear that global political solutions will be found for global problems.

Global communication – the shrinkage of social space

Many of the manifestations of the shrinkage of social space are only too familiar. While migration has been part of the story of humanity from the very beginning, its recent intensity and scale, in terms of both of numbers of people and distances travelled, is unprecedented. The more economically developed countries of the west have received increasing numbers of legal and illegal immigrants, not only from their former colonies as a legacy of empire, but from other poorer parts of the world. This has helped the economies of western states, but put some strains on their welfare services, as well as having some negative consequences for social political harmony, boosting far-right racist parties and movements exploiting hostility to migrant workers and asylum seekers. There have also been some adverse effects for the migrants' countries of origin, which have often lost some of their most skilled and enterprising former inhabitants.

Among the other consequences of global communication networks and the movement of peoples has been the globalization of crime. International drug trafficking is one manifestation. People trafficking on a global scale has also intensified, as desperate individuals and families commit life savings to criminal gangs of people smugglers. Some of this people smuggling is more sinister, as young people are effectively sold into slavery or prostitution. Such crimes have always taken place – although modern global communications have certainly intensified the numbers and distances involved. The new scope for international credit card crime and internet fraud is however a wholly new phenomenon. It is no longer necessary for criminals to risk their own necks in armed raids on banks or trains to steal huge sums; they can steal and use information. It is also easier for those bent on tax evasion to move their money to defraud the state, and effectively other taxpayers.

Global terrorism

One of the most publicized aspects of globalization has been the increase of international political **terrorism** (Booth and Dunne, 2002). Compared with casualties from various 'natural' disasters and ongoing wars and conflicts around the world, the victims of terrorism have been relatively few, although the random and unpredictable impact of terrorism has understandably aroused disproportionate fears. It has also demonstrated the impotence of **state governments** to protect its citizens and those within its borders from threats that it is difficult to predict or plan against. The most notorious of these new global terrorist networks, al-Qaida, has been credited with sponsoring and organizing terrorism across all the continents of the world, provoking a western 'war on terror' in response, which has already led to the invasion of Afghanistan and Iraq. Yet although acts of terrorism may have been inspired by al-Qaida, it seems more likely that much of the initiative and detailed organization has been largely local, stimulated by alienated residents and citizens within disaffected minority communities, whose own sympathies and loyalties lie outside the state.

Globalization and states

The impact of globalization on government and the exercise of political **power** has been extensive, although not perhaps as extensive as some have claimed. We do not yet live in a borderless world (Ohmae, 1990), as many would-be immigrants and asylum seekers could testify. For all the increase in international trade, significant barriers to the free movement of capital, goods and particularly labour still exist. Nor are the **nation-state** and the **ideology** of **nationalism** yet obsolete, at least to judge by the number of nations that have recently established or recovered recognition as independent states, as well as those still aspiring to the same goal.

> *For all the increase in international trade, significant barriers to the free movement of capital, goods and particularly labour still exist.*

However, it is difficult to deny that the world is less state-centred than it was. States remain very important, but the notion of state **sovereignty**, commonly dated from the Treaty of Westphalia (1648), has been significantly eroded. This had established the principle that each state would exercise supreme, comprehensive and exclusive power within its own borders, and would, along with other sovereign states, be exclusively responsible for cross-border relations between states. It followed that no state should interfere in the internal affairs of another sovereign state. Of course, this principle was fairly often violated in practice, as powerful states found pretexts for interfering in the internal affairs of their less powerful neighbours. Even so, the recognition of the sovereignty of other states was broadly accepted as a cardinal principle of international diplomacy from the mid-seventeenth to the twentieth centuries.

Globalization has substantially undermined this notion of state sovereignty. State governments no longer have exclusive control within their own borders, nor do they have comprehensive supervision over cross-border movements of information, finance, goods and people. This is perhaps most obviously the case with information. Once, through their control of national education and effective control also over the means of communication, governments could encourage the widespread acceptance of a common language and **culture**. If they wished, they could restrict the circulation of ideas that they considered harmful, banning books, suppressing newspapers, and later imposing government controls over film, radio and television. Thus the nation could be largely immunized from other cultures and rival ideologies. This was most obviously true of **dictatorships**, one-party **communist** states, and other regimes, such as South Africa under apartheid. However, information was often subtly controlled even in **democracies**, where the **mass media**, the press, and initially radio and television also, were national. Today, with satellite television, video and the internet, it is far more difficult for even the most autocratic regimes to exclude outside influences. Arabs in remote desert oases may be discovered watching American cartoons or Australian soaps. A truly global culture may not yet exist, but the logos of major multinational corporations are recognized almost everywhere.

Global institutions

State governments, particularly those of the great and middling powers, remain the most important political players on the world stage, but they now share that stage with other players. These include powerful transnational corporations (TNCs), and a rising number of **non-governmental organizations** (**NGOs**), as well as other levels of **governance** that increasingly affect their own citizens. Among supra-state levels of governance are the growing number of international organizations, such as the International Court, the United Nations, the World Trade Organization, the International Monetary Fund and the World Bank. There are also organizations representing what are sometimes called 'macro regions', such as the North Atlantic Treaty Organization, the European Union and the Organization for African Unity. While the members of these supra-state organizations are themselves state governments, sometimes with veto powers, there are often political costs associated with defying majority opinion. Increasingly, the decisions of such supra-state organizations have implications for states and their citizens.

More surprisingly, perhaps, according to some commentators, growing political decentralization within states may also be seen as both a product of globalization and a reaction against it. Globalization has contributed to the weakening of national sentiment which had previously sustained loyalty to established states, but has also created for many people a crisis of identity, that has stimulated an increased attachment to local **communities**, cities and micro-nations. This has created pressures for the decentralization and **devolution** of **power**, and sometimes for separatist **nationalism**. Smaller states, once seen as non-viable for purposes of defence and economic development, can survive and thrive within a political environment of multi-level governance. In response to such pressures for decentralization, devolution and separatism, state governments have often devolved more powers to regions and localities. Many of these sub-state levels of government already have extensive relations with comparable regional and city authorities in other states, as well as their own direct relations with supra-state authorities. Other political institutions have developed similar connections. **Political parties** and **pressure groups** have important links across state borders with others who share their aims and interests. Thus the European Union already has pan-European political parties and organized groups, as well as a formally constituted Committee of the Regions.

Yet for all this increased governance and associated political activity

> *Globalization has contributed to the weakening of national sentiment which had previously sustained loyalty to established states, but has also created for many people a crisis of identity, that has stimulated an increased attachment to local communities, cities and micro-nations.*

at a variety of levels, the most obvious point to be made about the political implications of globalization is its essentially undemocratic nature. At state level, democracy has increased substantially in recent decades. For most states, and for many other sub-global levels of governance, there are mechanisms for formal democratic **accountability** and control, based on principles of political **equality**, and one person, one vote, one value, no doubt imperfectly realized but substantially operative. None of this is the case at the global level. In international political organizations the heads that are counted are the heads of government, whose relative influence does not depend on the numbers of their citizens (whose own views are not canvassed). The 'international community', in so far as it exists, is largely a community of state governments, operating individually and collectively through international organizations, supplemented to an extent by some high-profile but not representative NGOs. Thus globalization has involved 'a politics of disempowerment' for ordinary people (Ake, 1999). Many scholars have struggled with the issue of remedying this situation, and creating a genuine global democracy (e.g Held, 1995). Some have perceived in the internet a potentially global forum of open democratic debate. However, while the growth of the 'blogosphere' has been impressive, and has given millions a platform, it is difficult to see how it could be transformed into a genuine global democracy in which each adult human being counted equally.

International relations in the twenty-first century

Perhaps no specialist area within the broad discipline of politics has been more transformed by relatively recent events and trends than international relations. Four significant developments (discussed in earlier parts and sections of this book) have enormously complicated its study: the end of the cold war, intensifying **globalization**, the increased salience of identity politics, and the growth of international **terrorism**, apparently reflecting new or rediscovered divisions between peoples.

> *Perhaps no specialist area within the broad discipline of politics has been more transformed by recent events and trends than international relations.*

The sudden and largely unpredicted end of the cold war following the implosion of the Soviet empire from 1989 transformed the long familiar landmarks of international relations, for several decades viewed in terms of a contest between two superpowers, two rival political **ideologies** and competing economic systems. Beyond this all-consuming conflict, nothing else appeared to matter very much. International relations involved concerns about deterrence, mutually assured destruction, the balance of **power**, and from a western perspective, the defence of the 'free world' of **liberalism**, **capitalism** and **democracy** from a perceived threat from the 'second world' of **communism**. The collapse of communism apparently left liberal democracy unchallenged and supreme. The USA remained the only surviving superpower from the old duopoly. Optimists looked forward to a 'peace dividend' from the 'new world order'. Yet it soon became apparent that other conflicts were emerging, or re-emerging, in place of the cold war.

Globalization (see preceding section) in many respects appeared to parallel and reinforce the end of the cold war. Liberal capitalism was triumphant. There was no longer appeared a credible alternative. Most former communist states eagerly embraced capitalism, the **free market** and prospects for greater material prosperity. The same global brands, such as McDonald's, which were already omnipresent in the west, found an enthusiastic welcome in new markets in the east. Aspects of western **culture** were widely imitated, although globalization should not simply be equated with westernization (Scholte, 2005: 58–9). Countries the world over appeared to be losing distinctive features and becoming more similar in interests and aspirations. In a more homogeneous world it might appear that old enmities would fade and there would be less to fight over between peoples who increasingly resembled each other. Indeed Scholte (2005: 198–9) observes 'perhaps it is no accident that states with McDonald's outlets in their jurisdictions have only once gone to war against each other' (the sole exception was the war over Kosovo). This is an interesting variation on the often-made point that democracies do not fight each other.

However, the point should not be exaggerated. One impact of global capital and global markets was to increase inequality between nations and peoples, and intensify the division between the haves and the have-nots (O'Brien and Williams, 2004: ch. 7). Moreover, while globalization appeared to reduce some of the differences between peoples, the growth of identity politics (see pages 243–8) had the reverse effect. Indeed the two apparently contradictory trends were perhaps not unconnected. The embrace of specific national, cultural or religious identities may be seen in part as a reaction against 'McWorld' and global capitalism. The growth of new forms of **nationalism**, including both 'micronationalist' movements and broader trans-state regional nationalism (such as Pan-African and Pan-Arab movement) is perhaps one manifestation of this. Also, another feature of globalization – increased migration – created many more minorities with a sense of rootlessness, often intensified by discrimination and prejudice, seeking something to cling to amid alien surroundings. Such minorities, unable or unwilling to assimilate in the host country, can come to feel they have more in common with those elsewhere who share their religion or culture. Thus some of the identities embraced are not territorial. The growth or revival of various forms of religious fundamentalism is one manifestation of this trend (Scholte, 2005: ch. 7; Brown, 2005: ch. 10).

The phenomenon of global terrorism is clearly fuelled by extreme forms of identity politics, particularly associated with religious fundamentalism. Yet most known terrorists seem to be products of globalization as well as reacting against it. They are not victims of increased global inequality, at least in material terms. Indeed, they are generally well educated and relatively prosperous. They have embraced western technology, to deadly effect, and some of them have for a time appeared to embrace western culture, only ultimately to reject it (Brown, 2005: 240–52).

> Most known terrorists seem to be products of globalization as well as reacting against it.

All this has transformed and complicated international relations. Security can no longer be sought by maintaining the 'balance of power', a consideration that has become almost irrelevant. Instead the preoccupation has been with potential trouble spots – rogue states which may harbour terrorists, or seek to acquire nuclear weapons; failed states, whose problems may lead to humanitarian disasters, and perhaps destabilize whole regions. The new threats to world peace appear shifting and diffuse. The old division between **realists** and **liberal idealists** in international relations has been largely superseded by more complex debates within and between neorealists, **neoliberals**, constructivists and others over national interest, international law, humanitarian intervention, and the conditions for a just war. In terms of specific foreign policies, there are some strange alliances between those working from contrary assumptions. Thus the Iraq war was both supported and opposed by neoliberals and neorealists.

Where does this leave the study of international relations today? What does seem to be clear is that ideas, cultures and identities matter far more in international relations, as the constructivists have been arguing (Reuss-Smit in Burchill et al, 2005), and the notion of enduring objective national interests appears more problematic. States may still pursue their interests defined in terms of power, as Morgenthau [1948] argued, but states change, interests change, and power takes different forms. Thus economic power may be more significant in the current climate than military power. Alliances and associations are shifting. International and transnational organizations and world opinion have become more important actors. International relations remains in a state of flux, which increases its interest and importance.

research

introduction to part VI:
what next?

Graduation involves an end and a beginning. It marks the end of your undergraduate degree studies and the beginning of the next phase of your life. This part of the book focuses on planning for your future after graduation, and the opportunities open to you. It explores the career prospects of politics graduates. These may be wider than you imagine. Your time at university should lead not just to a good degree, but, all being well, a fulfilled life and work after graduation.

Some of the knowledge you have acquired on the core politics programme and on subsidiary subjects and special options may have relevance for a variety of occupations. Many of the skills that you have developed are transferable to the world of work. For some students part-time jobs, formal work placements or political internships may have given you valuable practical experience, while a period of studying abroad may have widened your horizons, and made you more confident and independent. Even some of your leisure pursuits may add value to your academic qualifications. Practical guidance is given on how to make the most of yourself and your knowledge and skills, how to choose an appropriate career and how to apply for advertised posts.

Some students after graduation will consider further study to improve their qualifications still more. Whatever you decide, graduation will almost certainly not mark the end of studying. Increasingly, few jobs are for life, and most graduates can expect to have to retrain or update their qualifications to maintain and enhance their employability. Advice is given on some of the options you may face.

Yet ultimately a university education is not simply about equipping you for work but helping you to make the most of your life. A degree in politics should ensure you retain an enduring interest and involvement in public life and the community that will sustain you through the years.

next

Planning for the future

Some students have their whole future mapped out in their own mind, but most do not. They have little idea what they are going to do with the rest of their lives after graduating. To anyone just beginning a degree course, three or four years ahead seems an impossibly long time. Horizons are short term. Just getting through the course from one week to the next is the immediate concern. Even thinking as far into the future as to consider options for next year requires an effort of will. Some do not want to contemplate the necessary but unwelcome business of earning a living, even if (or perhaps especially because) they have already had to undertake to take poorly paid part-time work to make ends meet.

Yet a degree course does not last forever. Students who have just graduated invariably comment that it has all gone so quickly. The final year in particular seems to race by. In that final year, many students are so busy trying to do themselves justice in exams and other assessments that they can find little time to consider what they are going to do when the course is over. They dodge meetings with careers advisers, and ignore increasingly desperate enquiries from parents, who begin to fear their offspring are never going to 'settle down' and become financially self-supporting. They make only perfunctory attempts to apply for jobs or investigate further study. As a result they are not 'fixed up' when they have completed their course. Some drift into further part-time work after graduating, still having no clear ideas what they intend to do in the longer term.

> *If you do not plan, you risk closing down your options, and finding that choices are effectively made for you.*

However, it does make sense to think seriously about your future. Decisions you take or fail to take now may affect the rest of your life. If you do not plan, you risk closing down your options, and finding that choices are effectively made for you. Sometimes, when people come to look back on their careers close to retirement, they often regret lost opportunities. They think they might have done better for themselves, perhaps taken a different career path entirely. It is better to try to take control of your own life and decide what you want to do with it. No one else can or should take these decisions for you.

What can you do with a politics degree?

Probably, much more than you think. It is of course true that a politics course is not narrowly vocational. Like most other university degree courses, it is not geared towards a specific profession or area of work. Very few politics graduates can expect to pursue successful careers in politics, narrowly understood (although some have certainly done so). Yet that gives you far more choice. A politics degree can lead to wide variety of careers, unlike a narrowly vocational degree, geared to a specialized field, such as accounting, quantity surveying or information technology. Politics graduates in practice pursue a wide variety of careers, for example in government, the civil service and the public sector generally, in political research and lobbying, in business and industry, in law and accounting, in the media, including broadcasting, journalism and publishing, in information technology, and in education.

> *A politics degree can lead to wide variety of careers, unlike a narrowly vocational degree.*

Some of these career choices may be what you already expect, although others may surprise you. They may seem to involve a level of specialist knowledge and skills that you neither have nor anticipate acquiring on a university politics course. Surely, to pursue a career in accounting, law or information technology you need an appropriate degree in these areas? Yet in practice many of those who have enjoyed very successful careers in these areas have graduated in other subjects. Some of the knowledge and skills acquired on a politics degree may useful in these professions. However, politics graduates may pick up relevant expertise and professional qualifications subsequently, often while they are at work. (See below, on professional courses.)

You should be able to check what kind of work graduates on your own course have taken. This may give you some idea of what you might be able to do yourself. However, 'first destination' statistics, generally kept by universities, are not a wholly reliable guide to the final careers of many graduates. This is because some graduates initially take temporary jobs before they make up their mind on what they really want to do. If your university keeps good records of the longer-term progress of its 'alumni' this may provide a better indicator of what others have done, and you might be able to do.

Making the most of your knowledge and skills

Most degree courses that students take at university are like politics; they are broadly rather than narrowly vocational. They do not equip graduates to a do a specific job, but they do develop skills that are generic rather than specific, which means they are easily transferable to a wide range of different occupations. Today a politics degree involves the conscious and deliberate development of a variety of key skills. A politics graduate will have acquired skills in researching and assessing all kinds of information, analysing evidence and arguments, communicating effectively, both orally and in written reports and reviews, and using and applying information technology. Many politics graduates will have also acquired some statistical skills beyond simply interpreting statistics and applying statistical information. Many will have acquired skills of working with others on group projects. Some will additionally have undertaken a major piece of independent study, in the form of a dissertation or long essay. (These and other skills have already been discussed in some detail in Part I, Section 3 of this book.)

A politics graduate will have acquired skills in researching and assessing all kinds of information, analysing evidence and arguments, communicating effectively, both orally and in written reports and in using and applying information technology.

These skills are neither trivial nor only of use for academic studies. On the contrary, they are skills that are transferable to other environments, and vitally important in many careers and professions. Demonstrating that you have them when you apply for a post may sometimes be more of a problem. Sometimes you may be given aptitude tests to assess your suitability for a particular career. In those many careers where skills in oral communication are particularly important, you may be asked to give an oral presentation, which should be easy enough for those who already have extensive experience of this on their degree course. Some interviews are less organized and systematic, and you may have to 'sell yourself' more positively to make an impression. Here, it may help if you can talk confidently about the kind of work you have done on your degree course. If you have completed work on your degree programme that you and your tutors were particularly pleased with, you may want to consider taking a sample of your work (such as a dissertation, or final-year assignment) to a job interview.

The knowledge you have acquired on a politics degree may be particularly helpful in some occupations, particularly for any work in the public sector, or in those parts of the private and voluntary sectors that have extensive dealings with government in some shape or form. By the end of your course you should know quite a bit about the organization of government and decision-making processes, about pressure groups, the media, public law and the legislative process, about public finance and budgeting, both in your own country and more generally. You may have picked up more specialist knowledge of other governmental systems, of transnational government (such as the European Union), and of non-governmental organizations. You may have made a special study of international relations or global political economy. If you have studied abroad for a period, or taken a placement or internship, this will have broadened your experience and demonstrated your initiative, commitment and capacity to work in a different environment. Of course, if you have taken a joint honours programme, some of the knowledge and techniques you have picked up from other disciplines may also be relevant. How far any of this knowledge may have a practical application will depend on your ultimate career, but some of it could turn out to be very useful in specific professions. Indeed, if it has been formally assessed, it may earn you exemptions from some of the examinations of professional bodies.

Choosing a career

The career you choose after graduating may be the career you follow for the rest of your working life, so it is important to get it right. Of course an initial choice of career is not necessarily final. It is possible to change your career later, to move from one profession or area of work to another, and do something else. Indeed such a change may be forced by circumstances beyond your control, such as reduced demand and prospects over time for some specialist fields of employment. Increasingly, we are told there is no such thing as a job for life. Some who have built up skills and experience over many years may find that they have no choice but to start again, and retrain. Others may simply feel dissatisfied and unfulfilled by their initial career choice, and feel impelled to try something else. It may all prove worth it in the end, but a change of career is not something to be embarked upon lightly. It often involves starting again from the bottom, and almost inevitably, an immediate financial sacrifice. So, if possible, it is better to get it right first time.

It is perhaps best to leave more detailed advice on choosing a career to specialist careers advisers, although one or two general points can be made. One of the problems is that we tend to be influenced initially, perhaps too much, by the role models we have among our immediate family, friends or teachers. It is natural enough to want to stick with what is familiar. Without some knowledge or experience, it is very difficult to imagine what an unfamiliar career would be like as, for example, a lawyer, a journalist or a business manager. Some politics degree courses offer short work placements, and these may give some taste of what some careers are really like. You may get a chance to do part-time or vacation work in an area of employment you are considering, and find out more about it. Your extracurricular activities at university can also be helpful. Thus those who think they might fancy a career in journalism should try their hand at student journalism, to test whether they have any real interest or aptitude for it as a profession. (Indeed, if you apply for a job in journalism, experience on a student newspapers could be a definite plus, and if you did not try it, potential employers may reasonably ask you why.) Yet if you have no useful role models or work experience to guide your

If you have not already firmly made up your mind what you want to do, keep an open mind, and be prepared to do some research.

search for a suitable occupation, it is difficult. There may be something out there for which you are ideally suited, but which you now know little or nothing about.

If you have not already firmly made up your mind what you want to do, keep an open mind, and be prepared to do some research. Attend sessions with university careers advisers, and go to careers fairs, where you can seek information and advice without obligation. Make sure you understand what a specific career involves in terms of basic qualifications, opportunities to train on the job, working conditions and prospects before you make any serious applications.

The only career for which I have direct personal knowledge and experience is teaching. That is certainly one among many potential career choices for politics graduates. For a university career teaching politics you will need to undertake research for a higher degree, normally a Ph.D., and it may take some years to secure a permanent post, or 'tenure'. If you become particularly involved with studying and researching politics, university lecturing is the obvious way to combine your own academic interests with earning a living, although you will probably already know that you are most unlikely to make your fortune teaching at any level.

In some countries, such as the United Kingdom, there is a demand for specialist politics teachers in schools and colleges of further education. A higher degree may be useful to boost your CV but is not essential. On the other hand you will almost certainly need a specialist teaching qualification, and this will also be the case for those politics graduates who decide they want to teach a broader range of subjects to younger pupils. Broadly speaking, the higher the level of education you plan to teach at, the more important are your subject qualifications, and your teaching ability is rather less significant (although still important). The reverse is the case for those teaching younger and sometimes less able pupils at school. Here it is your teaching skills that are crucial rather than your expertise in particular subjects.

You are probably aware of the old cruel saying, 'Those who can, do. Those who can't, teach.' There is an element of truth in it. Some students drift into teaching without any real sense of vocation because they cannot think of anything else they want to do, and it is, after all, something they know about. I have come across a few university lecturers who neither like teaching nor have any particularly aptitude for it, but do it simply because it finances their research and writing. Others, more positively, have been inspired by their own teachers, and are keen to pass on their own enthusiasm for the subject to others. Would I recommend it? It can be a frustrating business. You can get a real buzz from it some days with a lively group of students, while at other times it seems like pulling teeth to obtain any response. I have no complaints. Yet most work is like that. If you choose teaching, rather than another career, do it for positive rather than negative reasons.

Applying for posts

Writing job applications and compiling CVs is inevitably time-consuming. There is no point in providing detailed advice here, as plenty should be available from your own institution, including examples of good practice. Seek advice, take time and trouble, and get someone to read your application to check it. Word processing packages make it much easier to produce professional-looking letters and CVs, and computer spell-check facilities help to avoid some of the grosser errors that might lead to your immediate rejection. Many employers have old-fashioned ideas about spelling, grammar and punctuation.

Make the most of yourself, but avoid exaggeration, and do not on any account invent experience or qualifications that you do not have.

One personnel manager, describing how he sifted applications, told me he immediately binned any with spelling mistakes. Make the most of yourself, but avoid exaggeration, and do not on any account invent experience or qualifications that you do not have. Others may do it, but do not imitate them. It is not worth it. It can be at least extremely embarrassing when you are found out, and could lead to more damaging consequences.

For interviews, again there is plenty of advice available, often illustrated by appropriate video clips. Prepare for the interview by rehearsing answers to the kind of questions you might expect. Think of questions that you can ask the interviewers yourself. Dress smartly, attend promptly, behave courteously. Try to look keen and interested. Do not be too distressed if you are given a hard time. Friendly interviews do not always promise success. A hard grilling may surprisingly be the preface to a job offer. Do not despair if things go badly. Sometimes they do, often for reasons outside your control. You will get better at it as you go along, although if you already plenty of experience of oral presentation you should have learned much about presenting yourself and communicating confidently.

If you are made an offer and you are not sure that you want to accept it, ask if you can have time to think about it. This may not be what the interviewers want to hear, but it is better than accepting, and later taking back your word, or worse, starting a job and pulling out in few weeks.

Further study

One option you may consider is further study. You may decide not to go straight into full-time employment immediately after graduating, but take another course, perhaps a higher degree, either at the same university or another institution. Some graduates may understandably feel that they have already had quite enough education to last them a lifetime, and have no inclination to prolong their studies any further. Instead, they are eager to throw themselves into a 'proper job', earning 'real money' as soon as possible. Others are quite the opposite. They have enjoyed student life so much that they never want it to end, and would sign up to any postgraduate course on offer to postpone the evil day of their entry into the 'real world' of work.

Both groups are liable to be disappointed. The 'Peter Pans' will discover they cannot remain perpetual students but have to grow up sometime and earn their keep. Their more worldly and materialist contemporaries will almost certainly find that they cannot turn their backs on education completely, as most careers involve the need for some serious further study at some stage. The notion of 'life-long learning' has become something a cliché, simply because it reflects reality. New knowledge and new skills will be necessary to adapt and survive in a fast-changing world.

There is thus not a stark 'either–or' choice between full-time employment and further study. Nearly all graduates can expect to have to do both. The only questions are, when and how? You can take another full-time course immediately after graduating. You can return to full-time study in a few years' time after a period in full-time employment. You can carry on part-time study while working, or take on a part-time course later. If you have learned to be self-motivated and self-directed you may be able to cope with what used to be called a 'correspondence course', but is now more commonly described as 'distance learning.'

next

All these options have advantages and disadvantages. 'Distance-learning' is commonly much cheaper than full-time courses, but also requires much more self-determination and persistence. One reason that some old correspondence courses were relatively cheap was because many students gave up in the early stages. The relative few who successfully persevered were effectively cross-subsidized by the more numerous drop-outs who had already paid their fees up-front. Yet as long as you appreciate the self-discipline that will be necessary, distance learning does have the advantage that you can fit your studying around work and family commitments, whenever you can find the time. Moreover, there are now some excellent courses run on a distance-learning basis, such as those developed by the UK 'Open University'. Indeed many prestigious traditional universities now offer some courses by distance learning.

Part-time courses involving college attendance require a regular commitment of time, which can be a problem, particularly if you miss a few weeks. Yet there are not only social benefits from attending classes, as tutors and fellow students help to keep each other going. Returning to full-time study later may be more rewarding but almost certainly much more expensive, both directly (in terms of course fees) and indirectly (in terms of lost earnings).

Thus if you want to extend your education and improve your qualifications there is something to be said for doing it sooner rather than later, before you will notice the substantial reduction in your living standards and before you have a family of your own whose needs must be considered. You will also be used to studying, and regularly producing work to be assessed. Those who return to study later sometimes find it difficult to cope with the demands of assessed work, and particularly examinations. Yet if you choose another full-time course immediately after graduating, do it for positive rather than negative reasons – because you really want to do a specific course, or really need a particular qualification. Do not undertake further full-time study simply to postpone a decision on what you are going to do for the rest of your life.

An 'academic' or 'professional' course?

One option is a higher degree, such as a Master's course, in politics, or a related subject. This can be a natural progression – carrying on your studies, commonly in a more specialized way at a more advanced level. There may be plenty of courses to choose between, and plenty of universities and staff only too eager to enrol you, because they need a sufficient number of students (and their fees!) if a particular course is to become and remain viable. So you may not have a problem with gaining acceptance. You may be able to opt for either 'part-time' or 'full-time' study, although at the postgraduate level the distinction between these two terms is relative, even more than at the undergraduate level, as nearly all postgraduate students will need to undertake some part-time work to maintain themselves.

Is a further qualification going to improve significantly your employability and prospects?

That is one reason you need to think carefully why you want to do it. Is a further qualification going to improve significantly your employability and prospects? In some cases the answer may be clearly, 'yes.' If for example you are keen to pursue an academic career at the university level, higher degrees are essential. Yet if you are thinking of becoming a school teacher or further education lecturer, a teaching qualification is more important than a higher degree, which may make only a marginal difference to your employability.

next

A different kind of option may be a professional course. A politics graduate may go on to practise as a lawyer or an accountant, for example, but to do this he or she will have to acquire a recognized professional qualification. This is, incidentally, often equally true for those who have degrees in law or accounting. They still have to pass their professional exams to achieve recognition as a full member of the profession. Practices vary between countries. However, many of the most successful accountants and lawyers originally studied another subject at degree level. Moreover, such professional qualifications may often be obtained while working as a trainee accountant or lawyer, sometimes on a day release or block release basis at college or university. Some students studying politics may have developed a particular expertise and interest in information technology, but need a recognized qualification if they are to proceed far in this area. Similarly, those interested in a career in the media may want to investigate postgraduate diplomas in newspaper or radio and television journalism. Do not simply assume that such qualifications will provide a passport for the career of your choice. Investigate very carefully the costs and benefits before you commit yourself. Seek hard information on the subsequent employment of those who have undertaken such courses.

In many professions there are further qualifications that may be useful or essential in progressing your career, but these similarly can often be obtained while you work or on a period of secondment from work, or part-time by studying in evenings or at weekends. These days it is highly unlikely that any skills acquired on a university degree will equip you for a lifetime at work. The new mantra is 'life-long learning'. You will need to acquire new skills and maintain, refresh and develop old skills over the course of a working life. Yet the generic skills you have developed on your politics degree should stand you in good stead for a lifetime.

A lifetime's interest and involvement in politics

This part of the book has necessarily concentrated on the important business of earning a living. Yet it is to be earnestly hoped that gainful employment is far from all you will have gained from undertaking a university course in politics. It should be an interest that you will carry with you for the rest of your life. Moreover, even if you do not pursue a political career full time, you will inevitably be involved to some degree in politics, beyond simply casting a vote periodically. The knowledge and understanding of politics you have picked up at university may prove unexpectedly valuable at various stages of your life.

> It is to be earnestly hoped that gainful employment is far from all you will have gained from undertaking a university course in politics.

You may become involved in a particular interest or cause, and in the practical business of pressure group politics. You may be aroused by a specific decision, such as new airport runway, or road, perhaps a hospital or school closure, and find yourself organizing opposition and demonstrations. Unforeseeable developments in your own life or that of your immediate family may impel you to seek a remedy for an injustice or advance a specific cause. You may become an active member of a political party, canvassing for support, and seeking to influence its policies and strategy. You may even seek election yourself. You make seek to influence the wider political debate by articulating your views in the media. Now, it is certainly true that you can do all this without studying politics at university, and so it should be, if democracy has any meaning. You should not need a degree to participate in politics. Yet your knowledge and understanding should help you to participate more effectively, and with more satisfaction.

However much or little you participate directly in politics yourself, politics in all its variety remains a subject that is not only intrinsically important but full of absorbing and never-ending interest. It will be surprising if you do not retain a keen concern in the subject, not only closely following political news around the world, but reading serious political analysis, perhaps even returning to its academic study at some later date. It is an interest you should be able to continue well into retirement after your full-time work is finished.

introduction to part VII:
resources for studying politics

The first section describes and explains some of the many academic and other resources available for politics students. It looks first at the vast range of relevant books and printed sources available through libraries, and explains how to access a range of catalogues to find the books and other sources that you need. It goes on to look at academic journals, and how to search for relevant articles. It reviews newspapers and periodicals dealing with politics and current affairs, and how to access relevant items through the internet. It discusses how to make the most of politics material on television and radio, and access recorded sources. It looks at the vast resources now available from the internet, including not only sites that can be accessed free by all users, but additional resources available through your own university library or learning centre. The section concludes with some information on politics associations and other relevant organizations around the world.

The second section provides guidance to further reading for each of the parts of this book, from Part I to Part V. (There is no additional reading recommended for Part VI.) These sources are cited using Harvard referencing, as elsewhere. Full references for all the sources cited in this section, and also for all those cited in the rest of the book, are to be found in the third section. This lists references, in alphabetical order by authors, of all books and journal articles cited. Where several references are given to various works by the same author, these are listed in order of year of publication. Multiple authored books and articles are listed alphabetically by the first named author.

Section 1: Resources for politics students

Books and catalogues

It is often difficult for politics students to access all the books they need for their course. Very few university libraries can hope to provide anything like a comprehensive collection of politics books on their shelves. Their budgets are limited, and their shelf space is limited. Many older books are out of print and it is difficult for relatively new institutions to obtain copies. Moreover they will only provide multiple copies of the more popular recommended texts (some of which you may be expected to purchase). Some important sources of information – encyclopaedias, specialist dictionaries, year books, statistical sources – may be available in the reference section. Other books recommended by tutors may be available in special short-term loan collections, to enable as many students as possible to access them. If you cannot find the books you need from these sources, what should you do?

> It is often difficult for politics students to access all the books they need for their course.

You should first access your own university catalogue online. This should provide full details of all the titles the library holds, the number of copies of each book, and where to find them. If a book is in the catalogue and not on the shelves but out on loan, you can reserve it, and pick it up later, although this is not much use if you need it urgently (one reason for checking on book availability well in advance wherever possible!). If the library does not have a copy it is possible to obtain copies on inter-library loan, although this also will take time. You can access the catalogues of many other libraries, including the Library of Congress and the British Library, free online, to discover what is available.

The full text of some older classics, particularly major works of political theory, can be accessed free online (e.g. from the Liberty Library of Government Classics at www.constitution.org/liberlib.htm) although this is not an easy way to read whole books, and it is expensive and time-consuming to download and print large numbers of pages. A number of official sources, including government reports and papers and collections of government statistics, are also available online.

You should consider purchasing some books that you need on a regular basis, and indeed you may be strongly advised by tutors to purchase certain texts. Sometimes you may be able to save money by purchasing them second hand, but be careful, because sometimes it is important to have the latest edition. The date of publication may be unimportant for classic politics texts that are regularly reprinted, although if it is a translated version of a foreign language source, you may be advised to obtain a particular translation. Browsing in bookshops can give you a good idea of recent and current politics titles being pushed by publishers, and you can obtain details of their catalogues in printed form or online. Very recent books, perhaps not yet catalogued and available at your university library, may be perused in bookshops.

Academic journals

For undergraduates studying politics there are a few journals that are designed to meet their needs (for example *Politics Review, Talking Politics*) containing generally fairly short articles on issues of current controversy, often written by experts, but in accessible language suitable for students. There are also large and still escalating numbers of academic politics journals, written by scholars, largely for scholars. These are what called 'refereed journals'. In other words, articles are only accepted for publication after a process of anonymous review by suitably qualified scholars, which often involves outright rejection and commonly involves changes to satisfy the requirements of reviewers and editors. It can be a long process before a revised article is finally accepted for publication.

> Politics undergraduates may increasingly find some academic journal articles on their reading lists, particularly in the later stages of their course.

Some refereed journals are very specialist, with limited readership; others are much broader in coverage. A few long-established journals are extremely prestigious. For many of those pursuing an academic career in researching and teaching politics, publication in such refereed journals is often more important than writing books. Specialists will need to read relevant journals to keep abreast of their chosen field.

Politics undergraduates may increasingly find some academic journal articles on their reading lists, particularly in the later stages of their course. Some of these may have become recognized as classics of the literature, regularly and routinely cited in later book and journal sources. Others may be new path-breaking studies that your tutors feel you should consult to keep abreast of the latest developments in theory and research. You will normally be given a precise reference and perhaps advice on how to access the item.

It is not normally useful to browse journals in the same way as you may browse books on the library shelves or in bookshops. Indeed, many journals may no longer found bound in volumes on the library shelves, although some of the older, more prestigious, journals may still be obtainable in this form. Considerations of costs and (particularly) space have led many libraries to restrict the back numbers of journals displayed in bound paper copies. However, many of these can be accessed online through your university catalogue if your university is a subscriber to the journal. If you only need a few pages, if necessary these can be downloaded and printed for studying at your leisure.

It is normally only on dissertations or extended essays that might require a literature search where undergraduates may need to trawl through journals as part of a literature search. (Graduate students will often need to do this on a more regular basis.) Here the problem is knowing what to look for. The solution is to access relevant electronic databases of the literature and search for all articles on the topic required. You will be able to obtain lists of journal titles and abstracts of their content. If your library is a subscriber to the journal you will be able to access the full text electronically if it is not available on the shelves. If your library is not a subscriber it may be part of a scheme to allow it to order items from other libraries on request. Your university librarians will normally be only too happy to advise on their facilities and how to use them, as many of these facilities are both expensive and under-used by students. (There are often clearly written pamphlets available giving practical advice on literature searches.)

Newspapers and magazines

Newspapers and magazines are a valuable source of information on current political developments. Often it is possible for students to purchase copies of quality newspapers and magazines dealing with politics and current affairs (such as *Time Magazine, Newsweek, The Economist, Spectator, New Statesman*) at a much reduced price. This is well worth considering. Indeed, you may want to cut out and keep relevant news items and articles, or print items from their accompanying websites (see below). Quality newspapers and magazines are a source not just of political news but of analysis and comment, and often feature articles by practising politicians, experienced political journalists and commentators, and sometimes leading academics. Indeed they may on occasion publish (commonly edited) versions of articles originally published in academic journals.

You may want to cut out and keep relevant news items and articles, or print items from their accompanying websites.

Of course, newspapers and magazines are not politically impartial and may be flagrantly partisan in their coverage, but politics students should be aware of bias and take account of it (see Part I, Section 3). Indeed, particularly for those studying aspects of political communication, it is useful to monitor how newspapers treat politics, what they include and exclude, and the interpretation they give to news stories. Those researching political communication will often focus on popular mass-circulation newspapers rather than the so-called 'quality' press, because the bias is more flagrant in the selection of political news and portrayal of political developments, and because they normally have more readers and potentially more extensive political influence.

It has to be admitted that even many quality newspapers have reduced their serious political coverage. Critics call this 'dumbing down'. Yet, by compensation, newspapers and magazines also now have accompanying websites where items from past issues can be accessed, and also additional material that has not been carried in the printed newspaper or magazine. These websites provide a (generally user-friendly) important source of information on recent and current political developments, invaluable for students.

Television, radio, video and other sources

Television and radio also have long provided extensive coverage of politics, although here again, as with the press, there are accusations of 'dumbing down'. Yet, as with the press, there remains much of value in news, discussion programmes and documentaries on radio and television. One problem used to be the fleeting impermanent nature of much of the output. This is perhaps less of a problem than it was, because of the increased availability of a wide range of recorded material. University libraries and learning centres may monitor and keep recordings for a limited period, and you may be able to access these. Also they may keep a range of programmes recorded on video or DVD. Some universities keep good collections of teaching material in this format. Some older feature films or documentaries with particular relevance to politics may also be available.

Needless to say, none of this material should be accepted uncritically. Because of greater legal and other restrictions on the broadcast media, often involving some obligation to political balance, particularly for (now generally declining) public service broadcasting, the political bias of television and radio is often less blatantly partisan. Thus the broadcast media in most democracies do not overtly favour one party or one set of politicians over others. However, critics detect other forms of bias in coverage, such as class bias, gender bias, ethnic bias, or a general 'establishment' bias. Indeed, this has become an important area of research for those with a special interest in political communication. It is also useful for students to be aware of the particular characteristics of media channels and their influence on the political output. So, for example, television is primarily a visual medium, and the main messages it conveys are through pictures.

For comparative politics it is worth noting also that through your university library you may be able to access television programmes (via satellite) from other countries, although this will require language skills for countries outside the English-speaking world.

The internet

Most modern students have grown up with the internet, and use it extensively. They are well aware of the wide range of websites relevant for the study of politics, and know how to access them, or search for what is available, for example via Google. For this reason it is hardly necessary to attempt to provide a list of all the websites that might be useful for studying politics. In any case, websites frequently change, and any list soon becomes dated. So the information and advice provided here is illustrative.

All websites have been established for a purpose, and you need to take that purpose into account when you visit them.

It is however important to reiterate the points made about political bias (above) in relation to other media. Many students take too much on trust. All websites have been established for a purpose, and you need to take that purpose into account when you access them. This is perhaps obvious when you access the website of a particular political party or campaigning group. You do not expect balanced coverage. But this is true to a greater or lesser degree for all organizations, including government departments, trade unions, international bodies, churches, charities and voluntary bodies. They all seek to accentuate the positive, and emphasize their successes. They have a message to put across. For any critical analysis of their work you will need to go elsewhere.

Yet the internet remains a fantastic resource, invaluable for politics students as long as it is used sensitively and critically. An illustrative list of sites is given below, although be warned that internet addresses can change.

Useful international sites

United Nations (www.un.org)
European Union (www.europa.eu) portal for links with all EU organizations
World Bank (www.worldbank.org)
NATO (www.nato.int)

US government and politics

Portal for US government (www.usa.gov)
White House (www.whitehouse.gov)
Senate (www.senate.gov)
House of Representatives (www.house.gov)
Congress Library (www.thomas.loc.gov)
Supreme Court (www.supremecourtus.gov)

UK government and politics

Portal for UK government and politics (www.direct.gov.uk)
Number 10 Downing Street (www.number10.gov.uk)
Cabinet (www.cabinetoffice.gov.uk)
Parliament (www.parliament.uk)
Electoral Commission (www.electoralcommission.gov.uk)

Main portals for the governments of selected other countries

Government of Australia (www.australia.gov.au)
Government of Canada (www.canada.gc.ca)
Government of India (www.india.gov.in)
Government of New Zealand (www.newzealand.govt.nz)
Government of South Africa (www.gov.za)

Politics associations and other relevant organizations

The main international body is the International Political Science Association (www.ipsa. ca) although of more use for students is the International Association for Political Science Students (IAPSS) (www.iapss.ca). There is also the International Studies Association, which publishes *International Studies Quarterly*. There are numerous national and regional organizations concerned with politics and political science, some of which are outlined below.

The British Isles

The Political Studies Association of the United Kingdom (PSA) (www.psa.ac.uk) mainly serves the needs of university politics lecturers and graduate students, although its website contains a wide range of useful links to other politics associations, university politics departments around the world, and a mass of other useful politics resources. It publishes several journals: *Political Studies, Political Studies Review* (devoted to reviews of recent politics books), *Politics* (a short-article journal which can be of more use to students than *Political Studies*), and the *British Journal of Politics and International Relations*.

There is also the British International Studies Association (BISA) (www.bisa.ac.uk), and for Public administration the Public Administration Consortium (www.ukpac.org). Particularly useful for undergraduates and those studying politics in schools is the Politics Association (UK) (www.politicsassociation.com), which publishes the journal *Talking Politics* and organizes conferences for students.

For the Irish Republic there is the Political Studies Association of Ireland (www.psai.ie).

The Americas

The leading body is the American Political Science Association (www.apsa.nct.org), which claims 15,000 members in 80 countries, and publishes *Political Science and Politics*. Canada has the Canadian Political Science Association (www.cpsa-acsp.ca) founded in 1913, which covers 50 departments of political science across Canada, and publishes the *Canadian Journal of Political Science*.

Elsewhere

Other organizations include:
Australasian Political Studies Association (www.auspsa.org)
French Political Science Association (www.afsp.msh-paris.fr)
Nordic Political Science Association (www.nopsa.org)
South African Association of Political Studies (www.saaps.org.za)

Section 2: Guidance on further reading

Suggestions are made here for further reading in association with Parts I to V of this book. (There is no additional reading recommended for Part VI.) As elsewhere, books and articles are cited using Harvard referencing. Note that the full references to all the books mentioned are in the bibliography (pages 288–300).

Further reading for Part I

For Part I, Section 1, most standard politics textbooks provide an introduction to the question, 'What is politics really about?' Particularly useful is the discussion provided in the first chapter of Andrew Heywood's *Politics* (3rd edition, 2007). The same question is addressed more extensively by a range of authors in a good collection of essays edited by Adrian Leftwich (2004). You may also want to consult the widely recommended and provocative book by Bernard Crick, *In Defence of Politics* ([1962] 2000) as well as the same author's contribution to Leftwich (2004) above. A more recent introduction to the literature is Gerry Stoker's stimulating and thoughtful *Why Politics Matters* (2006). You could look at some older classic texts, such as **Lasswell's** *Politics: Who gets what, when, how?* (1935). You may also want to consult entries on 'politics' in ordinary dictionaries and encyclopaedias, but more usefully in specialist politics dictionaries, such as McLean and McMillan (2003) and Scruton (2007).

On Part I, Section 2, 'What to expect from your politics course', there are handbooks that can be consulted, but it is probably quicker and easier to access current information on university politics departments and their courses on the internet. The Political Studies Association of the Unite Kingdom (www.psa.ac.uk) has an excellent website with links to university departments and courses around the world.

On Part I, Section 3, on study skills, if you are already enrolled for a politics course, check first what your own institution has to offer. Many universities now offer their own practical advice on the issues raised in this section, and some provide classes that you can attend. As you will be assessed substantially by your own university, it is only common sense to follow its guidance. You should pay particular attention to regulations on the submission of work, and any detailed recommendations on referencing, as well as guidance on the vexed topic of plagiarism.

One widely recommended book on the study skills required for a politics degree is Patrick Dunleavy's *Studying for a Degree in the Humanities and Social Sciences* (1986). The title accurately describes the breadth of the content, although the author is a distinguished British political scientist, and his own direct experience relates mainly to studying and teaching politics. It is certainly useful. However, as the publication date may suggest, on some topics it needs updating. Cottrell (2003) is more up to date (but even broader in

resources

scope). It is particularly good on some topics (such as plagiarism). The overall design is a matter of taste. Some may find the approach engaging and accessible, others perhaps a little patronizing.

Further reading for Part II

It is difficult to recommend books covering the whole time span of Section 1 on 'The evolution of the study of politics'. There are broad histories of political theory, but most of these are rather daunting in their depth and scope. Heywood (2004) and Morrow (2005) provide a thematic approach, Boucher and Kelly (2003) have edited a book on political thinkers, while Rosen and Wolff (1999) have provided a handy book of readings, arranged by topic. On particular periods there is Sinclair (1967) on the Greeks, Leff (1958) on medieval political thought and Hampsher-Monk (1992) on modern political thought. On the broader historical background I have found Robin Lane Fox (2006) very readable on Greece and Rome, and Maurice Keen (1969) good on medieval Europe.

On Section 2, I have found no satisfactory introduction to the development of the whole modern discipline of political science suitable for new students. Very useful, but difficult for beginners, is Colin Hay (2002) *Political Analysis: A critical introduction*. More comprehensive and much more weighty (in every sense of the word) is Goodin and Klingemann (eds) (1996) *A New Handbook of Political Science*. This contains an overview of the whole discipline with separate parts devoted to political institutions, political behaviour, comparative politics, international relations, political theory, public policy and administration, political economy and political methodology. It is as good a guide to the discipline as can be found, but difficult, and already a little dated. A British book by Bealey, Chapman and Sheehan (1999), *Elements in Political Science*, is easier but less comprehensive and authoritative. On theories and methods there is Marsh and Stoker (eds) (2002), *Theory and Methods in Political Science*, and Hay, Lister and Marsh (2006), *The State: Theories and issues*. Both books cover several of the theories and approaches discussed here.

On specific subjects, Hague and Harrop (2007) provide a good up-to-date survey of the whole field of comparative politics, while Guy Peters (1998) explores *Comparative Politics: Theory and methods*. Hindmoor (2006) can be recommended on *Rational Choice*. Brown, with Ainley (2005) provides a clearly written introduction to international relations, which can be supplemented by the essays in Burchill et al (2005). Will **Kymlicka** (1990) has written a useful and provocative guide to *Contemporary Political Philosophy*.

For particular concepts and key scholars and thinkers, see the entries in Parts III and IV and the guidance on further reading there.

Further reading for Part III

Students may wish to compare the accounts here of key political terms and concepts with those in other sources. You can look them up in an ordinary dictionary for a lay person's definition, but this may not take you very far, as many terms have a relatively specialized use in the academic study of politics, and of course their significance will not be explored. More useful are dictionaries of politics, which are sometimes multi-authored, with individual entries written by experts. One of the best is *The Concise Oxford Dictionary of Politics* (ed. McLean and McMillan, 2003) which has good coverage of both traditional political theory and modern political science. *The Blackwell Encyclopaedia of Political*

Thought (ed. David Miller et al, 1987) is very useful, although, as the title suggests, largely concerned with traditional political theory rather than political science. *The Penguin Dictionary of Politics* (Robertson, 1993) is more weighted towards modern politics, but contains many clearly written entries on contentious concepts. Hague and Harrop (2007) have a useful companion website (www.palgrave.com/politics/hague) which includes a dictionary of comparative politics with good brief definitions of relevant terms. Scruton's *A Dictionary of Political Thought* (3rd edn, 2007) is a valuable source for political theory. More specialist is *A Dictionary of Marxist Thought* (ed. Bottomore, 1991).

Andrew Heywood's excellent *Politics* (2007) has an extensive glossary with short (two to four-line) definitions of key terms, and additionally has fuller explanation and analysis of many terms in the text (use the index!). Even more useful is the same author's extremely lucid *Key Concepts in Politics* (Heywood, 2000). Concepts are fairly briefly defined and described and their significance is then explored rather more fully. (As the terms are discussed in different sections, you may to need to use the index to find a particular concept.) *Contemporary Political Concepts* (ed. Blakeley and Bryson, 2002) provides a more extended analysis of some selected concepts that have contemporary relevance.

Students today are only too familiar with the uses of the internet in searching for information. Entries posted on Wikipedia and other sites can be very helpful, but be warned, there is no quality control on the internet. Some material can be one-sided or idiosyncratic, or just plain wrong.

Further reading for Part IV

Some of the specialist politics dictionaries and other sources mentioned in the guidance on further reading for Part III on key concepts are also particularly useful for political theorists, especially Miller (1987), McLean and McMillan (2003) and Scruton (2007). In addition, there is Adams and Dyson (2003), *Fifty Major Political Thinkers*. This covers at rather greater length 44 of the thinkers on whom there are entries in Part IV. Rather more detail on some of the leading political theorists is provided in David Boucher and Paul Kelly (2003), *Political Thinkers: From Socrates to the present*. For further reading on particular thinkers follow up the suggestions here and in Miller (1987). However, while the above sources are good on political thinkers from the past and some more recent political philosophers, modern political scientists are either beyond their scope, or given very brief and selective treatment.

There is ultimately no substitute for reading the key works of leading thinkers, yet few of these can be tackled easily by those only just beginning the study of politics. **Plato's** early dialogues, particularly those included in the (1993) Penguin collection *The Last Days of Socrates* (containing *Euthyro, Apology, Crito* and *Phaedo*) are the most accessible, although sooner or later any serious student must tackle *The Republic* (many translations and editions, such as tr. Lee, 1955), preferably after reading an overview from a secondary source. **Aristotle's** *Politics* (tr. Sinclair, 1992) is also ultimately unavoidable, although (in my view at least) much less stimulating. **Machiavelli's** *The Prince* (many translations, for example that provided by Bondanella and Musa in Penguin's *The Portable Machiavelli*) is short and readable. You can also try dipping into **Rousseau's** *Social Contract*, **Paine's** key works (ed. Foot and Kramnick, 1987), **Burke's** [1790] *Reflections on the Revolution in France*, the contributions of **Madison** (especially) to *The Federalist Papers* ([1788, ed. Kramnick, 1987) and **Tocqueville** *Democracy in America* ([1835, 1840] tr. Bevan, 2003).

Relatively short and readable is John Stuart **Mill's** *On Liberty* ([1859], available in many modern editions, such as in the selection of Mill's work by Warnock (1962, Fontana). You could also try **Marx** and **Engels's** *The Communist Manifesto* ([1848], which is included in many selections of their work, such as that edited by Feuer, 1959).

Among what have come to be regarded as modern classics, **Schumpeter** (1943), **Downs** (1957), **Bell** (1960) and **Dahl** (1961), are all relatively accessible. **Rawls** (1971) effectively reinvigorated the study of political philosophy. Influential but controversial more recent texts include those by **Fukuyama** (1992), **Huntington** [1996], and **Putnam** (2000).

Further reading for Part V

Heywood (2007) and Hague and Harrop (2007) provide useful introductions to many of the topics considered in this part of the book. See also the guidance provided in their companion websites (www.palgrave.com/foundations/heywood and www.palgrave.com/politics/hague).

On public opinion, political culture and democracy, key works are those of **Almond** and Verba (1963, 1980), **Inglehart** (1971, 1977, 1990), and **Putnam** (2000, 2002). On elections and voting, Denver (2003) provides a readable survey of theories and research, applied to the United Kingdom, while Lane and Errson (1999) give useful analysis of voting in Europe. Wider comparative surveys of elections and voting are provided by Harrop and Miller (1987), and more recently by LeDuc et al. (2002). Farrell (2001) looks at electoral systems and their impact on voting.

Key works on types of political party are **Duverger** ([1954] 1970), Kirchheimer (1966), Panebianco (1988) and Katz and Mair (1995). On party systems see **Lipset** and **Rokkan** (1967), **Sartori** (1976) and Mair (1990). For a more up-to-date review, see Webb et al (2002).

On pressure groups Grant (2000) provides a good if explicitly UK focused survey. Hrebenar (1997) and Cigler and Loomis (2006) are valuable sources on interest group politics in the United States, while Mazey and Richardson (1993) look at pressure group influence on the European Union. On social movements, see Tarrow (1998). Landmark works in the literature on groups include **Bentley** ([1908] 1967), Truman (1951) and **Dahl** (1961, 1971).

On political communication, most emphasis in the literature is on the mass media; see for example Gunther and Mughan (2000), Norris (2000) and Street (2001). There is also a growing interest in the impact of the new media: see Sunstein (2001) and Chadwick (2006).

The transition from traditional public administration to the New Public Management, with its emphasis on market mechanisms, is analysed by Self (1993). See Osborne and Gaebler (1992), *Reinventing Government*, for their evangelical promotion of the new approach, involving 'steering' rather than 'rowing'. For an analysis of the impact of public choice theory, see Hindmoor (2006). For the new institutionalism, see March and Olsen (1984, 1989), and for an overview see Schmidt, in Hay et al (2006). On public policy and the policy process, Hill (1993) has edited a useful reader. For the debate over rationalism and incrementalism, see the contributions by Simon (1947), Lindblom (1959, 1979) and Etzioni (1967). For a discussion of governance see Rhodes (1997) and Pierre and Peters (2000).

On the issue of identity, until recently much of the debate was over nationalism and national identity. Key works in this literature include Gellner (1983), Anderson (1983), Greenfeld (1992) and Breuilly (1993). While pressure for further self-determination and the creation of new nation-states persists, some argue that the nation-state is obsolete (Ohmae, 1996). Others emphasize ethnic, cultural and religious identities that cut across state borders. One of the more influential and contentious analyses of the international implications of these trans-national identities was that of Huntington [1996] *The Clash of Civilizations and the Remaking of World Order.* Key contributions to the debate over multiculturalism and the rights and duties of minorities have been made by **Kymlicka** (1995), Parekh (2000) and **Barry** (2001b).

On democratization, Stoker (2006) chapter 1, 'The triumph of democracy?' provides a useful starting point. Huntington (1991) describes and analyses the uneven progress of democracy over the previous century. Chapters by Dalton and Whitehead in Goodin and Klingemann (1996) describe the early optimism of those researching the 'new democracies', following particularly the implosion of communism. Chapter 3 in Hague and Harrop (2007) sums up more recent research, and explores the distinction between 'liberal' and 'illiberal' democracies.

On the key but contentious issue of globalization see Ohmae (1990), Waters (2000) and especially Scholte (2005). Global political economy is explored by O'Brien and Williams (2004). Slaughter (2004) examines global governance. The notion of cosmopolitan democracy and world government is explored by Held (1995) and **Wendt** (2003). For the implications of globalization and other developments on international relations, see Baylis and Smith (2005) the later chapters of Brown with Ainley (2005) and Burchill et al (2005).

Section 3: References and bibliography

Adams, I. and Dyson, R. W. (2003) *Fifty Major Political Thinkers*, London, Routledge.

Adorno, T. W. et al (1950) *The Authoritarian Personality*, New York, Harper Row.

Ake, C. (1999) 'Globalization, multilateralism and the shrinking democratic space', in M. G. Schechter (ed.), *Future Multilateralism: The political and social framework*, Tokyo, United Nations University Press.

Albrow, M. (1970) *Bureaucracy*, London, Macmillan.

Almond, G. A. (1988) 'The return of the state', *American Political Science Review*, 82: 853–74.

Almond, G. A. and Verba, S. (1963) *The Civic Culture: Political attitudes and democracy in five nations*, Princeton, Princeton University Press.

Almond, G. A. and Verba, S. (eds) (1980) *The Civic Culture Revisited*, Boston, Little, Brown.

Alter, P. (1994) *Nationalism*, 2nd edn, London, Arnold.

Althusser, L. ([1965]1969) *For Marx*, London and New York, Allen Lane.

Anderson, B. (1983) *Imagined Communities: Reflections on the origins and spread of nationalism*, London, Verso.

Aquinas, T. (1948) *Aquinas: Selected Political Writings*, ed. A. P. d'Entreves, Oxford, Blackwell.

Arblaster, A. (1984) *The Rise and Fall of Western Liberalism*, Oxford, Blackwell.

Arendt, H. (1951) *The Origins of Totalitarianism*, New York, Harcourt Brace.

Arendt, H. (1963) *Eichmann in Jerusalem*, New York, Viking.

Aristotle ([c. 335–323 BC] 1992) *The Politics*, tr. Sinclair, London, Penguin.

Aristotle ([c. 335–323BC] 1953) *Ethics (The Nichomachean Ethics)*, tr. Thomson, Harmondsworth, Penguin.

Arrow, K. (1951) *Social Choice and Individual Values*, New York, Wiley.

Ashley, R. (1988) 'Untying the sovereign state: a double reading of the anarchy problematique', *Millennium*, 17(2).

Augustine ([413–425] 1972) *The City of God*, ed. Knowles, tr. Bettenson, Harmondsworth, Penguin.

Bachrach, P. and Baratz, M. S. (1962) 'Two faces of power', *American Political Science Review*, 56, 947–52.

Bachrach, P. and Baratz, M. S. (1970) *Power and Poverty: Theory and practice*, New York, Oxford University Press.

Bagehot, W. ([1867] 1963) *The English Constitution*, London, Fontana.

Barry, B. (1970) *Sociologists, Economists and Democracy*, London, Collier Macmillan.

Barry, B. (1977) 'Justice between generations', in P. Hacker and J. Raz (eds), *Law, Society and Morality: Essays in honour of H. L. A. Hart*, Oxford, Clarendon Press.

Barry, B. (1989) *Theories of Justice*, London, Harvester Wheatsheaf.

Barry, B. (1995) *Justice as Impartiality*, Oxford, Clarendon Press.

Barry, B. (2001a) *Culture and Equality: An egalitarian critique of multiculturalism*, Cambridge, Polity.

Barry, B. (2001b) 'Multicultural muddles', *New Left Review*, March/April.

Barry, B. (2005) *Why Social Justice Matters*, Cambridge, Polity.

Baylis, J. and Smith, S. (2005) *The Globalization of World Politics: An introduction to international relations*, Oxford and New York, Oxford University Press.

Bealey, F., Chapman, R. A. and Sheehan, M. (1999) *Elements in Political Science*, Edinburgh, Edinburgh University Press.

Beer, S. H. (1982) *Modern British Politics*, 2nd. edn, London, Faber and Faber.

Beetham, D. (1985) *Max Weber and the Theory of Modern Politics*, 2nd edn, Cambridge, Polity.

Beetham, D. (1987) *Bureaucracy*, Milton Keynes, Open University Press.

Bell, D. (1960) *The End of Ideology*, Glencoe, Free Press.

Bell, D. (1973) *The Coming of Post-Industrial Society*, Harmondsworth, Penguin.

Bell, J. (1993) *Doing Your Research Project*, Buckingham, Open University Press.

Bentham, J. ([1789] 1970) *An Introduction to the Principles of Morals and Legislation*, ed. J. Burns and H. Hart, London, Athlone Press.

Bentham, J. ([1776] 1977) *A Fragment on Government*, ed. J. Burns and H. Hart, London, Athlone Press.

Bentley, A. ([1908] 1967) *The Process of Government*, Chicago, Ill., University of Chicago Press.

Berlin, I. (1969) *Four Essays on Liberty*, Oxford, Oxford University Press.

Beveridge, W. H. (1942) *Social Insurance and Allied Services*, Cmnd 6404, London, HMSO.

Blakeley, G. and Bryson, V. (eds) (2002) *Contemporary Political Concepts*, London, Pluto Press.

Blumler , J. and McQuail, D. (1968) *Television in Politics: Its uses and influences*, London, Faber and Faber.

Booth, K. and Dunne, T. (eds) (2002) *Worlds in Collision: Terror and the future of global order*, Basingstoke, Palgrave Macmillan.

Bosanquet, B. ([1899]1920) *The Philosophical Theory of the State,* London, Macmillan.

Bottomore, T. (1966) *Elites and Society*, Harmondsworth, Penguin.

Bottomore, T. (ed.) (1991) *A Dictionary of Marxist Thought*, Blackwell, Oxford.

Boucher, D and Kelly, P. (2003) *Political Thinkers: From Socrates to the present*, Oxford, Oxford University Press.

Breuilly, J. (1993) *Nationalism and the State*, 2nd edn, Manchester, Manchester University Press.

Brown, C. with Ainley, K. (2005) *Understanding International Relations*, 3rd edn, Basingstoke, Palgrave Macmillan.

Brownmiller, S. (1977) *Against Our Will*, Harmondsworth, Penguin.

Bryson, V. (1992) *Feminist Political Theory: An introduction*, Basingstoke, Macmillan.

Buchanan, J. M. and Tullock, G. (1962) *The Calculus of Consent*, Ann Arbor, Mich., University of Michigan Press.

Bull, H. ([1977] 2002) *The Anarchical Society*, Basingstoke, Palgrave Macmillan.

Burchill, S., Linklater, A., Devetak, R., Donnelly, J., Paterson, M., Reuss-Smit, C. and True, J. (2005) *Theories of International Relations*, 3rd edn, Basingstoke, Palgrave Macmillan.

Burke, E. ([1790] 1975) *Burke on Government, Politics and Society* (includes *Reflections on the Revolution in France* and 'Speech to the electors of Bristol'), ed. B. W. Hill, London, Fontana/Harvester.

Butler, C. (2002) *Postmodernism: A very short introduction*, Oxford, Oxford University Press.

Butler, D. and Stokes, D (1969) *Political Change in Britain*, 2nd edn, London, Macmillan.

Byrne, P. (1997) *Social Movements in Britain*, London, Routledge.

Calvert, P. (2002) *Comparative Politics: An introduction*, Harlow, Longman.

Campbell, A., Converse, P. E., Miller, W. E. and Stokes, D. E. (1960) *The American Voter*, New York, Wiley.

Carr, E. H. ([1939] 2001) *The Twenty Years Crisis, 1919–1939*, ed. Cox, Basingstoke, Palgrave Macmillan.

Castells, M. (1977) *The Urban Question*, Cambridge, MA, MIT Press.

Chadwick, A. (2006) *Internet Politics: States, citizens and new communication technologies*, Oxford and New York, Oxford University Press.

Cigler, C. and Loomis, B. (eds) (2006) *Interest Group Politics*, Washington, Congressional Quarterly Press.

Cole, A. (1998) *French Politics and Society*, Hemel Hempstead, Prentice Hall.

Cottrell, S. (2003) *The Study Skills Handbook*, Basingstoke, Palgrave Macmillan.

Crenson, M. A. (1971) *The Unpolitics of Air Pollution*, Baltimore, Johns Hopkins Press.

Crick, B. ([1962] 2000) *In Defence of Politics*, 5th edn, London, Continuum.

Crosland, C. A. R. (1956) *The Future of Socialism*, London, Jonathan Cape.

Crozier, M. (1964) *The Bureaucratic Phenomenon*, London, Tavistock Press.

Curran, J. and Gurevitch, M. (1996) *Mass Media and Society*, 2nd edn, London, Arnold.

Dahl, R. A. (1956) *A Preface to Democratic Theory*, Chicago, Chicago University Press.

Dahl, R. A. (1957) 'The concept of power', *Behavioral Science*, 2 (July), 201–50.

Dahl, R. A. (1958) 'A critique of the ruling elite model', *American Political Science Review*, 52.

Dahl, R. A. (1961) *Who Governs? Democracy and power in an American City*, New Haven, Yale University Press.

Dahl, R. A. (1971) *Polyarchy: Participation and opposition*, New Haven, Yale University Press.

Dahl, R. A. (1989) *Democracy and its Critics*, New Haven, Yale University Press.

Dahl, R. A. and Lindblom, C. (1953) *Politics, Economics and Welfare*, New York, Harper and Row.

Dahrendorf, R. (1990) *Reflections on the Revolution in Europe*, London, Chatto and Windus.

De Beauvoir, S ([1949] 1972) *The Second Sex*, Harmondsworth, Penguin.

Dearlove, J. (1973) *The Politics of Policy in Local Government*, Cambridge, Cambridge University Press.

Denscombe, M (1998) *A Good Research Guide for Small-Scale Social Research Projects*, Buckingham, Open University Press.

Denver, D. (2003) *Elections and Voters in Britain*, Basingstoke, Palgrave Macmillan.

Deutsch, K. W (1963) *The Nerves of Government*, Glencoe, Ill., Free Press.

Dobson, A. (1990) *Green Political Thought*, London, Harper Collins.

Douglas, M. and Wildavsky, A. (1982) *Risk and Culture*, Berkeley, University of California Press.

Downs, A. (1957) *An Economic Theory of Democracy*, New York, Harper and Row.

Downs, A. (1967) *Inside Bureaucracy*, Boston, Little, Brown.

Drake, R. F. (2002) 'Disabled people, voluntary organisations and participation in policy making', *Policy and Politics*, 30, 3.

Dunleavy, P. (1979) 'The urban basis of political alignment: social class, domestic property ownership and state intervention in consumption processes', *British Journal of Political Science*, 9, 40–43.

Dunleavy, P. (1980) 'The political implications of sectoral cleavages and the growth of state employment', *Political Studies*, 28, 364–83 and 527–49.

Dunleavy, P. (1986) *Studying for a Degree in the Humanities and Social Sciences*, Basingstoke, Palgrave Macmillan.

Dunleavy, P. (1991) *Democracy, Bureaucracy and Public Choice*, Hemel Hempstead, Harvester Wheatsheaf.

Dunleavy, P. and O'Leary, B. (1987) *Theories of the State*, London, Macmillan.

Dunsire, A. (1973) *Public Administration: The word and the science*, London, Martin Robertson.

resources

Duverger, M. ([1954] 1970) *Political Parties*, London, Methuen.

Duverger, M. (1972) *The Study of Politics,* tr. R. Wagoner, Sunbury on Thames, Nelson.

Dworkin, A. (1979) *Pornography: Men possessing women*, London, Women's Press.

Dworkin, R. (1977) *Taking Rights Seriously*, London, Duckworth.

Easton, D. (1965) *A Systems Analysis of Political Life*, New York, Wiley.

Eckstein, H. (1960) *Pressure Group Politics: The case of the British Medical Association*, London, Allen and Unwin.

Eisenstadt, S. and Rokkan, S. (1973) *Building States and Nations*, Thousand Oaks, Calif., Sage.

Engels, F. ([1845] 1971) *The Condition of the Working Class in England* , trans. and ed. W.O. Henderson and O. Chaloner, Oxford, Blackwell.

Engels, F. ([1884] 1985) *Origin of the Family, Private Property and the State,* intro. by M. Barrett, Harmondsworth, Penguin

Etzioni, A. (1967) 'Mixed-scanning: a "third" approach to decision-making', *Public Administration Review*, 27.

Evans, P. B., Reuschemeyer, D. and Skocpol, T. (eds) (1985) *Bringing the State Back In*, Cambridge, Cambridge University Press.

Eysenck, H. J. (1957) *Sense and Nonsense in Psychology*, Harmondsworth, Penguin.

Farrell, D. (2001) *Electoral Systems: A comparative introduction*, London and New York, Palgrave Macmillan.

Figes, E. ([1970] 1978) *Patriarchal Attitudes*, London, Virago.

Finer, H. (1932) *The Theory and Practice of Modern Government*, 2 vols. London, Methuen.

Finer, S.E. (1958) *Anonymous Empire*, London, Pall Mall.

Finer, S. E. ([1962] 1988) *The Man on Horseback: The role of the military in politics*, Boulder, Colo., Westview.

Finley, M. I. (1963) *The Ancient Greeks*, Harmondsworth, Penguin.

Finley, M. I. (1972) *Aspects of Antiquity*, Harmondsworth, Penguin.

Firestone, S. ([1970] 1979) *The Dialectic of Sex*, London, Women's Press.

Foucault, M. (1965) *Madness and Civilisation*, tr. Howard, New York, Pantheon.

Foucault, M. (1972) *The Archaeology of Knowledge*, tr. Sheridan, London, Tavistock.

Foucault, M. (1977) *Discipline and Punish*, tr. Sheridan, London, Allen Lane.

Fox, R. L. (2006) *The Classical World: An epic history of Greece and Rome*, London, Penguin.

Freeden, M. (1996) *Ideologies and Political Theory*, Oxford, Clarendon Press.

Friedan, B. (1965) *The Feminist Mystique*, Harmondsworth, Penguin.

Friedan, B. (1982) *The Second Stage*, London, Michael Joseph.

Friedrich, C. J. and Brzezinski, Z. (1963) *Totalitarian Dictatorships and Autocracy*, New York, Praeger.

Fulton, Lord (Chair) (1968) *The Civil Service* (two volumes) Cmnd 3638, London, HMSO.

Fukuyama, F. (1992) *The End of History and the Last Man*, Harmondsworth, Penguin.

Fukuyama, F. (1996) *Trust: The Social Virtues and the Creation of Prosperity*, Harmondsworth, Penguin.

Fukuyama, F. (2002) *Our Posthuman Future: Consequences of the biotechnology revolution*, New York, Farrar, Straus and Giroux.

Galbraith, J. K. ([1952] 1956) *American Capitalism: The Concept of Countervailing Power*, Boston, Houghton Mifflin.

Galbraith, J. K. ([1955] 1992) *The Great Crash*, Harmondsworth, Penguin.

Galbraith, J. K. ([1958] 1999) *The Affluent Society*, London, Penguin.

Galbraith, J. K. ([1967]) *The New Industrial State,* London, Hamish Hamilton.

resources

Galbraith, J. K. ([[1973]]) *Economics and the Public Purpose*, Boston MA, Houghton Mifflin.

Gellner, E. (1983) *Nations and Nationalism*, Oxford, Blackwell.

Giddens, A. (1979) *Central Problems in Social Theory*, London, Macmillan.

Giddens, A. (1984) *The Constitution of Society*, Cambridge, Polity.

Giddens, A. (1994) *Beyond Left and Right*, Cambridge, Polity.

Giddens, A. (1998) *The Third Way*, Cambridge, Polity.

Giddens, A. (2000) *The Third Way and Its Critics*, Cambridge, Polity.

Giddens, A. (ed.) (2001) *The Global Third Way Debate*, Cambridge, Polity.

Godwin, W. ([1793] 1976) *An Enquiry Concerning Political Justice*, ed. I. Kramnick, Harmondsworth, Penguin.

Goodin, R. E. and Klingemann, H. (eds) (1996) *A New Handbook of Political Science*, Oxford, Oxford University Press.

Gramsci, A. ([1929-35] 1971) *Selections from the Prison Notebooks*, tr. Q. Hoare and G. Nowell Smith, London, Lawrence and Wishart.

Grant, W. (2000) *Pressure Groups and British Politics*, Basingstoke, Palgrave Macmillan.

Green, T. H. ([1881] 1986) *Lectures on the Principles of Political Obligation*, ed. P. Harris and J. Morrow, Cambridge, Cambridge University Press.

Greenfeld, L. (1992) *Nationalism: Five roads to modernity*, Cambridge, Mass., Harvard University Press.

Greenwood, J., Pyper, R. and Wilson, D. (2001) *New Public Administration in Britain*, London, Routledge.

Greer, G. (1970) *The Female Eunuch*, St Albans, Paladin.

Greer, G. (1984) *Sex and Destiny: The politics of human fertility*, London, Secker and Warburg.

Greetham, B. (2001) *How to Write Better Essays*, Basingstoke, Palgrave Macmillan.

Gunther, P. and Mughan, A. (eds) (2000) *Democracy and the Media: A comparative perspective*, Cambridge and New York, Cambridge University Press.

Habermas, J. ([1962]1989) *The Structural Transformation of the Public Sphere*, Cambridge, Polity.

Habermas, J. (1971) *Knowledge and Human Interests*, Boston, Mass., Beacon.

Habermas J. (1975) *Legitimation Crisis*, Boston, Mass., Beacon.

Habermas, J. (1984, 1986) *The Theory of Communicative Action*, 2 vols, Boston, Mass., Beacon.

Hague, R. and Harrop, M. (2001) *Comparative Government and Politics: An introduction,* 5th edn, Basingstoke, Palgrave Macmillan.

Hague, R. and Harrop, M. (2007) *Comparative Government and Politics: An introduction,* 7th edn, Basingstoke, Palgrave Macmillan.

Hall, P. A. (1999) 'Social capital in Britain', *British Journal of Political Science*, 29(3), 417–61.

Hampsher-Monk, I. (1992) *A History of Modern Political Thought*, Oxford, Blackwell.

Hampton, W. (1970) *Democracy and Community*, London, Oxford University Press.

Harrop, M. and Miller, W. L. (1987) *Elections and Voters: A comparative introduction*, Basingstoke, Macmillan.

Hay, C. (2002) *Political Analysis: A critical introduction*, Basingstoke, Palgrave Macmillan.

Hay, C., Lister, M. and Marsh, D. (eds) (2006) *The State: Theories and issues*, Basingstoke, Palgrave Macmillan.

Hayek, F. A. von ([1944] 1976) *The Road to Serfdom*, London, Routledge and Kegan Paul.

Hayek, F. A. von (1960) *The Constitution of Liberty*, London, Routledge and Kegan Paul.

Heclo, H. and Wildavsky, A. ([1974] 1981) *The Private Government of Public Money*, 2nd edn, London, Macmillan.

resources

Hegel, G. W. F. ([1821] 1991) *The Philosophy of Right*, ed. A. W. Wood, tr. H. B. Nisbet, Cambridge, Cambridge University Press.

Held, D. (1995) *Democracy and the Global Order: From the modern state to cosmopolitan governance*, Cambridge, Polity.

Held, D. (2006) *Models of Democracy*, 3rd edn, Oxford, Polity.

Hermon, E. and Chomsky, N. (1988) *Manufacturing Consent*, New York, Pantheon.

Heywood, A. (2000) *Key Concepts in Politics*, Basingstoke, Palgrave.

Heywood, A. (2003) *Political Ideologies: An introduction*, 3rd edn, Basingstoke, Palgrave Macmillan.

Heywood, A. (2004) *Political Theory: An introduction*, 3rd edn, Basingstoke, Palgrave Macmillan.

Heywood, A. (2007) *Politics*, 3rd edn, Basingstoke, Palgrave Macmillan.

Hill, M (ed.) (1993) *The Policy Process: A reader*, Hemel Hempstead, Harvester Wheatsheaf.

Hindmoor, A. (2006) *Rational Choice*, Basingstoke, Palgrave Macmillan.

Hirschman, A. (1970) *Exit, Voice and Loyalty*, Cambridge, Mass., Harvard University Press.

Hirst, P and Thompson, G. (1999) *Globalization in Question: The international economy and the possibilities of governance*, 2nd edn, Cambridge, Polity.

Hobbes, T. ([1651] 1968) *Leviathan*, ed. C. B. Macpherson, Harmondsworth, Penguin.

Hobhouse, L. T. ([1911] 1964) *Liberalism*, New York, Oxford University Press.

Hobhouse, L. T. ([1918] 1960) *The Metaphysical Theory of the State*, London, Allen and Unwin.

Hobsbawm, E. (1990) *Nations and Nationalism since 1780*, Cambridge, Cambridge University Press.

Hobsbawm, E. (1994) *Age of Extremes: The short twentieth century*, London, Michael Joseph.

Hobsbawm, E. (1996) 'The cult of identity politics', *New Left Review*, 217, May/June.

Hogwood, B. W. and Gunn, L. A. (1984) *Policy Analysis for the Real World*, Oxford, Oxford University Press.

Hooker R. ([1592] 1977) *Of the Laws of Ecclesiastical Polity,* in the Folgar Library Edition of the *Works*, ed W. Speed Hill, Cambridge, Mass., Harvard University Press.

Howard, K and Sharp, J. A. (1993) *The Management of a Student Research Project*, Aldershot, Gower.

Hrebenar, R. (1997) *Interest Group Politics in America*, 3rd edn, Englewood Cliffs, NJ, Prentice Hall.

Hughes, O. E. (2003) *Public Management and Administration*, 3rd edn, Basingstoke, Palgrave Macmillan.

Hume, D. ([1739–40] 1978) *A Treatise of Human Nature*, ed. L. A. Selby-Bigge, Oxford, Clarendon Press.

Hume, D. ([1748] 1947) *Of the Original Contract*, ed. E. Barker, London, Oxford University Press.

Hunter, F. (1953) *Community Power Structure*, Chapel Hill, University of North Carolina Press.

Huntington, S. P. ([1968]1969) *Political Order in Changing Societies*, New Haven, Conn., Yale University Press.

Huntington, S. P. (1991) *Third Wave: Democratization in the late twentieth century*, Cambridge, Mass., Harvard University Press.

Huntington, S. P. ([1996] 2002) *The Clash of Civilizations and the Remaking of World Order*, London, Free Press.

Inglehart, R. (1971) 'The silent revolution in Europe: intergenerational change in post-industrial societies', *American Political Science Review*, 65, 991–1017.

Inglehart, R. (1977a) *The Silent Revolution: Changing values and political styles amongst western publics*, Princeton, N.J., Princeton University Press.

Inglehart, R. (1997) *Modernization and Post-Modernization: Cultural, economic and social change in 43 societies*, Princeton, N.J., Princeton University Press.

Inglehart, R. (1990) *Culture Shift in Advanced Industrial Society*, Princeton, N.J., Princeton University Press.

Inglehart, R and Norris, P. (2004) *Sacred and Secular: Religion and politics worldwide*, Cambridge, Cambridge University Press.

Jordan, A. G. and Richardson, J. J. (1987) *British Politics and the Policy Process*, London, Allen and Unwin.

Kant, I. (1970) *Kant's Political Writings*, ed. H.S. Reiss, tr. H. B. Nisbet, Cambridge, Cambridge University Press.

Katz, R. and Mair, P. (1995) 'Changing models of party organization and party democracy: the emergence of the cartel party', *Party Politics*, (1), 5–28.

Kavanagh, D. (1990) *Thatcherism and British Politics: The end of consensus?*, Oxford, Oxford University Press.

Kedourie, E. (1993) *Nationalism*, 4th edn, Oxford, Blackwell.

Keen, M. (1969) *The Penguin History of Medieval Europe*, Harmondsworth, Penguin.

Keohane, R. and Nye, J. (eds) (1971) *Transnational Relations and World Politics*, Cambridge, Mass., Harvard University Press.

Keohane, R. and Nye, J. ([1977] 2000) *Power and Interdependence,* 3rd edn, Boston, Mass., Little, Brown.

Kesselman, M. and Krieger, J. (2002) *European Politics in Transition*, Boston, Mass., Houghton Mifflin.

Kesselman, M., Krieger, J. and Joseph, W. A. (2000) *Introduction to Comparative Politics*, Boston, Mass., Houghton Mifflin.

Key, V. O. (1942) *Politics, Parties and Pressure Groups*, New York, Crowell.

Key, V. O. ([1949] 1961) *Public Opinion and American Democracy*, New York, Knopf.

Key, V. O. (1950) *Southern Politics in State and Nation,* New York, Knopf.

Key, V. O. (1966) *The Responsible Electorate: Rationality in presidential voting*, Cambridge, Mass., Harvard University Press.

Keynes, J. M. (1919) *The Economic Consequences of the Peace*, London, Macmillan.

Keynes, J. M. ([1936] 1964) *The General Theory of Employment, Interest and Money*, New York, Harcourt Brace and World.

Kirchheimer, O. (1966) 'The transformation of the western European party systems', in J. LaPalombara and M. Weiner, *Political Parties and Political Development*, Princeton, N.J., Princeton University Press.

Kropotkin, P. (1902) *Mutual Aid*, London, Heinemann.

Kymlicka, W. (1989) *Liberalism, Community and Culture*, Oxford, Oxford University Press.

Kymlicka, W. (1990) *Contemporary Political Philosophy*, Oxford, Clarendon Press.

Kymlica, W. (1995) *Multicultural Citizenship*, Oxford, Oxford University Press.

Lane, J-E. and Ersson, S. O. (1999) *Politics and Society in Western Europe*, 4th edn, London, Sage.

Laslett, P. (ed.) (1956) *Philosophy, Politics and Society,* Oxford, Blackwell.

Lasswell, H. ([1935] 1958) *Politics: Who gets what, when, how?* New York, Meridian.

Lazarsfeld, P.F., Berelson, B. and Gaudet, H. (1944) *The People's Choice*, New York, Columbia University Press.

Leach, R. and Percy-Smith, J. (2001) *Local Governance in Britain*, Basingstoke, Palgrave.

LeDuc, L., Niemi, R. and Norris, P. (eds) (2002) *Comparing Democracies 2: New challenges in the study of elections and voting*, Thousand Oaks, Calif. and London, Sage.

resources

Leff, G. (1958) *Medieval Political Thought*, Harmondsworth, Penguin.

Leftwich, A. (ed.) (2004) *What is Politics?* Cambridge, Polity.

Lenin, V. I. ([1902] 1988) *What Is To Be Done?* ed. Service, London, Penguin.

Lenin, V. I. ([1916] 1970) *Imperialism, The Highest Stage of Capitalism*, Moscow, Progress.

Lijphart, A. (1967) *The Politics of Accommodation: Pluralism and democracy in the Netherlands*, Berkeley, Calif., University of California Press.

Lijphart, A. (1977) *The Politics of Plural Societies: A comparative exploration*, Berkeley, Calif., University of California Press.

Lijphart, A. (1984) *Democracies: Patterns of majoritarian and consensual government in twenty one countries*, London, Yale University Press.

Lijphart, A. (1994) *Electoral Systems and Party Systems*, New Haven, Yale University Press.

Lijphart, A. (1999) *Patterns of Democracy: Government forms and performance in thirty six countries*, New Haven, Yale University Press.

Lindblom, C. (1959) 'The science of muddling through', *Public Administration*, (19), 78–88.

Lindblom, C. (1977) *Politics and Markets*, New York, Basic Books.

Lindblom, C. (1979) 'Still muddling, not yet through', *Public Administration Review*, 19,2, 79–88.

Lindblom, C. (1980) *The Policy-Making Process*, 2nd edn, Englewood Cliffs N.J., Prentice Hall.

Linklater, A. (1998) *The Transformation of Political Community: Ethical foundations of the post-Westphalian era,* Cambridge, Polity Press.

Lipset, S. ([1960] 1983) *Political Man: The social bases of politics*, London and New York, Routledge.

Lipset, S. and Rokkan, S. (eds) (1967) *Party Systems and Voter Alignments*, New York and London, Free Press.

Lloyd, J. (2004) *What the Media are Doing to Our Democracy*, London, Constable.

Lloyd-Jones, H. (ed.) (1965) *The Greek World*, Harmondsworth, Penguin.

Locke, J. ([1689] 1963) *A Letter Concerning Toleration*, ed. M. Montuori, The Hague, Martinus Nijhoff.

Locke, J. ([1690] 1948) 'The second treatise on civil government', in *Social Contract*, ed. E. Barker, London, Oxford University Press.

Lovelock, J. (2007) *The Revenge of Gaia*, London, Penguin Books.

Lukes, S. (1974) *Power: A radical view*, London, Macmillan.

Lyotard, J-F. (1984) *The PostModern Condition: A report on knowledge*, Manchester, Manchester University Press.

Machiavelli, N. ([1513ff] 1979) *The Portable Machiavelli*, ed. and tr. P. Bondanella and M. Musa, London, Penguin.

MacIntyre, A. (1981) *After Virtue*, London, Duckworth.

MacKinnon, C. (1979) *Sexual Harassment of Working Women*, New Haven, Conn., Yale University Press.

MacKinnon, C. (1989) *Towards a Feminist Theory of the State*, London, Harvard University Press.

MacKinnon, C. (2007) *Sex Equality*, 2nd edn, New York, Foundation Press.

Macpherson, C. B. (1962) *The Political Theory of Possessive Individualism*, Oxford, Oxford University Press.

Madison, J., Hamilton, A. and Jay, J. ([1787–8] 1987) *The Federalist Papers*, ed. I. Kramnick, London, Penguin.

Mair, P. (1990) *The West European Party System*, Oxford, Oxford University Press.

Maloney, W. (2006) 'Political participation beyond the electoral arena' in Dunleavy et al, *Developments in British Politics* 8, 98–116, Basingstoke, Macmillan.

resources

Malthus, T. ([1798] 1970) *An Essay on the Principle of Population*, ed. A. Flew, Harmondsworth, Penguin.

March, J. G. and Olsen, J. P. (1984) 'The new institutionalism: organisational factors in political life', *American Political Science Review*, 78, 734–49.

March, J. G. and Olsen, J. P. (1989) *Rediscovering Institutions: The organizational basis of politics*, New York, Free Press.

Marcuse, H. (1964) *One Dimensional Man*, London, Routledge and Kegan Paul.

Margetts, H. (2002) 'Political participation and protest', in Dunleavy et al, *Developments in British Politics* 6A, Basingstoke, Macmillan.

Marsh, D. and Stoker, G. (eds) (2002) *Theory and Methods in Political Science*, 2nd edn, Basingstoke, Palgrave Macmillan.

Marx, K ([1840s] 1975) *Early Writings*, ed. L. Coletti, Harmondsworth, Penguin.

Marx, K (1977) *Selected Writings*, trans. D. McLellan, Oxford, Oxford University Press.

Marx, K. and Engels, F. (1959) *Basic Writings on Politics and Philosophy*, ed. L. S. Feuer, New York, Anchor/Doubleday.

May, J. D. (1973) 'Opinion structure of political parties: the special law of curvilinear disparity', *Political Studies*, 21, 135–51.

Mazey, S. and Richardson. J. (eds) (1993) *Lobbying in the European Community*, Oxford, Oxford University Press.

McKenzie, R. T. (1958) 'Parties, pressure groups and the British political process', *Political Quarterly*, 29(1).

McKenzie, R. T. (1963) *British Political Parties*, 2nd edn, London, Mercury.

McLean, I. and McMillan, A. (2003) *The Concise Oxford Dictionary of Politics*, 2nd edn, Oxford, Oxford University Press.

McLellan, D. (1976) *Karl Marx*, London, Paladin.

McLellan, D. (1980) *Marxism after Marx*, London and Basingstoke, Macmillan.

McLellan, D. (1995) *Ideology*, 2nd edn, Buckingham, Open University Press.

McNair, B. (2003) *An Introduction to Political Communication*, London, Routledge.

McQuail, D. (1992) *Media Performance*, London, Sage.

McShea, R. J. (1968) *The Political Philosophy of Spinoza*, New York, Columbia University Press.

Michels, R. ([1911] 1962) *Political Parties*, New York, Free Press.

Miliband, R. ([1963] 1972) *Parliamentary Socialism*, 2nd edn, London, Merlin.

Miliband, R. (1969) *The State in Capitalist Society*, London, Weidenfeld and Nicholson.

Miliband, R. (1973) *The State in Capitalist Society*, London, Quartet.

Miliband, R. (1994) *Socialism for a Sceptical Age,* Cambridge, Polity Press.

Mill, J. S. ([1859–61] 1972) *Utilitarianism, On Liberty, Considerations on Representative Government*, ed. H. B. Acton, London, Dent.

Mill, J. S. ([1869] 1988) *The Subjection of Women,* ed. S. Okin, Indianopolis, Hackett.

Mill, J. S. ([1873] 1989) *An Autobiography*, ed. Robson, Harmondsworth, Penguin.

Mill, J. S. and Bentham, J. (1987) *Utilitarianism and Other Essays*, ed. A. Ryan, Harmondsworth, Penguin.

Miller, D. (ed.) (1987) *The Blackwell Encyclopaedia of Political Thought*, Oxford, Blackwell.

Millett, K. ([1970] 1985) *Sexual Politics*, London, Virago.

Mills, C. Wright (1956) *The Power Elite*, Oxford, Oxford University Press.

Mishra, R. (1999) *Globalization and the Welfare State,* Cheltenham, Elgar.

Montesquieu, C.-L. de S. ([1748] 1949) *The Spirit of the Laws*, ed. F. Neuman, tr. T. Nugent, New York, Hafner.

More, T. ([1516 tr. Robinson, R. 1556] 1970) *Utopia*, Menston, Scholar Press.

Morgenthau, H. J. ([1948] 1978) *Politics Among Nations: The struggle for power and peace*, 5th edn, New York, Knopf.

Morrow, J. (2005) *History of Western Political Thought: A thematic introduction*, Basingstoke, Palgrave Macmillan.

Mosca, G. ([1896] 1939) *The Ruling Class*, tr. A. Livingston, New York, McGraw Hill.

Naess, A. (1989) *Ecology, Community and Lifestyle*, Cambridge, Cambridge University Press.

Nairn, T. (1981) *The Break-up of Britain*, London, NLB and Verso.

Nairn, T. (2000) *After Britain: New Labour and the return of Scotland*, London, Granta Books.

Newton, K. (1976) *Second City Politics*, Oxford, Oxford University Press.

Nietzsche, F. W. ([1883–9] 1968) *The Portable Nietzsche*, ed. and tr. W. Kaufmann, New York, Viking.

Niskanen, W. A. (1971) *Bureaucracy and Representative Government*, Chicago, Aldine-Atherton.

Norris, P. (2000) *A Virtuous Circle: Political communication in postindustrial societies*, Cambridge and New York, Cambridge University Press.

Norris, P. (ed.) (2001) *Britain Votes, 2001*, Oxford, Oxford University Press.

Nozick, R. (1974) *Anarchy, State and Utopia*, Oxford, Blackwell.

Oakeshott, M. (1962) *Rationalism in Politics and other Essays*, London, Methuen.

O'Brien, R and Williams, M. (2004) *Global Political Economy: Evolution and dynamics*, Basingstoke, Palgrave Macmillan.

Ohmae, K. (1990) *The Borderless World: Power and strategy in the interlinked economy*, New York, Harper Collins.

Ohmae, K. (1996) *The End of the Nation State*, London, Harper Collins.

Olson, M. (1965) *The Logic of Collective Action: Public goods and the theory of groups*, Cambridge Mass., Harvard University Press.

Olson, M. (1982) *The Rise and Decline of Nations,* New Haven, Yale University Press.

Olson, M. (2000) *Power and Prosperity: Outgrowing communist and capitalist dictatorships,* New York, Basic Books.

Orwell, G. (1945) *Animal Farm*, London, Secker and Warburg.

Osborne, D. and Gaebler, T. (1992) *Reinventing Government*, Reading, Mass. Addison-Wesley.

Ostrogorski, M. I. ([1902] 1964) *Democracy and the Organisation of Political Parties*, ed. S. Lipset, New York, Doubleday.

Owen, R. ([1813] 1991) *A New View of Society and Other Writings*, ed. G. Claeys, London, Penguin.

Paine, T. ([1772–1805] 1987) *The Thomas Paine Reader*, ed. M. Foot and I. Kramnick, Harmondsworth, Penguin.

Panebianco, A. (1988) *Political Parties: Organization and power*, Cambridge, Cambridge University Press.

Parekh, B. (2000) *Rethinking Multiculturalism: Cultural diversity and political theory*, Basingstoke, Macmillan.

Parsons, T. (1937) *The Structure of Social Action*, Glencoe, Ill., Free Press.

Parsons, I (1951) *The Social System*, New York, Free Press.

Parsons, T. (1956) *Economy and Society: A study in the integration of economic and social theory*, Glencoe, Ill. Free Press.

Parsons, T (1960) *Structure and Process in Modern Societies*, Glencoe, Ill. Free Press.

Parsons, W. (1995) *Public Policy: Introduction to the theory and practice of policy analysis*, Aldershot, Edward Elgar.

Pateman, C. (1970) *Participation and Democratic Theory*, Cambridge, Cambridge University Press.

resources

Pateman, C. (1979) *The Problem of Political Obligation: A critical analysis of liberal theory*, Chichester, Wiley.

Pateman, C. (1988) *The Sexual Contract*, Cambridge, Polity Press.

Peck, J. and Coyle, M. (1999)*The Student's Guide to Writing*, Basingstoke, Palgrave Macmillan.

Peters, B. G. (1997) 'Shouldn't row, can't steer: what's a government to do?' *Public Administration and Policy*, 12(2).

Peters, B. G. (1998) *Comparative Politics: Theory and methods*, Basingstoke, Palgrave Macmillan.

Phillis, R. (Chair) (2004) *An Independent Review of Government Communication*, London, Cabinet Office.

Pierre, J. and Peters, B. Guy (2000) *Governance, Politics and the State*, Basingstoke, Macmillan.

Plant, R. (1991) *Modern Political Thought*, Oxford, Blackwell.

Plato ([c. 404–394 BC] 1993) *The Last Days of Socrates* (*Euthyphro, Apology, Crito, Phaedo*), tr. H. Tredennick and H. Tarrant, Harmondsworth, Penguin.

Plato ([c. 390–385 BC] 1956) *Protagoras and Meno*, tr. Guthrie, Harmondsworth, Penguin.

Plato ([c. 388–387 BC] 1971) *Gorgias*, tr. W. Hamilton, Harmondsworth, Penguin.

Plato ([c. 386–380 BC] 1955) *The Republic*, tr. H. D. P. Lee, Harmondsworth, Penguin

Plato ([c. 350–347 BC] 1970) *The Laws*, tr. T. Saunders, Harmondsworth, Penguin.

Polsby, N. (1963) *Community Power and Political Theory*, New Haven, Yale University Press.

Popper, K. R. ([1934] 1959) *The Logic of Scientific Discovery*, London, Hutchinson.

Popper, K. R. ([1945] 1962) *The Open Society and Its Enemies*, 2 vols, London, Routledge and Kegan Paul.

Popper, K. R. (1957) *The Poverty of Historicism*, London, Routledge and Kegan Paul.

Potter, A. (1961) *Organised Groups in British National Politics*, London, Faber.

Poulantzas, N. (1968) *Political Power and Social Classes*, London, New Left Books.

Poulantzas, N. (1975) *Classes in Contemporary Capitalism*, London, New Left Books.

Poulantzas, N. (1976) 'The capitalist state: a reply to Miliband and Laclan', *New Left Review*, 95.

Poulantzas, N. (1978) *State, Power and Socialism*, London, New Left Books.

Pressman, J. and Wildavsky, A. (1973) *Implementation*, Berkeley Calif., University of California Press.

Przeworski, A. (1991) *Democracy and the Market: Political and economic reforms in Eastern Europe and Latin America*, Cambridge, Cambridge University Press.

Pulzer, P. (1967) *Representation and Elections in Britain*, London, Allen and Unwin.

Putnam, R. D. (1973) *The Beliefs of Politicians: Ideology, conflict and democracy in Britain and Italy*, New Haven, Yale University Press.

Putnam, R. D. (1976) *The Comparative Study of Political Elites*, Englewood Cliff, N.J., Prentice Hall.

Putnam, R. (1993) *Making Democracy Work: Civic traditions in modern Italy*, Princeton, N.J., Princeton University Press.

Putnam, R. (1995) 'Bowling alone: America's declining social capital', *Journal of Democracy*, (6), 65–78.

Putnam, R. (2000) *Bowling Alone: The collapse and revival of American community*, New York, Simon and Schuster.

Putnam, R. (ed.) (2002) *Democracies in Flux: The evolution of social capital in contemporary society,* New York and Oxford, Oxford University Press.

Rawls, J. (1971) *A Theory of Justice,* Oxford, Oxford University Press.

Rawls, J. (1993) *Political Liberalism*, New York, Columbia University Press.

Rawls, J. (1999) *The Laws of Peoples*, Cambridge, Mass., Harvard University Press.

Rhodes, R. A. W. (1997) *Understanding Governance*, Buckingham, Open University Press.

resources

Richardson, J. J. and Jordan, A. G. (1979) *Governing Under Pressure: The policy process in a post-parliamentary democracy*, Oxford, Martin Robertson.

Robertson, D. (1993) *Dictionary of Politics*, London, Penguin.

Robson, W.A. (1928) *Justice and Administrative Law*, London, Macmillan.

Robson, W. A. (1948) *The Development of Local Government*, 2nd edn, London, Allen and Unwin.

Robson, W. A. (1960) *Nationalised Industries and Public Ownership*, London, Allen and Unwin.

Rosen, M. and Wolff, J. (eds) (1999) *Political Thought*, Oxford, Oxford University Press.

Rousseau, J.-J. ([1755] 1984) *A Discourse on Inequality*, tr. M. Cranston, London, Penguin.

Rousseau, J.-J. ([1762] 1947) *The Social Contract*, ed. E. Barker, London, Oxford University Press.

Sabine, G. H. (1951) *A History of Political Theory,* 3rd edn, London, Harrap.

Said, E. (1978) *Orientalism: Western conceptions of the Orient*, New York, Vintage.

Sandel, M. (1982) *Liberalism and the Limits of Justice*, Cambridge, Cambridge University Press.

Sartori, G. (1976) *Parties and Party Systems: A framework for analysis*, Cambridge, Cambridge University Press.

Sartori, G. (1987) *The Theory of Democracy Revisited,* Chatham, N.J., Chatham House.

Sartre, J.-P. ([1943] 1957) *Being and Nothingness*, tr. H. E. Barnes, London, Methuen.

Saunders, P. (1980) *Urban Politics: A sociological interpretation*, Harmondsworth, Penguin.

Schattschneider, E. E. (1960) *The Semi-Sovereign People: A realist's view of democracy in America*, New York, Holt, Rinehart and Winston.

Schmitter, P. C. (1979) 'Still the century of corporatism?' in P. C. Schmitter and G. Lehmbruch (eds), *Trends Towards Corporatist Intermediation*, Thousand Oaks, Calif. and London, Sage.

Scholte, J. A. (2005) *Globalization: A critical introduction*, 2nd edn, Basingstoke, Palgrave Macmillan.

Schumacher, E. F. (1976) *Small is Beautiful*, London, Sphere.

Schumpeter, J. (1943) *Capitalism, Socialism and Democracy*, London, Allen and Unwin.

Scruton, R. (2007) *A Dictionary of Political Thought*, 3rd edn, London, Macmillan.

Self, P. (1993) *Government by the Market? The politics of public choice*, Basingstoke, Macmillan.

Seyd, P. (1987) *The Rise and Fall of the Labour Left*, Basingstoke, Macmillan.

Simon, H. A. (1947) *Administrative Behaviour*, Glencoe Ill, Free Press.

Sinclair, T. A. (1967) *A History of Greek Political Thought*, London, Routledge and Kegan Paul.

Singer, P. (1972) 'Famine, affluence and morality', *Philosophy and Public Affairs,* (1), 229–35.

Singer, P. (1975) *Animal Liberation: A new ethics for the treatment of animals*. New York, Random House.

Singer, P. (1979) *Practical Ethics*, Cambridge, Cambridge University Press.

Skocpol, T. (1979) *States and Social Revolutions*, Cambridge, Cambridge University Press.

Skocpol, T. (1994) *Social Revolutions in the Modern World,* New York, Cambridge University Press.

Skocpol, T. (1996) 'Unravelling from above', *The American Prospect*, March/April.

Slaughter, A.-M. (2004) *A New World Order*, Princeton, NJ, Princeton University Press.

Smith, A. ([1759] 1976) *The Theory of Moral Sentiments*, Oxford, Clarendon.

Smith, A. ([1776] 1976) *The Wealth of Nations*, ed. E. Cannan, Chicago, University of Chicago.

Sokal, A. and Bricmont, J. (1998) *Intellectual Impostors*.

Spencer, H. ([1884] 1981) *The Man versus the State*, ed. E. Mack, Indianapolis, Liberty Classics.

Spender, D. (1985) *Man Made Language*, London, Routledge and Kegan Paul.

Stewart, J. D. (1958) *British Pressure Groups*, Oxford, Oxford University Press.

Stoker, G. (2006) *Why Politics Matters: Making democracy work*, Basingstoke, Palgrave Macmillan.

Street, J (2001) *Mass Media, Politics and Democracy*, Basingstoke, Palgrave.

resources

Sunstein, C. (2001) *Republic.com*, Princeton, N.J., Princeton University Press.

Tansey, S. D. (2004) *Politics: The basics*, 3rd edn, London, Routledge.

Tarrow, S. (1998) *Power in Movement: Social movements and contentious politics*, Cambridge and New York, Cambridge University Press.

Tawney, R. H. ([1921] 1961) *The Acquisitive Society*, London, Fontana.

Tawney, R. H. ([1926] 1938) *Religion and the Rise of Capitalism*, Harmondsworth, Penguin.

Tawney, R. H. ([1931] 1964) *Equality*, London, Unwin.

Taylor, C. (1990) *Sources of the Self: The making of modern identity*, Cambridge, Cambridge University Press.

Teeple, G. (1995) *Globalization and the Decline of Social Reform*, Atlantic Highlands, N.J., Humanities Press.

Thoreau, H. D. ([1854] 1980) *Walden and On the Duty of Civil Disobedience*, New York, New American Library.

Thucydides ([late 5th century BC] 1972) *History of the Peloponnesian War*, tr. Warner, Harmondsworth, Penguin.

Tocqueville, A. de ([1835, 1840] 2003) *Democracy in America*, tr. G. Bevan, intro. I. Kramnick, London, Penguin.

Tocqueville, A de ([1856] 1947) *The Old Regime and the French Revolution*, tr. M. W. Patterson, Oxford, Blackwell.

Trotsky, L. (1937) *The Revolution Betrayed*, tr. M. Eastman, London, Faber and Faber.

Truman, D. (1951) *The Governmental Process,* New York, Knopf.

Tullock, G. (1965) *The Politics of Bureaucracy*, Boston, Mass., University Press of America.

Tullock, G. (1998) *On Voting: A public choice approach*, Aldershot, Edward Elgar.

Urwin, D. W. and Rokkan, S. (1983) *Economy, Territory and Identity,* Thousand Oaks, Calif., Sage.

Voltaire, F.-M. A. ([1759] 1970) *Candide,* tr. J. Butt, Harmondsworth, Penguin.

Walsh, K. (1995) *Public Services and Market Mechanisms: Competition, contracting and the New Public Management*, Basingstoke, Macmillan.

Walter, N. (1999) *The New Feminism*, London, Virago.

Waltz, K. (1979) *Theory of International Politics*, Reading, Mass., Addison-Wesley.

Walzer, M. (1983) *Spheres of Justice*, New York, Basic Books.

Walzer, M. (2000) *Just and Unjust Wars*, 3rd edn, New York, Perseus.

Waters, M. (2000) *Globalization*, London and New York, Routledge.

Watson, G. (1987) *Writing a Thesis: A guide to long essays and dissertations*, Harlow, Longman.

Webb, P., Farrell, D. and Holliday, I. (eds) (2002) *Political Parties in Advanced Industrial Democracies,* Oxford and New York, Oxford University Press.

Weber, M. ([1904] 1930) *The Protestant Ethic and the Spirit of Capitalism*, London, Allen and Unwin.

Weber, M. (1948) *From Max Weber: Essays in sociology*, tr. H. H. Gerth and C. W. Mills, London, Routledge and Kegan Paul.

Weber, M. ([1922] 1978) *Economy and Society*, ed. G. Roth and C. Wittich, tr. E. Fischoff, Berkeley, Calif., University of California Press.

Weber, M. (1978) *Selections in Translation,* ed. W. G. Runciman, tr. E/ Matthews, Cambridge, Cambridge University Press.

Wendt, A. (1987) 'The agent/structure problem in international relations theory', *International Organization*, 41, 335–70.

Wendt, A. (1992) 'Anarchy is what states make of it: the social construction of power politics', *International Organization*, 46, 391–426.

Wendt, A. (1999) *Social Theory of International Politics*, Cambridge, Cambridge University Press.

Wendt, A. (2003) 'Why a world state is inevitable', *European Journal of International Relations*, 9 (4).

White, T. H. (1962) *The Making of the President, 1960,* London, Jonathan Cape.

Wildavsky, A. (1980) *The Art and Craft of Policy Analysis*, Macmillan, London.

Williams, R. (1976) *Keywords*, Glasgow, Fontana.

Wolff, J. (1996) *An Introduction to Political Philosophy*, Oxford, Oxford University Press.

Wollstonecraft, M. ([1792] 1985) *A Vindication of the Rights of Women*, Harmondsworth, Penguin.

Young, M. ([1958] 1961) *The Rise of the Meritocracy 1870–2033: An essay on education and equality*, London, Pelican.

Index

Note Page numbers shown in **bold type** refer to specific relevant entries in Part III (key concepts) and Part IV (key thinkers).

Dunleavy, Patrick, 82, 92, 156, 196, 218, 283
Durkheim, Emile, 20
Dutch Republic, 61, 158
Duverger, Maurice, 14, **177**, 221, 224, 286
Dworkin, Angela, 102, **177**, 190
Dworkin, Ronald, 98, 138, **177**

E
Easton, David, 7, 86, 88, 94, 172, **177**
Ecole Nationale d'Adminisistration (ENA), 237
ecologism, **125** (*see also* environmentalism)
economic determinism, 74–5, 193
economics, 13, 23–4, 70, 87, 90
elections, **124**, 149, 152, 171, 216–20
electoral reform, 71
electoral systems, 86, **124**, 219, 224
electoral turnout, 219–20
electoral volatility, 218–19
elites and elitism, 72, 79, 80–83, 122, **124**,
    147, 148, 152, 176, 193–4, 195, 196,
    198, 201, 204, 227–9
empiricism, **124–5**, 132, 184
Engels, Friedrich, 74, 77, 79, 113, 141, 165–6,
    177–8, 192
England, 61–2, 158
English school (of international relations),
    174
Enlightenment, 63–8, 78, 118, 150, 156, 247
environment, 74, 115, 136, 189, 258
environmentalism, 79, **125**, 129, 133, 189
equality, 64, 66, 67, 71–2, 77, 78, 121, 122,
    125–6, 130, 137, 148, 153, 161, 175
essays, 38–40
essentially contested concepts, 17
ethnic cleansing, 67, 106, 254
ethnic minorities, **126–7**, 144, 157, 238, 244
ethnicity, 116, **126–7**, 133, 154, 244, 246
Etzioni, Amitae, 117, 134, 241
Europe
    European Community, 79
    European Convention on Human Rights,
        15, 67, 98, 159
    European Court of Human Rights, 136
    European Court of Justice, 136
    European Parliament, 139
    European Union, 120–1, 128, 139, 254,
        260

euro-communism, 77, 180
examinations, 50–52
executive, 119, **127**, 131, 136, 139
existentialism, 204

F
Fabian Society, 134, 208
failed states, 163, 262
fair trade, 70, 130
falsifiability, 85, 200
fascism, 10, 68, 72–3, 79, **127–8**, 132, 134,
    138, 156, 162, 164, 165, 169
federalism, 78, 87, 119, 123, **128**, 159, 161–2,
    190, 242–3, 249–250
feminism, 12, 68, 79, 98, 101–3, 115, 118,
    128–9, 130, 132, 133, 139, 148, 151,
    176, 177, 178, 180, 195
Figes, Eva, 102, 129
Filmer, R., 148
Finer, Herman, 95
Finer, Samuel, 11, 143, 227
Firestone, Shulamith, 102
foreign policy, 218
Foucault, Michel, 79, 97, 99, 102, 151, **178**,
    203
Fourier, Charles, 165
France, 61–2, 64, 65–6, 70, 71, 127, 133, 158,
    163, 224–5, 237
franchise, 75
Frankfurt school, 77, 169, 181, 191
Franklin, Benjamin, 64, 66
fraternity, 78, 125
Free Democratic Party (FPD), 224
freedom, 15, 64, 67, 69, 71, 114, 121, 122,
    125, **129–30**, 134, 140, 180, 194
free market, 69, 71–3, 80, 113, 116, 119,
    130, 139, 140, 146, 155, 205, 206, 239,
    261
free trade, 70, 130, 140
free will, 74
Friedan, Betty, 79, **178**
Friedman, Milton, 90, 146
Fukuyama, Francis, 172, **178–9**, 286

G
Gaebler, T., 9, 131, 241
Galbraith, John Kenneth, 83, 148, **179**